SOVIET UNION U.S.S.R.

MONGOLIA

NTH. KOREA
STH. KOREA

JAPAN

NORTH PACIFIC OCEAN

TURKEY

LEB
ISRAEL
Judaism

IRAQ

IRAN

AFGHANISTAN

PAKISTAN

CHINA

TAIWAN

HONG KONG

EGYPT

SAUDI
ARABIA

INDIA

BURMA

LAOS

SUDAN

Sikhism

THAILAND

KAMB

VIETNAM

PHILIPPINES

ETHIOPIA

Parsism
(Zoroastrianism)

SOMALIA

SOUTH PACIFIC OCEAN

UGANDA

KENYA

SRI LANKA

MALAYSIA

AIRE

TANZANIA

INDONESIA

PAPUA
NEW
GUINEA

MALAWI

ZAMBIA

ZIMBABWE

MOZAMBIQUE

INDIAN OCEAN

OTSWANA

SWAZILAND

UTH
RICA

LESOTHO

MADAGASCAR

AUSTRALIA

NEW ZEALAND

NLAND

RUM.

BULG

CE

D0005296

LIVING
RELIGIONS

LIVING RELIGIONS

MARY PAT FISHER
ROBERT LUYSTER

PRENTICE HALL
Englewood Cliffs, N.J. 07632

Prentice Hall Inc
A Division of Simon & Schuster
Englewood Cliffs, New Jersey 07632

10   9   8   7   6   5   4   3

ISBN 0-13-538604-7

This book was designed and produced by
CALMANN AND KING LTD, LONDON

Designer Karen Osborne
Picture researcher Sara Waterson
Maps by Eugene Fleury

Typeset by Black Box Graphics, Maidenhead
Printed in Hong Kong

Cover: MC 32985 – Michael Chase (living artist), *Sun God and
Charioteer*. Private Collection/Bridgeman Art Library.

Half title: The Jain saint Bahubali is honored by a colossal
57-foot-high statue. A Great Head-Annointing Ceremony is held
every ten to fifteen years in which pots of precious milk,
sandalwood, goldfoil, and gemstones are poured over the image.
Photograph courtesy Gurmeet Thukral.
Frontispiece: As part of the holy festival of Galungan, a procession
of women carry offerings into Pura Puseh, Desa Sempidi, near
the Holy Springs of Sempidi. Photograph courtesy Werner
Forman Archive.

The authors and publishers would like to thank all those who gave
permission to use text and photographs in this book. Text sources
are credited fully in the Notes, pages 349 to 356, and photographic
sources on page 361. Every effort has been made to trace copyright
holders and we apologise in advance for any unintentional
omissions. We would be pleased to insert the appropriate
acknowledgement in any subsequent edition of this book.

CONTENTS

Preface

Religion is not a museum piece. It is alive in people and places around the world. *Living Religions* is a sympathetic approach to what is living, and significant in the religious traditions of our world. It provides a clear, straightforward account of the development, doctrines, and practices of the major faiths practiced today. Our emphasis throughout is on the personal consciousness of believers and their own account of themselves, their religion, and reality at large.

Distinguishing features

Among the special features of this text are personal interviews with followers of each faith, providing first-person accounts of each religion as perceived from within. These are presented at length in boxes and also in excerpts woven throughout the text.

In addition, we have incorporated extensive quotations from primary sources to give a direct perception of the thinking and flavor of each tradition. Particularly memorable brief quotations are set off in boxes.

We also use illustrations to convey a living sense of each tradition. The book incorporates 41 color and 165 black and white illustrations, with an emphasis on contemporary religious life. Narrative captions that accompany them offer a deepened insight into the characteristics and orientation of each tradition and the people who practice it.

Three of our chapters are especially unique. The first chapter – "The Religious Response" – is a thoughtful exploration of religion in general. Religion is presented as a valid account of reality that takes many forms. This chapter includes a discussion of women and the feminine in religions, an area to which little attention has been paid in past surveys of world religions. It also examines the controversial side of religions, for they have at times evoked the lowest as well as the highest aspects of human nature.

The second chapter offers a sensitive, profound portrayal of the little-understood indigenous religions. We have tried to bypass the many misleading accounts of indigenous traditions written by outsiders, and to get at the heart of how real people experience their close-to-nature spiritual ways. As our world totters on the brink of ecological collapse, it is especially important that these surviving members of the ancient ways be heard correctly.

The final chapter is an original framework for understanding new religious movements. It is a rich, accurate, and up-to-date discussion of the novel and important religious trends of the late nineteenth and twentieth centuries, ending with interfaith dialogue.

Learning aids

We have tried to present each tradition clearly and without a clutter of less important names and dates. Key terms are defined when they first appear and also in an extensive glossary. Maps are used to give a sense of geographical reality to the historical discussions, as well as to illustrate the present distribution of the religions.

The history of each of the major religions is recapitulated in a time-line in the history section of that chapter. The simultaneous development of all religions can be compared in the overall time-line at the back of the book.

We assume that readers will want to delve further into the literature. At the end of each chapter, we offer an annotated list of books that might be particularly interesting and useful in further study of that religion.

Acknowledgements

In order to try to understand each religion from the inside, we have been travelling for many years to study with devotees and teachers of all faiths, and to interview them about their experience of their tradition.

The book has also been supported by a team of authorities in specific traditions: Robert Bee (Professor of Anthropology at the University of Connecticut, specializing in indigenous sacred lifeways), Reb Zalman Schacter-Shalomi (Professor Emeritus of Jewish Mysticism and Psychology of Religion from Temple University and a leader in the Jewish Renewal movement), Julia Gatta (Episcopal priest, spiritual director at Berkeley Divinity School at Yale, lecturer on ascetical theology at Yale Divinity School, member of the ecumenical committees of the National and World Council of Churches), and Willem A. Bijlefeld (Distinguished Senior Professor of Islamic Studies at the Hartford Seminary and editor of *The Muslim World*). They have shared resources, helped to frame the content, and reviewed and revised the chapters in their particular areas, offering invaluable aid for which we are deeply grateful. We authors nevertheless bear responsibility for the contents.

Living Religions has been extensively reviewed by professors teaching courses in world religions. They include: George Braswell of Southeastern Baptist Theological Seminary, Howard R. Burkle of Grinnell College, James Carse of New York University, Frances Cook of University of California, Ronald Flowers of Texas Christian University, Rita Gross of University of Wisconsin, Willard Johnson of San Diego State University, Anjum Khilji of Institute for Parapsychology at Durham Technical Community College, Dennis Klass of Webster University, Robert Minor of University of Kansas, Kusumita P. Pederson of New York University, Lynda Sexson of Montana State University, Paul Schwartz of San Francisco State University, and Herb Smith of McPherson College. In addition, Reverend Stan Possell, Rabbi Steven Razin, Mohammad T. Mehdi, and Prajapati O'Neill have read and commented on specific chapters. Their many suggestions and insights have been extremely valuable, and we would like to thank all of them.

Probably most important to the spiritual validity of the book are those many devotees, teachers, and scholars from each religion who were enthusiastic about the possibility of presenting their path truthfully and who gave generously of their own time, insights, and books. Some are quoted in the text; many more have helped. We would particularly like to thank those who appear in the featured interview boxes. All these people have offered great richnesses of information and experience, and for this we are sincerely grateful.

It has been an inspiring, deeply enriching journey.

Mary Pat Fisher
Robert Luyster

1 THE RELIGIOUS RESPONSE

Before sunrise, members of a Muslim family rise in Malaysia, perform their purifying ablutions, spread their prayer rugs facing Mecca, and begin their prostrations and prayers to Allah. In a French cathedral, worshippers line up for their turn to have a priest place a wafer on their tongue, murmuring, "This is the body of Christ." In a South Indian village, a group of women reverently anoint a cylindrical stone with clarified butter and fragrant sandalwood paste and place around it offerings of flowers. The monks of a Japanese Zen Buddhist monastery sit crosslegged and upright in utter silence, broken occasionally by the noise of the *kyosaku* bat falling on their shoulders. On a mountain in Mexico, men, women, and children who have been dancing without food or water for days greet an eagle flying overhead with a burst of whistling from the small wooden flutes they wear around their necks. By a stream in Iowa, a young woman sits with her eyes closed, praying to the mind and heart of the universe that her life may serve some sacred purpose.

These and countless other moments in the lives of people around the world are threads of the tapestry we call "religion." The word is probably derived from the Latin, meaning "to tie back," "to tie again." Despite the rich diversity of its expressions, all of religion shares the goal of tying people back to something behind the surface of life – a greater reality which lies beyond or invisibly infuses the world that we can perceive with our five senses.

Attempts to connect with this greater reality have taken many forms. Many of them are organized institutions, such as Buddhism or Christianity, with leaders, sacred scriptures, and historical traditions. Others are private personal experiences of individuals who belong to no institutionalized religion but nonetheless have an inner life of prayer, meditation, or direct experience of an inexplicable presence.

In this introductory chapter, we will try to develop some understanding of religion in a generic sense – why it exists and what general forms it takes – before studying the characteristics of the organized group religions that are practiced today.

Why are there religions?

We could account for the universality of religions from two different points of view: firstly that people have very strong psychological needs that religions satisfy, and secondly that there is a reality that transcends the physical world, which some people experience and respond to. Those who do not believe the second point of view think that humans have made up religions to meet their needs. Psychoanalyst Sigmund Freud

The heart of religion is the private spiritual experience of the individual. For members of the Krishna Consciousness movement, the nature of this experience is ecstasy.

described religion as a "universal obsessional neurosis," depicting it as a cosmic projection of our love/fear relationships with our parents. Others believe that religions have been invented or at least used to manipulate people. Historically, religions have often served as centers of secular power. Particularly vigorous anti-religious statements have come from the communist philosopher Karl Marx. He felt that religion (in particular, Christianity, the form with which he was most familiar) was a tool of oppression, a mirror of an unjust social system:

> *Man makes religion: religion does not make man. . . . The religious world is but the reflex of the real world. . . . Religion is the sigh of the oppressed creature, the sentiment of a heartless world, and the soul of soulless conditions. It is the opium of the people. . . . The social principles of Christianity declare all vile acts of the oppressors against the oppressed to be either the just punishment of original sin and other sins or trials that the Lord in his infinite wisdom imposes on those redeemed.* [1]

Yet others have rejected religion on the grounds that it is unscientific. This tendency arose with the glorification of Western science. From the seventeenth century onward, Western science considered mind and spirit separate from matter. The apparent physical

During the Enlightenment, worship of the Divine began to be replaced by faith in science and scientists, as suggested by Etienne-Louis Boullee's proposed Design for Monument to Isaac Newton, 1784.

realities of the universe were approached as a world unto themselves, a giant machine that could presumably be taken apart, understood, and used however humans chose. The belief that spirit creates, permeates, or intervenes in existence was set aside because spirit was not tangible, not scientifically verifiable. Religious concepts were not honored as they had been in all previous times and all places, for they seemed irrational. There were predictions that religions would fall by the wayside, since science was now on the verge of explaining everything.

In recent times, however, there has been a return to a more religiously sympathetic worldview, and some of the leaders of this shift have been our most respected scientists. Cynicism about religion is giving way to a search for spirituality, though not necessarily to the same faiths that sustained our ancestors.

Fulfillment of basic human needs

Many human needs are not met by the outer aspects of our life on earth. One of these is the difficulty of accepting the commonsense notion that this life is all there is. We are born, we struggle to support ourselves, we age, and we die. If there is nothing more, fear of death may inhibit enjoyment of life and make all human actions seem rather pointless. Confronting mortality is so basic to the spiritual life that, observes the Christian monk Brother David Steindl-Rast, whenever monks from any spiritual tradition meet, within five minutes they are talking about death.

> *It appears that throughout the world man has always been seeking something beyond his own death, beyond his own problems, something that will be enduring, true and timeless. He has called it God, he has given it many names; and most of us believe in something of that kind, without ever actually experiencing it.*
>
> *Jiddu Krishnamurti*[2]

Not only do we want a sense of some kind of eternal life; we also want this present life to have some meaning. For many, the desire for material achievement offers a temporary sense of purposefulness. But once achieved, these material goals may seem hollow. The Buddha said:

> Look!
> The world is a royal chariot, glittering with paint.
> No better.
>> Fools are deceived, but the wise know better. [3]

All religions help to uncover meaningfulness in the midst of the mundane. They do so by exploring the *transpersonal* dimension of life – the eternal and infinite, beyond limited personal or communal concerns. In doing so, some religions totally deny the value of earthly life; others seek to bring heaven to earth, infusing each moment with awareness of the whole.

There is in some of us a desire for perfection, which is confounded by the environmental degradation and human injustices of modern industrial life. That which is absolute, ultimate, and perfect does not seem to exist in the world that we perceive with our five senses. For example, if we look for perfection in human love, we are likely to be disappointed. Yet we can imagine an absolute, divine love that never ends and that accepts us unconditionally, despite our flaws. Religious practices may offer us access to this perfection.

Some of us also have a strong sense of our own imperfection and long to outgrow it. Religions describe ideals which can radically transform people. Mahatma Gandhi was

Some religions try to transcend the mundane, glimpsing what lies beyond. Others, such as the Zen Buddhism that influenced this 18th-century drawing of The Meditating Frog, *find ultimate reality in the here and now, intensely experienced.*

Nostalgia for perfection and beauty has inspired the creation of intricate temples such as Hagia Sophia in Istanbul. Built as an immense Christian church, it was transformed into a Muslim mosque when the city was taken over by Turks in 1453.

an extremely shy, fearful, self-conscious child. His transformation into one of the great political figures of our time occurred as he meditated single-mindedly on the great Hindu scripture, the Bhagavad-Gita. Gandhi was particularly impressed by the second chapter, which he says was "inscribed on the tablet of my heart."[4] It reads, in part:

> *He lives in wisdom*
> *Who sees himself in all and all in him,*
> *Whose love for the Lord of Love has consumed*
> *Every selfish desire and sense-craving*
> *Tormenting the heart. . . .*
>
> *He is forever free who has broken*
> *Out of the ego-cage of* I *and* mine
> *To be united with the Lord of Love.*
> *This is the supreme state. Attain thou this*
> *And pass from death to immortality.*[5]

People long to escape from personal problems. Those who are suffering severe physical illness, privation, terror, or grief often turn to the divine for help. Religious literature is full of stories of miraculous aid which has come to those who have cried out in their need. But sometimes help comes as the strength and philosophy to accept burdens. The eighteenth-century Hasidic Jewish master, the Baal Shem Tov, taught that the vicissitudes of life are ways of climbing toward the divine. Islam teaches patience, faithful waiting for the unfailing grace of Allah. An imprisoned Sikh saint saw the divine in all beings, even greeting his jailer with "Hallo! my friend ... devoted am I unto Thee."[6]

Rather than seeking help from without, an alternative approach is to seek freedom from problems in our "own" minds. According to some eastern religions, the concept that we are distinct, consistent individuals is an illusion; what we think of as "our" consciousnesses and "our" bodies are in perpetual flux. From this point of view, freedom from problems lies in recognizing and accepting the reality of temporal change and devaluing the "small self" in favor of the eternal self. Many contemplative spiritual traditions teach methods of turning within to discover and eradicate all attachments, desires, and resentments associated with the small self, revealing the purity of the true self. Once we have found it within, we begin to see it wherever we look. This realization brings a sense of acceptance in which, as philosopher William James observed:

> Dull submission is left far behind, and a mood of welcome, which may fill any place on the scale between cheerful serenity and enthusiastic gladness, has taken its place.[7]

In the midst of the turmoils of life, both inner and outer, people long to be happy and yearn for peace. The Christian apostle Paul wrote of "the peace of God, which passeth all understanding."[8] Gandhi was blissful in prison, for no human could bar his relationship with the Lord of Love. Kabir, a fifteenth-century Indian weaver who followed both Islam and Hinduism and who is also embraced by the Sikhs, described this state of spiritual bliss:

> The blue sky opens out farther and farther,
> the daily sense of failure goes away,
> the damage I have done to myself fades,
> a million suns come forward with light,
> when I sit firmly in that world.[9]

Some people feel that their true selves are part of that world of light, dimly remembered, and long to return to it. The poet William Wordsworth wrote:

> Our birth is but a sleep and a forgetting;
> The Soul that rises with us, our life's Star
>   Hath had elsewhere its setting
>   And cometh from afar;
>   Not in entire forgetfulness,
>   And not in utter nakedness,
> But trailing clouds of glory do we come
>   From God, who is our home.[10]

When we encounter nature in all its original beauty, or humans acting in pure love, we may be struck by another religious impulse – appreciation for this extraordinary creation. Ray Fadden, an elder of the Mohawk Nation, speaks of the native spiritual traditions as the "thank-you religion." For those who honor the miracles seen in all created beings, each day is begun in gratitude. Brother David Steindl-Rast observes that gratitude is the basis of the spiritual life. Religions teach us that there is a "someone" or "something" to thank for all of this. The Christian St. Francis of Assisi offered a beautiful Canticle to all creation:

Be praised, my Lord, with all your created things. Be praised, brother Sun, who brings the day and gives us light. He is fair and radiant with shining face and he draws his meaning from on high.

Be praised, my Lord, for sister moon and the stars in the heavens. You have made them clear and precious and lovely.

Praised be my Lord for our brother Wind, and for the air and the clouds and calm days and every kind of weather, by which you give your creatures nourishment.

Praised be my Lord for our sister water, which is very helpful and humble, precious and pure.

Praised be my Lord for our brother Fire, by which you light up the darkness; he is fair, bright and strong.

Praised be my Lord for our sister, Mother Earth, for she sustains and keeps us and brings forth all kinds of fruits together with grasses and bright flowers.

Praise be my Lord for our sister, bodily death, from which no living person can flee, praise be my Lord for all your creatures. We give you thanks. [11]

Storm system 1200 miles north of Hawaii, as seen from the Apollo 9 spaceflight, March 1969.

Behind the miracle of creation, there may be an intelligence. Some of us want to know who or what it is. We look to religions for understanding, for answers to our many questions about life. Who are we? Why are we here? What happens after we die? Why is there suffering? Why is there evil? Is anybody up there listening? For those who find security in specific answers, some religions offer *dogma* – systems of doctrines proclaimed as absolutely true and accepted as such, even if they lie beyond the domain of one's personal experiences. Religious dogmas provide some people with a sense of relief from anxieties, a secure feeling of rootedness, meaning and orderliness in the midst of rapid social change. Religions may also provide rules for living, governing everything from diet to relationships. Some religions, however, encourage each person to explore the perennial questions by themselves, and to live in the uncertainties of not-knowing intellectually, always breaking through old concepts until nothing remains but truth itself.

A final need that draws some people to religion is the discomforting sense of being alone in the universe. This isolation can be painful, even terrifying. The divine may be sought as a loving father or mother, or as a friend. Alternatively, some paths offer the way of self-transcendence. Through them, the sense of isolation is lost in mystical merger with the one, in communion with all.

Realities beyond the visible world

Religion therefore may be approached out of personal needs – such as longings for immortality, meaningfulness, perfection, personal growth, escape from problems, happiness, peace, understanding, and order, or the sense of gratitude or isolation. But the faithful would deny that the superhuman is simply a wishful projection of these needs. Either they have directly experienced a greater reality or they believe the words of a teacher who has done so. As we shall see, even Western science, long a bastion of religious scepticism, is now confirming that there is far more to life than the material world that we can touch and see with our normal senses.

MYSTICAL ENCOUNTERS WITH THE SACRED   Religious belief often stems from mystical experience – the overwhelming sensation that one has been touched by a reality that far transcends ordinary life. Those who have had such experiences find it hard to describe them, for what has touched them lies beyond the world of time and space to which our languages refer. These people usually know instantly and beyond a

The existential loneliness some feel is hauntingly depicted by the sculptures of Alberto Giacometti, such as his Walking Man, *c. 1947–48.*

> . . . *the things which are seen are temporal; but the things which are not seen are eternal.*
> *II Corinthians 4:18*

shadow of doubt that they have had a brush with spiritual reality. Teilhard de Chardin, a highly respected French paleontologist and Jesuit priest, became convinced that God is "the heart of All" because of his fiery personal encounters with "the unique Life of all things."[12] George William Russell, an Irish writer who described his mystical experiences under the pen name "AE," was lying on a hillside:

not then thinking of anything but the sunlight, and how sweet it was to drowse there, when, suddenly, I felt a fiery heart throb, and knew it was personal and intimate, and started with every sense dilated and intent, and turned inwards, and I heard first a music as of bells going away . . . and then the heart of the hills was opened to me, and I knew there was no hill for those who were there, and they were unconscious of the ponderous mountain piled above the palaces of light, and the winds were sparkling and diamond clear, yet full of colour as an opal, as they glittered through the valley, and I knew the Golden Age was all about me, and it was we who had been blind to it but that it had never passed away from the world. [13]

Encounters with a transcendent reality are given various names in spiritual traditions: enlightenment, God-realization, illumination, kensho, awakening, self-knowledge, gnosis, ecstatic communion, coming home. They may arise spontaneously, as in near-death experiences in which people seem to find themselves in a world of unearthly radiance, or may be induced by meditation, fasting, prayer, chanting, drugs, or dancing.

There are degrees of realization, just as there seem to be many levels of consciousness. In his classic study, *The Varieties of Religious Experience*, William James concluded:

Our normal waking consciousness, rational consciousness as we call it, is but one special type of consciousness, whilst all about it, parted from it by the flimsiest of screens, there lie potential forms of consciousness entirely different . . .

No account of the universe in its totality can be final which leaves these other forms of consciousness quite disregarded. [14]

A sense of the presence of the Great Unnamable may burst through the seeming ordinariness of life. (Samuel Palmer, The Waterfalls, Pistil Mawddach, North Wales, *1835–36.)*

Emersion or bathing is used in many religions as a symbol of spiritual cleansing.

Awakening to higher, more transcendent levels of consciousness may involve an expansion of our sense of who we are. Beyond egotism, we may discover that our beings do not stop at the boundaries of our skin but are instead continuous with the universe. An alternative experience is that a greater reality lies behind the material world, and encounters with this reality often send people to their knees in awe, in what has sometimes been called the "fear of God." German theologian Rudolf Otto, in his *Das Heilige* ("The Idea of the Holy"), found in the literature of many religions a sense of what he called the *mysterium tremendum*:

> *The feeling of it may at times come sweeping like a gentle tide, pervading the mind with a tranquil mood of deepest worship . . . It may burst in sudden eruption up from the depths of the soul with spasms and convulsions, or lead to the strangest excitements, to intoxicated frenzy, to transport, and to ecstasy. It has its wild and demonic forms and can sink to an almost grisly horror and shuddering . . . and again it may be developed into something beautiful and pure and glorious. It may become the hushed, trembling, and speechless humility of the creature in the presence of – whom or what? In the presence of that which is a mystery inexpressible and above all creatures.* [15]

[The ''flash of illumination''brings] a state of glorious inspiration, exaltation, intense joy, a piercingly sweet realization that the whole of life is fundamentally right and that it knows what it's doing.

Nona Coxhead[16]

EXPANSION OF SCIENTIFIC POSSIBILITY   Science shares with religion the goal of understanding the order of the cosmos. Like religion, science searches for universal principles that explain the facts of nature. Western science was born in the Greek philosophy of the sixth century BCE. Sages of the earliest school made no distinction between science, philosophy, and religion in their attempt to discover the essential nature of things (or "*physis*," from which the word "physics" is derived). These seekers did not have separate words for "spirit" and "matter." Like followers of Eastern traditions and ancient indigenous religions, they saw all of life as imbued with life and spirituality. This point of view is sometimes labelled *monism*: the concept that everything is reduceable to one fundamental reality.

Later Greek schools developed an opposite concept. They decided that matter can be broken down into its smallest building blocks, then thought to be atoms, and that these passive particles are moved by external spiritual forces. This division between spirit and matter, inner and outer, is called *dualism*. Most influential philosophers and religious thinkers, particularly Aristotle and the Christian church, were more interested in spirit. Matter was largely ignored in the West until the Renaissance, an era of great interest in nature, in which matter was subjected to experimentation and mathematical analysis. Nature was regarded as a giant machine made of many separate parts, ruled by God from above. But because the spiritual realm could not be mathematically assessed, scientific progress was based on ignoring spirit and quantifying matter. The idea of the divine seemed to be increasingly unnecessary to explaining the universe. Some later proclaimed, "God is dead!"

Contemporary Western science is now beginning to return to the original organic point of view that all of life is interrelated and that what has been called spiritual is a natural part of this wholeness. In biology, rather than the species-by-species struggle for survival depicted by Darwin, some scientists are asserting that the wisdom of nature includes many examples of seemingly purposeful creation, cooperation between species, and harmony of organisms and environment. In terms of purpose, for instance, geneticist Lucien Cuenot observes that "birds that fly can do so because a thousand details converge: long wing and tail feathers, pneumatic bones, air sacs, breast bone and pectoral muscles, design of the ribs, neck, feet, spinal column, pelvis, automatic hooking

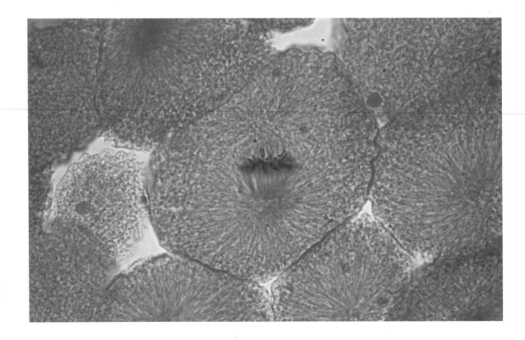

Things are not as they seem on the surface, as indicated by this electron micrograph photo of cell division.

of feather barbules, etc."[17] These characteristics cannot have converged accidentally by blind chance, says Cuenot.

After surveying the intelligence apparent in organic design, biologists Robert Augros and George Stanciu conclude:

> Nature wastes neither function nor structure. She provides all the equipment needed for each organism to live but does not burden it with useless organs . . . Every cell, every tissue, every organ serves a purpose. Every animal, every plant directs its activities to an end. The whole of nature is ordered by purpose.[18]

Transformation of the scientific point of view is particularly striking in twentieth-century quantum physics. In place of a machine-like universe separate from the human observer, those probing the world of subatomic particles have found that their behaviors can only be described in terms of a dynamic, interdependent whole. Furthermore, what we perceive with our five senses is not ultimate reality. For instance, the inertness and solidity of matter are only illusions. Each atom consists mostly of empty space with tiny particles whirling around in it. These subatomic particles – such as neutrons, protons, and electrons – cannot even be described as "things." In experiments they behave like energy as well as like mass, wavelike interconnections as well as separate particles. They have no precise location and may be found in several places at one time. And the interconnections do not exist separately from the mind of the person who is observing them. Human consciousness is inextricably involved in what it thinks it is watching. As physicist David Bohm puts it: "Everything interpenetrates everything."[19] This vision of reality was discovered long ago by the mystics of Hinduism, Buddhism, and Taoism. They uncovered it by meditation rather than experimentation, by looking beyond surface appearances to grasp the One.

Numerous scientifically unorthodox, but spiritually possible, explanations of the universe are now being proposed by highly respected scientists. Quantum physicist David Bohm suggests that the universe is multi-dimensional. The dimension we see and think of as "real" is the *explicate* order, but behind it lies the *implicate* order, in which separateness resolves into unbroken wholeness. Beyond may lie other subtle dimensions, all merging into an infinite ground that unfolds itself as light.

Biologist Rupert Sheldrake proposes that the forms and behaviors of living creatures are influenced by the forms and behaviors of other members of their species in ways that transcend physical heredity. He cites evidence of a non-material *morphogenetic field*, a sort of "group mind" that develops over time.

Some astrophysicists and mathematicians are overwhelmed by the odds against the development of life as we know it. For instance, if the force of gravitation were different by as little as one part in 10,000,000,000,000,000,000,000,000,000,000,000,000,000, stars would never have been formed. Amazingly fine balances are likewise required to hold atoms in equilibrium between diffusion and inward collapse. The mathematical improbability of such precise systems evolving by mere chance suggests to these scientists that there is an intelligent creative principle of some sort behind it all.

Although such theories are still highly controversial in scientific circles, they are based on evidence that we cannot fully trust the data of our senses. The world is not as it appears to be on the surface. Our bodies appear relatively solid, but they are in a constant state of flux and interchange with the environment. Our eyes, ears, noses, tongues, and skin do not reveal absolute truths. Rather, our sensory organs may operate as filters, selecting from a multi-dimensional universe only those characteristics that we need to perceive in order to survive. Imagine how difficult it would be simply to walk across a street if we could see all the electromagnetic energy in the atmosphere, such as X-rays, radio waves, gamma rays, and infrared and ultraviolet light, rather than only the small band we see as the colors of the visible spectrum. Scientific devices can perceive a greater range of energies, but we know that more lies beyond what we have yet been able to measure. And even our ability to conceive of what we cannot sense is limited by the way our brain is organized. To accept the possibility that absolute reality lies beyond our personal experience is not unscientific today.

> *The most beautiful and profound emotion that we can experience is the sensation of the mystical. It is the sower of all true science. He to whom this emotion is a stranger, who can no longer wonder and stand rapt in awe, is as good as dead. To know that what is impenetrable to us really exists, manifesting itself as the highest widsom and the most radiant beauty which our dull faculties can comprehend only in their most primitive forms – this knowledge, this feeling is at the center of true religiousness. . . . A human being is part of the whole. . . . He experiences himself, his thoughts and feelings as something separated from the rest – a kind of optical delusion of his consciousness. . . . Our task must be to free ourselves from this prison by widening our circle of compassion to embrace all living creatures, and the whole [of] nature in its beauty.*
>
> *Albert Einstein*[20]

Modes of knowing: reason and intuition

We have two basic ways of knowing what is: rational thought and direct intuition. To reason is to establish abstract general categories from the data we have gathered with our senses, and then organize these abstractions to formulate seemingly logical ideas about reality (for example, "Life is so precisely balanced that it must have been created intentionally by a great intelligence."). Intuition transcends the data of the senses and the manipulations of the mind to perceive truths that seem to lie beyond reason (for example, "Everything is permeated with meaningfulness!"). Some believe that this way of knowing perceives truth directly, rather than thinking about it. Intuitive wisdom cannot be verified by the senses or the scientific instruments that we use to extend the range of perception. It emerges into awareness in an entirely different way than does logical thought. Much of the stuff of religion originates in intuition. Some religions encourage followers to have faith in the intuitive wisdom of their founders, believing that the source of their teachings was divine revelation. The sacred teachings revealed to Muhammad, *The Qur'an*, acknowledge a divine source not only for these scriptures but also for the earlier Jewish and Christian scriptures.

Other religions encourage people to develop their own intuitive abilities to perceive spiritual truths. Some native American groups have the tradition of the vision quest, in which a person cries for a sacred vision of his or her purpose in this world. And many religions have developed meditation techniques that encourage intuitive wisdom to rise from the depths – or the voice of the divine to descend into individual consciousness. Whether this wisdom is perceived as a natural faculty within or an external voice, the

process is similar. In meditation, the consciousness is initially turned away from the world and even from one's own feelings and thoughts, letting them all go. Often a concentration practice, such as watching the breath or staring at a candle flame, is used to collect the awareness into a single unfragmented focus. Once the mind is quiet, distinctions between inside and outside drop away. The seer becomes one with the seen, in a fusion of subject and object where the inner nature of things often seems to reveal itself.

Understandings of the Divine

Approached by different ways of knowing, by different people, from different times and different cultures, the sacred has many faces. Labels that scholars have given to broad categories of belief are based on the word *theism*, meaning belief in the existence of a god or gods. Some people identify the universe or nature – or the total of its laws and forces – as "God." This concept is known as *pantheism*. Other believers perceive one high god who created and maintains the universe. This *monotheistic* divinity is usually conceived of as a being of sorts to whom one can address appeals and praise and who has personal attributes such as perfect love or all-pervading wisdom. A third possibility is the perception of numerous deities, a concept known as *polytheism*.

Anthropologists feel that human concepts of the divine mirror human social organization. Polytheistic concepts are often found among societies with distinct social classes (such as the castes of India) or occupational groups, whereas monotheistic beliefs tend to appear in societies in which one group or leader maintains order.

In addition to these perceptions of what constitutes the sacred reality, beliefs of where it resides differ. The divine may be conceived as present in creation (*immanent*) or as existing above and outside of the material universe (*transcendent*). *Animism* is the belief that many visible beings, objects, and natural phenomena are imbued with consciousness and spiritual energy and may share their wisdom or power with humans. Some people believe that the sacred reality is usually invisible but occasionally appears visibly in human *incarnations*, such as Christ or Krishna, or in special manifestations such as the flame Moses reportedly saw coming from the center of a bush but not consuming it.

Atheism is non-belief in any deity. Following Karl Marx, many communist countries discouraged or suppressed religious beliefs, attempting to replace them with secular faith in the party or state. Atheism may also arise from within, in those whose experiences give them no reason to believe that there is anything more to life than the mundane.

Agnosticism is not the denial of the divine but the belief that if it exists it is impossible for humans to know it. Buddha was largely silent about the nature of the divine, so the religion that he founded is sometimes called *nontheistic*.

These categories are not mutually exclusive, so attempts to apply the labels can sometimes confuse us rather than help us understand religions. In some "polytheistic" traditions there is a hierarchy of gods and goddesses with one highest being at the top. In Hinduism, each individual deity is understood as encompassing all aspects of deity. In the paradoxes that occur when we try to apply human logic and language to that which transcends linear thought, a person may believe that God is both a highly personal being and also present in all things. Or mystics may have deep personal encounters with the

The concept of God as an old man with a beard who rules the world from the sky has been supported by the art of patriarchal monotheistic traditions, such as William Blake's frontispiece to ''Europe'', The Act of Creation, 1794.

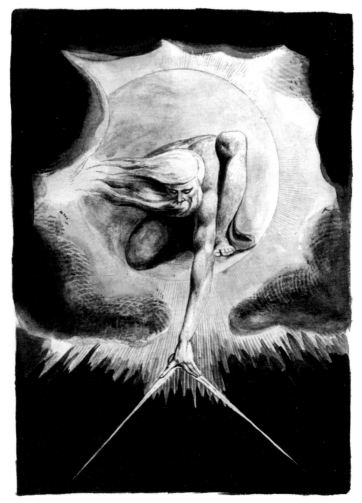

divine and yet find it so unspeakable that they say it is beyond human knowing.

Some people believe that the aspect of the divine that has revealed itself to them is the only one. Others feel that there is one being with many faces, that all religions come from one source. Father Bede Griffiths, a Catholic monk who lives in a Hindu community in India that attempts to unite Eastern and Western traditions, is among those who feel that if we engage in a deep study of all religions we will find their common ground:

> *In each tradition the one divine Reality, the one eternal Truth, is present, but it is hidden under symbols. . . . Always the divine Mystery is hidden under a veil, but each revelation (or ''unveiling'') unveils some aspect of the one Truth, or, if you like, the veil becomes thinner at a certain point. The Semitic religions, Judaism and Islam, reveal the transcendent aspect of the divine Mystery with incomparable power. The oriental religions reveal the divine Immanence with immeasurable depth. Yet in each the opposite aspect is contained, though in a more hidden way.* [21]

Worship and symbol

No matter how believers conceive of the divine, its greatness inspires their reverence. The outer forms of religions consist in large part of human attempts to express this reverence and perhaps enter the sacred state of communion with that which is worshipped. Around the world, rituals, sacraments, prayers, and spiritual practices are used to create a sacred atmosphere or state of consciousness in which people hope to touch or be touched by whispers of the eternal.

> *Our religious ceremonies are but the shadows of that great universal worship celebrated in the heavens by the legions of heavenly beings on all planes, and our prayers drill a channel across this mist separating our earthbound plane from the celestial ones through which a communication may be established with the powers that be.*
>
> Pir Vilayat Inayat Khan[22]

That which religions attempt to approach is beyond human utterance. Believers build statues and buildings through which to worship the divine, but these forms are not it. Because people are addressing the invisible, it can only be suggested through metaphor. Deepest consciousness cannot speak the language of everyday life; what it knows can only be suggested in images.

Many peoples have used similar images to represent similar sacred meanings. The sun is frequently honored as a symbol of the divine because of its radiance; the sky is the abode of many gods, for it is elevated above the earth. Great spiritual leaders are often said to have been born of virgin mothers, for their seminal source is not human but rather the Invisible One.

It is now common to interpret such symbols metaphorically rather than literally and to see them as serving functions for the society or the individual. For example, Joseph Campbell speculated that the sacred myths of a group serve four basic social purposes: awakening a sense of wonder at creation, incorporating the group's ethical codes, and helping individuals pass harmoniously through life-cycle changes. Following psychoanalyst Carl Jung's lead, Campbell interpreted legends of the hero's journey (with widespread stories of separation, initiation, and return bearing truth to the people) as a form of psychological instruction for individuals:

> It is the business of mythology to reveal the specific dangers and techniques of the dark interior way from tragedy to comedy. Hence the incidents are fantastic and ''unreal'': they represent psychological, not physical, triumphs. The passage of the mythological hero may be overground, [but] fundamentally it is inward – into depths where obscure resistances are overcome, and long lost, forgotten powers are revivified, to be made available for the transfiguration of the world.[23]

On the other hand, sometimes scholars have interpreted metaphorically that which believers find literally true. Indigenous medicine people experience their spirit allies as real, albeit often invisible. When we encounter the symbols of unfamiliar religions we may find them strange or unpleasant unless we can enter into the mystical truths they embody, empathize with those who believe in them, or develop an intellectual understanding of their metaphorical content.

Women and the feminine in religions

Many of the myths surviving in today's religions may be related to the suppression of early female-oriented religions by later male-oriented religious systems. Archaeological evidence from many cultures has recently been re-interpreted, suggesting that worship of a female high Goddess was originally widespread. Although there were and are now cultures that did not ascribe gender or hierarchy or personality to the divine, some that did may have seen the highest deity as a female.

Just as today's male high deity goes by different names in different religions (God, Allah), the Great Goddess had many names. Among her many identities, she was Danu or Diti in ancient India, the Great Mother Nu Kwa of China, the Egyptian Cobra Goddess Ua Zit, the Greek Creator Goddess Gaia, the Sun Goddess Arinna of Turkey, Coatlique the Mother of Aztec deities, Queen Mother Freyja of the Scandinavians, Great Spider Woman of the Pueblo peoples of North America, and Mawu, omnipotent creator of the Dahomey. A reverent address to Ishtar, supreme deity of ancient Babylon, dating from the eighteenth to seventh centuries BCE suggests some of the powers ascribed to her:

> *Unto Her who renders decision, Goddess of all things, Unto the Lady of Heaven and Earth who receives supplication; Unto Her who hears petition, who entertains prayer; Unto the compassionate Goddess who loves righteousness; Ishtar the Queen, who suppresses all that is confused. To the Queen of Heaven, the Goddess of the Universe, the One who walked in terrible Chaos and brought life by the Law of Love; And out of Chaos brought us harmony.* [24]

Temples and images that seem to have been devoted to worship of the Goddess have been found in almost every Neolithic and early historic archaeological site in Europe and the Near and Middle East. She was often symbolically linked with water, serpents, birds, eggs, spirals, the moon, the womb, the vulva, the magnetic currents of the earth,

An early image of what appears to be the Great Mother, creator and sustainer of the universe. (Tel Halaf, 5th millenium BCE.)

psychic powers, and the eternal creation and renewal of life. Some who worshipped her claimed knowledge about techniques of spiritual rebirth and illumination – or raising the lower earth energy represented by the serpent up the spine into the wings of higher spiritual knowledge and ecstatic communion with life. Sexuality was often a part of this process, with ritual intercourse honored as a means of accessing spiritual energies.

In these agricultural cultures that may have worshipped the Goddess, women frequently held strong social positions. Heredity lineages were often traced through the mother, and women were honored as priestesses, healers, agricultural inventors, counselors, prophetesses, and sometimes warriors.

What happened to these apparently Goddess-oriented religions? Contemporary scholars are now trying to piece together not only the reality, extent, and characteristics of Goddess worship, but also the circumstances of its demise. A recent cross-cultural survey by Eli Sagan (*The Dawn of Tyranny*) indicates that male-dominant social and religious structures accompanied the often violent shift from communal kinship groups and tribal confederations to centralized monarchies. In these kingdoms, social order was based on loyalty to the king and fear of his power. In Europe and the Middle East worship of the Goddess was suppressed by invading Indo-European groups (most probably from the steppes of southern Russia) in which males were dominant and championed worship of a supreme male deity. These conquests took place throughout the third and second millenia BCE with the help of horse-drawn chariots, a more devastating war technology than any previously used.

The Indo-Europeans' deity was often described as a storm god residing on a mountain and bringing light (seen as the good) into the darkness (portrayed as bad and associated with the female). Mythical accounts of the struggle between this male god and the female goddess for supremacy often involve a male god grappling with a serpent or dragon, as in the early Hebrew myth of Yahweh's defeat of the serpent Leviathan (an alternative name for Lotan, the Goddess of Canaan). In India, the Aryan god Indra, "he who overthrows cities," kills the Mother Goddess Danu and her son, who are described in the Vedic scriptures of the invaders as serpents and then as a dead cow and her calf.

In some cases, worship of the Goddess co-existed with or later surfaced within male deity worship. In India, the new gods often had female consorts or counterparts or were androgynous, both male and female. But the religion of the Goddess was especially stamped out by the patriarchal Hebrews and then by followers of Christ. Astarte, Queen of Heaven, had been worshipped for thousands of years in Palestine before the ascendency of the Hebraic followers of Yahweh, around 1800 to 1200 BCE. However, by 500 CE, goddess worship – other than devotion to Mary, the mother of Jesus – had been totally obliterated by the Roman and Byzantine Christian emperors.

As the Goddess was suppressed, so was spiritual participation of women. In patriarchal societies, women often became property and were expected to be obedient to the rule of men. Although Christ had honored and worked with women, his later male followers limited the position of women within the Christian church. The Apostle Paul wrote to the Corinthian congregation:

> *For the man is not of the woman, but the woman of the man. Let the women keep silence in the churches, for it is not permitted unto them to speak; but they are commanded to be under obedience, so saith the law. And if they learn anything, let them ask their husbands at home; for it is a shame for women to speak in the church. (I Corinthians 11:3, 7, 9)*

Not only was women's spiritual contribution cast aside; in replacing the Goddess, patriarchal groups may also have devalued the "feminine" aspect of religion – the receptive, intuitive, ecstatic mystical communion which was seemingly allowed freer reign in the goddess traditions. Fears of the force latent in the unconscious, unknown, and uncontrolled aspects of the psyche led to witch hunts, in which women were the major victims, and to a distrust of mystics of both sexes who dared to reveal their ecstatic and personal relationship with the divine.

Although women are still barred from equal spiritual footing with men in many religions, this situation is now being widely challenged. As we explore specific religions throughout this book, we will look at the position of women and any changes that seem to be taking place. Feminist Christian theologian Rosemary Ruether feels that the movement toward greater religious participation by women may transcend gender issues to heal other fragmentations in our spiritual lives:

> The feminist religious revolution ... reaches forward to an alternative that can heal the splits between ''masculine'' and ''feminine,'' between mind and body, between males and females as gender groups, between society and nature, and between races and classes.[25]

Fundamental and liberal interpretations

Within each faith people often have different ways of interpreting their traditions. The labels given to these modes of interpretation are often burdened by negative judgements, but the labels themselves are neutral and descriptive rather than judgemental.

Fundamentalists believe that scriptures or teachings are literally true – that Buddha's mother really was visited by a white elephant who implanted himself in her womb and was then born as the Buddha-to-be. In Christianity, fundamentalists believe that the Bible is factual history and that its teachings and prophecies are beyond dispute. The *orthodox* stand by the form of their religion; they claim to be strict followers of its established practices, laws, and creeds.

Other followers may be less rigid in their interpretations. They may not agree with all the established beliefs of the tradition, but still consider themselves faithful to the spirit, if not the letter of the law. *Liberals* favor individual freedom of interpretation; they may see scriptures as products of a specific culture and time rather than the eternal voice of truth, and may interpret passages metaphorically rather than literally. If activists, they may advocate reforms in the ways their religion is officially understood and practiced. Those who are labeled *heretics* publicly assert controversial positions that are unacceptable to the orthodox establishment. *Mystics* are guided by their own spiritual experiences, which may coincide with any of the above positions, from fundamentalist understandings to heresy.

The dark side of organized religion

Tragically, religions have often split rather than unified humanity, have oppressed rather than freed, have terrified rather than inspired.

Since the human needs that religions answer are so strong, those who hold religious power are in a position to dominate and control their followers. In fact, in many religions leaders are given this legitimized authority to guide people's spiritual lives, for their wisdom and special access to the sacred is valued. Because religions involve the unseen, the mysterious, these leaders' guidance may not be verifiable by everyday physical experience. It must more often be accepted on faith. While faith is one of the cornerstones of spirituality, it is possible to surrender to spiritual leaders who are misguided or unethical. Religious leaders, like secular leaders, may not be honest with themselves and others about their inner motives. They may mistake their own thoughts and desires for the voice and will of God. Some people believe, however, that the most important thing for the disciple is to surrender the ego; even an unworthy leader can help in this goal simply by playing the role of one to whom one must surrender personal control.

Because religions paint pictures of life after death, they may play on people's fear of death or fears of punishment, both here and hereafter. This excerpt from a sermon by the New England Calvinist minister Jonathan Edwards illustrates the terrifying images that can be conjured:

> *You are thus [sinners] in the hands of an angry God; 'tis nothing but his mere pleasure that keeps you from being this moment swallowed up in everlasting destruction. The God that holds you over the pit of hell, much as one holds a spider or some loathsome insect over the fire, abhors you, and is dreadfully provoked; his wrath towards you burns like fire; he looks upon you as worthy of nothing else, but to be cast into the fire.*[26]

Religions try to help us make ethical choices in our lives, to develop a moral conscience. But in people who already have perfectionist or paranoid tendencies, the fear of sinning and being punished can be exaggerated to the point of neurosis or even psychosis by blaming, punishment-oriented religious teachings. If they try to leave their religion for the sake of their mental health, they may be haunted with guilt that they have done a terribly wrong thing. Religions thus have the potential for wreaking psychological havoc in their followers.

Because some religions, particularly those that developed in the East, offer a state of blissful contemplation as the reward for spiritual practice, the faithful may use religion to escape from their everyday problems. Psychologist John Welwood observes that Westerners sometimes embrace Eastern religions with the unconscious motive of avoiding their unsatisfactory lives. He calls this attempt "spiritual bypassing":

> *Spiritual bypassing may be particularly tempting for individuals who are having difficulty making their way through life's basic developmental stages, especially at a time when what were once ordinary developmental landmarks – earning a livelihood through dignified work, raising a family, keeping a marriage together – have become increasingly difficult and elusive for large segments of the population. While struggling with becoming autonomous individuals, many people are introduced to spiritual teachings and practices which come from cultures that assume a person having already passed through the basic developmental stages. . . . The basic purpose of spiritual practice is to help liberate us from attachment to an imprisoning self-structure. In order to reap the full benefits of such a practice, however, we have to have a stable self-structure.*[27]

Because religions may have such a strong hold on their followers – by their fears, their desires, their deep beliefs – they are potential centers for political power. When church and state are one, the belief that the dominant national religion is the only true religion may be used to oppress those of other beliefs within the country. It may also be used as a rallying point for wars against other nations, casting the desire for control as a holy motive. Throughout history, huge numbers of people have been killed in the name of eradicating "false" religions and replacing them with the "true" religion. Our spirituality has the potential for uniting us all in bonds of love, harmony, and mutual respect. But often it has served instead to divide us by creating barriers of hatred and intolerance.

Because institutionalized religions attempt to follow the teachings of their founders, there is also the danger that more energy will go into preserving the outer form of the tradition than into maintaining its inner spirit. The living nature of any spiritual path can only be experienced. It cannot be solidified into dogma. If rituals are carried out without genuine inner experience, they become empty shells.

No religion is free from these distortions. To keep religion alive, true, and vibrant requires a genuine connection with the unseen, scrupulous honesty, and pure-heartedness. As we survey the various contemporary manifestations of the religious impulse, we will find people and groups who are keeping the spark of the divine alive today. They can be found in all traditions.

Suggested reading

Campbell, Joseph, *The Hero with a Thousand Faces,* second edition, Princeton, New Jersey: Princeton University Press, 1968. Brilliant leaps across time and space to trace the hero's journey – seen as a spiritual quest – in all the world's mythologies and religions.

Campbell, Joseph with Bill Moyers, *The Power of Myth,* New York: Doubleday, 1988. More brilliant comparisons of the world's mythologies with deep insights into their common psychological and spiritual truths.

Capra, Fritjof, *The Tao of Physics,* New York: Bantam Books, 1977, and London: Fontana, 1983. A fascinating comparison of the insights of Eastern religions and contemporary physics.

Eliade, Mircea, *The Sacred and the Profane,* translated by Willard R. Trask, New York: Harper and Row, 1959. Encompassing all religions, a study of religious myth, symbolism, and ritual as ways of creating a place for the sacred within a secular environment.

Ellwood, Robert S., Jr., *Mysticism and Religion,* Englewood Cliffs, New Jersey and London: Prentice-Hall, 1980. Good survey of kinds of mystical experiences and their relationship to religious thought.

Hixon, Lex, *Coming Home: The Experience of Enlightenment in Sacred Traditions,* Garden City, New York: Anchor/Doubleday, 1978. An exploration of the enlightenment experience in religious teachings from Plotinus to recent Hindu gurus.

Otto, Rudolf, *The Idea of the Holy,* second edition, London: Oxford University Press, 1950. An important exploration of "non-rational" experiences of the divine.

Sharma, Arvind, ed., *Women in World Religions,* Albany, New York: State University of New York Press, 1987. Analyses of the historic and contemporary place of women in each of the major religions.

Stone, Merlin, *When God was a Woman.* San Diego, California: Harcourt Brace Jovanovich, 1976. Pioneering survey of archaeological evidence of the early religion of the goddess.

2 INDIGENOUS SACRED WAYS

"Everything is alive"

Here and there around the globe, pockets of people still follow local sacred ways handed down from their remote ancestors and adapted to contemporary circumstances. These are the traditional *indigenous* people – descendants of the original inhabitants of lands now controlled by political systems in which they have little influence. Some who follow the ancient spiritual traditions still live close to the earth in non-industrial tribal cultures; many do not. But despite the disruption of their traditional lifestyles, many indigenous people maintain a sacred way of life that is distinctively different from all other religions.

These old ways which indigenous people may refer to as their Original Instructions on how to live were almost lost under the onslaught of genocidal colonization, conversion pressures from global religions, and economic changes. Much of the ancient visionary wisdom has disappeared. There are few traditionally trained elders left and few young people willing to undergo the lengthy and rigorous training necessary for spiritual leadership in these sacred ways. Nevertheless, in our time there is a renewal of interest in these traditions, fanning hope that what they offer will not be lost.

> *To what extent can [indigenous groups] reinstitute traditional religious values in a world gone mad with development, electronics, almost instantaneous transportation facilities, and intellectually grounded in a rejection of spiritual and mysterious events?* Vine Deloria, Jr.[1]

Barriers to understanding

Outsiders have little known or understood the indigenous sacred ways. When threatened with severe repression, many of these traditions have long been practiced only in secret. In Mesoamerica, the ancient teachings have remained hidden for five hundred years since the coming of the conquistadores, passed down within families as a secret oral tradition. In parts of aboriginal Australia, the real teachings have been underground for two hundred years since white colonialists and Christian missionaries appeared. As aborigine Lorraine Mafi Williams explains:

> *We have stacked away our religious, spiritual, cultural beliefs. When the missionaries came, we were told by our old people to be respectful, listen and be obedient, go to church, go to Sunday school, but do not adopt the Christian doctrine because it takes away our cultural, spiritual beliefs. So we've always stayed within God's laws in what we know.*[2]

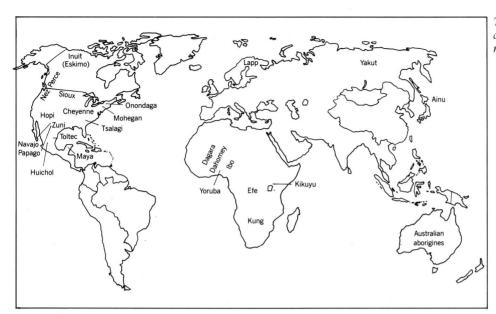

The approximate distribution of indigenous groups mentioned in this chapter.

Not uncommonly, the newer global traditions have either been adopted as a veneer over older ways or blended with them.

Until recently, those who attempted to ferret out the native sacred ways had little basis for understanding them. Most were anthropologists who approached spiritual behaviors from the non-spiritual perspective of Western science. Knowing that these researchers from other cultures did not grasp the truth of their beliefs, the native peoples have often teased them, purposely giving them information that was incorrect and even silly. They did so not only because it was fun, but also because they knew it was important to protect the sanctity of their sacred practices from the uninitiated.

In most native cultures, spiritual ways are shared orally. Teachings are experienced rather than read from books. There are therefore no scriptures of the sort that other religions are built around (although there once existed some texts which were destroyed by conquering groups, such as the Mayan codices). This feature helps to keep the indigenous sacred ways dynamic and flexible rather than fossilized. It also keeps the sacred experience fresh in the present. However, the dearth of tangible evidences of indigenous sacred ways, such as church buildings and scriptures, makes them even more inaccessible to outside investigators.

Indigenous peoples have generally had little interest in sharing their sacred ways with outsiders anyway. Their most sacred ceremonies are private. Some of their beliefs are tied to the land on which they live and their entire way of life; they are only meaningful within this context. The people respect the rights of others to their own beliefs and make no attempt to convert outsiders to their local ways.

Indigenous spirituality is a particular approach to all of life. Spirituality is not a separate experience, like meditating in the morning or going to church on Sunday. Rather, indigenous spirituality ideally pervades all moments, from reverence in gathering clay to make a pot, to respect within tribal council meetings. As an elder of

In the Kikuyu indigenous tradition of Kenya, it is very important to know intimately the land on which one lives, including its orientation to the sun and to Mt. Kenya, the sacred ''mountain of brightness.''

the Huichol in Mexico puts it:

> *Everything we do in life is for the glory of God. We praise him in the well swept floor, the well weeded field, the polished machette, the brilliant colors of the picture and embroidery. In these ways we prepare for a long life and pray for a good one.* [3]

The spiritual world view is not inevitably linked to materially simple ways of life. Tsalagi (Cherokee) priestess Dhyani Ywahoo lives in a modern frame house in Vermont; when her family lived in Brooklyn, they continued their ceremonial cycles in their backyard gardens. The neighbors thought their fireplaces were barbecue pits. She asserts:

> *The idea that to be a traditional Indian you have to go back into the past and throw everything away is not a realistic vision. A traditional Indian has a traditional state of mind that is respectful for the land and is always considering how to benefit as many people as possible.* [4]

Despite the hindrances to understanding of indigenous forms of spirituality, the doors to understanding are opening somewhat in our times. Firstly, the traditional elders are very concerned about the growing potential for planetary disaster. Some are beginning to share their basic values, if not their esoteric practices, in hopes of preventing industrial societies from destroying the earth. Secondly, those of other faiths are beginning to recognize the value and profundity of indigenous ways which were in the past abhorred and suppressed by organized religions. Thirdly, many people who have not grown up in native cultures are attempting to embrace indigenous spiritual ways, finding their own traditions lacking in certain qualities for which they long, such as love for the earth.

Indigenous traveling teachers who have revealed themselves are swamped with eager students. But many native peoples are wary of this trend. They feel that their sacred ways are all they have left and worry that even these may be sold, stolen, and ruined. Dhyani Ywahoo issues a strong warning about the dangers involved:

> *Caution: Native American religion is like fire. It's the fire that burns away confusion. It is the fire that warms the body and relieves suffering, and it is also the fire that destroys illusions. These are very powerful teachings. Native American teachings on the surface appear very simple. As one grows older, one realizes just how subtle and how deeply penetrating this wisdom is. There are certain rituals that people are very attracted to. They can really cause nervous breakdowns in someone who is not properly prepared, because Native American teaching is an internal process as well as an external process.* [5]

Cultural diversity

In this chapter we are considering the faith-ways of indigenous peoples as a whole. These traditions have evolved within materially diverse cultures. Some were once highly advanced in a material sense. Today's Mexican Indians are descendants of ancient great civilizations. When Cortes took over Tenochtitlan (which now lies beneath Mexico City) in 1519, he found it a beautiful clean city with elaborate architecture, indoor plumbing, a highly accurate calendar, and advanced systems of mathematics and astronomy. The Tsalagi people had an advanced theocracy before the time of Christ. When De Soto captured the female leader of the Tsalagi in the Mississippi Valley, the average city in this culture had eighteen to twenty-five thousand inhabitants, with elaborate sun temples and a highly developed philosophy. Former African kingdoms were highly culturally advanced.

At the other extreme are those few cultures that still maintain a survival strategy of hunting and gathering. For example, some Australian aborigines continue to live as mobile foragers, though constricted to government-owned missions. A nomadic survival strategy necessitates simplicity in material goods; whatever can be gathered or built rather easily at the next camp need not be dragged along. But material simplicity is not a sign of spiritual poverty. The Australian aborigines have a complex *cosmogony*, or model of the origins of the universe, supported by an elaborate system of stories told from memory and by a strong sense of their spiritual purpose within the cosmos.

Some traditional people live in their ancestral enclaves, somewhat sheltered from the pressures of modern industrial life, though not untouched by the outer world. The Hopi Nation has continuously occupied a harsh high plateau area of the Southwestern United States for eight hundred to one thousand years; their sacred ritual calendar is tied to the yearly farming cycle. Others visit their sacred sites and ancestral shrines but live in more urban settings because of job opportunities. The indigenous people who climb a mountain in Mexico to participate in the Sun Dance include subway personnel, journalists, and artists of native blood who live in Mexico City. Lorraine Mafi Williams is a filmmaker living in Sydney, Australia, but her people return to their sacred sites (some of them owned by non-native people) for spiritual and cultural renewal "whenever the industrial white world gets a bit too much for us."[6]

In addition to variations in lifestyles, indigenous traditions vary in their adaptations to dominant religions. Often native beliefs have become interwoven with those of global religions, such as Buddhism, Islam, and Christianity. Sometimes worshippers themselves are not clear which tradition they are following. In Southeast Asia, household Buddhist shrines are almost identical to the spirit houses in which the people still make offerings to honor the local spirits. The Dahomey tradition from West Africa was carried to Haiti by thousands of African slaves and called "Voodoo" from *Vodu*, one of the names for the chief non-human spirits. Forced by the European colonialists to adopt Christianity, worshippers of Voodoo fused their old gods with their images of Catholic saints.

Despite their different histories and economic patterns, indigenous sacred ways do tend to have certain principles in common. Some peoples even believe that their cultures were originally unified before the continents separated and/or the people began spiraling outward in their migrations. Scientific evidence for this concept includes recognition that some continents were once joined and that there are linguistic similarities between the languages of the Tsalagi in the Americas, Tibetans, and the aboriginal Ainu of Japan. When people of geographically far-flung indigenous traditions get together and start exchanging stories, they find many similarities.

The circle of right relationships

For indigenous peoples, everything in the cosmos is intimately interrelated. The symbol of unity among the parts of this sacred reality is a circle. Indigenous people hold the circle sacred because it is infinite – it has no beginning, no end. Time is circular rather than linear, for it keeps coming back to the same place. Life revolves around the generational cycles of birth, youth, maturity, and physical death, the return of the

Among the gentle Efe Pygmies of Zaire's Ituri Forest, children learn to value the circle by playing the "circle game." With feet making a circle, each names a circular object and then an expression of roundness (the family circle, togetherness, "a complete rainbow").

seasons, the cyclical movements of the moon, sun, stars, and planets. The earth is known to go through cyclical changes, with periods of relative stability separated by episodes of rapid shifts.

This understanding of life as a complex of circles is thought to be the perfect framework for harmony. As Lame Deer, a Sioux holy man, explains:

> Nature wants things to be round. The bodies of human beings and animals have no corners. With us the circle stands for the togetherness of people who sit with one another around the campfire, relatives and friends united in peace while the pipe passes from hand to hand. The camp in which every tipi had its place was also a ring. The tipi was a ring in which people sat in a circle and all the families in the village were in turn circles within a larger circle, part of the larger hoop which was the seven campfires of the Sioux, representing one nation. The nation was only a part of the universe, in itself circular and made of the earth, which is round, of the sun, which is round, of the stars, which are round. The moon, the horizon, the rainbow – circles within circles within circles, with no beginning and no end.[7]

To maintain the natural balance of the circles of existence, indigenous peoples are taught that they must develop right relationships with everything that is. Their relatives include the unseen world of spirits, the land and weather, the people and creatures, and the power within.

Relationships with spirit

Many indigenous traditions worship a Supreme Being who they believe created the cosmos. This being is known by the Sioux as Wakan tanka or Great Mysterious or Great Spirit of whom Black Elk speaks:

> We should understand well that all things are the works of the Great Spirit. We should know that He is within all things: the trees, the grasses, the rivers, the mountains, and all the four-legged animals, and the winged peoples; and even more important, we should understand that He is also above all these things and peoples.[8]

African names for this One are attributes such as "All-powerful," "Creator," "the one who is met everywhere," "the one who exists by himself," or "the one who began the forest." Usually the supreme being is referred to by male pronouns, but in some groups the Supreme Being is a female, such as Ala, earth mother goddess of the Ibo.

Awareness of one's relationship to the Great Power gives life meaning and makes it worthwhile. But it remains unseen and mysterious. An Eskimo shaman described his people's experience of:

> . . . a power that we call Sila, which is not to be explained in simple words. A great spirit, supporting the world and the weather and all life on earth, a spirit so mighty that [what he says] to mankind is not through common words, but by storm and snow and rain and the fury of the sea; all the forces of nature that men fear. But he has also another way of [communicating]; by sunlight and calm of the sea, and little children innocently at play, themselves understanding nothing. Children hear a soft and gentle voice, almost like that of a woman. It comes to them in a mysterious way, but so gently that they are not afraid; they only hear that some danger threatens . . . When all is well, Sila sends no message to mankind, but withdraws into his own endless nothingness, apart.[9]

In many cultures, this Great Mysterious is thought to have withdrawn a bit from the affairs of the earth. African myths suggest that the High God was originally so close to humans that they became disrespectful. The All-Powerful was like the sky, they say, which was once so close that children wiped their dirty hands on it, and women (blamed by men for the withdrawal) broke off pieces for soup and bumped it with their sticks when pounding grain. Although southern and central Africans believe in a high being who presides over the universe, including less powerful spirits, they consider this being either too distant or too powerful to worship or call on for help.

More accessible to humans and more involved in the daily workings of life are many unseen powers. Some of these are perceived without form, as mysterious and sacred presences. Others are perceived as having more definite, albeit invisible, forms and personalities. These may include deities with human-like personalities, the nature spirits of special local places such as venerable trees and mountains, animal spirit helpers, personified elemental forces, ancestors who still take an interest in their living relatives, or special beings such as the spirit keepers of the four directions.

The Dagara of Burkina Faso in West Africa are familiar with the *kontombili*, who look like humans but are only about one foot tall, because of the humble way they express their spiritual power. Other West African groups, descendents of hierarchical ancient civilizations, recognize a great pantheon of deities, the *orisha* or *vodu*, each the object of special cult worship. They are embodiments of the dynamic forces in life, such as Oya, goddess of death and change, experienced in tornadoes, lightning, winds, and fire; Olokun, ruler of the mysterious depths of consciousness; Shango, a former king who is now honored as the stormy god of electricity and genius; and Obatala, the source of creativity, warmth, and enlightenment.

John Redtail Freesoul, a Cheyenne-Arapahoe, explains his people's concept of the keepers of the four directions:

Of all the spirits populating the invisible world, there are four most friendly to man . . . They are the servants of Maheo (God), messengers to human beings, and act as guardian angels for each of the four cardinal points of the universe. When a Medicine Wheel [a sacred circle of rocks] is properly set up, these spirits are summoned. [10]

The spirits are available to reverent seekers as helpers and as teachers. Their teachings may come in frightening forms, such as thunder and lightning which test one's faith and courage. But right relationship with these spirit beings can be a sacred partnership. Sincere seekers respect, silently listen for, and learn from them and also purify themselves in order to engage their services for the good of the people. As we will later see, those who are best able to call on the spirits for help are the medicine men and women who have dedicated their lives to this service.

Kinship with all creation

In addition to the unseen powers, all aspects of the tangible world are imbued with the power of the great spirit and spiritually interconnected. Everything is therefore experienced as family. As Chief Seattle said in 1854:

We are part of the Earth and the Earth is part of us. The fragrant flowers are our sisters. The reindeer, the horse, the great eagle are our brothers. The rocky heights, the foamy

LIVING INDIGENOUS SACRED WAYS:
An interview with Mixashawn

 Mixashawn is an avant-garde jazz musician and founder of the Pequonawonk Canoe Society, dedicated to preserving the Native American heritage of the Connecticut River Valley. He also founded the Afro-Algonquin jazz group, drawing on the Native American rhythms which have influenced jazz as well as its more well-known African influences. Mixashawn's people were once part of the Maheekanew nation, or Mohegans. He grew up on the river and even though his family's home now sits in the midst of an urbanized area devoted to military manufacturing, he still maintains a sense of the river as a sacred relative:

"[Our relationship with the river] is a caretaker relationship. We see over the years they've really polluted this river. It's still beautiful, amazing as it is. But people don't realize that prayers are very important, too. Even the prayers of enjoying the river without a whole lot of pretensions – the river likes these things. That's why animals sing and do what they do, because that's part of the balance.

Nature is such a powerful structure naturally. People put too much organization in things. Organization is debilitating – the only reason we have it is because things keep on getting more scarce. So they have to organize so we won't use up what we already had before we were organized …

No matter how many books they burn, no matter how many people they persecute, how many No Trespassing signs they put up, the songs, the music, the culture all come to people, regardless of how many restrictions are put on it. Even if it's just through dreams, it will come. It will manifest. As long as people are receptive to the current, these things come about.

When you go into any barrio or any city in this country and you see the people who are the poorest, nine times out of ten, blood-wise and even culturally they are more Indian than these people who are getting all the benefits [of selling Indian art and culture]. They represent a great natural talent – the ability to make something beautiful from nothing. That's what I feel as a music-keeper, as an artist, is my responsibility to help preserve in any way that I can. I'm basically economically powerless, politically powerless, but on other realms I use the powers that I do have …

All religions involve sacrifice. When you go to a beautiful place and get something really nice, many times you'll have something with you and you'll lose it. You'll say, 'Oh, gee, I lost it,' but when you stop and think about it, you're supposed to be giving up something, whether you want to or not. Sacrifice is just part of the balance. People are so material that they hold onto things that they should be sacrificing and giving away; they hold onto them for themselves…

Flutes are universal throughout all cultures. The world is made up of atmospheres, [such as] the water atmosphere, air, and the stratosphere. In these atmospheres, these currents, the flute is the vessel that can be the mediator between humans and that Current which is in all atmospheres. To me that is why the flute is so universal and so healing and soothing for people, animals, everything. These birds can sing like that naturally. We humans have been given an instrument that can do the same thing. But we have to be careful with it, because it's powerful."

crests of waves in the river, the sap of meadow flowers, the body heat of the pony – and of human beings – all belong to the same family . . .

Humankind has not woven the web of life. We are but one thread within it. Whatever we do to the web, we do to ourselves. All things are bound together. All things connect. Whatever befalls the Earth befalls also the children of the Earth.

Native peoples everywhere know the earth as their mother. The land one lives on is loved, respected, and well-known. Oren Lyons, an elder of the Onondaga Nation Wolf Clan, speaks of this intimate relationship:

> [*The indigenous people's*] *knowledge is profound and comes from living in one place for untold generations. It comes from watching the sun rise in the East and set in the West from the same place over great sections of time. We are as familiar with the lands, rivers and great seas that surround us as we are with the faces of our mothers. Indeed we call the earth Etenoha, our mother, from whence all life springs . . . We do not perceive our habitat as wild but as a place of great security and peace, full of life.* [11]

In contrast to the industrial world's attempts to use and dominate the earth, native people have been taught to be caretakers of their mother, the earth. They are therefore very distressed about the destruction of the environment. Their prophecies warn of the potential for global disaster, and the more sensitive visionaries even hear the earth crying.

Take care how you place your moccasins upon the earth, step with care, for the faces of the future generations are looking up from earth waiting their turn for life.

Traditional saying [12]

The earth abounds with living presences, in the traditional worldview. Rocks, bodies of water, and mountains – considered inanimate by other peoples – are personified as living beings by indigenous peoples. Before one can successfully climb a mountain, one must ask its permission. Visionaries can see the spirits of a body of water. As a Pit River Indian explained, "Everything is alive. That's what we Indians believe. White people think everything is dead." [13]

All creatures are perceived as kin, endowed with consciousness and the power of the Great Spirit. As the original ecologists, native peoples know that all things depend on each other. They are taught that they have a reciprocal, rather than dominating, relationship with all beings. Hawaiian *kahuna* (shaman-priest) Kahu Kawai'i explains:

> *How you might feel toward a human being that you love is how you might feel toward a dry leaf on the ground and how you might feel toward the rain in the forest and the wind. There is such intimacy that goes on that everything speaks to you and everything responds to how you are in being – almost like a mirror reflecting your feelings.* [14]

Trees, animals, insects, and plants are all to be approached with caution and consideration. If one must cut down a tree or kill an animal, one must first explain one's intentions and ask forgiveness of the being. Western science now suggests that there can be a sort of communication between human and non-human species. Plants may actually grow better when loved and talked to; if a person even thinks of harming a plant, some polygraph tests show that the plant experiences a "fear" reaction.

Respect is always due to all creatures, in the indigenous world view, but sometimes a degree of coercion is also necessary. In traditional Eskimo whale hunts by kayak through rough, icy seas, the odds were stacked so heavily in favor of the whale that it was necessary to use song and ritual to charm and befuddle the whale.

There are many stories of indigenous people's relationships with non-human creatures. The Australian aborigines say they can still communicate with their relatives, the dolphins, and the women are adept at forming hunting partnerships with dogs.

Birds are thought to bring messages to the people from the spirit world. A Hopi elder said he spent three days and nights praying with a rattlesnake. "Of course he was nervous at first, but when I sang to him he recognized the warmth of my body and calmed down. We made good prayer together."[15]

The goal of right relationships with all beings is not just the short-range survival of the human group. The overall goal is to help everything remain in balance. Indigenous peoples know that there is both light and dark, birth and death, but they feel that these pairs are part of the natural order, held together in dynamic tension. To them, "evil" is a condition of imbalance or excess, and humans can cause imbalance by their actions.

Australian aborigines understand that the purpose they were given when placed on this planet was to protect its subtle energy grids. What some call *"ley lines"* are observed by many native peoples. They are thought to be channels through which the energy of the earth flows. Points where these channels converge are considered especially powerful, and especially critical places for praying for the earth's healthy balance. The aborigines have been told that the ley lines are what allow the earth to maintain its balance during the catastrophic pole shifts it experiences every seven thousand years. We are just entering such a period now, they say, and it is manifesting as severe droughts, floods, earthquakes, hurricanes, and the like. They are particularly concerned this time around because the minerals which are thought to hold the energy grids have all been taken out of the earth, except for one: uranium. They are fighting in Australia to prevent the mining of uranium, as the Hopi are in the United States, to protect the natural balance of the planet.

Science is beginning to support the idea of ley lines. In 1989, researchers at the U.S. National Center for Atmospheric Research announced evidence that:

> *The earth is made up in part by an interconnecting grid of electromagnetic energy connected to solar and lunar magnetic "shells." There are four focal points created within this energetic structure, and the electromagnetic balance at these points is particularly critical to the well-being of the earth system as a whole.* [16]

These four places are Tibet, Arizona, Hawaii, and Jerusalem.

Relationships with power

In certain places and beings, the power of spirit is believed to be highly concentrated. It is referred to as *mana* by the people of the Pacific islands. This is the vital force that makes it possible to act with unusual strength, insight, and effectiveness. It is not individual power; it is channeled through a being from the Great Spirit. Those who have developed their sensitivities can feel it and channel it for useful purposes.

> *All animals have power, because the Great Spirit dwells in all of them, even a tiny ant, a butterfly, a tree, a flower, a rock. The modern, white man's way keeps that power from us, dilutes it. To come to nature, feel its power, let it help you, one needs time and patience for that ... You have so little time for contemplation ... it lessens a person's life, all that grind, that hurrying and scurrying about.*
> Lame Deer, Sioux nation[17]

Tlakaelel, a contemporary spiritual leader of the descendants of the Toltecs of Mexico, describes how a person might experience this power when looking into an obsidian mirror traditionally made to concentrate power:

> *When you reach the point that you can concentrate with all your will, inside there, you reach a point where you feel ecstasy. It's a very beautiful thing, and everything is light. Everything is vibrating with very small signals, like waves of music, very smooth. Everything shines with a blue light. And you feel a sweetness. Everything is covered with the sweetness, and there is peace. It's a sensation like an orgasm, but it can last a long time.* [18]

Sacred sites may be recognized by the power that believers feel there. Concentrated power spots were known to ancient as well as contemporary peoples of the earth. Some sacred sites have been used again and again by successive religions, either to capitalize on the energy or to co-opt the preceding religion. Chartres Cathedral, for instance, was built on an ancient ritual site.

When indigenous people have been forced off their ancestral lands, many have felt the loss of access to their sacred power sites as a great tragedy. But when outsiders offer to buy these lands or mining rights to them, there is often a conflict within tribes between those of spiritual values and those who want the money.

Because power can be built up through sacred practices, the ritual objects of spiritually developed persons may have a lot of power. Special stones and animal artifacts may also carry power. A person might be strengthened by the spiritual energy of the bear or the wolf by wearing sacred clothing made from its fur. Power can also

Power objects are important tools of indigenous healers. In this 1890 photograph at Sia Pueblo, New Mexico, members of the medicine society have brought power objects such as feathers and rattles to help cure the sick boy in the foreground.

come to one through visions or by being given a sacred pipe.

Women are thought to have a certain natural power; men have to work harder for it. Women's power is said to be strongest during their menstrual period; many traditional men are afraid of them at this time and therefore bar them from ritual participation lest the strength of their power might overwhelm that of the men. In most native American nations that have *sweat lodge* ceremonies for ritual purification, menstruating women are not allowed to enter the lodge. Such rules are currently subject to debate and may be waived by the local spiritual leader.

Gaining power is both desirable and dangerous. If misused for personal ends, it becomes destructive and may turn against the person. To channel spiritual power properly, native people are taught that they must live within certain strict limits. Those who seek power or receive it unbidden are supposed to continually purify themselves of any selfish motives and dedicate their actions to the good of the whole. A pipe carrier must be ethically impeccable and must never turn away anyone who asks for help.

Power is not an end in itself. The goal of indigenous spiritual practices, which tend to develop power secondarily, is, according to Tlakaelel:

> *to identify yourself with nature, and to organize yourself with everything that exists so that you can use it for your service – to conserve life on this planet and to create the superior being of the future.*[19]

Spiritual specialists

In a few of the remaining hunting and gathering tribes, religion is a relatively private matter. Each individual has direct access to the divine. Although spirit is invisible, it is considered a part of the natural world. Anyone can interact with it spontaneously, without complex ceremony and without anyone else's aid.

More commonly, however, the world of spirit is thought to be rather dangerous – the fire that can burn those who are unprepared for its power, as Dhyani Ywahoo said. Although everyone is expected to observe certain personal ways of worship, such as offering prayers before taking plant or animal life, many ways of interacting with spirit are thought best left to those who are specially trained for the roles. These specialists are gradually initiated into the secret knowledge that allows them to act as intermediaries between the seen and the unseen. They sacrifice themselves through ritual purification and emptying practices in order to be clean vessels for the sacred knowledge and the sacred role.

Various sacred roles

Specialists' roles vary from one group to another, and the same person may play several of these roles. One specialization often present is that of storyteller. Because the traditions are oral rather than written, these people must memorize long and complex stories and songs so that the group's sacred traditions can be remembered and taught, generation after generation. It is very important to Australian aborigines that their children learn about the origin of the earth, the people, and the local creatures, and that they understand the weather and the patterns of the stars. Songs about these matters may have a hundred verses or more. The orally transmitted epics of the indigenous Ainu

A storyteller of the Kung people of Botswana, Africa, entertains an audience while passing on the oral teachings of the distant past.

of Japan are up to 10,000 lines long. What is held only in memory cannot be physically destroyed, but if a tribe is small and all its storytellers die, the knowledge is lost. This happened on a large scale during the nineteenth century in the United States as native people were killed by war and imported diseases.

There are also bards who carry the energy of ancient traditions into new forms. Rather than memory, they cultivate the muse. In Africa, poets are considered "technicians of the sacred," conversing with a dangerous world of spirits. They are associated with the flow and rhythms of water.

Many traditions have sacred clowns who must endure the shame of publicly foolish acts in order to teach the people through humor. Often they poke fun at the most sacred of rituals, keeping the people from taking themselves too seriously. A sacred fool, called *heyoka* by the Sioux, must be both innocent and very wise about human nature, and must have a visionary relationship with spirit as well.

> *Life is holiness and everyday humdrum, sadness and laughter, the mind and the belly all mixed together. The Great Spirit doesn't want us to sort them out neatly.*
> *Leonard Crow Dog, Sioux medicine man*[20]

A more coveted role is that of being a member of a secret society. Some indigenous cultures include groups in which one can participate by initiation or invitation only, whether to enhance one's prestige or to draw closer to the spirit world. When serving in ceremonial capacities, members often wear special costumes to hide their human identities and help them take on the personas of spirits they are representing. In African religions, some members of secret societies periodically appear as impersonators of animal spirits or of dead ancestors, helping to demonstrate that the dead are still watching the living and are available as awe-inspiring protectors of villages. The all-male Oro secret society in some Yoruba tribes uses this authority to enforce male domination; when Oro appears, "roaring" by swinging a piece of wood on a cord, women must stay inside their huts.

Sacred dancers, such as the masked Hopi and Zuni Kachinas, likewise offer themselves as personifications of the unseen powers. Their actions keep the world of the ancestors alive in the consciousness of succeeding generations.

In some socially stratified societies there are also priests and priestesses. These are specially trained and dedicated people who carry out the rituals that ensure proper functioning of the natural world, and perhaps also communicate with particular spirits or deities. Though West African priests or priestesses may have part-time earthly occupations, they are expected to stay in a state of ritual purity and spend much of their time in communication with the spirit being to whom they are devoted, paying homage and asking the being what he or she wants the people to do. In West Africa, there are also mediums associated with the temples; they enter a state of trance or allow themselves to be possessed by gods or spirits in order to bring messages to the people.

Shamans

The most distinctive spiritual specialists among indigenous peoples are the *shamans*, or *medicine people*. (They are called by many names, but the Siberian word "shaman" is used as a generic term by scholars.) They offer themselves as intermediaries between the physical and the non-physical world. According to archaeological research, shamanic methods are extremely ancient – at least twenty to thirty thousand years old. Ways of becoming a shaman and practicing shamanic arts are remarkably similar around the globe. Medicine people even practiced in Europe until they were wiped out in most areas by the Inquisition as "witches."

Black Elk, visionary and healer.

Contrary to the negative attitude of the Christian Inquisitors, medicine people are helpers to society. They are not to be confused with sorcerers, who practice black magic to harm others or promote their own selfish ends. "Medicine," in native American terminology, is the holy power to do good for all. It is not perceived as personal power. Black Elk explains:

Of course it was not I who cured. It was the power from the outer world, and the visions and ceremonies had only made me like a hole through which the power could come to the two-leggeds. If I thought that I was doing it myself, the hole would close up and no power could come through.[21]

There are many kinds of medicine. One is the ability to heal physical, psychological, and spiritual problems. Techniques used include physical approaches to illness, such as therapeutic herbs, dietary recommendations, sweatbathing, massage, cauterization, and sucking out of toxins. But the treatments are given to the whole person – body, mind, and spirit, with special emphasis on healing relationships within the group – so there may also be metaphysical divination, prayer, chanting, and ceremonies in which group power is built up and spirit helpers are called in. If an intrusion of harmful power, such as the angry energy of another person, seems to be causing the problem, the medicine person may attempt to suck it out with the aid of spirit helpers and then dry vomit the invisible intrusion into a receptacle.

These shamanic healing methods, once dismissed as quackery, are now beginning to earn respect from the Western medical establishment. Medicine people are permitted to attend indigenous patients in some hospitals, and in the United States, the National Institute of Mental Health has paid Navajo medicine men to teach young Indians the elaborate ceremonies that have often been more effective in curing the mental health problems of Navajos than has Western psychiatry.

In addition to healing, certain shamans are thought to have gifts such as talking with plants and animals, controlling the weather, seeing and communicating with the spirit world, and prophesying. A gift highly developed in Africa is that of divination, using techniques such as reading patterns revealed by a casting of cowrie shells. According to Mado Somé of the Dagara:

> Divination is a way of accessing information that is happening now, but not right where you live. Divination is something like your possession of a television. Thanks to that, you can know what is going on outside your immediate area or how something that is going on now is going to end up being. The cowrie shells work like an intermediary between us and the other world. Divination is actually the inscription of information on those physical things, allowing the shaman – whose eyes have been modified through the course of her various medicine journeys – to be able to read and interpret them. [22]

Shamans are contemplatives, Lame Deer explains:

> The wicasa wakan [holy man] wants to be by himself. He wants to be away from the crowd, from everyday matters. He likes to meditate, leaning against a tree or rock, feeling the earth move beneath him, feeling the weight of that big flaming sky upon him. That way he can figure things out. Closing his eyes, he sees many things clearly. What you see with your eyes shut is what counts.
>
> The wicasa wakan loves the silence, wrapping it around himself like a blanket – a loud silence with a voice like thunder which tells him of many things. Such a man likes to be in a place where there is no sound but the humming of insects. He sits facing the west, asking for help. He talks to the plants and they answer him. He listens to the voices of the wama kaskan – all those who move upon the earth, the animals. He is as one with them. From all living beings something flows into him all the time, and something flows from him. [23]

The role of shaman may be hereditary or it may be recognized as a special gift. Either way, training is rigorous. In order to work in a mystical state of ecstasy, moving between ordinary and non-ordinary realities, shamans must experience physical death and rebirth. Some have spontaneous near-death experiences, like the one described in Chapter 1. Uvavnuk, an Eskimo shaman, was spiritually initiated when she was struck by a lightning ball. After she came to, she had great power, which she dedicated to serving her people.

The great sea has set me in motion
Set me adrift,
Moving me as the weed moves in a river.
The arch of sky and mightiness of storms
Have moved the spirit within me,
Till I am carried away
Trembling with joy.

Uvavnuk, Netsilik Eskimo shaman[24]

Left *Traditional diviners of Mali rake sand and leave it overnight. The tracks of animals which run over it are interpreted the next day for information the client seeks.*
Right *Mexican* curandera (*healer*) *Maria Sabina has eaten hallucinogenic mushrooms to enter an ecstatic state. She chants, ''I am a doctor woman . . . I am the morning star woman . . . I am the moon woman . . . I am the heaven woman . . . they say it is like softness there.''*

Other potential shamans undergo rituals of purification, isolation, and bodily torment until they make contact with the spirit world. Igjugarjuk from northern Hudson Bay chose to suffer from cold, starvation, and thirst for a month in a tiny snow hut in order to draw the attention of Pinga, a helping female spirit:

My novitiate took place in the middle of the coldest winter, and I, who never got anything to warm me, and must not move, was very cold, and it was so tiring having to sit without daring to lie down, that sometimes it was as if I died a little. Only towards the end of the thirty days did a helping spirit come to me, a lovely and beautiful helping spirit, whom I had never thought of; it was a white woman; she came to me whilst I had collapsed, exhausted, and was sleeping. But still I saw her lifelike, hovering over me, and from that day I could not close my eyes or dream without seeing her . . . She came to me from Pinga and was a sign that Pinga had now noticed me and would give me powers that would make me a shaman.[25]

Left *This Nigerian priestess is dedicated to the river goddess Oshun.*
Right *The drum, ''voice of the ancestors,'' is used by shamans around the world to help enter a trance state in which they can commune with the spirit world, as in this historical photograph of an East Siberian Yakut shaman.*

In addition to becoming a familiar with death, a potential shaman must undergo lengthy training in shamanic techniques, the names and roles of the spirits, and secrets and myths of the tribe. Novices are taught both by older shamans and reportedly by the spirits themselves. If the spirits do not accept and teach the shaman, he or she is unable to carry the role.

The helping spirits that contact would-be shamans during the death-and-rebirth crisis become essential partners in the shaman's sacred work. Often it is a spirit animal who becomes the shaman's guardian spirit, giving him or her special powers. The shaman may even take on the persona of the animal while working. Many tribes feel that healing shamans need the powers of the bear; Lapp shamans metamorphosed into wolves, reindeer, bears, or fish.

Not only do shamans possess a power animal as an alter-ego, they also have the ability to enter parallel, spiritual realities at will in order to bring back knowledge, power, or help for those who need it. An altered state of consciousness is needed. Techniques for entering this state are the same around the world: drumming, rattling, singing, dancing, and in some cases hallucinogenic drugs. The effect of these influences is to open what the Huichol shamans of Mexico call the *Narieka* – the doorway of the heart, the channel for divine power, the point where human and spirit worlds meet. It is often experienced and represented artistically as a pattern of concentric circles.

The "journey" then experienced by shamans is typically into the Upperworld or the Lowerworld. To enter the latter, they descend mentally through an actual hole in the ground, such as a spring, a hollow tree, cave, animal burrow, or special ceremonial hole regarded as a navel of the earth. These entrances typically lead into tunnels which if followed open into bright landscapes. Reports of such experiences include not only what the journeyer saw but also realistic physical sensations, such as how the walls of the tunnel felt during the descent.

The shaman enters into the Lowerworld landscape, encounters beings there, and may bring something back if it is needed by the client. This may be a lost guardian spirit or a lost soul, brought back to revive a person in a coma. Often a river must be crossed as the boundary between the world of the living and the world of the dead. In West African tradition, there are three rivers separating these worlds and one must cross them by canoe. In another common variant, the journeyer crosses the underworld river on a bridge guarded by some animal. Often a kindly old man or woman appears to assist this passage through the underworld. This global shamanic process is retained only in myths, such as the Orpheus story, in cultures that have subdued the indigenous ways.

Contemporary rituals

Indigenous sacred rites revolve around two seemingly contradictory concepts. For one thing, the forces of life are mysterious and unseen. One can communicate with these forces in symbolic non-verbal ways, such as sprinkling cornmeal in thanks for the offerings of the earth or using pipe smoke to carry prayers up to the spirits. On the other hand, the people have observed that life operates according to strict natural laws.

Concentric circles and spirals appear throughout the visionary art of the world, including Australian aborigines' paintings of the Dreaming, a parallel and original reality. These patterns often suggest a journey through spiritual levels toward union with the Great Holy.

Humans can help to maintain the harmony of the universe by their ritual observances.

In order to maintain the natural balance and to insure success in the hunt or harvest, ceremonies must be performed with exactitude. For instance, there is a specific time for the telling of specific stories. Chona, a Papago medicine woman, told anthropologist Ruth Underhill:

> I should not have told you this [the origin of Coyote, who helped to put the world in order, with a few mistakes]. These things about the Beginning are holy. They should not be told in the hot time when the snakes are out. The snakes guard our secrets. If we tell what is forbidden, they bite. [26]

Ritual precision is not just an exercise in remembering the old traditions. According to Dhyani Ywahoo, there are strong psychological, as well as spiritual, reasons for doing things the right way. Paying attention to the proper forms brings clarity of attention and creates a sacred space in which many things can happen:

> What's important about ritual is that is has a beginning. And before that beginning there has been a preparation, so that people's bodies and minds are brought to a certain level of vibrancy. [After] abstaining from certain things, doing certain exercises, and living and behaving in a certain way, the sleepiness, the illusions that may veil our true nature are more transparent, more ready to let go. Also one is cultivating a more peaceful nature by having certain prescriptions about speech and behavior with other people.
>
> Then there is the beginning where everyone comes together, and there is the beginning of the family bonding. You also see what you need to correct in yourself in terms of relationship.
>
> Then the actual ceremonies begin, which [involve] much purifying, pacifying, and visioning – knowing what one's purpose is and seeing what needs to happen. And then there is generating of the energy through the ritual itself, so that vision can manifest for the benefit of family, clan, nation, all beings. [27]

Group observances

Each group has its own special ways of ritual dedication to the spirits of life, but they tend to follow certain patterns everywhere. Some honor major points in the human life cycle, such as birth, naming, puberty, marriage, and death. These rites of passage assist people in the transition from one state to another and help them become aware of their meaningful contribution to life. When a Hopi baby is twenty days old, it is presented at dawn to the rays of Father Sun for the first time and officially given a name. Its face is ritually cleansed with sacred cornmeal, a ceremony that will be repeated at death for the journey to the Underworld.

There are also collective rituals to support the group's survival strategies. In farming communities these include ways of asking for rain, of insuring the growth of crops, and of giving thanks for the harvest. In the Great Drought of 1988, Sioux holy man Leonard Crow Dog was asked by three non-native Midwestern communities to perform rainmaking ceremonies for them, thus honoring the power of the traditional medicine ways. Dhyani Ywahoo explains, "When Native American people sing for the rain, the rain comes – because those singers have made a decision that they and the water and the air and the Earth are one." [28]

Ritual dramas about the beginnings and sacred history of the people engage

The sacred pipe, such as the one held here by Little Bear, of the Cheyenne in this 1875 photograph, is considered an altar, used in offering reverence and praying to the spirits on behalf of the people.

performers and spectators on an emotional level through the use of special costumes, body paint, music, masks, and perhaps sacred locations. These dramas provide a sense of orderly interface among humans, the land, and the spiritual world. They also dramatize mysticism, drawing the people toward direct contact with the spirit world. Those who have sacred visions and dreams are supposed to share them with others, and often this is done through dramatization.

The Plains Indians were given, according to legend, the sacred pipe by White Buffalo Calf Woman as a tool for communicating with the mysteries and understanding the ways of life. The bowl of the pipe represents the female aspect of the Great Spirit, the stem the male aspect. When they are ritually joined, the power of the spirit is thought to be present as the pipe is passed around the circle for collective communion with each other and with the divine.

Groups also gather for ritual purification and spiritual renewal of individuals. Indigenous peoples of the Americas "smudge" sites and possessions, cleansing them with smoke from special herbs, such as sage and sweetgrass. Many groups make an igloo-shaped "sweat lodge" into which hot stones are carried. People huddle together in the dark around the stone pit. When water is poured on the stones, intensely hot steam sears bodies and lungs. Everyone prays earnestly. Leonard Crow Dog says of the *inipi* (sweat lodge):

> The *inipi* *is probably our oldest ceremony because it is built around the simplest, basic, life-giving things: the fire that comes from the sun, warmth without which there can be no life;* inyan wakan, *or* tunka, *the rock that was there when the earth began, that will still be there at the end of time; the earth, the mother womb; the water that all creatures need; our green brother, the sage; and encircled by all these, man, basic man, naked as he was born, feeling the weight, the spirit of endless generations before him, feeling himself part of the earth, nature's child, not her master.* [29]

Pilgrimages to sacred sites are often communal. The Huichol Indians of the mountains of western Mexico make a yearly journey to a desert they call Wirikuta, the Sacred Land of the Sun. They feel that creation began in this place. And like their ancestors, they gather their yearly supply of peyote cactus at this sacred site. To them, the psychotropic peyote is "the little deer," a spirit who helps them to communicate with the spirit world. The peyote is used ritually, rather than recreationally, and has thus been legalized in the north as well for use by members of the Native American Church.

When indigenous groups are broken up by external forces, they lose the cohesive power of these group rituals. Africans taken to the New World as slaves lost not only their own individual identity but also their membership in tight-knit groups. In an attempt to re-establish a communal sense of shared spiritual traditions among Afro-Americans, Professor Maulana Ron Karenga created a contemporary celebration, *Kwanzaa*, based on indigenous African "first fruits" harvest festivals. Using symbolic objects to help create a special atmosphere (such as candles, corn, fruits and vegetables, and a "unity cup," all called by their Swahili names) families and groups of families meet from December 26 to January 1 to explore their growth over the past year. They look at their own experiences of the Seven Principles – unity, self-determination, collective work, family-centeredness, purpose, creativity with limited resources, and confidence – and reward each other for progress by giving gifts.

This altar in the home of a Mexican healer illustrates the blending of indigenous ways with those of later religions. The serpent, masks, vegetables, eggs, and ''bird's nest'' derive from indigenous sacred ways, but are juxtaposed with Christian symbols.

Below left *To the Pygmies of the Ituri rain-forest, the Great Spirit is embodied in the forest itself, a benevolent presence that is both Mother and Father. Pygmy men perform a dance of gratitude to the forest for the animal food it provides.*

Below right *In West Africa, the gods and the spirits of the dead appear to the living in masquerade. The mysteries of spirit are made semi-visible by initiates wearing costumes such as layers of cloth or plant fibers.*

The Sun Dance Way of Self-Sacrifice

Sacrificing oneself for the sake of the whole is highly valued in most indigenous traditions. Through purification ceremonies, the people attempt to break through their small selves in order to serve as clear vehicles for the energy of the Great Spirit. In the Americas the most powerful ceremony for these purposes is the Sun Dance: dancing for four days without food or water, looking at the sun and praying for blessings for the people.

Those who live close to nature have always honored the sun, but the Sun Dance is a special ceremony that the Oglala Sioux say was first given to them through a vision received by a man named Kablaya. It has spread throughout the Americas, and now is performed in hundreds of sites each year during June or July. In theory, only those who have had visions that they should perform the dance should do so. Some come in penance, for purification; others offer themselves as vehicles to request blessings for all people or for specific people who need help. It is not considered proper to dance for one's own needs.

Dancers make a commitment to do the dance for four years. Some Sun Dances include women dancers; some who dance are children. Non-indigenous people are generally barred from dancing except in Mexico, where Tlakaelel has made the politically unpopular decision to allow a few carefully selected white people to dance. According to spokesperson Juan Salazar, he bases his decision on the traditional understanding that "we are all related" and on his elders' belief that the imbalance of the earth now requires sharing of the light of the sacred teachings, even though the indigenous peoples have been oppressed and misunderstood by past generations of white people.

The power of the Sun Dance requires that everything be handled in a sacred way. Dancers must do vision quests and purify themselves in sweat lodges before the ceremony begins. In spite of thirst and exhaustion, they must continue to participate in sweat lodges each day of the dance. A tree is chosen

Sweat lodges are used for physical and spiritual purification. A pole frame is covered with skins or blankets and heated rocks are splashed with water to create searing steam.

to be placed at the center of the circle (among the Sioux, it is always a cottonwood, which when cut crosswise reveals a multi-pointed star pattern representing the sun). The tree's sacrifice is attended with ritual prayers. Participants may string prayer flags onto its branches before it is hoisted in the center of the dancing circle.

During the dance itself, the participants are guided through patterns with symbolic meanings. The choreography varies from one group to another. The Sioux Sun Dancers do not move around the circle except to shift slightly during the day so that they are always facing the sun. In Mexico the patterns continually honor the powers of the four directions by facing each one in turn.

As they dance, the dancers blow whistles traditionally made from the bones of the spotted eagle, but now often whittled from hollow sticks. When giving instructions for the dance, Kablaya reportedly explained, "When you blow the whistle always remember that it is the voice of the Spotted Eagle; our Grandfather, Wakan-Tanka, always hears this, for you see it is really His own voice."[30]

A group of people support the dancers by singing special sacred songs and beating a large drum. If their energy flags, so does that of the dancers. A woman Sun Dancer says that after a while, "The drum is no longer outside of you. It is as if in you and you don't even know that you're dancing." The dancers also support each other in ways such as using the feathers they carry to fan those whose energy seems low.

Each dancer is the carrier of a sacred pipe. Between rounds, these may be shared with group onlookers who are led into the circle and who pass the pipes around among the dancers to strengthen them with the power of the smoke.

Non-dancers may also be led into the circle for a special healing round on the third or fourth day. By that time, the dancers have been so purified and empowered that they can all act as healers, using their eagle feathers as instruments to convey the divine power.

The suffering which each dancer willingly undergoes is heightened during piercing. For those whose visions suggest it – and whose tribes use piercing, for some do not – at some point during the dance incisions are made in the skin of their chest, back, or arms and sharpened sticks are inserted. There are then various ways of tearing through the skin. One reserved for chiefs is to drag buffalo skulls from ropes attached to the piercing sticks, symbolizing their carrying of the burdens of the people. More often, ropes are thrown over the trees and attached to the piercing sticks. Each person who pierces is then pulled upward, "flying" by flapping eagle wings, until the sticks break through the skin. It is thought that the more one asks when making the sacrifice the more difficult it will be to break free. One Sioux dancer was instructed in a vision that he should be hung from the tree for a whole night. They had to pierce him in many places in order to distribute his weight, and then pull him down in the morning.

Why must the dance involve so much suffering? A Sioux Sun Dancer explains, "Nobody knows why, but suffering makes our prayers more sincere. The sun dance tests your sincerity, pushes your spirit beyond its limits." And as the dance goes on, many of the dancers transcend their physical agony and experience an increasing sense of euphoria. A Mexican dancer explains:

It's not pain. It's ecstasy. We get the energy from the sun and from the contact with Mother Earth. You also feel the energy of the eagles [who often fly overhead], all the animals, all the plants that surround you, all the vegetation. That energy comes to sustain you for the lack of food and water. Also when you smoke the pipe it serves as food or energy; the smoke feeds you energy so that you can continue. And every so often we put our palms to the sun to receive the energy from the sun. You can feel it in your whole body, a complete bath of energy.

*Names of individual dancers interviewed are not given here, to preserve their privacy and the sacredness of the Dance.

Individual observances

In indigenous sacred ways, it is considered important for each person to experience a personal connection with the spirits. The people acknowledge and work with the spirits in many everyday ways. For instance, when searching for herbs, a person is not to take the first plant found; an offering is made to it with the prayer that its relatives will understand one's needs. Guardian spirits and visions are sought by all the people, not just specialists such as shamans. The shaman may have more spirit helpers and more power, but visionary experiences are available to all. Indigenous traditions have therefore been called "democratized shamanism."

To open themselves for contact with the spirit world, individuals in many indigenous cultures undergo a *vision quest*. After ritual purification, they are sent alone to a sacred spot to cry to the spirits to reveal something of their purpose in life and help them in their journey. This may also be done before undertaking a sacred mission, such as the Sun Dance. Indigenous Mexican leader Tlakaelel describes the vision quest as his people observe it:

> *You stay on a mountain, desert, or in a cave, isolated, naked, with only your sacred things, the things that you have gained, in the years of preparation – your eagle feathers, your pipe, your copal [tree bark used as incense]. You are left alone four days and four nights without food and water. During this time when you are looking for your vision, many things happen. You see things move. You see animals that come close to you. Sometimes you might see someone that you care about a lot, and they're bringing water. You feel like you're dying of thirst, but there are limits around you, protection with hundreds of tobacco ties. You do not leave this circle, and this vision will disappear when they come to offer the water or sometimes they will just drop it on the ground. Or someone comes and helps you with their strength and gives you messages.* [31]

In the traditional sacred ways, one is not supposed to ask for a vision for selfish personal reasons. The point of this individual ordeal, which is designed to be physically and emotionally stressful, is to ask how one can help the people and the planet.

When Brooke Medicine Eagle, a Nez Perce and Sioux poet, dancer, and healer, did her vision quest, she was visited by a spirit woman in a buckskin dress covered with tiny shimmering crystal beads. This being fed thoughts to her as if through her navel, which Brooke translated into these words:

> *She said to me that the earth is in trouble, that the land is in trouble, and that here on this land . . . what needs to happen is a balancing. She said that the thrusting, aggressive, analytic, intellectual, building, making-it-happen energy has very much overbalanced the feminine, receptive, allowing, surrendering energy. She said that what needs to happen is an uplifting and a balancing. And because we are out of balance, we need to put more emphasis on surrendering, being receptive, allowing, nurturing. . . . Not only do women need to become strong in this way; we all need to do this, men and women alike.* [32]

Such personal visions and ancient prophecies about the dangers of a lifestyle that ignores the earth and the spiritual dimensions of life are leading native elders around the world to speak to outsiders of their sacred traditions. They are not missionaries. They seek converts not to their path but to a respect for all of life which they feel is essential for the harmony of the planet. And they seek freedom to practice their Original

Instructions. A 1989 communique from the Traditional Circle of Indian Elders and Youth, meeting in the Queen Charlotte Islands, included these reminders of their spiritual rights and needs:

> *Increasingly, the world is beginning to recognize the integrity of indigenous religions. Our spiritual visions are gaining equality and support in international affairs. . . . Yet we must remind all people that the practices of our spiritual ways require certain elements. We need access to sacred sites, which must be protected. We need access to sacred animals, which must be kept from regulatory interference. We need the return of sacred objects, many of which are now in museums, historical societies, universities and private collections.*
>
> *Indigenous people around the world have a birthright and a responsibility to their ancestral lands. Our cultural and spiritual identity is dependent upon a land base. If the nations remain truthful to their traditional philosophy and values toward the land, their future is secure.* [33]

Suggested reading

Beck, Peggy V. and Walters, Anna L., *The Sacred: Ways of Knowledge, Sources of Life*, Tsaile (Navajo Nation), Arizona: Navajo Community College Press, 1977. A fine and very genuine survey of indigenous sacred ways, particularly those of North America.

Brown, Joseph Epes, *The Sacred Pipe*, 1953, New York: Penguin Books, 1971. Detailed accounts of the sacred rites of the Oglala Sioux by Black Elk, a respected holy man.

Brown, Vinson, *Voices of Earth and Sky: Vision Search of the Native Americans*, Happy Camp, California: Naturegraph Publishers, 1974. A survey of the old visionary traditions in the Americas.

Eliade, Mircea, *Shamanism: Archaic Techniques of Ecstasy*, translated from the French by Willard Trask, London: Routledge and Kegan Paul, 1964. The first scholarly book to examine shamanism as an authentic religious form rather than an anthropological oddity.

Freesoul, John Redtail, *Breath of the Invisible: The Way of the Pipe*, Wheaton, Illinois and London: Theosophical Publishing House, 1986. An inside look at some important indigenous spiritual ways by a Cheyenne-Arapahoe pipemaker.

Gill, Sam D., *Native American Religions*, Belmont, California: Wadsworth, 1982. A sensitive academic survey of indigenous sacred ways in the United States.

Gleason, Judith, *Oya: In Praise of the Goddess*, Boston: Shambhala Publications, 1987. A complex exploration of the Yoruba goddess which gives some insight into African traditions.

Halifax, Joan, *Shamanic Voices: A Survey of Visionary Narratives*, New York: E. P. Dutton, 1979, and Harmondsworth, London: Penguin, 1980. First-hand accounts of shamanistic visionary experiences.

Hultkrantz, Ake, *The Religions of the American Indians*, Berkeley: University of California Press, 1967, 1979 translation by Monica Setterwall. A survey from the point of view of the history of religions.

Lame Deer, John and Richard Erdoes, *Lame Deer: Seeker of Visions*, New York: Pocket Books, 1976. Fascinating first-hand accounts of the life of a rebel visionary who tried to maintain the old ways.

Ywahoo, Dhyani, *Voices of Our Ancestors: Cherokee Teachings from the Wisdom Fire*, Boston: Shambhala Publications, 1987. Inspiring words of a Tsalagi priestess.

3 HINDUISM

"With mind absorbed and heart melted in love"

In the Indian subcontinent there has developed a complex variety of religious paths. All those that honor the ancient scriptures called the Vedas are commonly grouped under the term "Hinduism." This label has now been adopted by many Indian people, but it is derived from a name applied by invaders to the faith of the people living in the region of the Indus River. The indigenous term for the Veda-based traditions in the entire Indian region is *Sanatana Dharma* ("eternal religion"). Sanatana, "eternal" or "ageless," reflects the belief that this religion has always existed. Dharma can be translated as "religion," "natural law," "duty," and "holding together."

What Sanatana Dharma encompasses are spiritual expressions ranging from extreme sensuality to extreme asceticism, from the heights of personal devotion to the heights of abstract philosophy, from metaphysical proclamations of the oneness behind the material world to worship of images representing a multiplicity of deities. According to tradition, there are actually thirty three million gods in India, some of them rocks or trees.

The extreme variations within Sanatana Dharma are reflections of its great tolerance and its great age. Indian teachers say that my soul is directing a path for me and your soul is directing a path for you. They may not be the same, but both are valid. Within a single family, one person might worship Mother Kali, another Krishna, and another Christ. The feeling is that the Divine has countless faces, and all are divine. Because of this exceptional tolerance, few of the myriad religious paths that have arisen over the millenia have been lost. They continue to co-exist in present-day India and share certain central beliefs.

Truth is one; sages call it by various names.	Rig Veda

One avenue into understanding this mosaic of beliefs and practices is to trace the supposed chronological development of patterns which co-exist today. But this approach is offered simply as an organizational framework. Historians of religion and devotees of the various forms have widely variant ideas about the historical origin of the threads that now compose Sanatana Dharma. The archaeological evidence is fragmented and Indians have not traditionally emphasized historical accuracy, readily interweaving reports of actual events and people with mythological embellishments and symbolism.

Pre-Vedic religion

Many of the threads of contemporary Hinduism may have existed in the religions practiced by the aboriginal peoples of India. Some of the ways of the ancient Dravidian

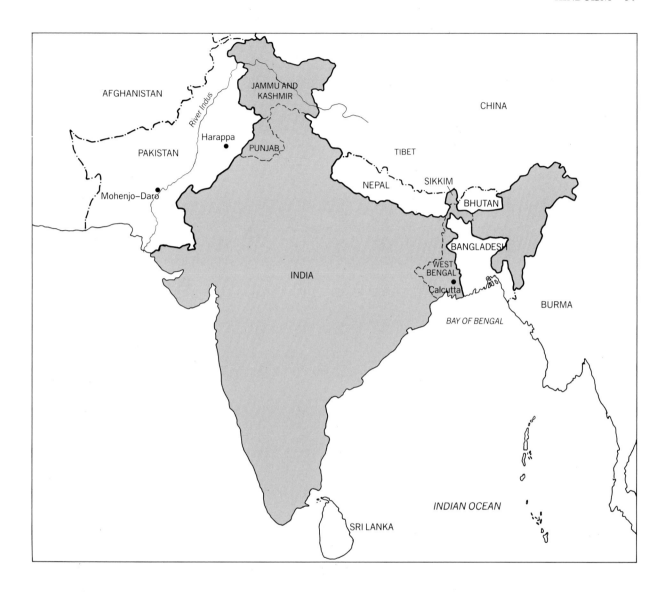

people seem to have persisted in southern Indian villages. There were also advanced urban centers in the Indus Valley of northwestern India from about 2500 BCE or even earlier until 1500 BCE. Major fortified cities were found by archaeologists at Harappa and Mohenjo-Daro; the culture they represent is labeled "Harappan."

Archaeologists have found little conclusive evidence of temples in the Harappan cities, but in south India folk wisdom says that there were once impermanent temples made of wood or actual living trees.

Whether or not the urbanities of the Indus Valley built what we would now consider temples, they lavished great care on their plumbing systems. Houses had wells, bathing rooms or drained bathing floors, and even built-in latrines, some of which had seats. Wastes were carried off in an elaborate system of communal brick drains. And the

The Indian subcontinent includes areas that are now politically separate from India. The Indus Valley, for instance, lies in what is now the largely Muslim state of Pakistan.

The river goddess Ganga. Appreciation of the feminine as a symbol of plenty, of sacred trees, and of the purifying powers of rivers may have been of pre-Vedic origin, but has persisted in Indian art and ritual practices.

major structure at Mohenjo-daro has been called the Great Bath by archaeologists. A large lined tank with steps leading down onto it is surrounded by an open courtyard; an adjoining structure has what appear to be private bathing rooms. Historians speculate from this evidence that the early Indus people placed a religious sort of emphasis on hygiene and/or ritual purification.

They also seemed to venerate life-giving power. Although few pieces of ritual art remain (some speculate that religious art was not intended to be permanent), seals have been found depicting an ascetic male figure in cross-legged yogic posture. He has an erect phallus, wears a great horned headdress, and is surrounded by strong animals. There were also stone *lingams*, natural elongated oval stones or sculptures up to two feet tall.

Both the seals and the lingams suggest that the early Indus people knew about yogic-like spiritual practices and were worshippers of Siva,[1] who is still one of the major forms of the Divine worshipped today. The word used in India to signify ritual worship, *puja*, is derived from an ancient Dravidian word meaning "to anoint." Worshippers may have reverently anointed the lingams, as so many people still do in India today.

Even more prominent among the artefacts are pieces that seem to honor a great goddess and stone images of the female vulva *(yoni)*. Sacred pots, like those still used in south Indian village ceremonies honoring the goddess, may have been associated then, as now, with the feminine as the receptacle of the primeval stuff of life. There is also considerable evidence of worship of local deities by stone altars placed beneath sacred trees. Each tree is still popularly believed to be the home of a tree spirit, and many are honored with offerings.

Certain animals appear frequently on the seals. Bulls are common motifs, perhaps associated with masculine power. *Nagas*, dragon-serpents, may have been honored as they still are by many indigenous peoples, as carriers of the primordial energy spiraling upward from the earth and initiators into timeless spiritual knowledge — or as they are by many Asiatic cultures, as guardian spirits of the waters.

Vedic religion

Western historians think that the highly organized farming cultures of the Indus Valley and the villages in other parts of the subcontinent were gradually overrun by nomadic invaders from outside India. Those whose influence became predominant were the *Aryans* (their Sanskrit word meaning "noble," or "one who knows the value of life"). They were among the Indo-European tribes who migrated outward from the steppes of southern Russia during the second millenium BCE.

The Aryans' material culture was crude, they were probably illiterate, and they had organized themselves into patriarchal tribes worshipping sky gods. Their advantage over the local populations was their emphasis on war technologies, primarily horse-drawn chariots.

The Vedas

The evidence used by archaeologists to piece together the theory of the Aryan invasion shows that the Indus Valley civilization was followed by a materially crude culture. But

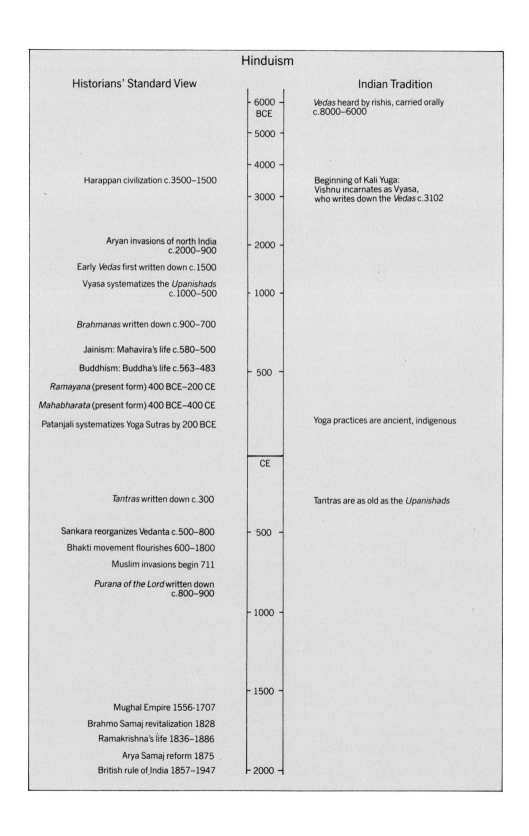

Hinduism

Historians' Standard View

Indian Tradition

6000 BCE — *Vedas* heard by rishis, carried orally c.8000–6000

5000

4000

Harappan civilization c.3500–1500 — 3000 — Beginning of Kali Yuga: Vishnu incarnates as Vyasa, who writes down the *Vedas* c.3102

Aryan invasions of north India c.2000–900 — 2000

Early *Vedas* first written down c.1500

Vyasa systematizes the *Upanishads* c.1000–500 — 1000

Brahmanas written down c.900–700

Jainism: Mahavira's life c.580–500

Buddhism: Buddha's life c.563–483 — 500

Ramayana (present form) 400 BCE–200 CE

Mahabharata (present form) 400 BCE–400 CE

Patanjali systematizes Yoga Sutras by 200 BCE — Yoga practices are ancient, indigenous

CE

Tantras written down c.300 — Tantras are as old as the *Upanishads*

Sankara reorganizes Vedanta c.500–800 — 500

Bhakti movement flourishes 600–1800

Muslim invasions begin 711

Purana of the Lord written down c.800–900

1000

1500

Mughal Empire 1556-1707

Brahmo Samaj revitalization 1828

Ramakrishna's life 1836–1886

Arya Samaj reform 1875

British rule of India 1857–1947 — 2000

the sacred literature that is traced back at least to this time reaches great spiritual heights. The works are called the *Vedas* ("body of knowledge") and are still held in greatest reverence as revealed scriptures which form the basis of all later scriptures. These sacred teachings seem to have originated by 1500 to 1000 BCE, though the Indian people and some scholars feel that they are far older. We know that the Vedas are much older than their earliest written forms; they were originally transmitted orally and may then have been written down over a period of eight or nine hundred years.

According to orthodox Hindus, the Vedas are not the work of any humans. They are believed to be the breath of the eternal, as "heard" by the ancient sages, or *rishis*. The scriptures are thought to transcend human time and are thus as relevant today as they were thousands of years ago. The *Gayatrimantra*, a verse in a Vedic hymn, is still chanted daily by the devout as the most sacred of prayers:

> *Aum* [*the primordial creative sound*],
> *Bhu Bhuvah Svah* [*the three worlds: earth, atmosphere, and heaven*],
> *Tat Savitur Varenyum,*
> *Bhargo Devasya Dheemahe* [*adoration of the glory, splendor, and grace that radiate from*
>   *the Divine Light that illumines the three worlds*],
> *Dhiyo Yo Nah Prachodayat* [*a prayer for liberation through awakening of the light of*
>   *the universal intelligence*]. [2]

The oldest of the known Vedic scriptures – and perhaps the oldest of all the world's existing scriptures – is thought to be the *Rig Veda*. It is addressed to the gods of natural phenomena, praising them and asking for blessings. Here, for example, is an excerpt from a hymn to Ushas, goddess of dawn:

> *Divine Ushas, thou art seen auspicious: thou shinest afar: thy bright rays spread over the*
> *sky, lovely and radiant with great splendours, thou displayest thy person . . . Bring to us,*
> *daughter of heaven, in thy spacious and beautiful chariot, desirable riches.* [3]

The controlling forces in the cosmos were perceived as *devas* ("shining ones"). Two of the most significant devas, Varuna and Indra, are no longer worshipped in India. *Varuna* was the god of cosmic order. *Indra*, the thunder god, was a passionate warrior against the enemies of the Aryans, particularly the indigenous peoples. It is possible that Indra was once a human warrior, later deified. Vishnu, a benevolent sun god, was of secondary importance but later became one of the major Hindu deities.

The fire sacrifice

Vedic worship centered around the fire sacrifice. In its earliest form, people seem to have gathered around a fire, placing offerings of food in it to be conveyed to the gods by *Agni*, the being of fire. The Vedic hymns sung to Agni are spiritually complex invocations of the power of truth against darkness.

Ritual use of fire is still central to contemporary Hindu worship. The twentieth-century seer Sri Aurobindo has written extensively about the metaphorical significances of Agni. His insights include these:

> *The Vedic deity Agni is the first of the Powers that have issued from the vast and secret*
> *Godhead. Agni is the form, the fire, the forceful heat and flaming will of this Divinity.*

[The word Agni] means a burning brightness, whence its use for fire. When man, awakened from his night, wills to offer his inner and outer activities to the gods of a truer and higher existence and so to arise out of mortality into the far-off immortality, it is this flame of upward aspiring Force and Will that he must kindle; into this fire he must cast the sacrifice. [4]

Over time elaborate fire rituals were created, controlled by priests. A portion of the Vedas, the *Brahmanas*, gave detailed instructions for the performance of the fire sacrifices. Specified verbal formulas, sacred chants, and sacred actions were to be used by the priests to invoke the breath behind all of existence (*Brahman*, the Absolute, the Supreme Reality). The verbal formulas were also called *mantras*, sounds which were believed to evoke the reality they connoted. The language used was Sanskrit (meaning "well-formed"), which was considered a re-creation of the sound-forms of objects, actions, and qualities, as heard by ancient sages in deep meditation.

The fire rituals were apparently held in the open air. The most auspicious places for their performance were at the confluence of two rivers. The place where the two major rivers of the early Aryan settlements, the sacred Ganga and the Jumna, joined was considered extremely sacred and is still a major pilgrimage spot for worshippers.

Offerings to Agni usually consisted of melted butter, grains, soma, and sometimes animals. Some researchers speculate that *soma* was a psychotropic liquid, perhaps made from an hallucinogenic mushroom mixed with milk and honey. Worshippers may have

The Vedas include hymns praising the cow, who is still beloved and treated as sacred by Hindus. The cow is our Mother, for she gives us her milk, and in her body are thousands of angels.

Brahmanic priestly rituals involve a series of prescribed acts and sacred objects, such as those being used by this priest in his homage to the Goddess Durga. The deity is invoked within the icon by hymns, mantras, and sacred gestures, and it is bathed with holy water and milk, anointed with oils, camphor and sandalwood, covered with flowers, offered foods, and entertained with lights.

used it for its consciousness-altering properties, and they offered it to their gods as well. Another possibility is that in some cases the word "soma" referred to a sweet liquid that drips from the roof of the mouth during transcendent yogic experiences. Ritual use of soma libations died out, but some spiritual seekers in present-day India continue to seek inspiration with ecstasy-inducing drugs.

Vedic worship was primarily sacrificial. The sacrifice offered by humans was metaphorically linked with the original personal sacrifice by which the universe was created: the dismemberment of the *Purusha*, the primal Being, by the gods. His mind, for example, became the moon, his eyes the sun, his breath the wind.

Origins of the caste system

Earthly sacrifices were designed to mirror the original cosmic sacrifice of Purusha and thus keep the world in proper order. If the sacrifices were offered correctly, the gods would be guided by the people's requests. Because the sacrifices were a reciprocal communion with the gods, priests who performed the public sacrifices had to be carefully trained and to maintain high standards of ritual purity.

Concerns about ritual proprieties, and also perhaps racial discrimination, led to the ranking of people according to their supposed degree of "pollution," based on their occupation. These distinctions, forming groups called *castes*, were given religious authority by the Vedic description of the dismemberment of Purusha:

> *His mouth became the brahman; his two arms were made into the rajanya; his two thighs the vaishyas; from his two feet the shudra was born.* [5]

Castes were defended as an idealized division of labor, thought to be the basis for an orderly society. The *brahmans* (or Brahmins) were to be the priests and philosophers, specialists in the life of the spirit. They had even higher status than the next group, referred to as rajanya in the Vedas but later called *kshatriyas*. They were the nobility of feudal India: kings, warriors, and vassals. Their general function was to guard and preserve the society; they were expected to be courageous and majestic. *Vaishyas* were the economic specialists: farmers and merchants. The *shudra* caste were the manual laborers and artisans.

In time, a fifth caste not mentioned in the Vedas developed: a casteless group called *"untouchables."* They had such impure functions in society (from working with animal products, such as making leather shoes, to street-sweeping and corpse-removal) that their touch, or even their shadow, was thought to pollute any of the higher classes.

Religion was increasingly controlled by the ritually pure and carefully trained priests, and contact between castes was limited. Caste membership became hereditary rather than a reflection of each individual's talents. This system became as important as the Vedas themselves in defining Hinduism until its social injustices were attacked in the nineteenth century. One of its opponents was the courageous leader Mahatma Gandhi, who renamed the lowest caste "the children of God." In 1948 the stigma of "untouchability" was legally abolished, though many caste distinctions still linger in modern India.

The Upanishads

Each of the Vedic books has been organized into four parts, composed over time. The *Upanishads* are thought by Western Indologists to have been created latest, around 1000 to 500 BCE or later. They represent the mystical insights of rishis who sought Ultimate Reality through their meditations in the forest. Many people consider them the cream of Indian thought, among the highest spiritual literature ever written. They were not taught to the masses but were rather reserved for advanced seekers of spiritual truth.

CONTEMPLATION OF THE LUMINOUS SELF   The word "Upanishad" connotes the devoted disciple's sitting down by the teacher to receive private spiritual instruction about the highest reality, loosening all doubts and destroying all ignorance. Emphasis is placed not on outward ritual performances, as in the earlier Vedic religion, but on inner experience as the path to realization and immortality.

In disciplined meditation, the rishis discovered Brahman, the Unknowable:

> *Him the eye does not see, nor the tongue express, nor the mind grasp.* [6]

From Brahman spring the multiplicity of forms, including humans. The joyous discovery of the rishis was that they could find Brahman as the subtle self *(Atman)* within themselves. Existence was like a wheel, with the One in the center and the

Diagram of Brahman
and Atman.

individual selves radiating outward like spokes. Humans were extensions of the center, but were not totally identical to it. One of the rishis explained this union thus:

In the beginning there was Existence alone – One only, without a second. He, the One, thought to himself; Let me be many, let me grow forth. Thus out of himself he projected the universe, and having projected out of himself the universe, he entered into every being. All that is has its self in him alone. Of all things he is the subtle essence. He is the truth. He is the Self. And that, ... THAT ART THOU.

Chandogya Upanishad[7]

Seekers are enjoined to meditate on the One in the "lotus of the heart," ten fingers above the navel, faithfully and reverently, with senses and heart purified and the inner energies under control:

Affix to the Upanishad, the bow incomparable, the sharp arrow of devotional worship; then, with mind absorbed and heart melted in love, draw the arrow and hit the mark – the imperishable Brahman ... Lose thyself in him, even as the arrow is lost in the target.

Mundaka Upanishad[8]

To realize Atman is to experience "pure unitary consciousness, wherein awareness of the world and of multiplicity is completely obliterated. It is ineffable peace."[9] As one of the rishis exclaimed:

Let him worship Brahman as Brahman, and he will become Brahman ... I am that Self! I am life immortal!
OM ... Peace – peace – peace.

Taittiriya Upanishad[10]

REINCARNATION   In addition to these profound descriptions of contemplation of the Absolute, the Upanishads express several doctrines that are central to all forms of Sanatana Dharma. One is the idea of *reincarnation*. In answer to the universal question, "What happens after we die?" the rishis taught that the soul leaves the dead body and enters a new one:

As a leech, having reached the end of a blade of grass, takes hold of another blade and draws itself to it, so the Self, having left his body behind it unconscious, takes hold of another body and draws himself to it.

Brihadaranyaka Upanishad[11]

KARMA   An important corollary to the idea that we are reborn into another body is the concept of *karma*. It means action, and also the consequences of action. Every act we make, and even every thought and every desire we have, shapes our future experiences. Our life is what we have made it. And we ourselves are shaped by what we have done: "As a man acts, so does he become ... A man becomes pure through pure deeds, impure through impure deeds."[12] Not only do we reap in this life the good or evil we have sown; they also follow us after physical death, affecting our next incarnation. Ethically, this is a strong teaching, for our every move has far-reaching consequences.

The ultimate goal, however, is not creation of good lives by good deeds, but a clean escape from the karma-run wheel of birth, death, and rebirth, which is called *samsara*. To escape from samsara is to achieve *moksha*, or liberation from the limitations of space, time, and matter through realization of the immortal Absolute. Many lifetimes of upward-striving incarnations are required to reach this transcendence of earthly miseries. This desire for liberation from earthly existence is one of the underpinnings of classical Hinduism, and of Buddhism as well.

Devotional religion of the epics and Puranas

It is difficult to pray to the impersonal Absolute, for it is formless and is not totally distinct from oneself. In time the desire for a personal relationship with a divine person became the heart of Sanatana Dharma as the majority of followers now experience it. This is *bhakti*: intense devotion to a personal manifestation of Brahman.

Although there are many devotional passages in the Upanishads, personal love for a personal deity flowered in the spiritual literature that followed the Vedas. Two major classes of scriptures that arose after 500 BCE (according to Western scholarship) were the *epics* and the *Puranas*. They were helpful vehicles to popularize spiritual knowledge and devotion through myths and legends of national events. They were particularly useful in spreading Hindu teachings to the masses at times when Buddhism and Jainism — movements born in India but not recognizing the authority of the Vedas — were winning converts.

In contrast to the rather abstract depictions of the Divine Principle in the Upanishads, the epics and Puranas are highly theistic. That is, they represent the Supreme as a Person. In fact, the Supreme is presented as various human-like deities. As T. M. P. Mahadevan explains:

> *The Hindu mind is averse to assigning an unalterable or rigidly fixed form or name to the Deity. Hence it is that in Hinduism we have innumerable god-forms and countless divine names. And, it is a truth that is recognized by all Hindus that obeisance offered to any of these forms and names reaches the one supreme God.* [13]

Two great epics, the *Ramayana* and the *Mahabharata*, present the Supreme usually as Vishnu, who intervenes on earth during critical periods in the cosmic cycles. In the unthinkable vastness of time as reckoned by Hindu thought, each world cycle lasts 4,320,000,000 years, the equivalent of one day in the life of Brahman. Each of the world cycles is divided into four ages, or *yugas*.

Dharma, as moral order in the world, is natural in the first age. The second age is like a cow standing on three legs; people must be taught their proper roles in society. During the darker third age, revealed values are no longer recognized, people lose their altruism and willingness for self-denial, and there are no more saints. The final age, *Kali Yuga*, is as imbalanced as a cow trying to stand on one leg. The world is at its worst, with egotism, ignorance, recklessness, and war rampant. According to Hindu figuring, we are in the midst of Kali Yuga, an age which began on a Friday in 3102 BCE. Such an age is described thus:

> *When society reaches a stage where property confers rank, wealth becomes the only source of virtue, passion the sole bond of union between husband and wife, falsehood the source of success in life, sex the only means of enjoyment, and when outer trappings are confused with inner religion . . .* [14]

Each of these massive cycles witnesses the same turns of events, with the balance inexorably shifting from the true dharma to dissolution and then back to the dharma as the gods are again victorious over the anti-gods. The Puranas list the many ways that the

Lord has incarnated in the world when dharma is decaying, to help restore virtue and defeat evil. For instance, Vishnu is said to have incarnated as Vyasa at the beginning of Kali Yuga to write down the Vedas, for humans no longer had good memories. It is considered inevitable that Vishnu will continually return in answer to the pleas of suffering humans, and equally inevitable that he will meet with resistance from "demonic forces" who are also part of the cosmic cycles.

THE RAMAYANA   The epics deal with this eternal play of good and evil, symbolized by battles involving the human incarnations of Vishnu. Along the way, they teach examples of the virtuous life. The Ramayana, thought to have been composed by about 100 or 200 BCE is much beloved and is acted out with great pageantry throughout India every year.

In the story, Vishnu incarnates as the virtuous prince Rama in order to kill Ravana, the ten-headed demon king of Sri Lanka. Rama is heir to his father's throne, but the mother of his stepbrother tricks the king into banishing Rama into the forest for fourteen years. Rama, model of morality, goes willingly, observing that a son's duty is to obey his parents implicitly, even when their commands seem wrong. He is accompanied into the ascetic life by his wife Sita, the model of wifely devotion in a patriarchal society, who may formerly have been an earth goddess in her own right. She refuses his offer to remain behind in comfort:

O my Lord! A father, mother, son, brother or daughter-in-law indeed abide by the results of their actions; but a wife, O best of men, shares in her husband's fate. Therefore I have been ordered no less than thou, to exile in the forest. If thou goest there I shall go before thee, treading upon thorns and prickly grass. I shall not cause thee trouble but will live on roots and fruits. And there will be pools, with wild geese and other fowl and bright with full-blown lotus flowers, where we may bathe. There I shall be happy with thee even for a hundred or a thousand years. [15]

Eventually Sita is kidnapped by Ravana, who woos her unsuccessfully in his island kingdom, guarded by all manner of terrible demons. Although Rama is powerful, he and his half-brother Lakshman need the help of the monkeys and bears in the battle to get Sita back. Hanuman the monkey becomes the hero of the story. He symbolizes the power of faith and devotion to overcome our human frailties. In his love for the Lord he can do anything.

The bloody battle ends in single-handed combat between Ravana and Rama. Rama blesses a sacred arrow with Vedic mantras and sends it straight into Ravana's heart. When he and Sita are reunited, he accuses her of possible infidelity, so to prove her innocence she successfully undergoes an ordeal by fire in which Agni protects her. After Rama's kingship is restored, he asks Sita to prove her purity several more times in order to preserve the integrity of his rule from the people's suspicions. After many ordeals, she utters these final words to Rama and the earth, becomes a field of radiance, and disappears into the ground:

O Lord of my being, I realize you in me and me in you. Our relationship is eternal.
Through this body assumed by me, my service to you and your progeny is complete now. I dissolve this body to its original state.

Mother Earth, you gave form to me. I have made use of it as I ought to. In recognition of its purity may you kindly absorb it into your womb. [16]

Rama and Lakshman shoot arrows into the breast of the demon Ravana, with Hanuman and the monkeys in the background. Sita waits within Ravana's compound, guarded by his demons. (North India, c. 19th century.)

Indian arts are designed to be interpreted on many levels. One way of interpreting the Ramayana is to see all the characters as parts of ourself. Rama, for instance, is the innate principle of goodness, while Ravana is our dark side, or ego – that which tends to greed, jealousy, and selfishness. Sita represents our devotion to the Supreme. If our good side loses its Sita, we will see evil all around, like the demons whom Rama had to confront. To restore our devotional connection with Brahman, we must kill the ego.

Sita's role in the story also illustrates two features of Hindu women's spirituality. One is the ideal of marriage, in which couples are spiritual partners. Marriage is a vehicle for spiritual discipline, service, and advancement toward a spiritual goal, rather than a means of self-gratification. Men and women are thought to complement each other, although the ideal of liberation has traditionally been intended largely for the male.

Second, the female is highly venerated. Women who follow role models such as Sita make major contributions to the good earthly life, consisting of dharma (order in society), material wealth (by bearing sons in a patriarchal society), and the aesthetics of sensual pleasure. Women are auspicious beings, mythologically associated with wealth, beauty, splendor, and grace. As sexual partners to men, they help activate the spiritualizing life-force.

Nevertheless, women are not encouraged to seek liberation through their own spiritual practices; their role is usually linked to that of their husband, who takes the position of their god and their guru. For many centuries, there was even the hope that a widow would choose to be cremated alive with her dead husband in order to remain united with him after death. This supreme self-sacrifice was called *sati*, meaning "good woman." It was treated as a religious ceremony, with the widow wearing her bridal sari and being blessed and bowed down to by the elders. According to the ideal, she sits serenely on the funeral pyre, tenderly cradling her husband's head in her lap, as the flames engulf them both.

Historically, there were apparently some women who chose to die thus. But this extreme ideal of duty and devotion became for some women a horrible death forced upon them rather than willingly chosen. Being a live widow put one in a difficult position as well; widows tended to be regarded as impure and unwanted by society unless they became strict ascetics. Sati was finally outlawed in 1829, and remarriage of widows was legalized in 1856. But controversy over the sati ideal continues in India.

THE MAHABHARATA   The other famous epic is the Mahabharata. Fifteen times as long as the Bible and apparently semi-historical, it may have been composed by about 300 BCE. The story revolves around the struggle between the sons of a royal family for control of a kingdom near what is now Delhi. Lessons inculcated in the course of the story revolve around the importance of sons, the duties of kingship, the benefits of ascetic practice and righteous action, and the qualities of the gods.

A portion of the Mahabharata that is of particular importance is the *Bhagavad-Gita* ("The teaching given in song by the Supreme Exalted One"). Krishna, the exalted one, appears as the charioteer of Arjuna, who is preparing to fight on the virtuous side of a battle that will pit brothers against brothers. Before they plunge into the battle, a metaphor for our struggles between our worldly ties and our spiritual aspirations, Krishna instructs Arjuna in the arts of self-transcendence and realization of the eternal. The eternal instructions are still central to spiritual practice in Sanatana Dharma.

Arjuna is enjoined to withdraw his attention from the impetuous demands of the

Above left *During the north Indian festival Ram-lila, giant effigies of Ravana and the demons from the epic Ramayana are dramatically burned, to the delight of the crowds.*
Above right *Legends about Krishna as a child are often reenacted by children as part of a holiday honoring Krishna's birthday, Janmashtami.*
Left *Krishna is often pictured as drawing humans to the divine by the power of love, symbolized by the lure of his flute.*

senses, ignoring all feelings of attraction or aversion. This will give him a steady, peaceful mind. He is instructed to offer devotional service and to perform the prescribed Vedic sacrifices, but for the sake of discipline, duty, and example alone rather than reward – to "abandon all attachment to success or failure ... renouncing the fruits of action in the material world."[17]

Actually, says Lord Krishna, those who do everything for love of the Supreme

Right *An Indian woman prepares a protective rice paste pattern, honoring the ancient tradition by which her female ancestors created intuitive designs to bring spiritual protection for their families.*

Below left *Kali is the archetype of the transcendental power of the Kundalini earth energy, and destroyer of hypocrisy and selfishness.*

Below right *At the end of Durga Puja, images of the ten-armed vanquisher of evil are carried to the river and consigned to the deep, so that she may return to her mate Shiva, who awaits her in the Himalayas.*

transcend the Vedic notion of duty. In offering everything they do to the Supreme, "without desire for gain and free from egoism and lethargy,"[18] knowing that their eternal self is separate from the experiences of the body, they feel peace, freedom from earthly entanglements, and unassailable happiness.

This yogic science of transcending the "lower self" by the "higher self" is so ancient that Krishna says it was originally given to the sun god and through his agents, to humans. But in time it was lost, and Krishna is now renewing his instructions pertaining to "that very ancient science of the relationship with the Supreme."[19] He has taken human form again and again to teach the true religion:

Whenever and wherever there is a decline in religous practice . . . and a predominant rise of irreligion – at that time I descend Myself.

To deliver the pious and to annihilate the miscreants, as well as to re-establish the principles of religion, I advent Myself millennium after millenium. [20]

Krishna says that everything springs from his being:

There is no truth superior to Me. Everything rests upon Me, as pearls are strung on a thread . . .

I am the taste of water, the light of the sun and the moon, the syllable om *in Vedic mantras; I am the sound in ether and ability in man . . .*

All states of being – goodness, passion or ignorance – are manifested by My energy. I am, in one sense, everything – but I am independent. I am not under the modes of this material nature. [21]

This Supreme Godhead is not apparent to most mortals. The Lord can only be known by those who love him, and for them, it is easy. Any small act of devotion offered in love for Krishna becomes a way to him: "If one offers Me with love and devotion a leaf, a flower, fruit, or water, I will accept it."[22] Sincere worship creates a direct path to the Divine: "To those who are constantly devoted and worship me with love, I give the understanding by which they come to Me."[23]

KRISHNA OF THE PURANAS   Despite the devotional quality of the passages quoted above, many of the instructions in the Bhagavad-Gita are quite austere. The way of devotion so beloved by the masses in India, and said to be the best path for Kali Yuga, is more evident in the *Purana of the Lord (Srimad Bhagavatam)*. Most Indologists think it was written about the eighth or ninth century BCE, but some Indians feel it was one of the works written down at the beginning of Kali Yuga by Vyasa. According to tradition, Vyasa had written down all the Vedas, Puranas, and the Mahabarata, but still he felt dissatisfied, as though something were missing. When he asked his spiritual master why this was so, his master said that the missing element was love of the Divine. What Vyasa then wrote was Srimad Bhagavatam, which describes the Supreme as a Person to be adored.

The Supreme Personality of Godhead is portrayed first in its vast cosmic dimensions: the Being whose body animates the material universe. For instance:

His eyes are the generating centers of all kinds of forms, and they glitter and illuminate. His eyeballs are like the sun and the heavenly planets. His ears hear from all sides and are receptacles for all the Vedas, and His sense of hearing is the generating center of the sky and of all kinds of sound. [24]

This material universe we know is only one of millions of material universes. Each is like a bubble in the eternal spiritual sky, arising from the pores of the body of Vishnu, and these bubbles are created and destroyed as Vishnu breathes out and in.

This cosmic conception is so vast that it is impossible for the mind to grasp it. It is much easier to comprehend and adore Krishna in his incarnation as Krishna the cowherding boy. Whereas he was a wise teacher in the Bhagavad-Gita, the Lord Incarnate of the Puranas is a much-loved child raised by cowherds in an area called Vrindavan near Mathura on the Jumna River. This area was actually home to a cowherding tribe, but whether the stories about Krishna have any historical basis is unclear.

The mythology is rich in earthly pleasures. The boy Krishna mischievously steals balls of butter from the neighbors and wanders garlanded with flowers through the forest, happily playing his flute. Between episodes of carefree bravery in vanquishing demons that threaten the people, he playfully steals the hearts of the *gopis*, the cowherd girls, many of them married. Through his magical ways, each thinks that he dances with her alone. He is physically beautiful.

Eventually Krishna is called away on a heroic mission, never returning to the gopis. Their grief at his leaving, their loving remembrances of his graceful presence, and their intense longing for him serve as models for the *bhakti* path – the way of extreme devotion.

In Hindu thought, the emotional longing of the lover for the beloved is one of the most powerful vehicles for concentration on the Supreme Lord. The Divine is known as a person rather than an impersonal principle. Some bhaktas interpret the scriptures literally, believing that this Divine Person is a reality rather than a metaphor. His Grace A. C. Bhaktivedanta Swami Prabhupada expounds this point of view:

> Personality of Godhead is not an imagination by the devotee for facility of worship, but He is the Supreme Person in fact and figure. The impersonal feature of the Absolute Truth is but His radiation, as the sun rays are but radiations from the sun. [25]

Spiritual disciplines

Another thread of Sanatana Dhama is spiritual discipline. The process of attaining spiritual realization or liberation is thought to take at least a lifetime, and probably many lifetimes. Incarnation in this world is prized as a chance of advancing toward spiritual perfection. The techniques seem to have been known in ancient times in India.

In the past, spiritual training was usually available to upper-caste males only; women and shudras were excluded. It was preceded by an initiation ceremony in which the boy received the *sacred thread*, a cord of three threads to be worn over the shoulder.

Students may live with their teacher, often in an *ashram*, a communal hermitage where rich and poor alike live simply apart from the world, serving their master as a spiritual parent. Celibacy is expected of those who take monastic vows.

The final stage is total detachment from the world for the life of the *sannyasin*. Living as a renunciate, the sannyasin is a contemplative who ritually cuts himself off from wife and family, declaring, "No one belongs to me and I belong to no one." He lives alone, with only a water jar, a walking staff, and a begging bowl for possessions. Some wandering sannyasins wear no clothes. In silence, the sannyasin concentrates on practices that will finally release him from samsara into cosmic consciousness.

The guru

Those who choose the path of study and renunciation often place themselves at the feet of a spiritual teacher, or *guru*. In Sanskrit, guru means "the venerable" or "the one who leads the disciple out of the darkness of ignorance." He or she does so not by academic teaching, but by being enlightened. Gurus do not declare themselves as teachers; people are naturally drawn to them because they have achieved spiritual states to which the seekers aspire.

A sannyasin, also referred to as a sadhu, renounces possessions and lives only for the spiritual life.

> Anyone and everyone cannot be a guru. A huge timber floats on the water and can carry animals as well. But a piece of worthless wood sinks, if a man sits on it, and drowns him.
>
> Ramakrishna[26]

Ramana Maharshi, who died in 1951, lived on a holy mountain in south India, so absorbed in Ultimate Consciousness that he neither talked nor ate and had to be

Above left
Sannyasins congregate in great numbers once every twelve years to celebrate Kumbha Mela, the victory of the gods over the demons. They are honored by other participants as they practice austerities.
Right   *Yogic adepts have developed extreme control of their bodies to amplify meditation efforts.*

force-fed by another holy man. But the needs of those who gathered around him drew out his compassion and wisdom, and he spontaneously counseled them in their spiritual needs. His glance alone was said to have illuminated many who visited him.

The Siddha tradition of south India specializes in "teaching" by the power of a glance, word, touch, or thought (called *shaktipat*). A disciple of the late Swami Muktananda (whom he calls "Baba," an endearing "Father" term for a holy man) describes the effect:

> When a seeker receives shaktipat, *he experiences an overflowing of bliss within and becomes ecstatic. Thus, by his divine power, Baba makes the seeker realize his true nature by giving him the experience of divinity within his own Self. In Baba's presence, all doubts and misgivings vanish, and one experiences inner contentment and a sense of fulfillment.* [27]

The great nineteenth-century saint Ramakrishna observed that no guru is necessary for the person who approaches God with sincere longing and earnest prayer. But such people are rare, he said – most seekers need a teacher.

When seekers find their guru, they love and honor him or her as their spiritual parent. The guru does not always behave as a loving parent; often the disciples are treated harshly, to test their faith and devotion or to strip away the ego. True devotees are nevertheless grateful for opportunities to serve their guru, out of love. They often bend to touch the feet or hem of the robe of the guru, partly out of humility (placing the dust from the guru's feet on top of their heads, signifying utter submission) and partly because great power is thought to emanate from the guru's feet. Humbling oneself before the guru is considered necessary in order to receive the teaching. A metaphor commonly used is that of a glass and a pitcher of water. If the glass (the disciple, or *chela*) is already full, no water (spiritual wisdom) can be poured into it from the pitcher (the guru). Likewise, if the glass is on the same level as the pitcher, there can be no pouring.

What is necessary is for the glass to be empty and below the pitcher; then the water can be freely poured into the glass.

Behaviors that outsiders often interpret as worship of the guru are ideally directed to that which comes through the guru. Swami Satchidananda explains:

Even if you find someone who is the right teacher for you, you should still know who the real guru is. Remember, it is not the physical body, but the Self, the light within. What you wish to acquire is the way he lives, the serenity he has … Ultimately all these forms and names should disappear into a formless and nameless One, who is the Absolute Guru. [28]

Yogic practices

Gurumayi Chidvilasanda, a contemporary female guru in the Siddha Yoga tradition, successor to Swami Muktananda. Devotees long for a glance from such beings, for through their eyes may flow the power and love of the divine.

Spiritual seekers are generally encouraged to engage in disciplines that clear the mind and support a state of serene, detached awareness. This desired state of balance, purity, wisdom, and peacefulness of mind is described as *sattvic*, in contrast with *rajasic* (active, restless) states or *tamasic* (lethargic, dull) states.

The practices for increasing sattvic qualities are known collectively as *yoga*, which means "yoke" or "union" of the individual consciousness with the Infinite Consciousness. The methods are called *sadhanas*. Some *sadhus* ("holy men") go to extremes of bodily mortification, such as standing always on one foot, naked, in hopes of denying the ego and thereby achieving liberation or union with the Supreme. But the essential focus of the sadhanas is on inner qualities rather than outer behaviors.

Yogic practices are extremely ancient. According to south Indian tradition, the sadhanas were developed by supreme masters known as the Tamil Yoga Siddhas. Some believe that they were known as long ago as the Paleolithic Age and were the basis for the great Indus Valley culture. As we noted earlier, the seals from the Indus Valley do show a siva-like deity in yogic posture.

A distinction can be made between yoga, the sattva-enhancing sadhanas practiced since ancient times by spiritual seekers, and Yoga, the philosophical system evolved to explain their use. The latter will be described in a later section.

HATHA YOGA   Techniques involving purification and discipline of the physical body are called *Hatha yoga*. Sustained physical postures *(asanas)* and care in eating are used to cleanse the body and develop the mind. The ability to concentrate the attention increases, and it is said that one is prepared for psychic currents later experienced during meditation. Without this preparation, the spiritual energies are thought powerful enough to "blow fuses" in the person, creating physical and psychological imbalances. Hatha yoga postures and diet are also considered quite beneficial to health.

In addition to postures and diet, hatha yoga includes regulated breathing exercises *(pranayama)*. They are thought to calm the nerves and increase the supply of *prana*. Food, water, and particularly air are reservoirs of prana, the invisible life energy that permeates the universe, according to Indian thought. By controlling the rhythm of breathing and taking deep breaths from the abdomen to the area beneath the shoulder blades, yogis are said to absorb more prana from the atmosphere and increase the electric potential of their cells. Demonstrations of the effectiveness of the practices include the Tibetan yogis' practice of sitting naked in the Himalayas, generating so much heat that they can reportedly dry wet towels placed on their bodies or melt the snow.

In Kundalini yoga, the body is thought to exist within a field of energy, which is most concentrated at the major chakras – subtle centers along the vertical axis of the body.

The Upanishads speak of the "pranic body" – an invisible energy field permeating and surrounding the physical body. Prana flows through channels in this invisible field, affecting the physical body. Breath is thought to shape this energy flow; controlled breathing brings it under the control of the mind and allows it to be directed at will. In addition to being a link between mind and body, breath is a ladder to higher levels of consciousness.

KUNDALINI YOGA   Another level of work with the body involves the subtle energy centers, or *chakras*, in the pranic body. They correspond to glands and nervous system junctions in the body and are believed to act as whirlpools where subtle energies can be exchanged with the outer environment. Focusing attention on these centers is said to "open" them, increasing the energy they funnel.

Seven major chakras have been identified by yogis. The lowest is at the base of the spine. It is associated with the basic desire for survival and with the latent energy called the *kundalini* power. It is often depicted as a coiled snake. The goal of kundalini practice is to raise and refine this energy, drawing it upward to stimulate the highest chakras, leading to the bliss of union with the Sublime. But if the kundalini energy is forced up the spine before the body is prepared and the chakras are purified and opened, the person may experience a kind of madness.

The energy of each chakra is said to be more refined than the one beneath it. The second chakra lies along the spine about three or four inches above the first. It is considered a center of sexual and creative energy. The third chakra is associated with the solar plexus and is thought to be a center of the emotions. Fourth is the heart chakra, seat of the higher spiritual emotions such as love, joy, and compassion. The fifth center is at the throat; its opening is said to be related to open communications.

The sixth chakra is called the *third eye*. Above and between the eyebrows, it is considered the center that manifests the power of the will and allows spiritual insight. The crown, or seventh chakra, is considered the seat of cosmic consciousness. In its fully opened state, it is perceived as a thousand-petaled lotus, effulgent with light.

The OM symbol, representing the original sound of creation, is topped by the sun and the moon, harmonized opposites. To chant OM is to commune with this cosmic sound vibration.

MANTRA YOGA   As indicated earlier, Indian thought has long embraced the idea that repetition of certain sounds has sacred effects. It is said that some ancient yogic adepts could discern supersonic sounds and that mantra (chanted sacred sounds) based on special seed syllables express an aspect of the Divine in the form of sound vibration.

Mystics say that the word "mantra" (or "mantrum") comes from the Sanskrit roots "man," or mind, and "tri," to cross. Chanting sacred syllables allows the consciousness to ride over the sea of the mind, directly affecting one's attitudes, emotions, states of consciousness, and chakras. Chanting a mantra calms and raises the vibration of the devotee, attuning him or her to the Divine Ground of Existence. By chanting "Om Shanti," for instance, slowly and reverently, a person becomes filled with the universal divine peace.

A mantra is also a tool for stilling the mind. Indians liken the mind to the trunk of an elephant, always straying restlessly here and there. If an elephant is given a small stick to hold in its trunk, it will hold it steadily, losing interest in other objects. Just so, the mantra gives the restless mind something to hold, quieting it by focusing awareness in one place.

DHYANA YOGA The path of meditation, *Dhyana yoga*, begins with concentration practices. A common yogic technique for bringing the mind to one-pointed remembrance of the Eternal is to concentrate on some visual form. Favorite images are a candle flame, the picture of a saint or guru, the OM symbol, and *yantras*. The latter are linear images with cosmic symbolism. The yantra on page 000 shows the physical core of the universe as a large dot surrounded by three rings representing the three qualities of nature: sattva (balance), rajas (activity), and tamas (inertia). Beyond these rings, two triangles are superimposed, symbolizing the linked male and female qualities of the Divine. The lotus petals symbolize the love and beauty of spirit manifesting as matter. The outer square is open on all sides, reminding the devotee that creation expands infinitely.

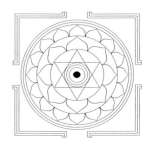

A yantra, cosmic symbol and focus for concentration.

In the state of meditation that follows concentration, all worldly thoughts have dissipated. Instead of ordinary thinking, the clear light of awareness allows insights to arise spontaneously as flashes of illumination. There may also be phenomena such as colored lights, visions, waves of ecstasy, or visits from immortal beings. The mind, heart, and body may gradually be transformed.

None of these phenomena are considered goals in themselves. The ultimate goal of yogic meditation is *samadhi*: a super-conscious state of union with the Absolute. Swami Sivananda attempts to describe it:

> *Words and language are imperfect to describe this exalted state . . . Mind, intellect and the senses cease functioning . . . It is a state of eternal Bliss and eternal Wisdom. All dualities vanish in toto . . . All visible merge in the invisible or the Unseen. The individual soul becomes that which he contemplates.* [29]

JNANA YOGA Another contemplative yogic path uses the mind rather than trying to transcend it by concentration practices. This is *jnana yoga* – "the way of wisdom." In this path, ignorance is considered the root of all problems in the world. Our basic ignorance is our idea of our selves as being separate from the Absolute. A method advocated by Ramana Maharshi is continually to ask, "Who am I?" Through intellectual effort, the seeker discovers that the one who asks the question is not the body, not the senses, not the pranic body, not the mind, but something eternal beyond all these:

> *After negating all of the above-mentioned as ''not this,'' ''not this,'' that Awareness which alone remains – that I am . . . The thought ''Who am I?'' will destroy all other thoughts, and, like the stick used for stirring the burning pyre, it will itself in the end get destroyed. Then, there will arise Self-realization.* [30]

In the jnana path, the seeker must also develop the spiritual virtues (calmness, restraint, renunciation, resignation, concentration, and faith) and have an intense longing for liberation. By cutting through all doubts and mental habits, the seeker finally graduates from theoretical knowledge of the self to direct experience of it. The ultimate wisdom is spiritual insight rather than intellectual knowledge.

> *Spiritual knowledge is the only thing that can destroy our miseries for ever; any other knowledge removes wants only for a time.*
>
> *Swami Vivekananda* [31]

KARMA YOGA In contrast to the ascetic and contemplative nature of the yogas already described, another way involves action in the world. *Karma yoga* is service rendered without any interest in its effects and without any personal sense of giving. The yogi knows that it is the Absolute who performs all actions, and that all actions are gifts to the Absolute. This consciousness leads to liberation from the self in the very midst of work. Krishna explains these principles in the Bhagavad-Gita:

> *A person in the divine consciousness, although engaged in seeing, hearing, touching, smelling, eating, moving about, sleeping and breathing, always knows within himself that he actually does nothing at all. Because while evacuating, receiving, opening or closing his eyes, he always knows that only the material senses are engaged with their objects and that he is aloof from them.*
>
> *The steadily devoted soul attains unadulterated peace because he offers the results of all activities to Me; whereas a person who is not in harmony with the Divine, who is greedy for the fruits of his labor, becomes entangled.* [32]

BHAKTI YOGA   The final yoga sadhana is the one embraced by most Indian followers of Sanatana Dharma. It is the path of devotion, *bhakti yoga.* "Bhakti" means "to share," to share a relationship with the Supreme. Bhaktas usually center their love on devotion to a personal deity, but teachers emphasize that it is the Supreme who is being worshipped in all forms.

Scriptures recognize many ways the devotee may feel related to the Divine. As is common in Hindu teachings, these are ranked from lowest to highest. The initial form of devotion is that of a servant to the master, exemplified by the monkey Hanuman in the Ramayana. A more evolved form is that of friend-to-friend. Higher and more intimate is a parent's love for a child, or a child's love for a parent. Above this is the love of a wife for her husband, as in Sita's devotion to Rama. Most intimate is the romantic love of lover for Beloved. The latter is depicted in many sensual images of Krishna and his consort Radha, but the intimacy implied is a rapturous surrender that transcends sensuality.

Bhaktas' devotion is considered more dear to the Supreme than ritualistic piety. The story is told that a pious Brahmin came daily to offer ritual worship to a stone statue of Siva. One day he was horrified to see wild flowers and partly-eaten pork decorating the shrine. These had been left by a hunter who stopped to worship Siva in his own fashion. Hoping to teach the Brahmin a lesson, Siva appeared to him in a dream commanding that he watch from hiding while the hunter expressed his devotion. When the hunter then came to worship, he saw blood oozing from the eye of the statue. Without hesitation, he plucked out his own eye to place it on that of the idol. The bleeding stopped, but then the statue's other eye started bleeding. The hunter prepared to pull out his other eye when Siva manifested himself, healed the hunter, and took him as one of his chosen devotees, thenceforth called "the beloved of the eye."

For bhaktas, the goal is not to lose themselves in cosmic consciousness but to remain separate from the deity, loving It. Ramakrishna explains why the bhakti way is more appropriate for most people:

> *As long as the I-sense lasts, so long are true knowledge and Liberation impossible . . . [But] how very few can obtain this Union (Samadhi) and free themselves from this ''I''? It is very rarely possible. Talk as much as you want, isolate yourself continously, still this ''I'' will always return to you. Cut down the poplar tree today, and you will find tomorrow it forms new shoots. When you ultimately find that this ''I'' cannot be destroyed, let it remain as ''I'' the servant.* [33]

The love between Radha and Krishna is the model for bhaktas' devotion to the Supreme Person.

Tantric practices

In contrast to the asceticism of yoga, another group of spiritual practices use the senses as vehicles to spiritual growth, rather than denying them. This approach is called *Tantra*. It appears in Hinduism, Buddhism, and Jainism, and is extremely ancient. Scriptures called *Tantras* were first written down around 300 BCE, but the practices may be prehistoric.

Tantra is a cluster of advanced secret practices, some of which are designed to awaken and harness the kundalini energy. Seed mantras – syllables whose sounds have no meaning but impact the subtle energy centers – may be used to awaken the chakras. Ritual sexual intercourse may be used as a way of raising the kundalini energy, for mutual transcendence of physical separation into the blissful awareness of mystical unity. Orgasm is delayed in the interest of allowing sexual energy to build and rise up the spinal columns of both partners. There may be an emphasis on the feminine as the center of creation and thus the most direct path back to its truths. Female deities are important, and many Tantric symbols are representations of the female genitalia. Yantras, for example, are often constructed of inverted triangles.

In Tantra, everything is considered holy, including the body. The five forbidden things of Brahmanism, wine, meat, fish, parched grain, and sexual intercourse, are intentionally used as sacraments. Ritual worship of deities is designed to arouse the emotions and senses, as powerful aids to spiritual realization. Whereas yoga aims at creating a sattvic state, Tantra inflames rajas, or passion, in order to transcend the limited personal consciousness.

Major theistic cults

After a period when Brahmanic ritual and philosophy dominated Sanatana Dharma, the Bhakti approach came to prominence around 600 CE. It opened spiritual expression to both shudras and women, and has been the primary path of the masses ever since. It may also have been the initial way of the people, for devotion to personal deities is thought to predate Vedic religion. Some theistic worship practices draw on the tantric tradition, for their goal is to uplift human awareness to sublime levels through worshipful use of the senses.

Of all the deities worshipped by Hindus, there are three major groupings: *Vaishnavites* who worship the Divine as Vishnu, *Saivites* who worship the Divine as Siva, and *Saktas* who worship the female creative power. Each devotee has his or her own "chosen deity," but will honor others as well.

Ultimately, Hindus rest their faith in one genderless deity with three basic aspects: creating, preserving, and destroying. The latter activity is seen as a merciful act that allows the continuation of the cosmic cycles.

Saktas

As we have seen, worship of the feminine aspect of the Divine probably dates back to the pre-Aryan ancient peoples of the Indian subcontinent. Her power is called *sakti* and is often linked with the kundalini energy. Lushly erotic, sensual imagery is frequently used to symbolize her abundant creativity. Secret tantric texts teach her devotees how to control and raise the kundalini energy.

The feminine principle is still worshipped in many forms, including those representing the totality of deity – eternal creator, preserver, destroyer. *Durga* is often represented as a beautiful woman with a gentle face but ten arms holding weapons with which she vanquishes the demons who threaten the dharma; she rides a tiger (see page 72).

Kali, by contrast, may be depicted dripping with blood and skulls symbolizing her aspect as the destroyer of evil. Her worship has had its dark "left-hand" side, with sacrifices of animals and purportedly even humans. A "right-hand" version of devotion to Mother Kali consists of asking her help in transforming oneself. What appears as destruction is actually a means of transformation. With her merciful sword she cuts away all personal impediments to realization of truth, for those who sincerely desire to serve the Supreme. At the same time, she opens her arms to those who love her. Two of her four arms hold a sword and a severed human head; one of the other two gestures "Fear not" and the other offers boons to her devotees.

In a sense, Kali represents life as it is, both the ugly and the beautiful. The divine reality is a wholeness encompassing both the pleasant and the unpleasant, creation and destruction. In India, death and birth are linked, each giving way to the other in eternal cycles.

Shiva as Lord of the Dance, trampling the demon of evil and bearing both the flame of destruction and the drum of creation. One of his two free hands gestures ''Fear not''; the other points to his upraised foot, connoting bliss.

Sakti worship has also been incorporated into worship of the male deities. Each is thought to have a female consort, shown in close physical embrace signifying the eternal unity of male and female principles in the oneness of the Divine. In these pairs, the female is often conceived as the life-animating force; the transcendent male aspect is inactive until joined with the productive female energy.

Saivites

Also quite ancient is worship of *Siva*, who was probably known before Vedic times and is still a major deity today, particularly in south India. In some systems he is one of the three major aspects of deity: Brahma (Creator), Vishnu (Preserver), and Siva (Destroyer). Saivites worship him as the totality, with many aspects. As Swami Sivasiva Palani, Saivite editor of *Hinduism Today*, explains: "Siva is the unmanifest; he is creator, preserver, destroyer, personal Lord, friend, primal Soul"; and he is the "all-pervasive underlying energy, the more or less impersonal love and light that flows through all things."[34] Siva is often depicted dancing above the body of the demon he has killed, reconciling darkness and light, good and evil, creation and destruction, rest and activity in the eternal dance of life.

Siva is also the god of yogis, for he symbolizes asceticism. He is often shown in austere meditation on Mount Kailas, clad only in a tiger skin, with a snake around his neck. The latter signifies his conquest of the ego.

Siva has various saktis, including Durga. He is often shown with his devoted spouse Parvati. Through their union cosmic energy flows freely, seeding and liberating the universe. Nevertheless, they are seen mystically as eternally chaste. Siva and his sakti are also expressed as two aspects of a single being. Some sculptors portray Siva as androgynous, with both masculine and feminine physical traits. This unity is often expressed abstractly, as lingam within yoni.

Lingams are naturally-occurring or sculpted cylindrical forms honored since antiquity in India (and apparently in other cultures as well, as far away as Hawaii). Those shaped by Nature, such as stones polished by certain rivers, are most highly valued, with rare natural crystal lingams considered unspeakably precious. While the lingam has often been interpreted sexually, as a phallic symbol, most Siva-worshippers do not perceive it as such and consider the sexual attribution the opposite of their beliefs. They feel that the original and pure understanding is that the lingam is a nearly amorphous, "formless" symbol for the unmanifest, transcendent nature of Siva — that which is beyond time, space, and cause, and form — whereas the yoni represents the manifest aspect of Sivaness.

Vaishnavites

In contrast to Sakti and Siva, Vishnu is beloved as the tender, merciful Deity. In one myth a sage was sent to determine who was the greatest of the gods by trying their tempers. The first two, Brahma and Siva, he insulted and was soundly abused in return. When he found Vishnu, the god was sleeping. Knowing of Vishnu's good-naturedness, the sage increased the insult by kicking him awake. Instead of reacting angrily, Vishnu tenderly massaged the sage's foot, concerned that he might have hurt it. The sage exclaimed, "This god is the mightiest, since he overpowers all by goodness and generosity!"

Worship of Vishnu, particularly his incarnation as Krishna, is especially prevalent in northern India. The ecstatic sixteenth-century Bengali saint and sage Sri Caitanya inflamed popular love for Krishna, adored as the flute-playing lover. Like Sri Caitanya, the devotee plays the role of Radha, Krishna's favorite among the gopis, making himself (if a male) like a loving female in order to experience the bliss of Lord Krishna's presence.

Major philosophical systems

Although the majority of followers of Sanatana Dharma are bhaktas, the spiritual wisdom of India has also expressed itself in elaborate intellectual systems of philosophy. Many distinct systems have evolved, but they all have certain features in common:
1 All have deep roots in the Vedas and other scriptures but also in direct personal experiences of the truth through meditation;
2 All hold ethics to be central to orderly social life – they acknowledge the existence of suffering and attribute it to the law of karma, thereby suggesting incentives to more ethical behavior;
3 All hold that the ultimate cause of suffering is people's ignorance of their true nature, the Self, which is omniscient, omnipotent, omnipresent, perfect, and eternal.

Two of the major philosophical systems born in India do not acknowledge the authority of the Vedas but nevertheless draw on many of the same currents as Sanatana Dharma. These two, Jainism and Buddhism, will be considered in the following two chapters. Of the others, Samkhya, Yoga, and Advaita Vedanta are most prevalent today.

Samkhya

The Samkhya system is thought to be the oldest in India, but no definite date has been set as its origin. Its founder, the partially mythical sage Kapila, was mentioned in the Mahabharata, which apparently took its current form somewhere between 400 BCE and and 400 CE. But Buddhism and Jainism, which developed simultaneously in the sixth century BCE, both include Samkhya principles, so the system probably preceded them and may be of pre-Vedic origin.

Samkhya philosophy puts forward two states of reality: *Purusha*, the Self which is eternally wise, pure, and free, beyond change, beyond cause: and *Prakriti*, the cause of the material universe. All our suffering, which is the focus of Kapila's concerns, stems from our false confusion of Prakriti with Purusha, the eternal Self. A dualistic understanding of life is essential, according to this system, if we are to distinguish the ultimate transcendent reality of Purusha from the temporal appearances of Prakriti, which bring us happiness but also misery and delusion.

An illuminating story is told about Indra, once king of the gods. He was forced by the other devas to descend into the body of a pig, and once there, began to enjoy the life, wallowing in the mud, mating, and having baby pigs. The devas were aghast; they came down to try to convince him to return, but Indra had forgotten his kingly state and insisted on remaining as a pig. Unable to talk him out of his delusion, the devas tried killing his babies; he was distraught but simply mated to have more piglets. Then the devas killed his mate. Indra grieved her loss but stayed in the mud. They finally had to kill him as well to bring him back to his senses. His soul then could see the body of the pig it had been inhabiting and was glad to return to heaven. The moral is that we, too, are like gods who forget the heights from which we came, so intent are we on the joys and sorrows of earthly life.

Yoga

Yoga is a system for recognizing earthly life for what it is and identifying with our eternal being. The system is closely linked to Samkhya philosophy, as the practical way of gaining direct experience of the distinction between Purusha and Prakriti.

As indicated earlier, the yoga sadhanas, or methods, are extremely ancient. By 200 BCE, a yogi named Patanjali (or perhaps a series of people taking the same name) had gathered them into a coherent system for attaining the highest consciousness. The 196 terse sayings are called *sutras*, "threads" on which meaning can be strung. For example, Book 2:5 contains this sutra: "Ignorance is regarding the impermanent as permanent, the impure as pure, the painful as pleasant, and the non-Self as the Self."

Yogis say that it is easier to calm a wild tiger than it is to quiet the mind, which is like a drunken monkey that has been bitten by a scorpion. The problem is that the mind is our vehicle for knowing the Self. If the mirror of the mind is disturbed, it reflects the disturbance rather than the pure light within. The goal of yogic practices is to make the mind absolutely calm and clear.

The mind is easily distracted from this clarity by the obstacles encountered by anyone who attempts to meditate: physical disease, dullness, doubt, carelessness, laziness, sensuality, false perception, failure to reach firm ground, and slipping from the ground gained. Patanjali prescribes the *eight limbs of yoga* as an integrated system for the seeker to outgrow the distractions:

1 *yama* (abstinence in our relationships with others: non-violence, truthfulness, non-stealing, celibacy, non-greed)
2 *niyama* (personal observances: purity, contentment, mortification, study, and devotion)
3 *asana* (postures)
4 *pranayama* (breath control)
5 *pratyahara* (withdrawal of attention from the senses)
6 *dharana* (concentration)
7 *dhyana* (meditation)
8 *samadhi* (contemplation or absorption in the superconscious state).

Samadhi cannot be achieved by the will; one can only surrender. Gerard Blitz, contemporary leader of yoga teachers in Europe, describes the effects:

The "I" disappears. Then you live with the stream of life every moment. You live without yourself. You have fantastic energy and an open heart and are full of love and you have intelligence and consciousness. [It is] being in life at every moment, completely, without fear, without being tired. You are always filling your batteries, so: action. You obtain siddhis – a larger state of consciousness in which you have more capacities. But this power [may be] an obstacle, and [you may use it to] influence people. You have to disappear. You have to become nothing. You have to serve. [35]

Advaita Vedanta

Whereas Samkya and Yoga are dualistic systems, Advaita ("not two") Vedanta is generally monistic, positing a single reality. It is based on the Upanishads (called Vedanta, or "the end of the Vedas"). Its founder is said to be Vyasa, systematizer of the Upanishads somewhere between 1000 and 500 BCE; Shankara reorganized the teachings many centuries later, probably between the sixth and ninth centuries CE. He is said to have been initiated by a thousand-year-old south Indian yogi, who received the tradition from the student of the student of Vyasa's son (some sages who live hidden from the world doing intense spiritual practices are thought to have become semi-immortal through inner alchemical processes).

According to Shankara, our material life is an illusion. It is like a momentary wave arising from the ocean, which is the only reality. Ignorance consists in thinking that the waves are different from the ocean. The absolute spirit, *Brahman*, is the essence of everything, and it has no beginning and no end. It is the eternal ocean of bliss within which forms are born and die, giving the false appearance of being real. That which makes us think the physical universe has its own reality is *maya*, the power by which the Absolute veils itself.

In Shankara's philosophical system, maya refers to the illusion that the world as we perceive it is real. He uses the metaphor of a coil of rope that, at dusk, is mistaken for a snake. The physical world, like the rope, does actually exist but we superimpose our memories and subjective thoughts upon it. Moreover, he says, only that which never changes is truly real. Everything else is changing, impermanent. Apparent phenomenal existence is not the same thing as reality.

In our ignorance we think that we exist as individuals, superimposing the notion of a separate ego-self on the underlying absolute reality of pure being, pure consciousness, pure bliss. It is a mistake to identify with the body or the mind, which exist but have no unchanging reality. When a person reaches transcendent consciousness, superimposition stops and the monistic oneness of reality is experienced.

Popular forms of worship

The subtleties of Hindu philosophy are not for the masses, but worship is for everyone. Personal and public opportunities abound for serving and celebrating the Supreme in many forms.

Devotions and rituals

There are rites for all occasions, such as first presentation of the child to the rising sun, first feeding of solid food, completion of studies, marriage, and death. Some of the ritual life of India seems to be of pre-Vedic origin. For instance, pilgrimages to holy places and purification rites at sacred rivers are important spiritual opportunities. And in the villages, women make special sacred drawings with rice paste on floors or walls for the protection of their households.

Nearly every home in India has a shrine with pictures or small statues of various deities, and many have a special prayer room set aside for their worship. Ritual purity is

The devout make pilgrimages to sacred rivers, particularly the Ganges, for ritual ablutions and prayers to the sun. Here Hindu women bathe in a river at the commencement of an eclipse.

still emphasized; the time for prayer and offerings to the deities is after the morning bath or after one has washed in the evening. Among orthodox families, menstruating women are still considered unclean and are not allowed to approach the shrines. Typically, a small oil lamp, symbolically invoking Agni, the fire deity, and a smoldering stick of incense are waved in a circle before the deities' images. If the devotee has a guru, a picture of him or her is usually part of the shrine, and one honors the guru as well as the deities as an adored guest.

In public worship ceremonies, called *puja*, the sacred presence is made tangible through devotions employing all the senses. Siva-lingams may be anointed with precious substances, such as ghee (clarified butter), honey, or sandalwood paste, with offerings of rose water and flowers. In a temple, devotees may have the great blessing of receiving *darsan* (visual contact with the Divine) through the prominent eyes of the images. One hears the sounds of mantras and ringing bells. Incense and flowers fill the area with uplifting fragrances. *Prasad*, food that has been sanctified by being offered to the deities and/or one's guru, is passed around to be eaten by devotees, who experience it as sacred and spiritually charged.

The deity image is treated as if it were a living king or queen. Fine-haired whisks are waved before it, purifying the area for its presence. Aesthetically pleasing meals are presented on the deity's own dishes at appropriate intervals; fruits must be perfect, without any blemishes. During visiting hours, the deity holds court, giving audience to devotees. In the morning, the image is ritually bathed and dressed in sumptuous clothes for the day; at night, it may be put to rest in bedclothes. If it is hot, the deity takes a nap in the afternoon, so arrangements are made for its privacy. For festivals, the deity is carefully paraded through the streets.

To an outsider, such observances look like children playing with dolls. But for the devout, loving service to the Divine makes It real and present. The statue is not a symbol of the deity; the deity is *in* the statue, reciprocating the devotee's attentions with a tangible exchange of energy. According to Swami Sivasiva Palani:

> *It is thought that the subtle essences of these things given in devotion are actually absorbed by the Divine, in an invisible and rather mystical process. It's as though we are feeding our God in an inner kind of a way. It's thought that if this is done properly, with the right spirit, the right heartfulness, the right mantras, that we capture the attention of the personal Lord and that he actually communes with us through that process, and we with him. Of course, when I say ''us'' and ''him'' I connote a dualism that is meant to be transcended in this process. One uses the dualism of the puja to find the monism that is at the heart of it.* [36]

In addition to worshipping the Divine through services to images, orthodox Brahmins observe many days of fasting and prayer, corresponding to auspicious points in the lunar and solar cycles or times of danger, such as the four months of the monsoon season.

Festivals

Sanatana Dharma honors the Divine in so many forms that almost every day a religious celebration is being held in some part of India. Sixteen religious holidays are honored by the central government so that everyone can leave work to join in the throngs of worshippers. These are calculated partially on a lunar calendar, so dates vary from year to year. Most Hindu festivals express spirituality in its gayest aspects. Group energy attracts the gods to overcome lurking evils, and humorous abandon helps merry-makers transform their fears.

Holi is the riotously joyful celebration of the death of winter and the return of colorful spring. In northern Indian areas where Vaishnavism is strong, the holiday is associated with Krishna, for as an infant he is said to have killed a demon employed by the king of winter. Pilgrims flock to Mathura for re-enactments of Krishna's playful exploits with the gopis. The festivities are probably of ancient indigenous origin, and in some areas, the two-day craziness is dedicated to Kama, the god of sexual love. Whatever the excuse, bands of people take to the streets with pistols for squirting colored liquids at anyone they meet. Their uninhibited gaiety is increased by liberal consumption of a marijuana and water paste. At the end, everyone hugs and old grudges are dropped as the new year begins.

In July or August a special day, *Naga panchami*, is devoted to the *Nagas*, or snakes. Snakes were considered powerful gods by the indigenous peoples, and the tradition persists. In south Indian villages, where they are especially honored, thousands of live snakes are caught and exhibited by brave handlers. Worshippers sprinkle vermilion and rice on the hoods of cobras, considered especially sacred. On Naga Panchami, farmers abstain from ploughing to avoid disrupting any snake-holes.

Three days later Vaishnavites celebrate Krishna's birthday (*Janmashtami*). At his birthplace, Mathura, Krishna's devotees fast and keep a vigil until midnight, retelling stories of his life. Elsewhere, pots of milk, curds, and butter are strung high above the ground to be seized by young men who form human pyramids to get to their prize. They romp about with the pots, drinking and spilling their contents like Krishna, playful stealer of these milk products he loved.

At the end of the summer, it is Ganesh who is honored, especially in west and south India, during *Ganesh Chaturti*. Special potters make elaborate clay images of the jovial elephant-headed remover of obstacles, son of Parvati, who formed him as a boy from the flour and oil of her beauty-cream and set him to stand guard while she bathed. Since he wouldn't let Siva in, her angry spouse smashed the boy's head into a thousand pieces. Parvati demanded that the boy be restored to life with a new head, but the first one found was that of a baby elephant. To soothe Parvati's distress at the peculiarity of the transplant, Siva granted Ganesh the power of removing obstacles. The elephant-headed god is now the first to be invoked in all rituals. After ten days of being sung to and offered sweets, the Ganesh images are carried to a body of water and bidden farewell with prayers for an easy year until Ganesh Chaturti comes around again.

In different parts of India, the first nine or ten days of Asvina, the lunar month corresponding to September or October, are dedicated either to the *Durga Puja* (in which elaborate images of the many-armed goddess celebrate her powers to vanquish the demonic forces) or to *Dussehra* (in which huge effigies of the wicked Ravana and his helpers may be burned, re-enacting the climax of the Ramayana and the triumph of Rama, his brother Lakshman, and the beloved monkey Hanuman). Or both aspects may be incorporated into the same ceremonies, in which the same theme is the triumph of good over evil.

Twenty days later is *Divali*, the happy four-day festival of lights. Variously explained as the return of Rama after his exile, the puja of Lakshmi (goddess of wealth, who visits only clean homes), and the New Year of those following one of the Indian calendars, it is a time for tidying business establishments and financial records, cleaning and illuminating houses after the mess of the monsoon season, wearing new clothes, gambling, feasting, honoring clay images of Lakshmi and Ganesh, and setting off fireworks.

Initially more solemn is *Mahashivaratri*, in which a day of fasting and a night of keeping vigil to earn merit with Siva are followed by gaiety and eating. During the ascetic part of the observance, many pilgrims go to sacred rivers or special tanks of water for ritual bathing. Siva lingams and statues are venerated, and the faithful chant and tell stories of Siva to keep each other awake. A reformist group, *Arya Samaj*, decries what it considers superstition and idolatry and honors the day as the end of a weeklong celebration of their reform. They carry out Vedic fire sacrifices and hold spiritual talks, throwing personal offerings into the fire on the last day.

Modern world Hinduism

Sanatana Dharma did not develop in India in isolation from other religions and national influences. Groups continued to flow into the subcontinent from outside. Muslims began taking over certain areas beginning in the eighth century CE; during the sixteenth and seventeenth centuries CE a large area was ruled by the Muslim Mogul Emperors. Islam and Hinduism generally co-existed, despite periods of intolerance on the part of

Muslim leaders, along with Buddhism and Jainism which had also grown up within India. Indian traders carried some aspects of Sanatana Dharma to Java and Bali, where Hinduism survives today with unique Balinese flavor.

When the Mughal Empire collapsed, European colonialists moved in. Ultimately the British dominated and in 1857 India was placed under direct British rule. Christian missionaries set about to correct abuses they perceived in certain Hindu practices, such as sati (widow-burning) and the caste system. But they also taught those who were being educated in their schools that Hinduism was "intellectually incoherent and ethically unsound."[37] Some Indians believed them and drifted away from their ancient tradition. Others felt that this accusation was untrue, but wondered how to make Hinduism palatable to modern tastes, how to reconcile it with contemporary life.

To counteract Western influences, *Mahatma* ("Great Soul") *Gandhi* (who died in 1948) encouraged grassroots nationalism, emphasizing that the people's strength lay in awareness of spiritual truth and in non-violent resistance to military-industrial oppression. He claimed that these qualities were the essence of Hinduism, which he considered the universal religion.

In addition to being made a focus for political unity, Sanatana Dharma itself was revitalized by a number of major figures. One of these was *Ramakrishna*, who lived from 1836 to 1886. He was a devotee of the Divine Mother in the form of Kali. Eschewing ritual, he communicated with her through intense love. He practiced Tantric disciplines, which brought him spiritual powers, spiritual insight, and reportedly a visible brilliance, but he longed only to be a vehicle for pure devotion:

I seek not, good Mother, the pleasures of the senses! I seek not fame! Nor do I long for those powers which enable one to do miracles! What I pray for, O good Mother, is pure love for Thee – love for Thee untainted by desires, love without alloy, love that seeketh not the things of the world, love for Thee that welleth up unbidden out of the depths of the immortal soul![38]

Ultimately, Ramakrishna worshipped the Divine through many Hindu paths, as well as Islam and Christianity, and found the same One in them all. Intoxicated with the One, he had continual visions of the Divine Mother and ecstatically worshipped her in unorthodox, uninhibited ways. For instance, once he fed a cat some food that was supposed to be a temple offering for the Divine Mother, for she revealed herself to him in everything, including the cat. He also placed his spiritual bride, Sarada Devi, in the chair reserved for the Deity, honoring her as the Great Goddess.

> *Do not care for doctrines, do not care for dogmas, or sects, or churches, or temples; they count for little compared with the essence of existence in each [person], which is spirituality . . . Earn that first, acquire that, and criticise no one, for all doctrines and creeds have some good in them.*
> *Ramakrishna*[39]

The pure devotion and universal spiritual wisdom Ramakrishna embodied inspired what is now known as the Ramakrishna Movement, or the Vedanta Society. A famous disciple named *Vivekananda* (1863–1902) carried the eternal message of Sanatana Dharma to the world beyond India, and excited so much interest in the West that Hinduism became a global religion. He also reintroduced Indians to the profundities of their great traditions.

Within India Sanatana Dharma was also influenced by reform movements such as Brahmo Samaj and Arya Samaj. The former defended Hindu mysticism and bhakti devotion to an immanent Deity. The latter advocated a return to what it saw as the purity of the Vedas, rejecting image worship, devotion to a multiplicity of deities, priestly privileges, and popular rituals. Though different, both movements were designed to convince intellectuals of the validity of "true" Hinduism. Today many liberal Hindus practice only those portions of the traditions which they find meaningful. They refuse to follow the old ways out of fear of the Deity or blind habit.

Gurus have kept the teacher-to-pupil transmission alive, training the many contemporary gurus, both male and female, who now offer training in Hindu thought and practice in ashrams and study centers around the globe. Many of the major scriptures of Sanatana Dharma have been translated into other languages. Yoga has a wide following, though many outside India learn the asanas and breathing practices without knowing anything of the spiritual framework of their traditional use. At the other extreme, Western-born ascetics of the Krishna Consciousness movement renounce their possessions, wear the orange robes of sannyasins, study all the literature about Krishna, and humbly offer chants and devotional services to the Lord.

The international Vedanta Society and the Ramakrishna Movement teach a simplified version of Sanatana Dharma, based on these central principles:

Truth or God is One.
Our real nature is divine.
The purpose of our life is to realize the One in our own soul.
There are innumerable spiritual paths, all leading to this realization of divinity. [40]

There is a highly ecumenical spirit of tolerance in many of the ways that Sanatana Dharma is being shared with the world. For example, Swami Sivananda (1887–1963) wrote 340 books and pamphlets to disseminate spiritual knowledge in English. He founded the Yoga-Vedanta Forest Academy for research and practice of Hindu philosophies, yoga sadhanas, comparative religion, and mysticism, as well as the nonsectarian Divine Life Society for "anyone devoted to the ideals of truth, non-violence, and purity." Spiritual seekers from many paths and many countries flock to ashrams with living gurus, such as Mother Krishnabai in south India, whose Anandashram resonates with continual repetition of the "Ram" mantram. At the same time, India is now experiencing violent clashes between its own Hindus, Muslims, and Sikhs; some have turned to religious fundamentalism and intolerance as an antidote to the insecurities of rapid modernization.

Brahmanic orthodoxy is, however, on the wane, and many modern Indians are less in touch with their traditions than were their parents and grandparents. But the multifaceted traditions of Sanatana Dharma are being kept alive by interest both within and without India. The late saint Paramhansa Yogananda observed:

India, China, and other Eastern lands can greatly benefit from emulation of the practical grasp of affairs, the material efficiency, of Western nations like America. The Occidental peoples, on the other hand, require a deeper understanding of the spiritual basis of life, and particularly of scientific techniques that India anciently developed for man's conscious communion with God. [41]

Suggested reading

The Bhagavad-Gita, available in numerous translations. Central teachings about how to realize the immortal soul.

Eck, Diana, *Darsan: Seeing the Divine Image in India*, second edition, Chambersburg, Pennsylvania: Anima Books, 1985. A lively explanation of deity images and how the people of India respond to them.

Eliade, Mircea, *Yoga: Immortality and Freedom*, translated by Willard R. Trask, Princeton, New Jersey: Princeton University Press, 1969, and London: Arkana, 1989. A classic study of mystical yogic aspects of Hinduism by a famous Western historian of religions.

Mahadevan, T. M. P., *Outlines of Hinduism*, second edition, Bombay: Chetana Limited, 1960. One of the clearest general introductions to the intricacies of Sanatana Dharma.

Stillson, Judah, J., *Hare Krishna and the Counterculture*, New York: John Wiley and Sons, 1974. A sympathetic and scholarly description of the International Society for Krishna Consciousness, the most visible bhakti path outside India.

Sahi, Jyoti, *The Child and the Serpent*, London: Routledge and Kegan Paul, 1980. An artist's attempt to rediscover the inner meanings of traditional visual symbols by living in the villages of south India.

Swami Prabhavananda, *The Spiritual Heritage of India*, Hollywood, California: Vedanta Press, 1979. A scholarly summary of the complexities of Hindu philosophy, with relatively little emphasis on bhakti or popular ways of worship.

Swami Prabhavananda and Frederick Manchester, trans., *The Upanishads: Breath of the Eternal*, The Vedanta Society of Southern California/New American Library, 1957. A lyrical translation of these sublime scriptures, slightly confused by the consistent substitution of Self for Atman.

Swami Satchidananda, trans., *Integral Yoga: The Yoga Sutras of Patanjali*, Yogaville, Virginia: Integral Yoga Publications, 1984. A fascinating opportunity to compare literal translations of the terse Sanskrit sutras with an insider's interpretation of their meaning, plus interesting commentaries.

Swami Satchidananda, ed., Philip Mandelkorn, *To Know Your Self*, Garden City, New York: Anchor Press/Doubleday, 1978. The yogic way to Ultimate Consciousness, explained in contemporary language without reference to scriptures, but studded with relevant stories.

Yogananda, Paramhansa, *Autobiography of a Yogi*, Los Angeles: Self-Realization Fellowship, 1956, and London: Rider and Company, 1987. First-hand account of the growth of a great spiritual leader, with explanations of many aspects of Sanatana Dharma.

Zimmer, Heinrich, *Philosophies of India*, New York: Bollingen Foundation/Pantheon Books, 1951. An advanced analysis of Indian philosophies (including Jainism and Buddhism) which assumes some prior knowledge of the traditions.

4 JAINISM

"Be careful all the while!"

Although the majority of Indians who are religious continue to follow the Hindu paths, Mother India has given birth to several other religions. One of them is Jainism. Until recently, it has been little known outside India. Even within India (according to perhaps low government estimates) there are only four to five million Jains. Yet its gentle ascetic teachings offer valuable clues to our global survival.

Earlier descriptions of Jainism by Western observers are strangely negative. It was accused of having an "empty heart," of being a self-centered search for personal salvation, of having no savior, and worst of all, from the Western point of view, of having no personal God. Yet Jainism is in itself a complete and fruitful path with the potential for uplifting human awareness and inculcating high standards of personal ethics. It has never condoned war, the caste system, or the killing of animals for any reason.

The Tirthankaras and Mahavira

The present form of Jainism can be traced to a teacher known as Mahavira ("The Great Hero"). He was a contemporary of the Buddha who died approximately 526 BCE. Like the Buddha, he was the prince of a kshatriya clan, and renounced his position at the age of thirty to wander as a spiritual seeker. The austerities he tolerated are legendary. For example, when he was meditating, villagers are said to have treated him miserably to make him leave:

> Once when he [sat in meditation], his body unmoving, they cut his flesh, tore his hair, and covered him with dirt. They picked him up and then dropped him, disturbing his meditational postures. Abandoning concern for his body, free from desire, the Venerable One humbled himself and bore the pain. [1]

Finally after twelve years of meditation, silence, and fasting he achieved liberation and perfection. For thirty years until his death at Pava, now a sacred pilgrimage site, he spread his teachings. His community is said to have consisted of 14,100 monks, 36,000 nuns, and 310,000 female and 150,000 male lay followers. They came from all castes, for Jainism does not acknowledge the caste system.

The Jain teachings are not thought to have originated with Mahavira. He is considered the last of twenty-four *Tirthankaras* ("Fordmakers") of the current era. In Jain cosmology, the universe is without beginning or end. Eternally it passes through long cycles of progress and decline. At the beginning of each downward cycle, humans are happy, long-lived, and virtuous; they have no need for religion. As these qualities decline, humans look at first to patriarchs for guidance but as things get worse Tirthankaras must create religion in order to steer people away from the growing evilness of the world.

The "wretched" fifth period of the cycle of decline began three years after Mahavira died. It will last 21,000 years, while Jainism itself will slowly disappear, along with human virtue and longevity. A "very wretched" period of another 21,000 years is to follow. Humans of this period will be amoral and short-lived, and civilization will be lost. At the end of this stage, almost everyone will be destroyed by storms. The few survivors will gradually work their way back upward in the ascent phase of the cycle.

Historians of religion cannot comment on the truth of this vast view of unrecorded history, but they do feel that Jainism is of ancient, non-Vedic, indigenous origins in India. Some Eastern scholars believe that the twenty-third Tirthankara, who is said to have lived about 250 years before Mahavira, and perhaps the twenty-second, were also historic rather than mythological figures.

Jain teachings were carried by memory but Bhadrabahu (eleventh successor to Mahavira), the only person who perfectly remembered all of them, left the world to end his life in solitary penance when he felt that the purity of the ancient ways had been corrupted. The existing written sacred texts – a canon of forty-five books – were later reconstructions by other monks.

The influence of Jainism was overshadowed by the growing popularity of devotional bhakti ways in India, but the tradition has never died out. Jain merchants, monks, and nuns still practice teachings which have not changed much in two thousand years, with the monastics practicing much stricter forms of the religion than lay people.

Rishabhadeva, the First Tirthankara of the present era. The Tirthankaras are always depicted either in cross-legged lotus position or standing up, a form of deep meditation for enlightened beings who are said never to sleep. (North-east India, 12th–13th century.)

Freeing the soul: the ethical pillars

In the midst of a world of decline, as they see it, Jains are given great room for hope. The *Jiva* – the individual's higher consciousness, or soul – can save itself by discovering its own perfect, unchanging nature and thus transcend the miseries of earthly life. This process may require many incarnations. Jains, like Hindus and Buddhists, believe that we are reborn again and again until we finally free ourselves from *samsara*, the Ferris wheel of birth and death, and of life's ups and downs.

The gradual process by which the soul learns to extricate itself from the lower self and its attachments to the material world involves purifying one's ethical life until nothing remains but the purity of the jiva. In its true state, it is omniscient and one with all beings.

One who has thus brought forth the highest in his or her being is called a *Jina* (a "winner" over the passions), from which the term Jain is derived. The Tirthankaras were Jinas who helped others find their way, regenerating the community by teaching inspiring spiritual principles.

Karma

The soul is veiled by the debris of karmic accumulations. Like Hindus and Buddhists, Jains believe that our actions influence the future course of our current life, and of those lives to come. But there is a difference: in Jain belief, karma is actually subtle matter –

minute particles that we accumulate as we act and think. Mahavira likened karma to coats of clay that weigh down the soul.

Jains are very careful to avoid accumulating karma. Three of the chief principles to which they adapt their lives are *ahimsa* (non-violence), *aparigraha* (non-possessiveness), and *anekantwad* (non-absolutism).

Ahimsa

The principle of non-violence espoused by Mahatma Gandhi can be traced in part to Jain teachings, but the Jains carry ahimsa even farther. They believe that every centimeter of the universe is filled with living beings, some of them minute. All of them want to live. Humans have no special right to supremacy: all things deserve to live and evolve as they can. To kill any living being has negative karmic effects.

> *All breathing, existing, living, sentient creatures should not be slain, nor treated with violence, nor abused, nor tormented, nor driven away. This is the pure, unchangeable, eternal law. . . . Correctly understanding the law, one should arrive at indifference for the impressions of the senses, and not act on the motives of the world.* [2]
>
> *Akaranga Sutra, IV: Lesson 1*

It is difficult not to do violence to other creatures. As we walk, we squash insects unknowingly. Even in breathing, Jains feel, we inhale tiny organisms and kill them. Jains avoid eating after sunset, so as not to inadvertently eat unseen insects who might have landed on the food, and some Jain ascetics wear a cloth over their mouth to avoid inhaling any living organisms.

Human life is inevitably destructive; the best that can be hoped for is to do as little damage as possible. The higher the life-form, the heavier the karmic burden of its destruction. Levels of life are determined by their degree of sensitivity. The highest group of beings are those with many senses, such as humans, gods, and higher animals (such as horses, snakes, monkeys, and elephants). Lower forms have fewer senses. The "one-sensed" beings have only the sense of touch. They include plants and the elements: the earth-bodies in soil, minerals, and stones, the water-bodies in rivers and lakes; fire-bodies in fires and lightning, and wind-bodies in winds and gases. The Jain sutras describe the suffering of even these one-sensed beings: Their agony at being wounded is like that of a blind and mute person who cannot see who is hurting him or express his pain.

Jains are therefore strict vegetarians, and they treat everything with great care. Even to kick a stone while walking is to injure a living being.

Ahimsa also extends to care in speaking and thinking, for abusive words and negative thoughts can injure another. One's profession must also not injure beings, so most Jains work at jobs considered harmless, such as banking and clerical occupations. Agriculture is considered harmful, for in digging into the soil one harms minute organisms in the earth.

Aparigraha

Another central Jain ideal is non-attachment to things and people. One should cut one's

Jain women on their way to worship wear mouth-cloths to prevent injury to inhaled minute beings

living requirements to a bare minimum. Possessions possess us; their acquisition and loss drive our emotions. Some Jain monks wear no clothes; the Tirthankaras are always depicted as naked, and therefore free. Even attachments to our friends and relatives bind us to samsara. Jainism advocates compassion for all beings, but this is not the same as dependent love. We are to live helpfully and consciously within the world, but not be drawn into its snares.

Aparigraha, or non-acquisitiveness, is considered the way to inner peace. If we can let go of things and situations, moment by moment, we can be free. The story is told of a *muni* (monk) who saw twelve stray dogs chasing another dog who was racing away with a bone he had found. When they caught him, they attacked him to wrest it from his jaws. Wounded and bleeding, he let go of it. The others immediately abandoned him to chase the one who picked it up. The monk saw the scene as a moral lesson: So long as we cling to things, we have to bleed for them. When we let them go, we will be left in peace.

Aparigraha is of value to the world community as well. Contemporary Jains point out that their principle of limiting consumption offers a way out of the global poverty, hunger, and environmental degradation that result from unequal grasping of resources by the wealthy. As His Holiness Acharya Sushil Kumar explains:

If we live simply, limit our needs and do not try to fulfill every desire, collecting more and more, automatically we will protect the environment. Because we will not need so many things, we will not need big industries to produce unnecessary things. . . . If we live simply, automatically the environment will stay clean. [3]

Anekantwad

The third central ethical principle is *anekantwad*, roughly translated as "relativity." Jains try to avoid anger and judgementalism, remaining open-minded by remembering that any issue can be seen from many angles, all partially true. They tell the story of the blind people who are asked to describe an elephant. The one who feels the trunk says an elephant is like a snake hanging from the sky. One feeling a leg argues that an elephant is a tree trunk. The one holding the tail is sure that neither of the others is right, that an elephant is a long hairy thing. The one feeling an ear argues that an elephant is not at all like any of the above. Each has a different version, each a partial grasp of the truth.

In the Jain way of thinking, the fullness of truth has many facets. There is no point in finding fault with others; our attention must be directed to cleansing and opening our own vision. Shree Chitrabhanu, a contemporary Jain teacher, describes the results of eliminating false impressions and allowing the pure consciousness to flow in:

> *Once you have closed the open gates, dried up all the polluted water, and cleaned out all the debris, then you can open them again to receive the fresh, clean rainfall. What is that rainfall? It is the flow of* maitri *– pure love, compassion, and communication. You feel free and flowing with all. . . . You meet to share. See how easily you meet people when there is no feeling of greater or lesser, no scar or bitterness, no faultfinding or criticism.*[4]

Spiritual practices

Jainism is an ascetic path and thus is practiced in its fullest by monks and nuns. In addition to practicing meditation, monks and nuns adopt a life of celibacy, physical penance and fasting, and material simplicity. They may sleep on the bare ground or wooden slabs, and are expected to endure any kind of weather with indifference. At initiation, they may pull their hair out by the roots rather than be shaved. They must learn to accept social disapproval, to depend on others for their food, and to feel no pride at being more spiritually advanced than others. The *Digambaras* ("sky-clad") wear no clothes, symbolizing their innocence of shame and their non-attachment to material goods; the *Svetambaras* ("white-clad") feel that wearing white robes does not stand in the way of liberation.

No Jain nuns are nude; they all wear white. All nuns, no matter how long or earnestly they have practiced, are considered inferior to monks. The Digambaras believe that no woman can achieve liberation unless she is reborn as a man; the Svetambaras think the nineteenth Tirthankara was a woman, but this belief is controversial.

Jain monks and nuns carry ahimsa to great extremes in their wariness of injuring one-sensed beings. Among the many activities they must avoid are digging in the ground (because of the earth-bodies there), bathing, swimming, or walking in the rain (because of the water-bodies they might injure), extinguishing or lighting fires (because even to light a fire means that a fire-body will eventually be destroyed), fanning themselves (to avoid sudden changes in air temperature that would injure air-bodies), and walking on vegetation or touching living plants. They must move slowly with eyes downward, to avoid stepping on any being. In general, they will do the least harm if they devote their time to sitting or standing in meditation rather than moving around.

LIVING JAINISM
An interview with Padam and Laxmi Jain

Dr. Padam Jain is a psychiatrist, now living in the United States with his wife Laxmi. They have three grown children and an extended family in India. Like many Jains, they are moderately wealthy. Dr. Jain begins by relating this fact to the principle of aparigraha.

Padam: There is not a good explanation why, although Jains have talked about aparigraha – limiting wealth and attachment to possessions – they have been the owners of that much wealth. But they have practiced aparigraha in a way. My father, for example, has limited his clothing, how many shirts he has. He and others do this as a constant reminder that attachment causes pain and greed, which is also the root cause of disparity among people. It is as if the wealthy get rich because of the poorness of others.

Also, I think the Jains are honest and hardworking and that can bring prosperity. There is a lot of discipline of the mind and body, and this discipline in generations also helps. In my large extended family, where Jainism has been for ages, no one has used drugs or alcohol or smoked.

Laxmi: You earn the money, but then you spend for the good cause also. Your wealth is not bad, but is used for the good cause.

Padam: What I see in Jainism is that principles are not only for a particular aim such as to be in heaven. It is to be healthy and peaceful here on earth. For example, not eating after sunset has a lot of advantages.

Laxmi: One reason was that in India, in three months of rainy season we get a lot of rain and mosquitos and dark and all that. And sometimes the lights go off and it's difficult to cook. When you're eating you might get insects because of the weather. It's a warm climate and sometimes in the rainy season, in the remote villages, it happens. These principles were like they thought thousands of years ago before there was electricity, but they still apply.

And the second thing is that they thought it good to wind up early, to get free after six or seven or eight o'clock. You send the kids to bed and then you do your own things. The women go for a walk, they go with their husbands and spend some time with them, or go to visit the family in the evenings. Otherwise up to ten o'clock you would be busy in the kitchen. If you have big joined families, it's a lot of work. And if you finish eating by like seven o'clock, you can digest the food easily.

Padam: I apply the Jain principle of anekantwad in my psychiatry practice. What we are trying to teach people in my practice is equanimity – to look more objectively at what the problem actually is. And then after looking you act rather than react automatically and irrationally.

The karmas – the very subtle particles that cling to the soul that Jains talk about – are something we are able to grasp a little bit more now because of recent scientific discoveries that subatomic particles can be very, very small. Even passions are like matter – they have very small particles, which we can think of like particles of light or electricity. Sometimes you become aware of them, such as the pleasant vibrations you feel when you are with a nice person or the heaviness you feel when there is grieving, pain, or violence going on. When we die, the soul leaves, and all those particles are going with it. When it goes it is not seen. It is probably even difficult to weigh.

Householders cannot carry renunciation as far as monks and nuns, but they can nonetheless purify and perfect themselves. Jains believe that the universe is without beginning and that it has no creator; only the individual can work out his or her own salvation. Padma Agrawal explains:

A monk at the feet of the Jain statue of Gomateshwara, (renunciate son of the first Tirthankara) in Mysore, India.

A monk at the feet of the Jain statue of Gomateshwara, (renunciate son of the first Tirthankara) in Mysore, India.

In Jainism, unlike Christianity and many Hindu cults, there is no such thing as a heavenly father watching over us. To the contrary, love for a personal God would be an attachment that could only bind Jainas more securely to the cycle of rebirth. It is a thing that must be rooted out.[5]

The world operates by the power of nature, according to natural principles. Jains do believe in gods and demons, but the former are subject to the same ignoble passions as humans. In fact, one can only achieve liberation if one is in the human state, because only humans can clear away karma. Ideally, one should be very grateful to be born as a human, for this is the highest stage of evolution short of liberation.

Householders can journey toward the final state by passing through fourteen stages of ascent of the soul, or *gunasthana*. The first four are efforts to remove false mental impressions. Moral effort to purify oneself begins with the fifth stage. Jains attempt to plumb the depths of what psychoanalysts call the "shadow self" in order to free themselves from emotional problems. Then as spiritual inertia is overcome, self-control and relinquishing of the passions follow. Throughout this process, the veils of karma are lifting and the soul experiences more and more of its natural luminosity. In the highest state of perfection, known as *kevala*, all gross activities have come to an end, and the liberated being has "boundless vision, infinite righteousness, strength, perfect bliss, existence without form, and a body that is neither light nor heavy."[6]

Although severe vows of renunciation can be taken by householders, lay spiritual life is more likely to consist of six duties: the practice of equanimity through meditation, praise of the Tirthankaras, veneration of teachers, who live as mendicants, making amends for moral transgressions, indifference to the body, often by holding a particular position for a length of time, and renunciation of certain foods or activities for specific periods.

The Tirthankaras are honored through images. They all look alike for the perfect soul is non-particularized; symbols such as the bull always shown with the first Tirthankara are used to help worshippers identify each of the twenty-four.

The worshipper's feeling is one of reverence rather than supplication; the Tirthankaras are elevated beyond the human plane and are not available as helpers. They are instead models for one's own life and since there can be no divine intervention, there is not a great emphasis on priesthood. Laypeople can carry out worship services themselves, either alone or in groups.

When participating in *devapuja* (worship of the Tirthankara images), a Jain has to feel that he or she is approaching a living Jina, radiant and omniscient, with teachings issuing from his body in the form of a divine sound. People pay their respects with offerings and waved lamps, but unlike Hindu pujas, Jain rituals do not expect any reciprocation from the object of veneration. Salvation from samsara is a result of personal effort, often symbolically portrayed by a symbolic diagram laid out with rice grains.

The new Jain symbol: Ahimsa is inscribed on the open palm. The swastika represents the wheel of samsara. The three dots symbolize insight, knowledge, and conduct. The crescent and dot above symbolize the liberated soul in the highest region of the universe.

In Jain worship, the image of the Tirthankara is venerated, but will not respond personally by communicating with or helping the worshippers.

World Jainism

Through the centuries, Jainism managed to survive as a small heterodox minority within largely Hindu India. In our time, it has been carried to the outside world by several teachers. One of them, Shree Chitrabhanu, was for twenty-nine years a monk who walked barefoot over 30,000 miles of Indian soil to teach Jain principles to the populace. When he was invited to address the Temple of Understanding Spiritual Summit Conferences in Switzerland and the United States in 1970 and 1971, his controversial decision to attend in person marked the first time in five thousand years of known Jain history that a Jain monk had traveled outside India. For a time he was president of the World Fellowship of Religions and has now established Jain meditation centers in the United States, Brazil, Canada, Kenya, England, and India.

Acharya Shri Sushil Kumar has likewise established Jain centers in the United Kingdom and the United States as well as India. He points out that the Jain scriptures consider as "Jains" all those who practice Jain principles:

> In the Jain system, there is no concern that a person has to use the same terminology as a Jain or has to be Jain by birth or by practice. There is not any baptism, by which before you were a Christian and today you became a Jain. [You don't become a Jain] by uniform, by virtues, by rules or regulations, no! By your system. If a person's experience, his conduct, is like a Jain, he is a Jain. If somebody is a real symbol of non-violence, love, compassion, peace, harmony, oneness, then he is the perfect Jain. We can't convert any Jains, but you can convert your habits, your mind.[7]

Suggested reading

Chitrabhanu, Gurudev Shree, *Realize What You Are: The Dynamics of Jain Meditation*, New York: Jain Meditation International Center/Dodd, Mead and Company, 1978. A useful introduction to a path of meditation designed to overcome negativity, release blocks to fulfilling one's potential, and to identify the eternal in oneself.

Chitrabhanu, Gurudev Shree, *Twelve Facets of Reality: The Jain Path to Freedom*, New York: Jain Meditation International Center/Dodd, Mead and Company, 1980. Classic Jain reflections on the realities of life, in engaging, contemporary language, with many teaching tales.

Fischer, Eberhard, and Jain, Jyotindra, *Jaina Iconography*, parts 1 and 2, Leiden: E.J. Brill, 1978. An inside look at Jainism through its visual representations of its beliefs.

Jaini, Padmanabh S., *The Jaina Path of Purification*, Berkeley: University of California Press, 1979. A rarity: An appreciative, scholarly analysis of the Jaina path.

Kumar, Acharya Sushil, *Song of the Soul*, Blairstown, New Jersey: Siddhachalam Publishers, 1987. Insights into Jain mantra practice, as taught by a respected contemporary monk.

Muller, F. Max, ed., *Gaina Sutras*, vols. XLV and XXII of *Sacred Books of the East*, Oxford: Clarendon Press, 1884 and 1895. Engaging translations of various sorts of sutras, including both philosophical treatises and rules of conduct for Jain ascetics.

Rosenfield, Clare, and Segall, Linda, "Ahimsa is not a religion: It is a way of life," New York: Jain Meditation International Center. A brief but profound explanation of Jain tenets in contemporary terms, relating the principles to planetary concerns.

5 BUDDHISM

"He will deliver by the boat of knowledge the distressed world"

At the same time that Mahavira was serving the role of the last Tirthankara, teaching the way of Jainism, the man who came to be known as the Buddha preached another alternative to the ritual-bound Brahmanism of sixth-century BCE India. In many ways his teachings parallel those of Sanatana Dharma. Yet the religion he founded has distinguished itself organizationally from Hinduism and indeed is no longer linked with its Indian birthplace.

Buddhism generally focuses on earthly suffering and its cure. Many religions offer comforting supernatural solutions to the difficulties of earthly life. Buddhism is quite different: In its traditional form, it holds that our salvation from suffering lies only in our own efforts. The Buddha taught us that only in understanding how we create suffering for ourselves can we become free.

We might imagine that the discomfort of having to face ourselves and take responsibility for our own liberation would be a highly unappealing path that would attract few followers. But the way of the Buddha spread from his native India throughout the Far East, becoming the dominant religion in many eastern countries. In some, it took on devotional and mystical qualities from earlier local traditions. And now, more then two and a half thousand years after the Buddha's death, the religion that he founded is also attracting considerable interest in the West.

The life of the Buddha

What we know about the Buddha himself is sketchy. His prolific teachings were probably not collected in written form until at least four hundred years after his death. In the meantime they were apparently held, and added to, as an oral tradition chanted from memory by monks, groups of whom were responsible for remembering specific parts of the teachings. Only a few factual details of the Buddha's own life have been retained. Most of what is usually taught about the life of the Buddha is rich in symbolic meanings but not verifiable as historical fact.

The one who became the Buddha (a title that means "Enlightened One") was born about 563 years before the beginning of the Christian calendar. His father was apparently a wealthy landowner serving as one of the chiefs of a kshatriya clan, the Shakyas. They lived in the foothills of the Himalayas and could probably see these great mountains looming in the distance.

Legends describe a miraculous conception in which his mother dreamed that she was taken up the Himalayas by guardian spirits and placed on a divine couch in a golden

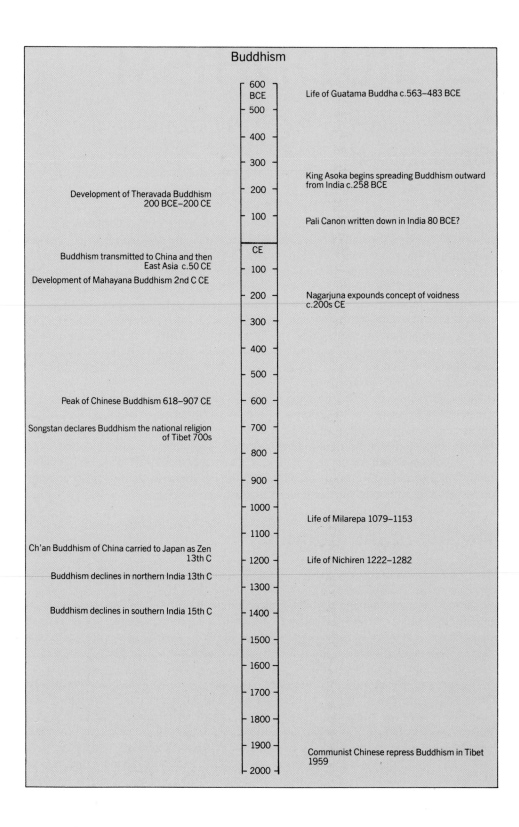

Buddhism

	600 BCE — Life of Guatama Buddha c.563–483 BCE
	500
	400
	300
Development of Theravada Buddhism 200 BCE–200 CE	200 — King Asoka begins spreading Buddhism outward from India c.258 BCE
	100 — Pali Canon written down in India 80 BCE?
	CE
Buddhism transmitted to China and then East Asia c.50 CE	100
Development of Mahayana Buddhism 2nd C CE	200 — Nagarjuna expounds concept of voidness c.200s CE
	300
	400
	500
Peak of Chinese Buddhism 618–907 CE	600
Songstan declares Buddhism the national religion of Tibet 700s	700
	800
	900
	1000
	1100 — Life of Milarepa 1079–1153
Ch'an Buddhism of China carried to Japan as Zen 13th C	1200 — Life of Nichiren 1222–1282
Buddhism declines in northern India 13th C	1300
Buddhism declines in southern India 15th C	1400
	1500
	1600
	1700
	1800
	1900 — Communist Chinese repress Buddhism in Tibet 1959
	2000

mansion. The Future Buddha came to her in the form of a white elephant and entered her womb. He had incarnated many times before and was drawn to earth once again by his compassion for all suffering beings. Legends also tell of the Brahmins' interpretation of his mother's dream (and of marks on the baby himself): A son would be born whose greatness would lead to his either becoming king of all India or one who retires from earthly life to become an enlightened being, sharing his own awakening with the world.

The heralded birth occurred in Lumbini, a garden retreat. The boy was named Siddartha*, "wish-fulfiller," or "He who has reached his goal." His family name, Gautama, honored an ancient Hindu sage whom the family claimed as ancestor or spiritual guide. It is said that Siddartha's father, hoping to encourage his son's kingship, tried to make the boy's earthly life so pleasant that he would not choose to retire from it. Siddartha later described a life of fine clothes, white umbrellas for shade, perfumes, cosmetics, a mansion for each season, the company of female musicians, and a harem of dancing girls. He was also trained in knightly sports and married to at least one wife, who bore a son.

In the midst of this life of ease, Siddartha was apparently unconvinced of its value. An early indication of his future direction had occurred as a mystical experience during his youth. While sitting beneath a rose-apple tree, he spontaneously entered an extremely blissful state of meditation. By contrast, he was struck by the stark fact that despite its temporary pleasures, life always leads to decay and death. According to the legend, the gods arranged for him to see four sights that his father had carefully tried to hide from him: a bent old man, a sick person, a dead person, and a monk seeking eternal rather than temporal pleasure. Increasingly dissatisfied with the futility of sensual delights, at the age of twenty-nine Siddhartha renounced his wealth, left his wife and baby, shaved his head, and donned the coarse robe of a wandering ascetic.

The new role he had adopted was not unique. Many Hindu sannyasins were already leading the homeless life of poverty considered appropriate for seekers of spiritual truth. Although the future Buddha would later develop a new religion that departed significantly from certain orthodox Hindu beliefs, he initially tried the traditional methods. He headed southeast to study with a famous Brahmin teacher who had many followers. This teacher sought to liberate the soul *(atman)* from its material cage into unity with *Brahman.* Although Siddartha is said to have achieved the Sphere of No-thing-ness under these teachings, he resumed his search, apparently feeling that a still higher state of realization lay beyond. His next Brahmin teacher helped him to realize an even higher level, the Sphere of Neither-Perception-nor-non-Perception. But again he moved on, unsatisfied that he had reached his ultimate goal: the way of total liberation from suffering. He sought out temple priests but was disturbed by the cruelty of their animal sacrifices to the gods. Before leaving them, he tried to teach them that it was hypocritical and futile to try to atone for misdeeds by destroying life.

Still searching, Siddartha found five pupils of his second teacher living as ascetics in the forest. Admiring their efforts to subdue the senses, he decided to try their practices himself as an experiment in liberation. For six years he outdid them in extreme

---

*Buddhist terms have come to us both in Pali, an Indian dialect first used for preserving the Buddha's teachings (the Buddha himself probably spoke a different ancient dialect), and in Sanskrit, the language of Indian sacred literature. For instance, the Pali *suta* ("that which is heard or learned") is equivalent to the Sanskrit *sutra.* In this chapter Sanskrit will be used, as it is more familiar to Westerners, except in the section on Theravada, which uses the Pali.

The Buddha gives his first sermon, using the mudra (sacred gesture) representing the karmic wheel of birth, death, and rebirth.

self-denial techniques: nakedness, exposure to extreme heat and cold, breath retention, a bed of brambles, severe reduction of food. Finally he recognized that this extreme ascetic path had not lead to enlightenment.

Siddhartha then shifted his practice to a Middle Way of neither self-indulgence nor self-denial. To the disillusionment of the five ascetics, who left him, he revived his failing health by accepting food once more and taking reasonable care of his body. Placing his faith in clarity of mind, he began a period of reflection. On the night of the full moon in May as he sat in deep meditation beneath a sacred fig tree at Gaya, he finally experienced Supreme Enlightenment.

After passing through four states of serene contemplation, he first recalled all his previous lives. Then he had a vision of the wheel of deaths and rebirths, in which past good or bad deeds are reflected in the next life. Finally he had a revelation of the existence of suffering, its source, and the means for removing suffering. After this supreme experience, it is said that he literally radiated light. According to the legend, he was tempted by Mara, the personification of evil, to keep his insights to himself, for they were too complex and profound for ordinary people to understand. But the Buddha, as he now knew himself, compassionately determined to set the wheel of teaching in motion, even if only for the sake of a few who would understand: those with "only a little dust" in their eyes.

The first people with whom the Buddha shared the essence of his insights were the five ascetics who had abandoned him, thinking he had given up. In his famous Deer Park sermon at Sarnath, he taught them what became the essence of Buddhism: The Four Noble Truths about suffering and the Eightfold Path for liberation from suffering. Convinced, they became the first disciples of the new techniques.

The Buddha continued to teach the *Dharma* (Pali: *Dhamma*) — which in his system means the truths of reality, and the right conduct for each person's state of evolution — for forty-five years. As he walked through the northern Indian countryside, still as a voluntarily poor teacher with a begging bowl, he gave sermons and converted people of all sects and classes. Some became *bhikshus* (Pali: *bhikkhus),* monks emulating his life of poverty and spiritual dedication; others continued as householders. One who became a lay disciple was his father; his son joined the order of bhikkshus. His wife and stepmother joined the order of nuns, or *bhikshunis* (Pali: *bhikkhunis)* despite the Buddha's considerable reluctance to admit women. He thought that his teachings would last only five hundred years rather than a thousand years if women entered the order, but his teachings have far outlasted both predictions. Even today, however, the Buddha's suspicion of women is reflected in the fact that women seeking ordination in some contemplative Buddhist orders must observe more precepts, or rules, than men.

The circumstances of the Buddha's death at the then extraordinary age of eighty bespeak his selfless desire to spare humankind from suffering. His last meal, served by a blacksmith, seemingly included some poisonous mushrooms or tainted pork. Severely ill and recognizing his impending death, the Buddha nevertheless pushed on to his next teaching stop at Kusinara, converting a young man along the way. He sent word back to the blacksmith that he must not feel remorse or blame himself for the meal, for his offering of food brought him great merit.

When he reached his destination, he lay down on a stone couch, at which point, it is said, the trees above rained blossoms down upon him. As his monks came to pay their last respects, he urged them to tend to their own spiritual development:

You must be your own lamps, be your own refuges . . . A monk becomes his own lamp
and refuge by continually looking on his body, feelings, perceptions, moods, and ideas in
such a manner that he conquers the cravings and depressions of ordinary men and is
always strenuous, self-possessed, and collected in mind.[1]

The last words attributed to the Buddha, according to one translation, were, "All
composite things must pass away. Strive onward vigilantly."[2]

The Dharma

Buddhism is often described as a "nontheistic religion." There is no personal God who
creates everything and to whom prayers can be directed. This is not to say that life on
earth is all there is, but unlike other Indian sages, the Buddha did not focus on
descriptions of ultimate reality, the nature of the soul, life after death, or the origin of
the universe. He said that curiosity about such matters was like a man who, upon being
wounded by a poisoned arrow, refused to have it pulled out until he was told the caste
and origin of his assailant, his name, his height, the color of his skin, and all details
about the bow and arrow. In the meantime, he died.

> *Being religious and following Dhamma has nothing to do with the dogma that the world*
> *is eternal; and it is has nothing to do with the other dogma that the world is not eternal.*
> *For whether the world is eternal or otherwise, birth, old age, death, sorrow, pain, misery,*
> *grief, and despair exist. I am concerned with the extinction of these.*[3]

The Buddha spoke of his teachings as a raft to take us to the farther shore, rather than a

*The Buddha's final
liberation into Nirvana
when he physically died
is symbolized by this
enormous Sri Lankan
statue in which he is
serenely lying down with
eyes closed to the world.*

description of the shore or something to be carried around once we get there. The basic planks of this raft are insights into the truths of existence and the path to liberation; *Nirvana* (Pali: *Nibbana*) is the farther shore, the goal of spiritual effort.

The facts of existence

In his very first sermon, the "Deer Park" sermon preached to the five ascetics, the Buddha set forth *The Four Noble Truths* around which all his later teachings revolved. These were: **1** that life inevitably involves suffering; **2** that suffering has its roots in desire for things to be different than they are or to stay as we want them; **3** that the only way out of suffering is to relinquish desire, to become totally detached from our likes and dislikes; and **4** that only through a life of morality, concentration, and wisdom, which he set forth as the Eightfold Path, can desire and therefore suffering be extinguished.

The reason that desire leads us to suffering, the Buddha taught, is that we do not understand the nature of things, of that which we desire. Everything is actually impermanent, changing all the time. We seek to grasp and hold life as we want it to be, but we cannot, since everything is in constant flux.

In Buddhism, happiness is not the goal of life, for unhappiness is understood as the inevitable companion of happiness. The sun will give way to rain; a lovely flower will decay; beloved friends will die; our bodies will surely age. As the contemporary monk Ajahn Sumedho points out, "trying to arrange, control and manipulate conditions so as to always get what we want, always hear what we want to hear, always see what we want to see, so that we never have to experience unhappiness or despair, is a hopeless task."[4]

What a Buddhist strives for instead is the realization of *dukkha* (the fact of suffering: of discomfort and frustration with our life situations), *anicca* (impermanence), and *anatta* (no eternal self). Suffering is actually useful to us because it helps us to see things as they really are. When our attention is drawn to the fact that everything changes and passes away, moment by moment, we can become aware that nothing in this world has an independent, solid character. There are only momentary configurations within a continual process of change. There is no continual "I". What we regard as our self is simply an ever-changing bundle of fleeting feelings, sense impressions, ideas, and evanescent physical matter. We have no eternal, unchanging soul; one moment's identity leads to the next like one candle being lit from another. Once we have fully grasped these basic facts of life, we can be free in this life, and free from another rebirth.

The wheel of birth and death

Buddhist teachings about reincarnation are slightly different from those of Hindu orthodoxy, for there is no eternal soul to be reborn. In Buddhism, one changing state of being sets another into motion, every event depends on a cause. One of these is *karma* (Pali: *kamma*) – our acts of will. These influence the level at which that personality-developing process we think of as "me" is reborn. The impressions of our good and bad actions help to create our personality moment-by-moment. When we die, this process continues, passing on the flame to a new life on a plane that reflects our past karma.

The Wheel of Life: In the center are animals representing lust, hatred, and delusion. The next circle shows the fate of those with good karma (left) and bad karma (right). The third circle represents the six spheres of existence, from the gods to the infernal regions. The outer rim shows the chain of cause and effect. Grasping the wheel is a monster representing death, impermanence.

There are thirty-one planes of existence, interpreted as psychological metaphors by some Buddhists. Metaphors or metaphysical realities, these include hells, famished demons ("hungry ghosts," tormented with unsatisfied desires), animals, humans, and gods. Like the lower levels, the gods are imperfect and impermanent. Round and round we go, life after life, repeatedly experiencing ageing, decay, suffering, death, and painful rebirth, unless we are freed into Nirvana, which is beyond all the cause-and-effect-run planes of existence.

The Eightfold Path of liberation

To help us escape from these facts of suffering, the Buddha set forth a systematic approach by which dedicated humans could pull themselves up and achieve the final goal of liberation. The Eightfold Path offers ways to burn up all past demerits, avoid accumulating new demerits, and build up merit for a favorable rebirth. Perfection of the path means final escape from the cycle of death and rebirth, into the peace of Nirvana. The eight factors in this system are not sequential steps. They must be developed simultaneously, for they are related to each other.

The first factor is *right understanding*. Initially this means seeing through illusions, such as the idea that a little more wealth could bring happiness. Gradually one learns to question old assumptions in the light of the Four Noble Truths.

Second is *right thought or motives*. The Buddha encourages us to uncover any "unwholesome" emotional roots behind our thinking, such as a desire to hide our imperfections or avoid contact with others. As we discover and weed out such emotional blocks, our thought becomes free from the limitations of self-centeredness – relaxed, clear and open.

Third is *right speech*. The Buddha cautions us to relinquish our propensity to vain talk, gossip, tale-bearing, harsh words, and lying, and to use communication instead in the service of truth and harmony.

The fourth factor, *right action*, begins for the layperson with observing the five basic precepts for moral conduct: avoid destroying life, stealing, sexual misconduct, lying, and intoxicants. Beyond these, we are to base our actions on clear understanding. A story used to illustrate this principle is the Jataka Tale, purported to derive from one of the Buddha's previous incarnations, of the monkeys who in trying to be helpful, pulled up the trees to see if they needed water. "Evil deeds," said the Buddha, are those "done from motives of partiality, enmity, stupidity, and fear."[5]

Fifth is *right livelihood* – being sure that one's way of making a living does not violate the five precepts. One's trade should not harm others or disrupt social harmony.

Right effort, the sixth factor in the Eightfold Path, bespeaks continual striving to cut off "unwholesome states," past, present, and future. This is not a way for the lazy.

The seventh factor, *right mindfulness*, is particularly characteristic of Buddhism, for the way to liberation is said to be through the mind. We are urged to be aware in every moment. In the *Dhammapada*, short verses about the way of truth, said to have been uttered by the Buddha, there appears this pithy injunction:

Check your mind.
Be on your guard.
Pull yourself out
as an elephant from mud. [6]

The eighth factor, *right meditation*, applies mental discipline to the quieting of the mind itself. "It is subtle, invisible, treacherous,"[7] explains the Buddha. Skillful means are therefore needed to see and transcend its restless nature. When the mind is fully stilled, it becomes a quiet pool in which the true nature of everything is clearly reflected. The various schools of Buddhism that have developed over the centuries have taught different techniques of meditation, but this basic principle remains the same.

> *Try to be mindful, and let things take their natural course. Then your mind will become still in any surroundings, like a clear forest pool. All kinds of wonderful, rare animals will come to drink at the pool, and you will clearly see the nature of all things. You will see many strange and wonderful things come and go, but you will be still. This is the happiness of the Buddha.*
>
> Achaan Chah, meditation master, Wat Ba Pong, Thailand[8]

Nirvana

About the goal of Buddhist practice, Nirvana, the Buddha had relatively little to say. The word itself refers to the extinguishing of a flame from lack of fuel. The only way to end the cycle in which desire feeds the wheel of suffering is to end all cravings and lead a passion-free existence which has no karmic consequences.

For the *Arhant* (Pali: *Arhat* or *Arahat*), or saint, who has found Nirvana within this life:

*No suffering for him
who is free from sorrow
free from the fetters of life
free in everything he does.
He has reached the end of his road. . . .*

*Like a bird invisibly flying in the sky,
he lives without possessions,
knowledge his food, freedom his world,
while others wonder. . . .*

*He has found freedom –
peaceful his thinking, peaceful his speech,
peaceful his deed, tranquil his mind.*[9]

What happens when such a being dies? One enters a deathless, peaceful, unchanging state that cannot be described. Individuality disappears and one enters the realm of ultimate truth, about which the Buddha was silent. Why? At one point he picked up a handful of leaves from the forest floor and asked his disciples which were more numerous, the leaves in his hand or those in the surrounding forest. When they replied, "Very few in your hand, lord; many more in the grove," he said:

Exactly. So you see, friends, the things that I know and have not revealed are more than the truths I know and have revealed. And why have I not revealed them? Because, friends, there is no profit in them; because they are not helpful to holiness; because they do not lead from disgust to cessation and peace, because they do not lead from knowledge to wisdom and Nirvana.[10]

Buddhism south and north

As soon as he had attracted a small group of disciples, the Buddha sent them out to help

Training of Buddhist monks often begins at an early age, with study of the ancient scriptures.

teach the Dharma:

> *Walk, monks, on tour for the blessing of the manyfolk, for the happiness of the manyfolk, out of compassion for the world, for the welfare, the blessing, the happiness of devas and men . . . There are beings with little dust in their eyes who, not hearing Dhamma, are decaying, but if they are learners of Dhamma they will grow.* [11]

This missionary effort spread in all directions. Two hundred years after the Buddha died, a great Indian king, Asoka, was converted to Buddhism. Under his leadership Buddhism was carried throughout the kingdom and outward to other countries as well, beginning its development as a global religion. After Asoka's death, Brahmins reasserted their political influence and Buddhists were persecuted in parts of India. In the Buddha's homeland, Buddhism nearly died out and never became the dominant religion.

Many Buddhist sects have developed as the Buddha's teachings have been expanded upon and adapted to local cultures in different areas. There are two primary divisions. The remaining form that tries to adhere closely to what it considers the original teachings is called *Theravada*, or Teaching of the Elders. It is prevalent in the south Asian countries of Sri Lanka, Burma, Thailand, Kampuchea (Cambodia), and Laos and is therefore referred to as the Southern School. The other major grouping is the Northern School, which is the dominant Buddhist path in Nepal, Tibet, China, Korea, Mongolia, and Japan. Those of this group call it *Mahayana*, the "Greater Vehicle," because they feel that theirs is a bigger raft that can carry more people than the stark teachings of the Theravadins, which they call the *Hinayana*, or "Lesser Vehicle."

Both groups are in general agreement about the Four Noble Truths, the Eightfold Path, and the teachings about karma and Nirvana described above, but the Theravadins try to stay close to the supposed earliest scriptures whereas the Mahayanists have more freely interpreted and adapted the Dharma, leading to numerous subsects within Mahayana. There are also differences in emphasis: Mahayana focuses more on compassion and metaphysics, while Theravada emphasizes discipline of the mind. Each claims to be a purer representative of the essence of the Buddha's teachings.

Theravada: the path of mindfulness

Theravada is noted for its adherence to early scriptures, its emphasis on the monastic life of renunciation, and its mindfulness meditation teachings. These characteristics are more obvious among the intellectuals and monastics; the common people are more devotional in their practices.

THE PALI CANON   The doctrine and quotations cited thus far all come from the *Pali Canon*, the "Bible" of Theravada Buddhism. Because the Buddha taught tirelessly for decades, sayings attributed to him fill forty-five volumes in the Thai edition of the canon. This compilation is also referred to as the *Tipitaka* – "the three baskets of the Law." When the teachings were first written down, they were inscribed on palm leaves, which were stored in baskets (some are still preserved on palm leaves and have not been transcribed). The "three baskets" were: rules for monks and nuns, discourses of the Buddha, and "the basket of further discipline." According to legend, the last pitaka was

Map showing the approximate distribution of Theravada and Mahayana Buddhism in the world today.

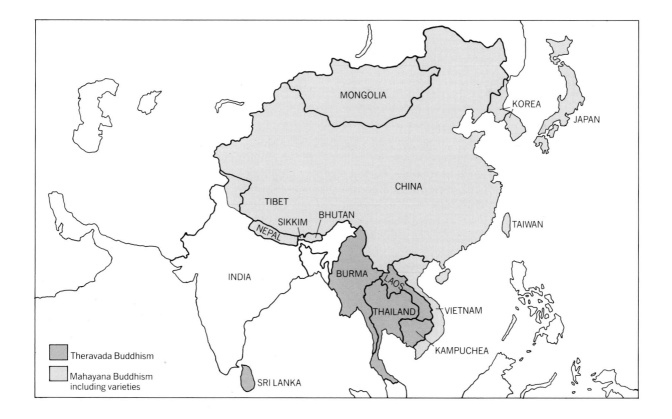

preached by the Buddha to the gods in heaven, but scholars think that this highly philosophical, academic part of the canon probably represents later attempts to systematize the Buddha's ideas.

In addition to the Tipitaka, Theravadins also honor other non-canonical Pali works, such as later commentaries and commentaries-on-the-commentaries. The 547 lively Jataka Tales, such as the story of the foolish monkeys, appear in the commentaries as explanations of the context of the pithy sayings found in the discourses ("A foolish man, even when he tries to do good..."). These folk tales are said to have been told by the Buddha and to represent scenes from his own previous incarnations, but they are also used to demonstrate Buddhist virtues, such as wisdom and compassion.

THE TRIPLE GEM   Like all Buddhists, those of the Southern School soften the discipline of the mind with devotion to the *Triple Gem*: Buddha (the Enlightened One), Dhamma (the doctrine he taught, ultimate reality), and Sangha (the order of his disciples). To become a Buddhist, and then afterwards to reassert the basis of one's faith, a person "takes refuge" in these three jewels by reciting the Pali formula, *Buddham saranam gacchami* ("I go to the Buddha for refuge"), *Dhammam saranam gacchami* ("I go to the Dhamma for refuge"), *Sangham saranam gacchami* ("I go to the Sangha for refuge"). One takes refuge in the Buddha not by praying to him for help but by paying homage to him as supreme teacher and inspiring model. In a sense, taking refuge in the Buddha is honoring the Buddha-wisdom within each of us.

The Dhamma is like a medicine, but it will not cure our suffering unless we ourselves take it. In the Pali chanting, the Dhamma is described as immediate, timeless, leading to calmness, and only known through our direct experience and personal effort.

The Sangha is the order of bhikkus and bhikkunis who have renounced the world in order to follow, preserve, and share the Dhamma. The Buddha established one of the world's first monastic orders, and this core remains strong in Theravada. There are presently about half a million Theravadin monks in Southeast Asia. To simplify their worldly lives and devote themselves to studying and teaching the Dhamma, monks must shave their heads, dress in simple robes, own only a few basic material items, eat no solid foods after noon, practice celibacy, and depend upon the laity for their food, clothing, and medical supplies. Early every morning they set forth with begging bowl, and the laypeople regard it as a merit-making opportunity to set up sidewalk kitchens to feed them. In this interdependent system, the monks reciprocate by offering spiritual guidance, chanted blessings, and various social services, often including secular advice and education. Monks offer discourses on the Dhamma in the preaching hall of the large monasteries and also, when invited, in private homes.

Buddhist monasteries are at the center of village life, rather than separated from it. The monasteries are open, and people come and go. The monks hold a revered social position as models of self-control, kindness, and intelligence; no one can sit on a higher level than a bhikkhu. In Theravadin countries it is common for young men to take temporary vows of monkhood – often for the duration of the rainy season when little farmwork can be done. They wear the saffron robes, set forth with shaven heads and begging bowls, and receive religious instruction while they practice a life of simplicity. This background is considered so valuable and socially desirable that even the present king of Thailand spent some time as a monk.

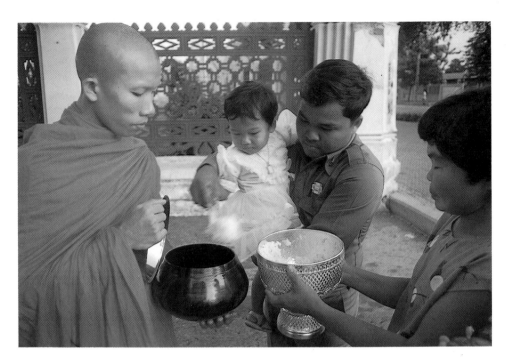

In Southeast Asia a large population of monks is supported by laypeople, who offer food daily.

By contrast, there has traditionally been little social support for bhikkunis, or Buddhist nuns, in Southeast Asia. Provisions were made during the time of the Buddha for women monastics to live in the same monasteries as men, with the same lifestyle, but the order of fully ordained nuns disappeared completely in Theravadin countries about a thousand years ago. Many of the early Buddhist scriptures take an egalitarian position toward women's capacity for wisdom and attainment of Nibbana, but spiritual power was kept in the hands of monks. Nuns were by rules of the order forever subservient to the monks, seniority notwithstanding, so there was little opportunity for them to grow into positions of leadership. Nevertheless, some women's desire for spiritual freedom is strong today. As part of attempts to revive fully ordained orders of nuns in Theravadin countries such as Sri Lanka, a landmark meeting occurred in Bodh Gaya in 1987: The First International Conference of Buddhist Nuns.

VIPASSANA MEDITATION   In addition to trying to preserve what are thought to be the Buddha's original teachings, Theravada is the purveyor of mindfulness meditation techniques. *Vipassana* literally means "insight" but the meditation methods used to develop insight begin by increasing one's attentiveness to every detail as a way of calming, focusing, and watching the mind. As taught by the Burmese meditation master Mahasi Sayadaw, the beginning vipassana practice is simply to watch oneself breathing in and out, with the attention focused on the rise and fall of the abdomen. To keep the mind concentrated on this movement, rather than dragged this way and that by unconscious, conditioned responses, one continually makes concise mental notes of what is happening: "rising," "falling." Inevitably other mental functions will arise in the restless mind. As they do, one simply notes what they are — "imagining," "wandering,"

LIVING BUDDHISM:
An interview with two Thai Buddhists

In Thailand, over ninety-three per cent of the population is Buddhist, and there are historically close ties between State and Sangha. The people are unusually happy and free, perhaps partly because of their Buddhist faith. Below are interviews with two women from Bangkok.

Komkai Charoensuk, a grandmother who practices meditation and studies with monks and nuns:

"I'm just beginning to become a good Buddhist. I practice meditation, but not continuously. It needs a lot of patience and great attention. Not time. The present moment – that's the most important thing we must know.

When somebody else is angry and starts to curse us, it is very easy for us to feel that we are hurt by them. But we can try to find out what is the cause of their suffering, their anger. The longer you keep the pain in yourself, the worse it will become. You stay angry, angry, and angry. That's the way that you are hurting yourself. And it's foolish to hurt one's own heart or one's mind. But we need a lot of practice before we can overcome these sorts of things.

We don't want to start and end and come back and start and end again and come back and start again. We don't want to be born again and suffer, another time be happy, another time suffer. You laugh and you cry, and you laugh and you cry all your life. That's why we want to go to Nirvana: No more happiness, no more unhappiness. And then when anyone scolds you, you are smiling, you understand why they are scolding you. You understand everything. Nobody can hurt you."

Prachoomsuk Achava-Amrung, a professor of educational research with a background in chemistry, and past president of the International Association of Educators for World Peace:

"I am a scientist and Buddhism is very scientific. Everything is cause and effect relationships. There is no God or anything holy. You have to help yourself. In some other religions, you pray for God to help you, but not in Buddhism. Buddha said, 'I can guide you. I cannot help you. I can point your way, but you have to do it yourself. Not me.'

The whole Buddhist teaching is peace, peace of mind. You know the word 'Thai' means 'free.' This is a very interesting case history: Thailand was never colonized during the period of European colonization. Did Thailand have powerful weapons? Huge armies? Not a bit. We can stay free because we have Buddhism in our hearts. We are smiling. We see everybody as a friend. We have a proverb that you can find friends everywhere, but you cannot find enemies anywhere unless you make them.

In that time it was very funny that the British battleship sailed to Bangkok through the Gulf of Thailand, and also the French, and the Thai people said, 'What a big ship! Let's everybody go and see!' instead of shooting at them. Just, 'What can we do for you? What's wrong with your ship?' And the captain came down and they signed a contract, a treaty of friendship. They made that treaty so that the British had the advantage. We didn't know – we just signed. We are friendly, so we didn't fall, we were not colonized. But other countries had fighting and the Europeans had more powerful weapons and conquered them.

So when I work with the peace movement, I try to let people know that peaceful mind, like we have in Thailand. We have freedom and peaceful mind and right attitude toward people. We see everybody as friend. This is the way we are trying to teach the world to help children develop peaceful minds."

"remembering" – and then returns the attention to the rising and falling of the breath. Body sensations will appear, too, and one handles them the same way, noting "itching," "tight," "tired."

Periods of sitting meditation are alternated with periods of walking meditation, in which one notes the exact movements of the body in great detail: "lifting," "moving," "placing." This same mindfulness is carried over into every activity of the day. If ecstatic states or visions arise, the meditator is told simply to note them and let them pass away without attachment. The truths of existence as set forth by the Buddha – dukkha, anicca, anatta – will become apparent during this process, and the mind becomes calm, clear, attentive, and flexible, detached from likes and dislikes.

THE LAITY Although meditators from all over the world are now traveling to Southeast Asia to study with the masters of meditation, their demanding discipline is embraced by relatively few Theravadins. The majority of monasteries are not meditation centers. Most laypeople's religious lives are more devotional than intellectual. Recognizing this natural tendency, Theravada developed two separate paths for bhikkhus and the laity: the path for monks and nuns was based on development of morality, concentration, and wisdom, leading to freedom, whereas the laity was expected only to give alms and to observe the Three Refuges and the Five Precepts, with some attention to the development of tranquility. Laypeople are not expected to know much about the Buddha's teachings; few of them try to gain Enlightenment.

Stupas such as these bell-shaped monuments at the Great Stupa complex in Borobudur, Java, may house relics or statues of the Buddha and are sacred places for pilgrimage. The Buddha's long ears signify wisdom; the topknot represents higher consciousness.

Even within the relatively austere Theravada path there have arisen a number of ways of worship. One is the veneration of relics thought to be from the Buddha. These are placed in *stupas*, architectural mounds reaching into the sky, perhaps derived from the indigenous spiritual traditions. A tiny bone chip from the Buddha, for instance, is enshrined at Doi Suthep temple near Chiang Mai in Thailand. To share this sacred relic with the people, the ruler was said to have placed it on the back of a sacred white elephant – legendary symbol of the Buddha – so that it would choose the best place for the temple. The elephant climbed a nearby hill until it reached the auspicious spot, where it circled three times and then went down on its knees. Thousands of pilgrims climb the 290 steps to the temple today, praying for blessings by acts such as pressing squares of gold leaf onto an image of the Buddha, lighting three sticks of incense to honor the Triple Gem, lighting candles, and offering flowers to the Buddha images.

Loving images of the Buddha proliferate in the temples and roadside shrines (which are almost identical to the indigenous spirit shrines, still quite common in Southeast Asia for Theravada has related itself to indigenous ways rather than displacing them). These physical images of the Buddha give a sense of his protective, guiding presence even though according to Theravadin orthodoxy the Buddha no longer exists as an individual, having entered Nibbana. Even the monks are regarded as magical protectors of sorts, and the faithful can request chantings of blessings for protection. For instance, in the books of Pali chants there is a special prayer for protection from unwanted crawling creatures, such as spiders and rats. It addresses them in a spirit of loving-kindness *(metta)* and then requests, "May those beings go away!"[12]

Left *Buddhists sit on the floor in their temples, honoring statues of the Buddha as an eternal principle in the universe.*
Right *In Southeast Asia roadside shrines of the Buddha, some of them on busy city streets, are visited by laypeople bringing offerings such as food and drink, elephant figures, flowers, candles, and incense. They are quite similar to the earlier spirit shrines.*

Mahayana: the path of compassion and metaphysics

This human tendency to devotion and metaphysical beliefs is given fuller rein in the Mahayana tradition, and indeed was part of the reason for its development. Rather than enforcing a gap between the intellectuals and monastics on one hand and the common people on the other, many schools of Buddhism take a more liberal approach designed to encompass everyone. They honor the scriptures in the Pali Canon but derive many of their teachings from other scriptures. Some of these are attributed to the Buddha and are said by Mahayanists to be esoteric teachings given only to the Arhats and the Bodhisattvas, the compassionate enlightened beings described below. The body of scriptures is open-ended, enriched by the *sutras* (wisdom teachings: literally, a thread on which jewels are strung) of those who have grasped the Dharma. The Dharma is not embodied only in scriptures; in Mahayana, it is carried as a living tradition, transmitted mind-to-mind. The student must experience the truth directly in order to pass it on.

Each school, and there are many branches within Mahayana, offers a special set of methods, or "skillful means," for awakening. They are quite varied, in contrast to the relative uniformity of Theravada, but most Mahayana traditions have a few characteristics in common.

THE BODHISATTVA VOW   A major shift in emphasis is the motive of the individual. In Theravada, one contemplates the fact of suffering in one's life and tries to achieve individual liberation through ardent practice. In Mahayana, by contrast, the ideal is to be aware of the suffering of others and speed one's own enlightenment in order to effectively serve the suffering world. People are taught that because we have all incarnated so often, it is likely that we have been closely related to everyone in some previous lifetime. One practice is to regard every person as having been one's mother, or some other favorite relative, at some point. How then could we be indifferent to anyone?

The feeling of active responsibility for everyone's welfare is embodied in the Bodhisattva ideal. "Bodhi" means perfected wisdom; "sattva" means essence. Mahayana reveres those beings who have achieved enlightenment and thereby recognized truth directly, but who in their boundless compassion have chosen to stay connected with the earth to help free all sentient beings from suffering in *samsara* (the world of birth and death) rather than enter the final bliss of Nirvana. The following passage from the Diamond Banner Sutra exemplifies the supreme altruism of the Bodhisattva:

Kuan-yin, "hearer of cries," Bodhisattva of mercy.

> *A Bodhisattva resolves: I take upon myself the burden of all suffering, I am resolved to do so, I will endure it. I do not turn or run away, do not tremble, am not terrified, nor afraid, do not turn back or despond.*
>
> *And why? Because it is surely better that I alone should be in pain than that all these beings should fall into the states of woe. There I must give myself away as a pawn through which the whole world is redeemed from the terrors ... and with this my own body I must experience, for the sake of all beings, the whole mass of all painful feelings ... I must not abandon all beings.*[13]

The Bodhisattva is not one who runs about mindlessly trying to help. He or she is like a lotus flower whose purity is undefiled by the muck of human ignorance, serene in wisdom and boundless compassion. Bodhisattvas joyously offer their own great store of merits to help lift others toward liberation. As all who have felt the sufferings of others know, none of us is truly free until we are all free. Bodhisattvas do not carry martyr complexes. In their awakened experience, there is no self who gives. In the perfection of giving, a Bodhisattva "surrenders that gift to all beings, but he apprehends neither beings nor self."[14]

Mahayanists who have awakened from worldly goals and have turned toward spiritual development may take the Bodhisattva vow themselves once they have passed certain preparatory stages. That is, if they have sought the companionship of friends with similar interests ("spiritual friends"), and have become broadminded, purehearted, sincerely faithful, virtuous, Buddha-serving, and wholeheartedly compassionate, the true will for enlightenment may arise. Seeking enlightenment not for their own sake but for all beings, they can ask for a ceremonial ordination. This vow can be taken by anyone who is well prepared, whether monk or layperson, and it includes a set of precepts for behavior that is more demanding than that expected of others.

Bodhisattvahood is not just an ideal for earthly conduct; numerous heavenly Bodhisattvas are available to hear the pleas of those who are suffering. The heavenly Bodhisattvas are seen as aspects of the eternal Buddha. Each has a specific attribute, such as wisdom or compassion, and worshippers can pray to them for help.

THE THREE BODIES OF BUDDHA   The idea of the eternal Buddha principle is a major departure from Theravadin tradition. In Theravada, Buddha is an historical figure who no longer exists but who left his Dharma as a guide. Mahayana regards the Buddha as a universal principle. Metaphysically, Buddha is said to be an eternal presence in the universe with three aspects, or "bodies": The essence of knowledge and compassion, "Consciousness merged in the Universal Consciousness"; the body of bliss, that radiant aspect of Buddhahood that communicates the Dharma to Bodhisattvas; and the body of transformation, by which the Buddha principle becomes human to help liberate humanity. It was in this third body that the Buddha appeared for a time on the earth as the historical figure Siddartha Gautama of the Shakyas. He is called Shakyamuni Buddha by Mahayanists to distinguish him from other manifestations of the Buddha.

Whereas Theravada is non-theistic, Mahayana has thus elevated Buddhahood to somewhat theistic status. The common people therefore recognize a multitude of Buddhas and Bodhisattvas to whom they can pray for help. But some Mahayanists interpret teachings about the Bodhisattvas and the three bodies of the Buddha symbolically rather than literally, as metaphors for aspects of consciousness within the mysteries of the cosmos. From this point of view, Nirvana can be described as the state of pure, blissful, and radiant consciousness.

EMPTINESS   Although literal interpretation of Mahayana metaphysics supports the idea of heavenly forms, to higher understanding Mahayana Buddhism denies attachment even to these. Some of the most complex and paradoxical of Mahayana teachings concern the concept of *sunyata*, meaning voidness or emptiness, They were first propounded by Nagarjuna around the second century CE and echoed in Hinduism hundreds of years later in Shankara's Advaita Vedanta philosophy.

According to Nagarjuna, all earthly things are conditional – they arise and pass away, having no eternal reality. They are thus devoid of true power, ultimately empty. "Like

The region where Siddartha grew up is in full view of the high peaks of the Himalayas.

Buddhist nuns have traditionally been given lower status than monks, but as a group they are growing in strength today.

Left *The Buddhist framework for life in Tibet revolved around mountain monasteries until they were closed by the Chinese, who also allegedly killed a large proportion of the monks.*
Right *The fourteenth Dalai Lama, spiritual leader of Tibetan Buddhists from his government-in-exile in Dharamsala, in the Himalayan foothills of northern India, is also revered around the world as a compassionate voice for global peace.*

something borrowed, or a city founded on sand, they last a short while only."[15] A Buddhist is therefore unmoved by either pleasure or pain, gain or loss, and "is not allured by the things of the world, because they have no basis."[16] Apparent reality is just a projection of the mind, like the rope that appears in the dusk of human ignorance to be a snake.

Nagarjuna extends this doctrine of voidness to metaphysics as well. Our ideas about the unseen worlds are also empty, he claims, for ultimate reality is beyond the grasp of human thought and speech. The concept of Nirvana is therefore just as illusory as our concepts of the physical world. This fact suggests a paradoxical conclusion: What is real is emptiness. It is everywhere, all-embracing. There is therefore no difference between the changing physical world of *samsara* and Nirvana. Both are conditioned human perceptions of the underlying undifferentiated reality.

As perceived by the empty mind that precedes thinking, says Korean Zen Buddhist master Seung Sahn:

> *Everything is the same substance. You are the universe – the universe is you. In pure emptiness, all minds are the same. You get to Great Meaning through No Meaning, to Great Choice through No Choice.* [17]

Tibetan Vajrayana: short-cut to the Palace of Unity

Of the many branches of Mahayana Buddhism, perhaps the most prolific in creating elaborations developed in Tibet. Prior to the introduction of Buddhism, the mountainous region had been home to a shamanistic religion called Bon (pronounced "pern"). In the seventh century CE a particularly powerful king of Tibet, Songtsan, became interested in the religion that surrounded his isolated kingdom. He sent a group of students to study Buddhism in India, but they all died in the searing heat of the plains. Only one member of a second group survived the arduous trip across the

Himalayas, returning with many Sanskrit texts. After some of these works were translated into Tibetan, Songtsan declared Buddhism the national religion and encouraged Buddhist virtues in his subjects.

The Bon shamans kept trying to sabotage this threat to their power until a tantric adept, Padmasambhava, was invited to the country from Kashmir in the eighth century CE. Along the way, it is said, he subdued and converted the local Bon deities. He developed Tibetan Buddhism by splicing elements of the Bon ways and esoteric tantric practices into Mahayana Buddhism. Many of the Bon gods and goddesses were adopted as lower-grade tantric guardian deities, but animal sacrifice was replaced with symbolic forms of worship and black magic gave way to inner purification practices. When people interpreted tantric teachings literally, indulging freely in alcohol and sex in the name of spirituality, another teacher named Atisha from the great center of Buddhist learning at Nalanda, India, was called in to set things right.

Under Atisha, Tibetan Buddhism became a complex path with three stages, said to have been the *yanas* – vehicles, means of progress, or responsibilities – prescribed by the Lord Buddha. While the Buddha did not develop them to their current state, he is said to have supported the idea of different levels of teachings for the less and more evolved. The first of these is called Hinayana by the Tibetans: quieting of the mind and relinquishing of attachments through meditation practices. The second is Mahayana: training in compassion and loving-kindness. The third is an advanced esoteric path called *Vajrayana* ("the indestructible diamond vehicle") or *Tantrayana*, said to be the speeded-up path that allows enlightenment within a single lifetime. It includes extremely rigorous practices derived from the tantric yoga of India. Adepts in this path attempt to construct a "diamond-body" for themselves that will allow them physically to sustain entries into the intense energies of higher levels of consciousness.

After developing tranquility, freedom, and loving-kindness – no small feats in themselves – dedicated Vajrayana aspirants are guided through a series of tantric practices by gurus, the highest of whom are *lamas*. The latter are revered as incarnate Bodhisattvas and carefully trained from a young age for their role as those who have realized the Supreme Truth and can help others advance toward it. As in Hinduism, submission to the guru in gratitude for the teachings is the only way to receive them.

Tantric meditations always begin and end with dissolving into emptiness, not only because this is the enlightened awareness of how things are but also because the psychic powers developed on the tantric path could be misused by those who have not understood their essential emptiness. Initiates are then given practices in the *deity yoga* of divine pride and radiant appearance. That is, each aspirant meditates on one of the many deities who embody various manifestations of energy in the universe. The forms of the deities must be recognized as constructions of the mind, and therefore ultimately empty, having only the power that the mind gives them. At the same time, meditating on these radiant beings brings out their qualities in the meditator.

The highest stage of Vajrayana is the use of the subtle vital energies of the body to transform the mind. Through esoteric practices, the vital energies flowing through the body are purified and their channels opened so that the purified energy from the spiritual center atop the head and behind the navel unite in the spiritual heart. This union produces a very high state of consciousness in which the mind "rides" upon such subtle energy that it becomes what Tibetans call "the clear light of bliss." Using this subtle mind of clear light, one is then said to be capable of attaining Buddhahood in a

In Tibetan Buddhist art, the yantras of Hinduism have become highly elaborated thang-ka paintings, created in a sacred manner as aids to devotional concentration. (Mandala of Akshoboya, probably Tibetan, 18th century.)

single lifetime.

The yogic practices used to transform the mind also have as side-effects such abilities as levitation, clairvoyance, meditating continuously without sleep, and warming the body from within while sitting naked in the snow. Milarepa, the famous Tibetan poet-saint whose enlightenment was won through great austerities, once sang this song:

Blissful within, I don't entertain
The notion ''I'm suffering,''
When incessant rain is pouring outside.

Even on peaks of white snow mountains
Amidst swirling snow and sleet
Driven by new year's wintry winds
This cotton robe burns like fire. [18]

Tibetans have suffered persecution by the communist Chinese, who overran the country in 1951, destroying ancient monasteries and scriptures and forcing the highest of the lamas — the beloved fourteenth Dalai Lama, spiritual and political leader of the people — into exile. But religious fervor and ceremony still pervade every aspect of Tibetan life, from house-raising to ardent pilgrimages. Monks and laypeople alike meditate on *thang-kas*, or *mandalas*, visual aids to concentration and illumination which portray a Buddha or Bodhisattva surrounded by deities in a diagram symbolically representing the universe. Both also chant mantras. A favorite one is the phrase associated with the beloved Tibetan Boddhisattva of mercy, Avalokitesvara: *Om mani padme hum.* It evokes awareness of the "jewel in the lotus of the heart," that beautiful treasure lying hidden within each of us. Because some emphasis is placed on the number of repetitions, mantras are written out thousands of times and spun in prayer wheels or placed on prayer flags which continue the repetition of the mantra as they blow in the wind.

Zen: the great way of enlightenment

As Buddhism was transmitted to China around 50 CE and thence to Japan, Korea, and Vietnam, absorbing elements of Taoism along the way, another radical form of the religion developed that came to be called Zen (*Ch'an* in Chinese – which in turn is derived from the Sanskrit *dhyana*, the yogic stage of meditation). It claims to preserve the essence of the Buddha's teachings through direct experience, triggered by mind-to-mind transmission of the Dharma. It dismissed scriptures, Buddhas, and Boddhisattvas in favor of training for direct intuition of cosmic unity, known as the Buddha-nature or the Void.

A central way of directly experiencing the underlying unity is *zazen*, sitting "meditation." "To sit," said the Sixth Zen Patriarch, "means to obtain absolute freedom and not to allow any thought to be caused by external objects. To meditate means to realize the imperturbability of one's original nature."[19]

Prescriptions for the manner of sitting are quite rigorous: One must take a specific upright posture and then not move during the meditation period, to avoid distracting the mind. Skillful means are then applied to make the mind one-pointed and clear. One beginning practice is simply to watch and count each inhalation and exhalation from one to ten, starting over from one if anything other than awareness of the breath enters the mind. Although this explanation sounds simple, the mind is so restless that many people must work for months before finally getting to ten without having to start over.

The Chinese communists dismantled the system whereby a fourth of the men in Tibet were ''unproductive'' monks, supported by the laity and holding considerable secular power. But spirituality persists among the people, who include full-length prostrations in their prayers.

Getting to ten is not really the goal; the goal is the process itself, the process of recognizing what comes up in the mind and gently letting it go without attachment or preferences.

> The Great Way is not difficult
> for those who have no preferences.
> When love and hate are both absent
> everything becomes clear and undisguised.
> Make the smallest distinction, however,
> and heaven and earth are set infinitely apart.
>
> *from the Hsin hsin ming by Sengtsan, third Zen patriarch*[20]

Left to right *The Zen Oxherding Pictures illustrate stages along the spiritual path. The ox represents our true nature. By State 6, the seeker has found the ox and rides it home. In the eighth stage both ox and self are forgotten: ''Whip, rope, Ox and man alike belong to Emptiness.'' And in the tenth stage, the enlightened one happily returns to everyday life, ''entering the marketplace with helping hands.'' Brush and ink drawings by Gyokusei Jikihara.*

As one sits in zazen, undisturbed by phenomena, the natural mind is revealed. This "original mind" is spacious and free, like an open sky. Thoughts and sensations may float through it like clouds, but they arise and then disappear, leaving no trace. What remains is reality, "True Thusness." In some Zen schools, this perception of thusness comes in a sudden burst of enlightenment, or *kensho*.

When the mind is calmed, action becomes spontaneous and natural. Zen practitioners are taught to have great confidence in their natural functioning, for it arises from our essential Buddha-nature. It is said that two Zen monks, upon becoming enlightened, ran naked through the woods scribbling on rocks.

On the other hand, the Zen tradition links spontaneity with intense, disciplined

concentration. In the art of calligraphy, the perfect spontaneous brushstroke – executed with the whole body, in a single breath – is the outcome of years of attentive practice. Giving ourselves fully to the moment, to be aware only of pouring tea when pouring tea, is a simplicity of beingness that most of us have to learn. Then whatever we give ourself to fully, be it painting, or serving tea, or simply breathing, reveals the Thusness of life, its unconditioned reality.

Another tool used in one Zen tradition is the *koan*. Here the attention is focused ardently on a question that boggles the mind, such as "What is the sound of one hand clapping?" or "What is your face before your parents' birth?" As Roshi [venerable teacher] Philip Kapleau observes, "Koans deliberately throw sand into the eyes of the intellect to force us to open our Mind's eye and see the world and everything in it undistorted by our concepts and judgments." To concentrate on a koan, one must look closely at it without thinking about it, experiencing it directly. Beyond abstractions, Roshi Kapleau explains, "The import of every koan is the same: that the world is one interdependent Whole and that each separate one of us is that Whole."[21]

The aim of Zen practice is enlightenment, or *satori*. One directly experiences the unity of all existence, often in a sudden recognition that nothing is separate from oneself. As one Zen master put it:

The moon's the same old moon,
The flowers exactly as they were,
Yet I've become the thingness
Of all the things I see![22]

The purpose of zen meditation and arts such as archery, the tea ceremony, calligraphy, garden design, and flower arrangement is to train the mind to return to its original unselfconscious union with ultimate reality.

All aspects of life become at the same time utterly precious, and utterly empty, "nothing special." This paradox can only be sensed with the mystically expanded consciousness; it cannot be grasped intellectually.

Enlightenment is not an end in itself, however. As Zen master Seung Sahn explains, one first attains an empty, "don't know" mind. This mental emptiness brings the direct experience of truth – "Sky is blue, tree is green, sugar is sweet" – and of the "mystical energy" of life. The true goal lies even beyond this:

> *The correct function of mystical energy is only to help other people. Somebody is hungry –*
> *What? Somebody is suffering – What? Moment to moment, keep correct situation, correct*
> *function, correct relationship. That is the human being's original job.*[23]

Pure Land: calling on Amida Buddha

Zen is essentially a strict monastic practice in which great attention is given to every action; it has little appeal for the laity. Other forms developed in the Far East that have much greater popular appeal. One of the major trends is known as Pure Land Buddhism. At a time of great social upheaval (for instance, the old feudal aristocracy in Japan was falling apart), it was widely thought that people had become so degenerate that it was nearly impossible for them to attain enlightenment through their own efforts. Instead, many turned to Amida Buddha to save them. Amida (Sanskrit: Amitabha) is the Buddha of Boundless Light. According to scriptures, he had vowed to prepare a special place of bliss, the Pure Land, for all those who called on his name with total faith and devotion.

Many people contributed to the growth of Pure Land Buddhism into a mass movement. In the tenth century, for example, a Japanese monk named Kuya encouraged others to join him as he danced through the streets with a bell about his neck, singing songs of devotion and calling on Amida Buddha by chanting the *nembutsu*: "Namu Amida Buddha" ("Imperfect myself, I take refuge in the immeasurable light, in the immeasurable life"). This profession of faith is available to everyone, male or female, monks or laity, so it allows a spiritual life for the devout who live family-centered lives in the world.

The results of loving trust in Amida Buddha were described very vividly by the monk Genshin. After graphic depictions of the eight hells, such as the burning vat in which people are cooked like beans, he describes the ineffable pleasures of being reborn into the Pure Land upon death:

> *Rings, bracelets, a crown of jewels, and other ornaments in countless profusion adorn his*
> *body. And when he looks upon the light radiating from the Buddha, he obtains pure*
> *vision, and because of his experiences in former lives, he hears the sounds of all things.*
> *And no matter what color he may see or what sound he may hear, it is a thing of marvel.*[24]

Many believers interpret these passages literally, anticipating that if they are sufficiently faithful they will enjoy a beautiful life after death. But some understand the Pure Land as a state that can be achieved in this life; a metaphor for the mystical experience of enlightenment, in which one's former identity "dies" and one is reborn into an expanded state of consciousness. According to this view, the lotus symbolizes the blooming of the pure lotus from the mire of ignorance and suffering, which the Buddha identified as the human condition. As contemporary Pure Land Buddhist priest and scholar Taitetsu Unno explains:

> *To be reborn into that state one has to be reborn here and now in awakening. There is no such thing as after death. Buddhism sees time not past, present, and future, but as present to present to present ... When one's life is fulfilled in this moment, the next moment is fulfilled. And if death is the next moment, that, too, is fulfilled. One can't be in total confusion and say, ''When I die I will be saved and be reborn in Pure Land.'' You've got to be careful because that may not be true. But if you have some understanding, some major awakening now, then even if people say ''That's a bunch of baloney!'' you don't care, because each moment is fulfilled, each moment.*[25]

Amida appears to welcome the faithful to the Western Paradise. (Konkai Komyo-ji, Kyoto, 14th century.)

Nichiren: salvation through the Lotus Sutra

While Pure Land Buddhists despair of purifying themselves by their own efforts, and therefore humbly submit to the grace of Amida Buddha, a thirteenth-century Japanese fisherman's son, who named himself Nichiren, stressed the importance of striving to reform not only ourselves but also society. He blamed the political struggles of the time on false Buddhist paths, including the Pure Land focus on the next life rather than this one. For Nichiren, the highest truths of Buddhism were embodied in the Lotus Sutra, a large compilation of parables, verses, and descriptions of innumerable forms of beings who support the teachings of the World-Honored One, the Buddha. Nichiren gave particular attention to two of these beings: the Bodhisattva of Superb Action, who staunchly devotes himself to spreading the Perfect Truth, even in evil times, and the Bodhisattva Ever-Abused, who is persecuted because of his insistence on revering everyone with unshaken conviction that each person is potentially a Buddha. Nichiren himself was repeatedly abused by authorities but persisted in his efforts to reform Buddhism in Japan and then spread its purified essence, the bodhisattva ideal, to the world.

The phrase chanted by Nichiren and his followers, ''*Namu myoho rengekyo,*'' refers to faith in the entire Lotus Sutra. Today it is chanted by Nichiren monks and nuns by the hour, slowly revealing its depths as it works inwardly, beyond thought. In our time, some in the Nichiren tradition undertake long peace walks, beating small hand drums while chanting "Namu myoho rengekyo," and contributing to world peace by truly bowing to the Buddha in each person, even if they encounter abuse. As the Most Venerable Nichidatsu Fujii, who passed away in 1985 at the age of one hundred and influenced Gandhi's doctrine of non-violence, has explained:

> *We do not believe that people are good because we see that they are good, but by believing that people are good we eliminate our own fear and thus, we can intimately associate with them. To believe in the compassionate power of the Supreme Being which we cannot see is a discipline in order to believe in the invisible good in others.*[26]

The chanting of "Namu myoho rengekyo" has also caused seventy Peace Pagodas to arise thus far in Japan, England, Austria, and the United States, in fulfillment of the prophecy in the Lotus Sutra that wherever this Scripture of the Lotus Blossom of the Fine Dharma is preached, a beautiful stupa will spontaneously emerge as a physical reminder of the Buddha's "supernatural penetrations." These pagodas are built with

Life in a Western Zen Monastery

Side-by-side in still rows, with birdsong and sunlight streaming in through the tall windows, sit the monks and laypeople of Zen Mountain Monastery. For thirty-five-minute blocks separated by periods of attentive walking, they support each other by practicing zazen together in silence. With this group structure, many find it easier to carry on the rigorous discipline of serious Zen training than they would by themselves.

This particular monastery, located in the Catskill Mountains near Mt. Tremper, New York, reflects the changing face of religion in the United States. A hundred years ago the main building was handcrafted of stone as a Benedictine Monastery; later it became a Lutheran summer camp. Now back-to-back with the Christ on the cross on the outside of the building is a statue of Buddha on the altar in the zendo. The monastery houses five fully ordained monks who have taken lifetime vows of service (two of them women), several novices and postulants in training (an aspect adopted from Western monasticism), lay residents who stay for up to a year, and groups of people who come for special retreats and classes. Increasingly these are professionals and family people from the mainstream culture, rather than the hippies who embraced Buddhism in the 60s and 70s. They do not come for a comfortable vacation, for zazen is hard work and the teachers are dedicated to creating snags that help people discover the places where they are not free. They are expected to practice intensely and then leave, carrying what they have learned back into the world. As the monk Shugen observes, "If Zen doesn't work in the world, it's not working."

In addition to long sessions of silent sitting and walking, Dharma talks by the resident Zen master John Daido Loori Sensei (an American ordained in both authentic Zen lineages), and private coaching by the monks, monastery residents participate in structured non-theistic liturgical services designed to foster attentiveness and appreciation. They chant in Japanese and English, with frequent bowing to each other, to their meditation cushions, and to the Buddha on the altar in identification with all beings and gratitude for the teachings. Zen master Daido notes that liturgy reflects the innards of a religion: "In Catholicism, cathedrals are awe-inspiring, the chants expansive; in Zen the form is simple and the chanting is grounded, not other-worldly."

The rest of the day is devoted to caretaking of the buildings and 200-acre nature sanctuary, mindful practice done in silence, and to work practice. Those with office jobs combine ancient and modern arts: They sit cross-legged on low cushions before their computers and use calligraphic skills to hand-letter signs. Meals are simple and include coarse breads donated by a nearby whole-grain bakery. Every action – even brushing one's teeth – is treated as liturgy, in the sense of bringing total attentiveness to the sacredness of even the most "mundane" activity as a teaching that enlightenment takes place in one's everyday experience.

Following the lead of their teacher Daido, who is at once highly disciplined in the pure mind-to-mind Dharma transmission and very down-to-earth, approachable, and compassionate, monastery residents are human, playful, and loving. The women monks shave their heads when ordained and keep it very short thereafter, but for them near-baldness feels like freedom rather than self-sacrificing asceticism. The monk Myotai observes:

I could feel every breeze, and being bald definitely altered the way I saw the habit patterns I brought to my interactions with other people, clarifying how much "extra" was still there, to a degree that surprised me. There is a several-year entry period before ordination, to get clear on what it means, but one aspect of actually having no hair was that it really opened up the male-female dynamic. I no longer felt myself relating to men as a woman. That was very freeing. It was also wonderful to have this daily reminder of what I was doing with my life.

Above *The stillness of the zendo at Zen Mountain Monastery.*
Above right *Oriyoki, a ceremonial meal, at Zen Mountain Monastery.*
Right *John Daido Loori Sensei, abbot of Zen Mountain Monastery.*

donated materials and labor by people of all faiths who support the belief expressed by Nichidatsu Fujii, in hopes of world peace.

Another Nichiren branch has gained a tremendous following in Japan and the United States during the twentieth century: Nichiren Shoshu Soka Gakkai. One of its temples at the foot of Mount Fuji is the largest in the world. The organization has considerable nationalistic political influence in Japan (to be discussed in the final chapter) but its leader Daisaku Ikeda is also an international activist for world peace. He calls for a peaceful world revolution, through transformation of individual consciousness.

Buddhism in the West

Images of the Buddha are now enshrined around the world, for what began in India has gradually spread to the West as well as the East. Much of this transmission has occurred in the twentieth century, with the United States becoming a vibrant center of Buddhism. Scholars are studying Buddhist traditions in great depth at many universities, and many people are trying to learn Buddhist meditation practices. A number of the highest Tibetan lamas, forced out of Tibet, have established spiritual communities in the United States, complete with altars full of sacred Tibetan artefacts. Intensive vipassana retreats of up to three months are carried out in centers such as the Insight Meditation Society in rural Barre, Massachusetts. Theravadin teachers from Southeast Asia and Europe make frequent appearances to conduct retreats, and American teachers undertake rigorous training in Southeast Asia under traditional meditation masters. In addition to numerous Zen centers where Westerners who have undergone training in the East serve as teachers to lay practitioners of meditation, there are a number of Zen monasteries giving solid training in zazen and offering a monastic lifestyle as a permanent or temporary alternative to life in the world. In England, the American monk Ajahn Sumedho guides a monastic forest community in the Thai Theravada style in which he was trained.

The Buddha's compassion has not yet been the dominant theme in Western interest in Buddhism. Buddhism has more often been embraced by Westerners because of their longing for the peace of meditation. In the midst of a chaotic materialistic life, there is a desire to discover emptiness, to let the identity with self fall away, or to become familiar with the mind's tricks in the still simplicity of a *zendo*, a Zen meditation hall. Many psychotherapists are studying Buddhism for its insights into the mind and human suffering. Richard Clarke, who is both a Zen teacher and a psychotherapist, feels that a discipline such as Zen should be part of the training of therapists:

> [*We must*] *come holding to nothing. Zen is to guide people into experiencing the realm of emptiness and to let that experience penetrate all of life and be the ground from which one lives. Then a person could be very effective anywhere, not just as a therapist, but particularly as a therapist. Any human interaction becomes more than superficial interaction.*
>
> *Emptiness is also the source of infinite compassion in working with people: to really feel a person without any agenda, to be spacious to that person, to will that they be the way they*

are. When a person experiences that in someone's presence, then they can drop away those things that they've invented to present themselves with. Those faces, those armors, those forms of the self become unnecessary. Learning that, they are able to find how wonderful it is not to have to carry those around. [27]

The growing interest in Buddhism in the West, where new books on Buddhism and translations of traditional scriptures are rapidly appearing, is helping to revitalize Buddhism in Asia. As Asia entered the modern world, many of its peoples lost interest in their traditional religions, which became superficial re-enactments of ceremonial practices. But as Westerners themselves are taking strong interest in Buddhism, those who have grown up as Buddhists are reassessing their religion and finding new depths in it. Buddhist principles and practices may become increasingly important parts of our universal path to world peace.

Suggested reading

de Bary, William Theodore, ed., *The Buddhist Tradition in India, China, and Japan*, New York: Modern Library, 1969. An excellent survey with useful commentaries and selections from Buddhist scriptures.

Fremantle, Francesca, and Trungpa, Chogyam, trans., *The Tibetan Book of the Dead*, Boston and London: Shambhala Publications, 1975. The classic Tibetan Buddhist scripture on the projections of the mind and the practices of deity yoga to attain enlightenment.

Friedman, Lenore, *Meetings with Remarkable Women: Buddhist Teachers in America*, Boston and London: Shambhala Publications, 1987. Wisdom from Buddhist traditions shared in very personal, perceptive interviews.

Levine, Stephen, *A Gradual Awakening*, Garden City, New York: Doubleday, 1979 and London: Rider and Company, 1980. Gentle, poetic presentation of vipassana techniques in their relevance to contemporary life.

Lal, P., trans., *The Dhammapada*, New York: Farrar, Straus and Giroux, 1967. A basic book attributed to the Buddha that covers the essentials of the Dharma in memorable, pithy verses.

Morgan, Kenneth W., *The Path of the Buddha*, New York: Ronald Press Company, 1956. The varying paths of Buddhism as presented by respected scholars from each tradition.

Sangharakshita, Bhikshu, *The Three Jewels: An Introduction to Buddhism*, London: Rider and Company (distributed in the U.S. by The Theosophical Publishing House), 1967. Use of Buddha, Dharma, and Sangha as a framework for presenting a wealth of information about Theravada and Mahayana teachings.

Suzuki, Shunryu, *Zen Mind, Beginner's Mind*, New York and Tokyo: Weatherhill, 1970. A beautiful book leading one gracefully and seemingly simply through the paradoxes of Zen.

6 TAOISM AND CONFUCIANISM

The unity of opposites

While India was giving birth to Hinduism, Jainism, and Buddhism, three other major religions were developing in East Asia. Taoism and Confucianism grew largely in China and Korea and later spread to Japan; Shinto was distinctively Japanese. These are not missionary traditions and have thus remained associated primarily with their homelands. In this chapter we will explore the two that developed in China from similar roots but with different emphases: Taoism and Confucianism. Shinto will be the subject of Chapter 7. Buddhism, Christianity, and Islam have also infused East Asia, and their practice is often mixed with the native traditions.

In East Asia, religions that will be treated as separate entities in this chapter and the next are in fact more subtly blended and practiced. Furthermore, twentieth-century political shifts in China have made it difficult to pin-point or predict the continued existence of religious ways there.

Ancient traditions

In ancient Chinese tradition, the universe arises from the interplay of yin and yang. They are modes of energy commonly represented as interlocking shapes, with dominance continually shifting between the dark, receptive yin mode and the bright, assertive yang mode.

The indigenous spiritual ways permeate all later religious developments in China and Korea. One major feature is the veneration of ancestors. Dead ancestors and live descendants are closely bonded, with the ancestors providing boons for the living if treated with proper respect (or trouble if ignored). Respect is shown primarily through *li* – the funerals, mourning rituals, and continuing sacrifices to the deceased ones' spirits. The degree to which they are venerated depends upon their place in the patriarchal hierarchy; most important is the family's founding ancestor. The practice of this family religion is of central importance; individual spirituality and group institutions that transcend the family are of less importance.

There are also, however, shrines and temples to other deities, from nature spirits to widely-admired dead humans who are still available to help the people. For instance, coastal peoples honor "The Holy Mother in Heaven," a woman who is said to have been born in the tenth century CE. As a teenager, she reportedly used her miraculous powers to save her father and brother from drowning when their boat sank. One can make offerings to these deities and seek their aid with personal problems. Sometimes their help can be sought through the mediumship of a person who serves as a shaman and enters trance states in order to commune with the supernatural beings.

In addition to these ancient folkways, contemporary beliefs have roots in the ancient Chinese philosophy of the nature of the universe. Its central idea is that there is one

Absolute Reality, sometimes referred to as *T'ai Chi* ("Supreme Ultimate"). It has two aspects, yin and yang, whose interplay causes the ever-changing phenomena of the universe. *Yin* is the dark, receptive, "female" aspect; *yang* is the bright, assertive, "male" aspect. Wisdom lies in recognizing their ever-shifting, but regular and balanced, patterns and moving with them. This creative rhythm of the universe is called the *Tao*, or "way."

In the Chinese diagram of the T'ai Chi (see page 134), yin and yang interpenetrate each other (represented by the small circles). As soon as one aspect reaches its fullest point, it begins to diminish, accompanied by an increase in its polar opposite.

In order to be aware of these shifts and harmonize one's actions with them, the ancients devised a system of divination. It became extremely sophisticated and was written down in 1150 BCE as the *I Ching*, or Book of Changes. It contains information on sixty-four hexagrams created by six throws of yarrow stalks or coins. Yin is represented by a broken line and yang by a straight line. One respectfully purifies the divining objects, asks a question, casts the objects, and then consults the I Ching for the symbolic meaning of the results. Some configurations yield two sets of results: one indicating the present and one the direction of the future.

Each hexagram is built from two of eight basic trigrams. Each trigram is a metaphorical embodiment of an attribute, a natural phenomenon, and a "family" relationship, with each family member symbolizing a different life function. The combination of two trigrams yields multi-leveled explanations, all open to individual interpretation. For example, hexagram number 46, Sheng, consists of the earth trigram on top of the wood trigram. It is called "Pushing Upward," like a tree growing up from the earth. Like all the hexagrams, it has been interpreted by various commentators over time, including Confucius. One description of the significance of Sheng is based on nature – the image of the slow, invisible growth of a tree:

Thus the superior man of devoted character
Heaps up small things
In order to achieve something high and great. [1]

Another set of commentaries on the same hexagram is based on the attributes: devotion and yielding in the upper trigram and gentleness in the lower. These non-aggressive qualities, it is said, will ultimately lead to "supreme success."

Taoism – The Valley Way

Taoism, called Doism in Korea, is as full of paradoxes as the Buddhist tradition it influenced: Ch'an or Zen Buddhism. It has been adored by Westerners who seek a carefree, natural way of life as an escape from the industrial rat race. Yet beneath its words of the simple life in harmony with nature is an esoteric tradition of great mental and physical discipline. Taoism includes both efforts to align oneself with the unnamable original force, and ceremonial worship of deities from the Jade Emperor to the Kitchen god. Some Taoist scriptures counsel indifference about birth and death; others teach ways of attaining physical immortality. These variations developed within an ancient tradition that had no name until it had to distinguish itself from Confucianism. "Taoism" is actually a label invented by scholars and awkwardly stretched to cover both a philosophical tradition *(Tao-chia)* and a religion *(Tao-chiao)*.

The hexagram Sheng is a visual symbol of the various meanings attached to ''pushing upward.''

Tao-chia: teachings of Taoist sages

Aside from its general basis in ancient indigenous ways, the specific origin of Taoist philosophy and practices is unclear. In China, tradition attributes the publicizing of Tao-chia to the Yellow Emperor, who supposedly ruled from 2697 to 2597 BCE. He was said to have studied with an ancient sage and to have developed meditation, health, and military practices based on what he learned. After ruling for a hundred years, he ascended to heaven on a dragon's back and became one of the immortals.

In Korea, Doism is said to have begun among the sun- and sky-worshipping tribes of what is now northern China and southern Siberia, who were driven to the Korean peninsula by perhaps 3000 BCE. Long before the Chinese Yellow Emperor, the chief of a "Korean" tribe in southern Siberia is said to have developed a strong practice of breathing meditation in order to increase his physical, mental, and spiritual powers and thus rule effectively. This proposed origin of Doism is thought to have occurred some seven to eight thousand years ago.

The philosophical basis of Taoism is expounded in the famous scripture, the *Tao-te Ching* ("The Classic of the Way and the Power"). It is second only to the Bible in number of translations, for its ideas are not only fascinating but also elusive for translators working from the terse ancient Chinese ideograms. For one thing, many ideograms have multiple meanings; a single word, for instance, connotes both thinking and feeling, and can be translated as either "mind" or "heart." A second difficulty is the succinctness of the original Chinese. Many parts of speech are non-existent and subjects are often dispensed with, but to render the ideas into English sentences translators try to fill in the concepts, with widely mixed results. One recent translation, by Stephen Mitchell, alternately refers to sages as "she" and "he," for there are no gender distinctions in the Chinese. A third problem is that extant Chinese copies of the book vary in places. Fourthly, it is a book of mystical wisdom which can better be understood intuitively than intellectually.

Even the supposed author of the *Tao-te Ching* is obscure. According to tradition, the book was dictated by Lao-tzu (or Lao-tse, meaning "Old Boy"), a curator of the royal library of the Chou dynasty, to a border guard as he left society for the mountains at the reported age of 160. The guard recognized Lao-tzu as a sage and begged him to leave behind a record of his wisdom. Lao-tzu reportedly complied by inscribing the five thousand characters now known as the Tao-te Ching. This is said to have happened during the sixth century BCE, with Lao-tzu purportedly fifty-three years older than Confucius. But some historians think the Tao-te Ching was the work of several sages and question whether Lao-tzu ever existed.

The book itself counsels "invisibility." Its central philosophy, which shines through widely varying translations, is that one can best harmonize with the natural flow of life by being receptive and quiet.

These teachings were expressed more emphatically and humorously by a sage who lived perhaps two centuries later, Chuang-tzu. He, too, was a minor government official for a while but left political involvement for a hermit's life of freedom and solitude, radically rejecting the idea that government can fix society. Writings attributed to him are called the *Chuang-tzu*.

FLOWING WITH TAO   At the heart of Taoist teachings is *Tao*, the "unnamable," the

Lao-tzu, one of the major conveyers of the Taoist tradition, is often depicted as a humorous old man riding off into the mountains after reportedly drawing the five thousand characters of the Tao-te Ching.

"eternally real."[2] Contemporary Master Da Liu asserts that Tao is so ingrained in Chinese understanding that it is a basic concept that cannot be defined, like "goodness." Moreover, Tao is a mystical reality that cannot be grasped by the mind. Lao-tzu writes:

The Tao that can be told of
  Is not the Absolute Tao,
The Names that can be given
  Are not Absolute Names.

The Nameless is the origin of Heaven and Earth;
The Named is the Mother of All Things . . .

These two (the Secret and its manifestations)
  Are (in their nature) the same; . . .
They may both be called the Cosmic Mystery:
Reaching from the Mystery into the Deeper Mystery
Is the Gate to the Secret of All Life.[3]

In Chapter 25 of the *Tao-te Ching* he is more explicit about the mysterious Unnamable:

Before the Heaven and Earth existed
There was something nebulous:
  Silent, isolated,

> *Standing alone, changing not,*
> *Eternally revolving without fail,*
> *Worthy to be the Mother of All Things.*
> *I do not know its name*
>   *And address it as Tao.*
> *If forced to give it a name, I shall call it ''Great.''*
> *Being great implies reaching out in space,*
> *Reaching out in space implies far-reaching,*
> *Far-reaching implies reversion to the original point.*[4]

Although we cannot know Tao, we can become one with it: "You can't know it but you can be it, at ease in your own life."[5] There are several basic principles for the life in harmony with Tao. One is to experience the transcendent unity of all things, rather than separation. Professor Chang Chung-yuan observes that "the value of Tao lies in its power to reconcile opposites on a higher level of consciousness."[6] This higher level can only be attained when one ceases to feel any personal preferences. Chuang-tzu:

> *When there is no more separation between ''this'' and ''that,'' it is called the still-point of Tao. At the still-point in the center of the circle one can see the infinite in all things. Right is infinite; wrong is also infinite. Therefore it is said, ''Behold the light beyond right and wrong.''*[7]

Everything has its own nature and function, says Chuang-tzu. But disfigured or beautiful, small or large, they are all one in Tao.

Taoism is concerned with mystical communion with life, accepting things as they are, not with outer standards of morality. Chuang-tzu asserts that herein lies true spirituality:

> *Such a man can ride the clouds and mist, mount the sun and moon, and wander beyond the four seas. Life and death do not affect him. How much less will he be concerned with good and evil!*[8]

In addition to experiencing oneness, the Taoist sage takes a low profile in the world. He or she is like a valley, allowing everything needed to flow into his or her life, or like a stream. Flowing water is a Taoist model for being. It bypasses and gently wears away obstacles rather than fruitlessly attacking them, effortlessly nourishes the "ten thousand things" of material life, works without struggling, leaves all accomplishments behind without possessing them. Lao-tzu observes:

> *Water is the softest thing on earth,*
> *Yet its silken gentleness*
> *Will easily wear away the hardest stone.*
> *Everyone knows this;*
> *Few use it in their daily lives.*
> *Those of Tao yield and overcome.*[9]

This is the uniquely Taoist principle of *wei wu wei*: "doing not-doing," or taking no action contrary to nature. Chuang-tzu uses the analogy of a butcher whose knife always stays sharp because he works with the spirit, finding the spaces between the bones where a slight movement of the blade will glide through without resistance. Even when difficulties arise, the sage does not panic and take unnecessary action.

> *Do you have the patience to wait*
> *till your mud settles and the water is clear?*
> *Can you remain unmoving*
> *till the right action arises by itself?*
>
> *Lao-tzu*[10]

A third central Taoist principle is non-interference. Much of Taoist teaching is directed to rulers, that they might guide society without interfering with its natural course. Chuang-tzu:

> *Let your mind wander in the pure and simple. Be one with the infinite. Allow all things to take their course. Do not try to be clever. Then the world will be ruled!*[11]

The world is naturally in harmony; Tao is our original nature. But according to tradition, the Golden Age of Tao declined as humans departed from the Way. "Civilization," with its intellectual attempts to improve on things and its rigid views of morality, actually leads to world chaos, the Taoists warn.

How much better, Lao-tzu advises, to "reveal Simplicity and hold the Uncarved Block," to accept not-knowing, to "draw nourishment from the Mother" by moving freely with the boundaryless, changing universe rather than trying to impose controls on it.[12]

Fourth, Taoism places great value on withdrawal from the madding crowd to a contemplative life in nature. Whether in a peaceful or chaotic environment, the Taoist seeks to find the still center, save energy for those times when action is needed, and take a humble, quiet approach to life. Things of importance to the worldly are seen as having little value. Chuang-tzu even goes to some lengths to point out that it is the useless who survive; the tree which is good for nothing does not get chopped down.

> *Sweet music and highly seasoned food*
> *Entertain for a while,*
> *But the clear, tasteless water from the well*
> *Gives life and energy without exhaustion.*
>
> *Lao-tzu*[13]

SPIRITUAL ALCHEMY   Flowing with Tao is easy and natural. But paradoxically, it is based on masterful spiritual discipline. Lao-tzu describes the appearance of mastery:

> *The ancient Masters were profound and subtle.*
> *Their wisdom was unfathomable. . . .*
> *They were careful*
> *as someone crossing an iced-over stream.*
> *Alert as a warrior in enemy territory.*
> *Courteous as a guest.*
> *Fluid as melting ice.*
> *Shapable as a block of wood.*
> *Receptive as a valley.*
> *Clear as a glass of water.*[14]

Sites for Taoist and Buddhist temples in China were traditionally chosen according to the ancient art of feng-shui, or geomancy, the awareness of the presence and movement of natural energies. The energies of waterfalls and mountains were considered conducive to spiritual practices. (Buddhist Temple Amid Clearing Mountain Peaks, *Northern Sung, c. 940–967* CE.)

The mastery to which Taoist writers refer is the result of powerful ascetic practices traditionally passed down secretly from teacher to pupil. These teachers lived in the mountains; Taoist teachers are said to be still hidden in the remote mountains of China and Korea. In Korea, for instance, early in the twentieth century a young boy named Chung Sahn reportedly encountered a strange man in the mountains who said, "If I teach you to break stones, will you follow me?" Curious, the boy agreed, and the teacher, Chung Woon Tosa, did indeed break stones with his fingers. Chung Sahn lived with him and his teacher for twenty years as an ascetic until he was told to return to civilization, for it was time to share the arts with the general public. He returned to Seoul, where he opened schools of Kouk Sun Do ("The Highest [Mountain] Way") practice now attended by thousands of Koreans, often for self-healing. Some of the instructors he trained have spread the teaching to other countries. In 1984, Chung Sahn himself withdrew again to the mountains to the ascetic life of a Doist hermit.

The aim of the ascetic practices is to unify spiritually dedicated human beings with the universe by working with the mind and body. Within our body is the spiritual microuniverse of the "three treasures": generative force *(ching)*, vitality *(ch'i)*, and spirit *(shen)* [*chong, ki,* and *shin* in Korean]. Using breath and the subtle energy channels in the body, the practitioner builds a reservoir of *ching* energy in the "cauldron" several inches below the navel, whence it rises up the spine as a vapor, transmuted into *ch'i* energy. *Ch'i* is in turn transmuted into *shen* in an upper cauldron in the head (an area similar to the Third Eye of Indian yogic practice), drops down to illuminate the heart center, and then descends to an inner area of the lower cauldron. There it forms what is called the Immortal Fetus, which adepts can raise through the Heavenly Gate at the top of the head and thus leave their physical body for various purposes, including preparation for life after death. Along the way, the adept learns to draw the *ch'i* of the macrouniverse of heaven and earth into the microuniverse of the body, unifying and harmonizing inner and outer, heaven and earth. This can only occur if the "three treasures" are brought to a state of serenity, of voidness, through which they return to the "one source."

> *The secret of the magic of life consists in using action in order to attain non-action.*
> *The Secret of the Golden Flower*[15]

This process, called *ch'i-gung*, takes many years to complete. It is described in two esoteric manuscripts that have now been translated into Western languages: *Hsin Ming Fa Chueh Ming Chih* ("The Secrets of Cultivating Essential Nature and Eternal Life"), written down by a Taois Master born in 1860 (translated as *Taoist Yoga* by Lu K'uan Yu), and *T'ai I Chin Hua Tsung Chih* ("The Secret of the Golden Flower"), transmitted orally in China until its first printing in the eighteenth century. The latter was translated into German by Richard Wilhelm in 1929, with a foreword by Carl Jung. The language is often that of alchemy, of transforming base metals to gold, but the references are to the potential for transforming the human body into a vehicle for the spirit.

One of the goals of esoteric Taoist practice is to separate the spirit from the body so that the former can operate independently, both before and after death.

THE LURE OF IMMORTALITY   Taoist secrets have long been sought after by those desiring physical longevity or spiritual immortality. Chuang-tzu had counseled indifference to birth and death: "The Master came because it was time. He left because he followed the natural flow. Be content with the moment, and be willing to follow the flow."[16] In Chapter 33 of the *Tao-te Ching*, Lao-tzu referred enigmatically to some kind of immortality or long life realized through spiritual death of the individual self. The goal of spiritual alchemy is to transmute the body and mind into selfless vehicles for the eternal. However, as Professor Huai-Chin Nan puts it, people who are interested in Taoist practices:

> *usually forget the highest principles, or the basis of philosophical theory behind the cultivation of Tao and the opening of the* ch'i *routes for longevity. . . . Longevity consists of*

maintaining one's health, slowing down the ageing process, living without illness and pain, and dying peacefully without bothering other people. Immortality does not mean indefinite physical longevity; it indicates the eternal spiritual life. [17]

A quiet contemplative life in natural surroundings, with sexual abstinence, peaceful mind, health-maintaining herbs, practices to strengthen the inner organs and open the meridians (subtle energy pathways known to Chinese doctors), and *ch'i-gung* breath practices to transmute vital energy into spiritual energy, does seem to bring a marked tendency to longevity. Chinese literature and folk knowledge contain many references to venerable sages thought to be centuries old. They live hidden in the mountains, away from society, and are said to be somewhat translucent. Their age is difficult to verify. The Chinese sage Li Ch'ing Yuen claimed that he was two hundred and fifty years old, shortly before he died early in the twentieth century, apparently from the effects of being exposed to "civilization." The most famous of the legendary long-lived are the Eight Immortals, humans who were said to have gained immortality, each with his or her own special magical power.

Another way of flowing with Tao, and thereby living long and effectively, is the body-centered practice of *T'ai-chi chuan*. Of unknown origin, it appeared in China many centuries ago as a martial art and is still practiced daily by many Chinese at dawn and dusk for their health. It looks like slow swimming in the air, with continual circular movement through a series of dance-like postures. They are ideally manifestations of the unobstructed flow of *ch'i* through the body. According to the *T'ai-chi Ch'uan Classics*, "In any action the entire body should be light and agile and all of its parts connected like pearls on a thread." [18] *Ch'i* is cultivated internally but not expressed externally as power. In combat, the practitioner of T'ai-chi is advised to "yield at your opponent's slightest pressure and adhere to him at his slightest retreat," [19] using mental alertness to subtle changes rather than muscular strength in order to gain the advantage.

Al Huang embodies the fluidity of Tai-chi chuan, practiced both for physical health and for teaching the mind to flow with change so that action is effortless.

LIVING TAOISM:
An interview with Master Hyunmoon Kim

Hyunmoon Kim is a teacher of Taoist practices known in Korea as Kouk Sun Do. His teacher is said to have been trained by elderly Taoist recluses in the mountains.

"In Korea, we believe that five to seven thousand years ago, Korea covered over half of China, from the southern part of Siberia. We think we migrated to Korea as ancient China attacked Korea, so we started to lose territory. We didn't call it Korea; it was many tribes. We think that Taoist history started in one of these tribes, with a chief of a tribe. A chief of the tribe has to have some kind of power, not just inheritance from the parents. This Taoist tradition descended from this chief of the tribe; they basically practiced breathing meditation. We think this was about seven to eight thousand years ago.

For a long time, Korea has forgotten these Taoist traditions and teachings. Foreign religions have dominated for a long time. But we heard the legends: When you go to a mountain there's some supernaturally powerful person there, and if you practice for years you also learn how to control the energy. In Korea, fortunately or unfortunately, there was no opportunity for Taoism to become a religion with a priesthood. Only a few people, and they stayed in the mountains. Almost one teacher for one student. They stayed in the mountains, in caves, with just nature life and nature food. The traditional diet is pine tree leaves and roots.

My teacher, Chung Sahn, learned this Taoist tradition and practice from two hermits, his teacher and his teacher's teacher. [He spent] twenty years in the mountains, quite isolated from society. He brought the arts into the city, for his teacher's teacher wanted to publicize them to the people. [He thought] this is the time, people need this art, and people will understand.

Still for Korean people, unless they experience this art – not written material – even though they start to believe now, they still resist. They don't want it for spiritual reasons; the biggest reason is for healing. They start with that, and once they're healed, they realize, 'Oh, there is some spiritual reasoning here.'

One of the characteristics of Taoist practices is to treat the body as priority. We want the physical body to survive forever. Through the practice we make our body as gold, alchemically.

In order to find the truth, there are two ways of approach, two opposite poles. One side is you really live in this crazy and hectic life, and that's one of the possibilities to find nature. Everything is nature; we try to find the five elements inside our body. The five elements are the inner organs, and once you open the channels, you clearly see how they work together. This is the real nature – not necessarily trees and the outside world. The other one is the totally serene life. You can be able to find the real nature either way. It depends on your system, your background, your inheritance, former life. Nobody knows unless you practice.

Reading scriptures is not part of our Korean system. The *Tao-te Ching*, of course, comes from the practice. So if you practice you don't really need a *Tao-te Ching*. You will learn these things. Basically what the Taoists always say, how we learn from nature, is the balance between yin and yang, right in the middle. The whole system works with the balance."

T'ai-chi is also a physical way of becoming one with the eternal interlocking of yin and yang, and of movement and stillness. T'ai-chi master Al Chung-liang Huang says:

Think of the contrasting energies moving together and in union, in harmony, interlocking, like a white fish and a black fish mating. If you identify with only one side of the duality, then you become unbalanced. . . . Movement and stillness become one. One is not a static point. One is a moving one, one is a changing one, one is everything. One is also that stillness suspended, flowing, settling, in motion.[20]

Despite the development of these techniques for body-mind harmony with Tao, the desire for shortcuts to longevity has persisted from ancient times to the present. From aristocrats to peasants, the Chinese people sought to prolong life through the advice and potions of Taoist alchemists. Some of them have been frauds; others have taken the allegorical references to spiritual alchemy literally, trying to compound actual chemical formulas to make the body immortal. These efforts persist. In 1988 "Laoshan Taoist Beverage" went into mass production. The secret brew's lifespan-lengthening formula is said to have been guarded by the chief priest of Mount Laoshan for a thousand years.

Tao-chiao: Taoist religion

Within the umbrella of what scholars call "Taoism" there are also several religious sects, *Tao-chiao*, that developed somewhat independently of *Tao-chia*. They are characterized by belief in numerous gods and ancestral spirits, magic-making, ritual, and the aid of priests.

Although practices such as alchemy, faith-healing, sorcery, and the use of power objects seem to have existed from ancient times in China, their conversion into organized religion apparently dates from the first-century CE efforts of Chang Tao Ling. He was a Taoist philosopher, alchemist, and magician. Mahayana Buddhism was growing in popularity in China, and Chang Tao Ling and his successors are said to have borrowed the appeal of its colorful mythology of gods, its rituals, and its magical practices. They played up existing indigenous Chinese beliefs in feared demons, gods, and ancestor spirits, added priestly rituals, and soon had followers contributing grain (thus the label, "Five Bushels of Rice Religion") to support Taoist priests. They were at times politically powerful. Successors to Chang Tao Ling were called "Celestial Masters," a line that has been maintained for seventeen centuries, but now in Taiwan rather than mainland China.

In contrast to the namelessness of original Tao, religious Taoism followed the ancient practice of acknowledging certain deceased humans as deities. Lao-tzu and the Yellow Emperor were both said to have ascended into the heavens and were worshipped as heavenly immortals. Indeed, anybody who had created anything thought to be of great benefit to society or who died in a war for the country was elevated to the status of *Shen,* or god. At the top of this burgeoning pantheon were the Three Pure Ones: rulers of the past, present, and future. The *Jade Emperor,* god of the present, was considered the heavenly partner of the earthly emperor, whose power thus incorporated the claim of divine help.

In addition to reverence for heaven, the early reverence for nature – mountains, rivers, animals, plants, stars, constellations, sun and moon – was also expressed in Taoist religion. Each mountain and river was thought to be governed by a special god who meditated there. At one time, almost every mountain in China had either a Taoist or Buddhist temple on it. As we have seen, ancestors were also worshipped as godlike spirits who could help the living, if properly treated.

All this changed with the death of the imperial tradition in the nineteenth and early twentieth centuries and then the revolution that ultimately established the current Communist government. It does not claim to draw its authority from the gods. On the contrary, it has at times acted rigorously to uproot what it considers backward, unscientific, and wealth-stealing superstitions. Schoolchildren are taught to glorify the state and the common cause, rather than the supernatural. During the Cultural Revolution of 1966 to 1976, zealous young Red Guards destroyed Taoist, Buddhist, and Confucian temples and books.

In recent years a certain freedom of religion was allowed once again, although the future is uncertain after the brutal crackdown in 1989 on those seeking more political freedom. Some temples are maintained as historic sites, and the old people still make pilgrimages to sacred Taoist mountain temples. Temples are popular tourist attractions both for Chinese and foreigners. A revival of interest in religion had begun before the 1989 massacres, but generations educated to believe that religion is simply illusion may not change their minds.

In Chinese communities elsewhere, such as Taiwan and Hong Kong, Taoist priests and priestesses still perform ceremonies for private families, such as rituals designed to purge sins at death and thus thwart punishment by the gods. They use water, incense, music, whips, and invocations to the gods to exorcize evil presences from homes and in public ceremonies held at the beginning of November. In August, they join with

Left *Taoist priest.*
Right *Taoist religion is still practiced in non-communist Chinese areas. These people are worshipping at the Matsu Yen Tao Temple in Anping, Taiwan.*

Buddhist priests in a festival designed to feed the hungry ghosts and allow the drunken ghosts to escape from the rivers into which they have fallen. Taoist priests are also sought for their skills in foretelling the future by various divination methods, predecessors of the ubiquitous fortune cookies offered globally by Chinese restaurants.

Individuals also carry on certain ceremonies without priests, such as the farewell party for the god of the kitchen on January 23 or 24, near the end of the Chinese year. In hopes that the god of the kitchen, who sits in the corner watching what the family does, will speak well of them in his annual report to the Jade Emperor, families offer sweets, incense, and paper horses, with the prayer, "When you go to heaven you should report only good things, and when you come down from heaven you should protect us and bring peace and safety to us."[21]

Confucianism – perfect virtue

The period when Lao-tzu supposedly lived, the sixth century BCE, was a spiritual high point in many cultures. It roughly coincided with the life of the Buddha, the Persian empire, the Golden Age of Athens, the great Hebrew prophets, and in China, with the life of another stellar figure. Westerners call him Confucius and his teaching Confucianism; his name was Kung Fu-tzu ("Master K'ung," his family name) and Chinese call his teaching *Juchiao*, "the religion of the scholar."

This philosophy became highly influential in China as the central faith of the ruling class and still permeates the society despite great political changes. For two thousand years Taoism, Buddhism, and Confucianism co-existed in China, contributing mutally to the culture. Like the teachings of Taoists and the Buddha, the philosophy of Confucius was eventually converted into a religion of sorts.

Master K'ung's life

Young Ch'iu K'ung was born in approximately 551BCE, during the Chou dynasty, into a family whose ancestors had been prominent in the previous dynasty. They had lost their position through political struggles, and Ch'iu's father, a soldier, died when the boy was only three years old. Although young Ch'iu was determined to be a scholar, the family's financial straits necessitated his taking public service jobs to earn a living. His responsibilities included such humble work as overseeing granaries and livestock. He married at the age of nineteen and had at least two children.

Ch'iu's mother died when he was twenty-three, sending him into three years of mourning. During this period he lived ascetically and studied ancient ceremonial rites *(li)* and imperial institutions. When he returned to social interaction, he gained some renown as a teacher of li and of the arts of governing.

It was a period of political chaos, with the stability of the early Chou dynasty having given way to disorder. Feudal lords held more power than kings of the central court, ministers assassinated their rulers, and sons killed their fathers. Confucius felt that a return to classical standards of virtue was the only way out of the chaos, and he earnestly but unsuccessfully sought rulers who would listen to his ideas.

Confucius turned to a different approach: training young men to be wise and altruistic public servants. He instructed them in the "Six Classics" of China's cultural heritage: the I Ching, poetry, history, rituals, music and dance, and the Spring and Autumn Annals of events in his state, Lu. According to tradition, it was Confucius who edited older documents pertaining to these six areas and who put them into the form now known as the *Confucian Classics*. There are now only five; the treatises on music were either destroyed or never existed. Of his role, Confucius claimed only:

> *I am a transmitter and not a creator. I believe in and have a passion for the ancients.* [22]

Although great value was later placed on study of the Confucian Classics in China, Confucius's work and teachings were considered relatively insignificant during his lifetime. After his death in 479 BCE, his emphasis on virtue and scholarship gradually predominated over the mysticism of other philosophies. By the second century BCE Confucianism was declared the national creed and the Confucian Classics were the basic wisdom studied and discussed by scholars and government officials. The life of the gentleman-scholar devoted to proper government became the highest ideal. Eventually temples were devoted to the worship of Confucius himself as the model for unselfish public service, human kindness, and scholarship.

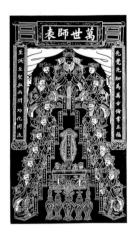

Confucianism idealized gentleman scholars, who became the highest class in China until the 20th-century revolution.

The Confucian virtues

Foremost among the virtues that Confucius felt could save society was *jen*. Translations of this central term include innate goodness, love, benevolence, perfect virtue, and human-heartedness. At one point he defined it as a matter of reciprocity (later called The Golden Rule in the Christian tradition). Confucius said: "Do not do to others what you would not want others to do to you." [23]

Rulers were enjoined to rule not by physical force but by the example of personal virtue:

> *Confucius said: "If a ruler himself is upright, all will go well without orders. But if he himself is not upright, even though he gives orders they will not be obeyed . . . One who governs by virtue is comparable to the polar star, which remains in its place while all the stars turn towards it."* [24]

Asked to define the essentials of strong government, Confucius listed adequate troops, adequate food, and the people's confidence. But of these, troops are least important, he said, followed by food. The only true necessity is that the people have faith in their rulers. To earn this faith, the ruling class should "cultivate themselves," leading lives of virtue and decorum. They should continually adhere to *jen*, always reaching upward, cherishing what is right, rather than reaching downward for material gain.

The ideogram for *jen* is a combination of "two" and "man," conveying the idea of relationship. In a patriarchal society, those relationships emphasized by Confucius referred to males – filial piety and brotherly love:

> *A youth should be filial at home, and fraternal when abroad. He should be earnest and sincere; he should show an affection for all and be disposed towards* jen. [25]

In Confucius's ideal world, there is a hierarchy in which each knows his place and respects those above him. Social order is based on this system of conduct according to status: "Let the prince be prince, the minister be minister, the father father and the son son." [26] Social order begins in the family and then extends to society, expressed as the virtues of loyalty and altruism.

Confucius also supports the ancient Chinese custom of ancestor veneration, as an extension of filial piety:

Filial piety is the force that continues the purposes and completes the affairs of our forefathers . . . To gather in the same place where they earlier have gathered; to perform the same ceremonies which they earlier have performed; to play the same music which they earlier have played; to pay respect to those whom they honored; to love those who were dear to them; in fact, to serve those now dead as if they were living, and those now departed as if they were with us still. This is the highest achievement of filial piety. [27]

Confucius said relatively little about the supernatural, preferring to focus on the here-and-now: "While you are not able to serve men, how can you serve the ghosts and spirits?" [28] He made a virtue of *li* (the rites honoring ancestors and deities), but with the cryptic suggestion that one make the sacrifices "as if" the spirits were present. According to some interpreters, he encouraged the rites as a way of establishing earthly harmony through reverent, ethical behavior. The rites should not be empty gestures; he recommended that they be outwardly simple and inwardly grounded in jen.

Divergent followers of Confucius

The Confucian tradition has been added to by many later commentators. Two of the most significant were Mencius and Hsun Tzu, who differed in their approach.

A little over a hundred years after Confucius died, the "Second Sage" Meng Tzu (commonly latinized to Mencius) was born. During his lifetime Chinese society became even more chaotic. Like his predecessor, the Second Sage tried to share his wisdom with embattled rulers, but to no avail. He, too, took up teaching, based on his studies of stabilizing aspects of the earlier feudal system.

Mencius's major addition to the Confucian tradition was his focus on the virtue of *yi*, or righteous conduct. It begins at the top. Mencius emphasized the moral duty of rulers to govern by the principle of humanity and the good of the people. If rulers are guided by profit motives, this self-centered motivation will be reflected in subordinates all down the line and social chaos will ensue. On the other hand, "When a commiserating government is conducted from a commiserating heart, one can rule the whole empire as if one were turning it in one's palm." [29] This is a natural way, says Mencius, for people are naturally good: "The tendency of human nature to do good is like that of water to flow downward." [30] Heaven could be counted on to side with the righteous, empowering their good cause.

Another follower quite disagreed with this assessment. This was Hsun Tzu, who seemingly was born when Mencius was an old man, and whose life as a would-be reformer resembled that of his predecessors. He argued that human nature is naturally evil and that heaven is impersonal, operating according to natural laws rather than intervening on the side of good government or responding to human wishes ("Heaven does not suspend the winter because men dislike cold. . . ." [31]). Humans must hold up their own end. Their natural tendency, however, is to envy, to hate, and to desire personal gain and sensual pleasure. The only way to constrain these tendencies is to teach and legally enforce the rules of *li* (rites and rules of decorum) and *yi* (guides to righteous conduct). Though naturally flawed, humans can gradually attain sagehood by persistent study, patience, and good works and thereby form a cooperative triangle with heaven and earth.

Although Hsun Tzu's careful reasoning eventually lost ground to Mencius's idealism, their points of agreement are basic to Confucianism: perfect virtue is of great value; humans can attain it; and study and emulation of the ancient sages and rulers are the path to harmony in the individual, family, state, and world. This scholar's approach is quite different from Taoism, in which not-doing and emptiness are cultivated as the path to Tao.

Confucianism as a state cult

During the Han dynasty (205 BCE to 220 CE) Confucius's teachings were at last honored by the state. The Han scholar Tung Chung-shu set up the educational system based on the Confucian Classics that lasted until the twentieth century. He used Confucian ideals to unite the people behind the ruler, also noting that the ruler himself should be subject to Heaven. Despite ups and downs in official favor, Confucius himself was elevated to the status of a savior and worshipped in special temples by those of the scholar class. Apocryphal stories were told about his divine conception and birth – very similar to those told about the Buddha – and the divine mandate for his teachings.

Although Confucius had counseled the restrained use of li, a tenth-century CE Sung dynasty revival of Confucianism (which Western scholars call "neo-Confucianism" and Chinese "the Sung learning") developed with a great emphasis on religious ritual and sacrifice. These were thought to preserve harmony between humans, heaven, and earth. At the family level, offerings were made to propitiate the family ancestors. Government officials were responsible for ritual sacrifices to beings such as the gods of fire, literature, cities, mountains, waters, the polar star, sun, moon, and former rulers, as well as spirits of the earth and sky.

The most important ceremonies were performed by the emperor, to give thanks and ask blessings from heaven, earth, gods of the land and agriculture, and the dynastic ancestors. Of these, the highest ritual was the elaborate annual sacrifice to Shang Ti at the white marble Altar of Heaven by the emperor. He was considered Son of Heaven, the "high priest of the world." Both he and his retinue prepared themselves by three days of fasting and keeping vigil. In a highly reverent atmosphere, he then sacrificed a bull, offered precious jade, and sang prayers of gratitude to the Supreme, such as this one:

> With reverence we spread out these precious stones and silk, and, as swallows rejoicing in the spring, praise Thy abundant love ... Men and creatures are emparadised, O Ti, in Thy love. All living things are indebted to Thy goodness, but who knows whence his blessings come to him? It is Thou alone, O Lord, who art the true parent of all things. [32]

The performance of rituals was a time-consuming major part of government jobs, carried out on behalf of the people. But as China gradually opened to the West, beginning in the seventeenth century, a reaction set in against these old sacred ways. The New Culture movement of the 1920s Republic glorified science and social progress, and the last of the imperial dynasties was overthrown. Under the Communist regime established in 1949, Communism took the place of religion, attempting to transform the

society by secular means "into a world of light that never existed before." Party Chairman Mao tse-Tung was venerated almost as a god, with the little red book of quotations from Chairman Mao replacing the Confucian Classics.

During the Cultural Revolution (1966-1976), Confucianism was attacked as one of the "Four Olds" — old ideas, culture, customs, and habits. The Cultural Revolution attempted to destroy the hierarchical structure that Confucianism had idealized and prevent the intellectual elite from ruling over the masses. Contrary to the Confucian virtue of filial piety, young people even denounced their parents at public trials, and scholars were made objects of derision. An estimated one million people were attacked. Some were killed; some committed suicide.

Mao said that he had hated Confucius from his childhood. What he so disliked was the intellectual emphasis on study of the Classics and on rituals. But in some respects, Confucian morality continued to form the basis of Chinese ethics. Communist ideology subordinates the individual to the group, as Confucius had advocated. Mao particularly emphasized the (Confucian) virtues of selfless service to the people and of self-improvement for the public good:

All our cadres, whatever their rank, are servants of the people, and whatever we do is to serve the people. How then can we be reluctant to discard any of our bad traits?[33]

For decades, Communist China prided itself on being the most law-abiding country in the world. The streets were safe, and tourists found that if they could not understand the currency, they could trust taxi drivers to take the exact amount, and no more, from their open wallets. But recently there has been a rapid rise in crime and official corruption. The society has changed abruptly since China opened its doors to the West in 1978, undermining traditional Confucian virtues. The government blames the influx of materialistic values, from undiscriminating embrace of the underside of Western culture and the rapid shift toward a free market economy. In early 1989, Zhao Ziyang, then Communist Party leader, urged officials to maintain Confucian discipline (without naming it that) in the midst of the changes: "The Party can by no means allow its members to barter away their principles for money and power."[34] But when the people picked up this cry, ageing leaders chose brutally to suppress popular calls for greater democracy and an end to official corruption; they did so in the name of another Confucian-like virtue: order in society.

With the fall of Mao and before him, Confucius, on what can the contemporary appeal for honesty and selfless service be based? After two thousand years of ascendency, Confucius's teachings are no longer the primary texts of schoolchildren and scholars. They may only encounter his teachings as college students if they happen to major in the study of Chinese philosophy or literature. Only a few old Confucian priests remain from the old days, and they live mainly in the countryside.

One solution of the government has been to idolize citizens whose behaviors reflect Confucian virtues, holding them up as models for others. Chinese newspapers frequently carry contemporary stories about selfless public servants, such as Yuan Jingliang. He is a doctor at a time when that profession earns little money in return for long hours of hard work. *China Daily* describes him and his work in ways that still reflect the idealization of Confucian virtues:

> *Tall, thin, and with glistening, kind eyes, Yuan, 50, looks the model of the Chinese intellectual of his generation. . . .*
>
> *Yuan doesn't take advantage of the loopholes in the hospital's administration, common in hospitals, to loaf on the job. He makes his rounds conscientiously, always looking to his patients' needs. He generally finds time for a comforting word or two.*
>
> *''His voice is always so gentle and his face looks caring and sympathetic,'' said Wu Qihong [a patient].*[35]

As for Confucian religion, philosopher Peimin Ni speculates that there may be a return of religious sentiment in his country:

> *Now they don't have Mao tse Tung as a god, and they've got to have something to believe. Many young people may fall into Taoist or Confucian beliefs because they already have deep roots in Chinese culture. That makes it easier to believe in the pursuit of a long life, to believe that there are other worlds with gods as models for this life.*[36]

In Japan, Confucianism survives as an ethical system. It was imported during the sixth and seventh centuries CE as a way of harmoniously unifying the Japanese tribes into a centralized empire. Although the central government eroded, the ethics of the system lived on, and were re-invigorated with an infusion of neo-Confucianist thought during the seventeenth to early nineteenth centuries. The arguments for the primacy of the imperial family were carried to an extreme under the Meiji regime, which emphasized loyalty to the emperor and to the nation and led Japan into a devastating role in World War II. But Confucian idealization of education, order, duty, earnestness, and public-mindedness still permeate the Japanese culture and are particularly prominent in business, in which the Japanese excel. Japanese politics, however, have been rocked by claims that many top leaders accepted bribes, so when Uno Sosuke took over as Prime Minister in 1989, it was with this appeal to Confucian ideals: "I would like to make the party clean, and thus restore the trust of the people."[37]

Suggested reading

de Bary, William Theodore, Chan, Wing-tsit, and Watson, Burton, eds., *Sources of Chinese Tradition*, New York: Columbia University Press, 1960. Useful commentaries and extensive texts from Confucian and Taoist schools.

Chai, Ch'u, and Chai, Winberg, *Confucianism*, Woodbury, New York: Barron's Educational Series, 1973. An accessible historical view of Confucian tradition, ancient and contemporary.

Chai, Ch'u, and Chai, Winberg, eds. and trans., *The Sacred Books of Confucius and other Confucian Classics*, New Hyde Park, New York: University Books, 1965. Useful introduction and selected texts.

Chung-yuan, Chang, *Creativity and Taoism*, New York: Harper Colophon Books, 1963. An exquisite inside view of Taoism, through quiet, poetic, and sensitive exploration of Chinese art, poetry, and Taoist and Ch'an Buddhist philosophy.

Feng, Gia-Fu, and English, Jane, trans., *Chuang-tsu: Inner Chapters*, New York: Vintage Books, 1974. A classic energetic, humorous exposition of Taoist principles, accompanied in this translation by photographs that help one enter the essence of Tao.

The I Ching, translated into German by Richard Wilhelm and thence into English by Cary Baynes, third edition, Princeton, New Jersey: Princeton University Press, 1967. Fascinating insights into the multiple possibilities of the interplay of yin and yang in our lives.

The Secret of the Golden Flower, translated by Richard Wilhelm into German and thence into English by Cary Baynes, New York: Harcourt Brace Jovanovich, 1962, and London: Arkana, 1984. An esoteric explanation of Taoist spiritual alchemy, with psychological commentary by Carl Jung.

Tao-te Ching, attributed to Lao-tzu, available in numerous translations, including the popular English translation by Lin Yutang: *The Wisdom of Laotse*, New York: Modern Library, 1948. Reading several translations of this short book of wisdom helps one to experience the essence of the Taoist teachings, which defy literal translation.

Thompson, Laurence G., *Chinese Religion*, fourth edition, Belmont, California: Wadsworth Publishing Company, 1989. A well-organized, clear presentation of the many strands of religion in China.

7 SHINTO

The way of the Kami

Japan has embraced many religions that originated in other countries, but it also developed its own unique path: Shinto. It is an organized version of the indigenous religion of the country, closely tied to nature and the unseen world. Of those modern Japanese who are religious, many combine practices from several religions, for each offers something different. Confucianism informs organizations and ethics, Buddhism and Christianity offer ways of understanding suffering and the afterlife, traditional veneration of ancestors links the living to their family history, and Shinto harmonizes people with the natural world.

The core of Shinto

Shinto has no founder, no orthodox canon of sacred literature. It seems to have begun as the local religion of agricultural communities and had no name until Buddhism was imported in the sixth century CE. To distinguish the indigenous Japanese way from the foreign one, the former was labeled "shin" (divine being) "do" (way). During one period it was used by the central government to inspire nationalism, but since the forced separation of church and state after World War II Shinto has quietly returned to its roots. They can be described through three central aspects of the path: affinity with natural beauty, harmony with the spirits, and purification rituals.

LOVE OF NATURAL BEAUTY   Before industrial pollution and urbanization, Japan was a country of exquisite natural beauty, and to a certain extent, it still is. The islands marry mountains to sea, and the interiors are laced with streams, waterfalls, and lush forests. Even the agriculture is beautiful, with flowering fruit trees and terraced fields. The people lived so harmoniously with this environment that they had no separate word for "nature" until they began importing modern Western ideas late in the nineteenth century.

Living close to nature, the people experienced life as a continual process of change and renewal. They organized their lives around the turn of the seasons, honoring the roles of the sun, moon, and lightning in their rice farming. Mount Fuji, greatest of the volcanic peaks that formed the islands, was honored as the sacred embodiment of the divine creativity that had thrust the land up from the sea. The sparkling ocean and rising sun so visible along the extensive coastlines were loved as earthly expressions of the sacred purity and brightness at the heart of life.

The Japanese people have traditionally honored the natural beauty of their land and have considered Mt. Fuji to be its most sacred peak. Pilgrims have long made the arduous climb up Fuji seeking purification and good fortune.

> *To be fully alive is to have an aesthetic perception of life because a major part of the world's goodness lies in its often unspeakable beauty.*
>
> *Rev. Yukitaka Yamamoto, Shinto priest*[1]

Although industrialization and urbanization have blighted some of the natural landscape, the sensitivity to natural beauty survives in small-scale arts. In traditional rock gardening, flower arranging, the tea ceremony, and poetry, Japanese artists continue to honor the simple and natural. If a rock is placed just right in a garden, it seems alive, radiating its natural essence. In a tea ceremony, great attention is paid to each natural sensual delight, from the purity of water poured from a wooden ladle to the genuineness of the clay vessels. These arts are often linked with Zen Buddhism, but the sensitivities seem to derive from the ancient Japanese ways.

HONORING THE KAMI   Surrounded by natural beauty, the Japanese people found the divine all around them. In Shinto, the sacred is both immanent and transcendent. In Japanese mythology, the divine originated as one essence:

> *In primeval ages, before the earth was formed, amorphous matter floated freely about like oil upon water. In time there arose in its midst a thing like a sprouting reedshoot, and from this a deity came forth of its own.*[2]

This deity gave birth to many *kami*, or spirits, two of whom were told to organize the material world. Standing on the Floating Bridge of Heaven, they stirred the ocean with a jeweled spear. When they pulled it out of the water, it dripped brine back into the ocean, where it coagulated into eight islands, with mountains, rivers, plants, and trees (these may be interpreted either as Japan or the whole world). To rule this earthly kingdom they created the kami Amaterasu, Goddess of the Sun.

Although the word *kami* (a way of pronouncing the character "shih") is usually translated as "god" or "spirit," these translations are not exact. *Kami* can be either singular or plural, for the word refers to a single essence manifesting in many places. Rather than evoking an image, like the Hindu or Mahayana Buddhist god-idols, *kami* refers to a quality. It means that which evokes wonder and awe in us. The kami harmonize heaven and earth and also guide the solar system and the cosmos. It/they tend to reside in beautiful or powerful places, such as mountains, certain trees, rocks, waterfalls, whirlpools, and animals. In addition, it/they manifest as wind, rain, thunder, or lightning. Some humans also have kami-nature. Kami also appears in abstract forms, such as the creativity of growth and reproduction.

Recognizing the presence of kami, humans have built shrines to honor it/them. There are even now approximately eighty thousand Shinto shrines in Japan. Some honor kami protecting the area; some honor kami with special responsibilities, such as protecting crops from insects. The shrines are situated on sites thought to have been chosen by the kami for their sacred atmosphere. At one time, every community had its

Shinto shrines are set apart by a torii, an ever-open sacred gateway at the entrance to all shrine precincts. This floating torii is the symbolic gate to Itsukushima Jjinja shrine, Miyajima.

own guardian kami, and the people maintained and worshipped at their local shrine, going there to make offerings of food to the kami and to ask for their help. One way of doing so is to write the request on a wooden prayer tablet and hang it on a tree – or today, a board with many hooks. Thirty-two or -three days after an infant's birth, its parents take it to the shrine for the kami's blessing. Couples may also visit a shrine if they desire to conceive a child.

The kami are not necessarily pictured as forms, for at times Shintoism has been strongly iconoclastic. In the eighteenth century, for instance, a famous Shinto scholar wrote:

Never make an image in order to represent the Deity. To worship a deity is directly to establish a felt relation of our heart to the living Divinity through sincerity or truthfulness on our part. If we, however, try to establish a relation between Deity and man indirectly by means of an image, the image will itself stand in the way and prevent us from realizing our religious purpose to accomplish direct communion with the Deity. So an image made by mortal hands is of no use in Shinto worship. [3]

Within the most sacred part of a shrine, the only representation of the kami may be a mirror. It reflects the revered light of brightness and purity, considered the natural order of the universe. Some kami are represented by stones. Even more abstract, some shrines are completely empty at the center.

Followers of the way of the kami may also make daily offerings to the kami in their home. Their place of worship usually consists of a high shelf on which rests a miniature shrine, with only a mirror inside. The daily home ritual may begin with greeting the sun in the east with clapping and a prayer for protection for the household. Then offerings are placed before the shrine: rice for health, water for cleansing and preservation of life, and salt for the harmonious seasoning of life. When a new house is to be built, the blessings of the kami are ceremonially requested.

To acknowledge and follow the kami is to bring our life into harmony with nature, Shintoists feel. The word used for this concept is *kannagara*, which is the same word used for the movements of the sun, moon, stars, and planets. Yukitaka Yamamoto, 96th Chief Priest of the Tsubaki Grand Shrine, says kannagara could be translated as "Natural Religion":

The life of man is located in Daishizen, Great Nature, the vast cosmic setting into which we are born, where we live and within which our lives find any meaning. Natural Religion is the spontaneous awareness of the Divine that can be found in any culture. . . . The Spirit of Great Nature may be a flower, may be the beauty of the mountains, the pure snow, the soft rains or the gentle breeze. Kannagara means being in communion with these forms of beauty and so with the highest level of experiences of life. When people respond to the silent and provocative beauty of the natural order, they are aware of kannagara. When they respond in life in a similar way, by following ways "according to the kami," they are expressing kannagara in their lives. They are living according to the natural flow of the universe and will benefit and develop by so doing. [4]

PURIFICATION In traditional Shinto, there is no concept of sin. The world is beautiful and full of helpful spirits. Sexuality per se is not sinful; the world was created by mating deities, and people have traditionally bathed together communally in Japan. However, by evil behaviors humans can accumulate impurities that cover their original innocence

Modern Japanese visit Shinto shrines for many purposes, asking the blessings of kami on the patterns of their lives. Most Shinto shrines are built with an appreciation for simple natural materials, and the larger ones are periodically rebuilt with great ceremony.

and purity and offend the spirits.

The quality of impurity or misfortune is called *tsumi*. It can arise through unkind interaction between humans or between humans and the environment or through natural catastrophes. Followers of the way of the kami have various means of removing tsumi. One is paying attention to problems as they arise:

> *To live free of obstructing mists, problems of the morning should be solved in the morning and those of the evening should be solved by evening. Wisdom and knowledge should be applied like the sharpness of an axe to the blinding effect of the mists of obstruction. Then may the* kami *purify the world and free it of* tsumi.[5]

The kami of the high mountain rapids will carry the tsumi to the sea, where the whirlpool kami will swallow it and the wind kami will blow it to the netherworld, where kami of that place absorb and remove it.

> *After this has been completed, the heavenly* kami, *the earthly* kami *and the myriad of* kami *can recognise man as purified and everything can return to its original brightness, beauty and purity as before since all* tsumi *has wholly vanished from the world.*[6]

People may also be purified spontaneously by a kind of grace that washes over them, often in nature, bringing them into awareness of unity with the universe. Hitoshi Iwasaki, a young Shinto priest, says that he likes to look at the stars at night in the mountains where the air is clear:

> *When I am watching the thoroughly clear light of the stars, I get a pure feeling, like my mind being washed. I rejoice to think this is a spiritual Misogi [purification ritual] .... Master Mirihei Ueshiba, the founder of Aikido, is said to have looked upon the stars one night, suddenly realized he was united with the universe, and burst into tears, covering his face with his hands. We human beings, not only human beings but everything existing in this world, are one of the cells which form this great universe.* [7]

In addition to these personal ways of cleansing, there are ritual forms of purification. One is *oharai*, a ceremony commonly performed by Shinto priests which includes the waving of a piece of wood from a sacred tree, to which are attached white streamers (the Japanese version of the shaman's medicine fan of feathers or the Hindu yak-tail whisk, all used to sweep through the air and thus purify an area). This ceremony is today performed on cars and new buildings. A version used to soothe a kami who is upset by an impurity was called for in 1978 when there was a rash of suicides in a Tokyo housing complex by residents jumping off roofs.

The cleansing powers of water, plentiful in natural Japan, is often used. One may take a ritual bath in the ocean, source of life. Or, in a lengthy ritual called *misogi*, a believer may stand beneath a waterfall, letting its force hit the shoulders and carry impurities and tensions away. Before even entering the waterfall, those seeking purification must undergo preliminary purification practices because the waterfall itself is kami. The women put on white kimonos and headbands, the men white loincloths and headbands.

It is customary to ask a Shinto priest to ritually purify building sites so that the kami will consider them acceptable habitations. Even cars are sometimes purified.

The misogi ritual proceeds with shaking the soul by bouncing the hands up and down in front of the stomach, to help the person become aware of the soul's presence. Next comes a form of warm-up calisthenics called Bird Rowing. Following a leader, the participants then shout invocations that activate the soul, affirm the potential for realizing the infinite in one's own soul, and unify the people with the kami of earth, guidance, water, life, and the *ki* energy (which the Chinese know as *ch'i*).

Before entering the waterfall, the participants raise their metabolism and absorb as much ki as possible by practicing a form of deep breathing. They are sprinkled with purifying salt and are given sake to spray into the stream in three mouthfuls. The leader counts from one to nine, to symbolize the impurity of the mundane world and then cuts the air and shouts "Yei!" to dispel this impurity. With ritual claps and shouts the participants then enter the waterfall, continually chanting "Harae-tamae-Kiyome-tamae-ro-kon-sho-jo!" This phrase requests the kami to wash away all tsumi from the six elements that form the human being, from the senses, and from the mind. This part of the ritual has been scientifically proven to lower the blood pressure.

After this powerful practice, participants dry off, spend time in meditation to calm the soul, and share a ceremonial drink to unify themselves with the kami and with each other. The whole misogi ceremony is designed to restore one's natural purity and sense of mission in life. As Rev. Yamamoto explains:

> As imperfect beings, we often fail to recognize our mission. These failures come about because we have lost something of our natural purity. This is why purification, or misogi, is so central to Shinto. It enables man to cultivate spirituality and to restore his or her natural greatness.[8]

Buddhist and Confucian influences

Over time, the essence of Shinto has been blended with other religions imported into Japan. The two religions with which Shinto has been most blended are Buddhism, first introduced into Japan in the sixth century CE, and Confucianism, first imported early in the seventeenth century CE.

Buddhism is still practiced side-by-side with Shinto. The fact that their theologies differ so significantly has been accepted by the people as covering different kinds of situations. The Japanese often go to Shinto shrines for life-affirming events, such as conception, birth, and marriage, and to Buddhist temples for death rites. Shingon Buddhist monks tried long ago to convince the Japanese that the Shinto kami were actually Buddhist deities. The two religions were therefore closely interwoven in some people's minds until the Meiji government extricated its version of Shinto from Buddhism in the nineteenth century. But the parallel worship of the two paths continues, with some villages having stone monuments to the kami and statues of Nichiren placed next to each other.

As for Confucianism, seventeenth-century Japanese Confucian scholars attempted to free themselves from Buddhism and to tie the Chinese beliefs they were importing to the ancient Japanese ways. One, for instance, likened *li* to the way of the kami as a means of social cohesion. Another stressed reverence as the common ground of the two paths and was himself revered as a living kami. The neo-Confucianists' alliance with Shinto to throw off the yoke of Buddhism actually revived Shinto itself and made the ancient, somewhat amorphous tradition more self-conscious. Scholars began to study and interpret its teachings. The combination of Confucian emphasis on hierarchy and Shinto devotion helped pave the way for the establishment in 1868 of the powerful Meiji monarchy.

State Shinto

The Meiji regime distinguished Shinto from Buddhism and took steps to promote Shinto as the spiritual basis for the government. Shinto, amplifying the Japanese traditions of ancestor veneration, had long taught that the emperor was the offspring of Amaterasu, the Sun Goddess. *Naobi no Mitama* ("Divine Spirit of Rectification"), written in the eighteenth century, expressed this ideal:

> This great imperial land, Japan, is the august country where the divine ancestral goddess Amaterasu Omikami was born, a superb country. . . . Amaterasu deigned to entrust the country with the words, ''So long as time endures, for ten thousand autumns, this land shall be ruled by my descendants.''
>
> According to her divine pleasure, this land was decreed to be the country of the imperial descendants, without disturbances from harsh gods, without any unsubmissive person. It is a land where, for ten thousand autumns, to the end of time, the emperors, as descendants of Amaterasu Omikami, would make theirs the mind of the heavenly gods, so that even now, without deviation from the divine age, the land might continue in tranquility and in accord with the will of the kami, a country ruled in peace.[9]

It had been customary for the imperial family to visit the shrine to the Sun Goddess at Ise to consult the supreme kami on matters of importance. But the Emperor Meiji carried this tradition much farther. He decreed that the way of the kami should govern the nation. The way, as it was then interpreted, was labeled *State Shinto*. It was administered by government officials rather than bona fide Shinto priests, whose objections were silenced, and many of the ancient spiritual rituals were suppressed. State Shinto became the tool of militaristic nationalists as a way to enlist popular support for guarding the throne and expanding the empire.

By the time that Japan was defeated in World War II, the emperor Hirohito, Meiji's grandson, may have been little more than a ceremonial figurehead. But he had been held up as a god, not to be seen or touched by ordinary people. At the end of the war he officially declared himself human. The traditional spiritual Shinto, however, was left with the stigma built up by State Shinto. It was also confused with new religious sects that often had little to do with Shinto traditions but were nonetheless labeled *Sect Shinto* by the Meiji regime. These new sects will be considered separately in Chapter 13.

Shinto today

Japanese reaction to the horrors of the war and desire for modernization threatened to leave Shinto in the shadows of the past. As Hitoshi Iwasaki notes (see Interview), for a time it was difficult for young people to learn about Shintoism. But the shrines remain and are visited by over eighty million Japanese at New Year. People often visit more as tourists than as believers, but many say they experience a sense of spiritual renewal when they visit a shrine. Long-established households still have their kami shelf, often

LIVING SHINTO:
An interview with Hitoshi Iwasaki

Hitoshi Iwasaki is a young Shinto priest struggling to educate himself in the suppressed ancient ways of his people. He officiates at the new Shinto shrine in Stockton, California, and maintains close ties with its parent shrine in Japan, Tsubaki Grand Shrine in the Mie Prefecture, where a fine waterfall is used for misogi.

"We Japanese are very fortunate. We give gratitude for every natural phenomenon and we worship the mountain, we worship the river, we worship the sea, we worship the big rocks, waterholes, winds.

Unfortunately, after World War II, we were prohibited to teach the Shinto religion in schools. We never learned about Shinto at school. Many young Japanese know the story of Jesus Christ, but nothing about Shinto. The government is not against Shinto. [The silence comes from] newspapers, the media, and the teachers' union, because they were established just after World War II. They have a very left-wing mind [and associate Shinto with State Shinto]. Ordinary Japanese people don't link Shinto with politics nowadays, but the teachers' union and newspapers never give the side of religion, Shinto, or Japanese old customs.

Against this kind of atmosphere, we learned in the school that everything in Japan was bad. Shinto and Japanese customs were bad. Many young people are losing Japanese customs. But I went to Ise Shrine University, where I learned that Shinto is not just State Shinto. Some young people like me study Japanese things and they become super-patriots. That's the problem. No middle. Just super-left or super-right.

I learned Shinto partly by learning aikido. The founder was a very spiritual person who studied in one of the Shinto churches. In Shinto we don't have services, we don't preach, we don't do anything for people who want to be saved. But I want to introduce the idea of Shinto to the people of the United States and young Japanese and I can do it through aikido. I think I learned the way of nature through aikido practice. We are born as a child of kami, which means we are part of the universe, like a tree. People practice aikido not to fight but to be a friend, to unite.

In Japan some people are going to Shinto. They were all doing Zen before, but Zen is very difficult. In waterfall purification, no choice. Just standing under the waterfall.

My friend, a Shinto priest, went to the Middle East, in complete desert. He says it was difficult to explain Shinto. For them, nature is enemy. They have to fight nature.

In Japan we have water everywhere. Now the big rivers and streams are polluted. But people come to the shrines. Some are now vacation spots. People gather because this is a sacred place from ancient times where people come to pray. And other people want to go where people are gathered, so some of the shrines become vacation places, surrounded by souvenir shops. Many come to Shinto shrines and pray Buddhist prayers. Why not? Buddha is one of the kami. Everything has kami."

next to the Buddhist family altar, which combines tablets memorializing the dead with scrolls or statues dedicated to a manifestation of the Buddha.

Some Shintoists now explain their path as a universal natural religion, rather than an exclusively Japanese phenomenon, and try to explain the way of harmony with the kami to interested non-Japanese, without striving for conversions. A Shinto shrine has been built in California, offering ritual ways of experiencing one's connection with nature and learning to see the divine in the midst of life. Reverend Yamamoto, who travels around the world explaining the wisdom Shinto has to offer, in 1969 performed a two thousand-year-old ceremonial address to the kami at the United Nations Chapel in New York as a request for the well-being of humanity and the safeguarding of the Apollo moon flight. He explains:

> *Three brave men were flying to the moon for the purposes of peace and science. If the hearts and minds of these men were not united and pure, they could not succeed in their mission. There was nothing out of order in offering a proper prayer by a priest so that these men might leave the earth in a purified state.* [10]

In Japan, Shinto also survives as the basis for the seasonal holidays. These became exuberant affairs in which the people and the kami join in celebrating life. Many have an agricultural basis, insuring good crops and then giving thanks for them. Often the local kami is carried about the streets in a portable shrine.

Among the many local and national Japanese festivals with Shinto roots, one of the biggest is New Year's. It begins in December with ceremonial housecleaning, the placing of bamboo and pine "trees" at doorways of everything from homes to offices and bars to welcome the kami, dressing in traditional kimonos, and on December 31, there is a national day of purification. On New Year's day, people may go out to see the first sunrise of the year and will try to visit a shrine as well as friends and relatives.

Left *On November 15, or the nearest Sunday, boys of five and girls of three and seven dress up in traditional clothes and visit a Shinto shrine to pray for health and good fortune. This is called The Seven-Five-Three Festival or Shichi-go-san.*
Right *Contemporary Japanese often honor both the Shinto kami and dead relatives at their home shrines.*

Two ceremonies honor those reaching a certain age: On January 15, those who are twenty years old are recognized as full-fledged adults, and on November 15, children who are three, five, or seven years old (considered delicate ages) are taken to a shrine to ask for the protection of the kami. On February 3, the end of winter, people throw beans to toss out bad fortune and invite good, and at shrines the priests shoot arrows to break the power of misfortune. A month-long spring festival is held from March to April, with purification rites and prayers for a successful planting season. The month of June is devoted to rites to protect crops from insects, blights, and bad weather. Fall brings thanksgiving rites for the harvest, with the first fruits offered to the kami and then great celebrating in the streets.

Despite the fact that Japan is now one of the most technologically advanced countries in the world, with business its primary focus, there still seems to be a place for ritual — and in some cases, heart-felt — communion with the intangible kami that, in Shinto belief, permeate all of life.

Suggested reading

Hori, Ichiro, *Folk Religion in Japan*, Chicago and London: University of Chicago Press, 1968. A lively study of Japanese folk traditions such as shamanism and mountain worship which contributed to Shinto.

Kitagawa, Joseph M., *On Understanding Japanese Religion*, Princeton, New Jersey and Guildford, Surrey: Princeton University Press, 1987. A scholarly history including Shinto and "new religions."

Picken, Stuart D. B., *Shinto: Japan's Spiritual Roots*, Tokyo: Kodansha International, 1980. An appreciative and well illustrated view of Shinto by a minister of the Church of Scotland who is also a practitioner of misogi.

Smith, Robert J., *Ancestor Worship in Contemporary Japan*, Stanford, California: Stanford University Press, 1974. A sociological study of the continuing tradition of venerating family ancestors in contemporary Japan, including historical chapters which are of help in understanding the roots of State Shinto.

Yamamoto, Yukitaka, *Way of the Kami*, Stockton, California: Tsubaki America Publications, 1987. A highly accessible introduction to Shinto, seen as a universal natural way.

8 ZOROASTRIANISM

"May the evil mind be vanquished"

From East Asia, we move to the Middle East, cradle of three major living religions, Judaism, Christianity, and Islam, and one religion of few living representatives but considerable historical significance, Zoroastrianism. Born in what is now Iran, Zoroastrianism is in some ways a bridge between Eastern and Western religions. Its origins are synchronous with and similar to those of Hinduism, and yet it proclaimed doctrines that later showed up in Judaism, Christianity, and Islam – such as belief in one Creator God, an evil force, an afterlife, heaven and hell, and a dramatic apocalyptic end of the world with final resurrection of the dead.

The extent of Zoroastrianism's direct influence on later faiths is not clear. The theology of ancient Zoroastrianism is subject to debate, for over the centuries a large portion of its sacred scriptures were destroyed or forgotten and the meanings of the old language were lost. Nevertheless, Zoroastrianism is of great interest to scholars of the history of religion and to the remaining practitioners of this ancient way.

Origins in ancient Iran

In Iran, this faith is called *Mazdayasna* – "the worship of Ahura Mazda," or the Creator and Lord. Westerners label it Zoroastrianism after its great prophet Zarathushtra (called Zoroaster by the Greeks). He is thought to have lived some time between 1100 and 500 BCE. But many elements of the faith pre-dated Zarathushtra. He was considered the last and greatest of numerous reformers who came to restore pure religion whenever its practice had lapsed.

The early elements came from the faith of the Indo-Iranians, a branch of the same Aryan tribes who made their way down from the steppes of southern Russia into the Indian subcontinent. Semi-nomadic pastoralists from a cold climate, they seem to have revered fire, which they tried to keep ever burning. Like the Indian Aryans, they honored the divinities of nature in daily priestly rituals called *yasna* (known as *yagna* in India). These rituals, held on an open-air plot like the early Brahmanic rituals, included use of a sacred drink called *haoma*, comparable to the mysterious Vedic *soma* potion. Libations were offered to the god of fire and the goddesses of water, the two most precious sustainers of life.

When people died, their bodies were offered to the birds to be picked clean, to avoid contaminating the earth with decaying flesh. The bones were then buried and the memorial treated with special care by the next generation, for it was believed that at some point the person would be bodily resurrected.

In devotional art, the prophet Zarathushtra is often portrayed in communion with the divine, which he knew as the Lord of Life and Wisdom, Ahura Mazda.

The Indo-Iranian people also worshipped a pantheon of gods representing the elements, aspects of nature, and abstract principles, such as justice and obedience. These often corresponded with those worshipped by the Vedic Indians. As a group they were called *Daevas* (Sanskrit: *Devas*), or "Shining Ones", with the highest gods called *Ahuras* ("Lords"). The ritual worship conducted by the priests was designed, as in India, to maintain the natural order, truth and righteousness of the universe by re-enacting the original sacrifice which led to its creation.

Zarathushtra's mission

Trained as a priest in this tradition, Zarathushtra ("He of the Golden Light") was also apparently a mystical seeker who spent many years in spiritual retreat, asking for revelations of spiritual truth. He is said to have had a great vision at the age of thirty. After wading into a river up to his neck, he was symbolically purified of all lower aspects of his being. Radiant, he returned to the bank, where according to legend he saw a great shining being – Vohu Manah, the embodiment of the good mind – who led him into the presence of Ahura Mazda, the high Indo-Iranian god of wisdom. Ahura Mazda was surrounded by angelic presences manifesting six attributes of the divine.

Zarathushtra said he experienced communion with Ahura Mazda and his attributes on many occasions. Framroz Rustomjee explains these visitations as the result of Zarathushtra's own spiritual progress:

> When by years of training and meditation upon the sublime, a man is able to be oblivious of the physical surroundings in which he finds himself and is able to work in the mental plane upon things of sublime consequence, then he arrives at a stage when there is gradual unfoldment of the Divine Spark in him, . . . the link between God and man . . . . Zarathushtra had trained the powers of his mind to such a depth of perfectness, and had so lived a life of righteousness, that there took place within his mind a gradual unfoldment of the Indwelling Divinity. [1]

From these direct contacts with the divine, Zarathushtra learned that of all the Indo-Iranian gods, Ahura Mazda was the Supreme Lord, from whom all good things flowed. The prophet had been troubled by violent aspects of the old religion, perhaps those carried by nomads worshipping the warlike Indra and plundering the pastoralists' settlements. He is also said to have disapproved of the worship of the nature spirits through fear, accompanied by requests for personal benefits. Zarathushtra denounced all cruelty, selfishness, distortion, and hypocrisy in the name of religion. He insisted that Ahura Mazda creates only goodness and should be worshipped by good thoughts, words, and deeds.

He poured forth his adoration for the Supreme in metric verses called *Gathas*. These are the only words of the prophet that have been retained over centuries of vicissitudes. "Speak to me as friend to friend," he implores Ahura Mazda. "Grant us the support which friend would give to friend." [2] The Gathas are mantric chants, designed to induce a state of ecstatic communion in the worshipper. They are not theological treatises, but they are our only source of information about Zarathushtra's beliefs.

Despite his ecstatic visions, Zarathushtra was long unable to convince anyone else to follow him in honoring Ahura Mazda above all others. He did not seek to extricate people from the older religion but rather to appeal to them to use their Good Mind, to think for themselves, rather than blindly following anyone. Priests of the ancestral religion denounced him as a heretic. After ten years, his only convert was his cousin. Some of the gathas seem to refer to his despair at being unable to fulfill his divine mission:

> To what land shall I bend my steps? Whither shall I turn for homage? They have separated me from the Strong in Spirit and the Friend. Neither does the Fellow-worker seek to rejoice me, nor, by any chance, the cruel despots of the country who are Followers of the Druj [the Lie]. How then shall I rejoice Thee, O Mazda Ahura? . . . [3]

At last Zarathushtra journeyed to another kingdom and convinced its king, Vishtapa, of the truth of his understanding. Legend has it that the other priests of the court tried to frame the newcomer as a sorcerer. He revealed their deception and performed a miraculous healing on the king's ailing horse, an allegorical reference to the mind. King Vishtapa adopted Zarathushtra's creed and proclaimed it the state religion. It spread throughout Iran. Zarathushtra guided the Magi Brotherhood of spiritual adepts and preached for almost fifty years until his death by assassination at a fire temple at the age of seventy-seven.

Post-Zarathushtran history

Over the centuries Zoroastrianism was in and out of political favor. Its popularity peaked when it was the state religion of the great Persian empire, which was the largest the world had known. It was built in the mid-sixth century BCE by King Cyrus, who seems to have been a follower of Ahura Mazda (even though he and succeeding kings left no written mention of the prophet Zarathushtra). Cyrus's reign was noted for its religious tolerance as well as its power and wealth. The Jewish poet Second Isaiah (Isaiah 45:1) proclaimed him "God's anointed," for he released the Jews from their Babylonian exile and authorized their return to Judea.

The empire Cyrus created by far-reaching conquests stretched from the Indus Valley to what is now Greece. The Jews within this territory were allowed to practice their own religion but may have adopted certain Zoroastrian beliefs, such as the belief in an evil force, an immortal soul, reward or punishment in an afterlife, and final resurrection of the body at the apocalypse – for these doctrines were absent from earlier Judaic religion. From Judaism, they may have passed indirectly into Christianity and Islam.

The spiritual tradition of devotion to Ahura Mazda was severely threatened by the 331 BCE invasion of Alexander, known as "The Great" in the West but "The Accursed" in Iran. He ransacked the beautiful capital of Persepolis, destroying fire temples, burning the library containing the holy scriptures of Zarathushtra, and killing so many Zoroastrian priests that oral transmission of many scriptures was lost. The Gathas of Zarathushtra survived, however, for many people knew them by heart, as did the most commonly used ritual prayers.

Two centuries later Zoroastrianism was re-established as the state religion of a shrunken Iranian empire by the Parthians, who ruled for almost five hundred years. Under the Parthians the surviving revealed teachings of Zoroastrianism were reassembled as the *Avesta*, or "holy texts." Also during this time the commentaries on the Avesta and detailed instructions about the rituals and customs were compiled as the *Pahlavi texts*, named for the medieval Persian language in which they were written or translated.

The next major threat to Zoroastrianism came from the spread of Islam after the death of Muhammad in 632 CE. Arabic Muslims defeated the Zoroastrian Iranian forces, and when Mongols also invaded from the east, they were gradually converted to Islam rather than Zoroastrianism. Islam is said to have had the appeal of a new and living faith; the older faith of Iran may have descended into empty ritualism by that time.

Iranians who struggled to remain faithful to Zarathushtra's teachings were persecuted and their numbers dwindled until in the tenth century CE a small band emigrated to India in search of religious freedom. India's spiritual origins were similar to their own, and Mother India was noted for her religious tolerance. On promising that they would not try to convert Indians to their faith, the immigrants were given land to settle and allowed to build a fire temple. The sacred fire they consecrated upon reaching their new home is said to have been kept burning for over a thousand years and its temple in Udwada is a major pilgrimage spot for Indian Zoroastrians, known as *Parsis* ("Persians"). Today India, particularly the Bombay area, is the center of Zoroastrianism, rather than Iran.

Zoroastrian teachings

After Zarathushtra's death, his teachings seem to have been merged with earlier polytheistic trends. Today there is uncertainty about exactly what he taught, but enough is known that his theology can be sketched, along with its later transformations.

The primacy of Ahura Mazda

Zarathushtra is considered the first of the monotheists of the Western traditions, in the sense that he elevated one god above all others worshipped by the earlier Iranians. His mystical visions convinced him that there is only one divine being who creates and orders the universe. This God, Ahura Mazda, is referred to as masculine. It is he who creates all good things, gives life, "pours out His Holy Wisdom on every thing that lives," is eternal, mighty, and bountiful, "most worthy to be loved, radiant in action, Lord of Life and Truth."[4]

In the Gathas Zarathushtra makes impassioned pleas to Ahura Mazda to make him a more fit spiritual vehicle, so that he can "dedicate to Mazda the life-breath of his whole being."[5] He asks for Ahura Mazda's guidance in the mission of protecting the selfless, voluntarily poor devotees, "the poor in spirit, the meek and lowly of heart, who are Thine." He particularly emphasizes the need for clear thought in this mission:

> *O Lord of Life, we long for Thy mighty Fire of Thought which is an enduring, blazing Flame bringing clear guidance and joy to the true believer, but as for the destruction-loving, this quickening Flame overcomes his evil in a flash.*[6]

O Lord of Life and Wisdom, I will for ever uphold Thy Divine Law and Thy Good Mind. Teach me Thyself, through Thy spoken Word which springs from the Spirit, and with Thy very own Mouth, whence life first came into being.   Gatha Ahunavaiti, Yasna 28:11

Although Zarathushtra perceived Ahura Mazda as the one Eternal Being, he also described six divine powers that radiate from the godhead. They are Vohu Manah (The Good Mind), Asha Vahishta (Order, Eternal Truth, Righteousness), Khshathra Vairya (Absolute Power), Armaiti (Devotion), Haurvatat (Perfection), and Ameretat (Immortality).

After the prophet's death, these six attributes were personified and worshipped as beings, and uttering their names was thought to bring great power. These Bountiful Immortals were called the *Amesha Spenta*. They were described as luminous deities with shining eyes and beautiful forms, guardians of Ahura Mazda's creation who held celestial councils in the heavens and descended to earth on radiant paths. The Amesha Spenta are chief among the *Yazata*, or angels, who bring the light of the sun to earth and help those who dedicate offerings and prayers to them.

The Yazata include many of the deities worshipped by the earlier Iranians. Prominent among the Yazata is Sraosha, the guardian spirit of humankind and the model of obedient listening and service to the Divine. In the Gathas Zarathushtra invokes this quality of divine obedience as the highest of all traits. Another frequently mentioned Yazata is the popular Mithra, guardian of the light, protector of the truth, and bestower of wealth.

The choice between good and evil

In addition to adoring the good creator, Zarathushtra wrestled with the problem of evil.

The Adam and Eve account of the origin of evil apparently derives from an ancient Mesopotamian legend. In Zoroastrian tradition, it was the Evil Spirit, Angra Mainyu, who tempted the father and mother of humanity. (Persia, 14th century.)

Precisely where evil comes from and whether it is a being, such as Satan, is controversial in contemporary interpretations of the Gathas. Although some Western scholars describe Zarathushtra's theology as cosmic dualism, with Ahura Mazda opposed by a dark force of equal power, most Zoroastrians disagree. They feel that Ahura Mazda created only good, not evil. Evil either has independent existence or is a trait of the human mind. It is not an anti-god equal to Ahura Mazda; unlike Ahura Mazda, it will not last forever.

Zarathushtra did speak of two opposing powers; *Spenta Mainyu*, the good spirit, and *Angra Mainyu*, the evil spirit. Spenta Mainyu is life, order, perfection, health, happiness, increase; Angra Mainyu is not-life, chaos, imperfection, disease, sorrow, decrease. The two principles will always actively oppose each other in humans and in creation as a whole until the good spirit is at last victorious. Evil, Zarathushtra asserts, is not all-powerful or eternal, but to assure the victory of good over evil, humans must dedicate themselves as spiritual warriors on the side of Spenta Mainyu.

According to many scholars' interpretation of Yasna 30 (Zarathushtra's sermon on the origin of evil) the Twin Mainyu are the two aspects of the human mind. Human beings are given the free will and mental capacity to choose between the two powers. In their thoughts, words, and deeds, they can grow in love, devotion, and service, or they can contribute to evil. Zarathushtra felt that non-loving acts in the name of religion aided the cause of evil. He railed against worship of the Daevas, using the old word for the "shining gods" for what he considered dark forces, magic, and selfish ritualism. It is not clear precisely what gods and practices he was referring to, but the cult of Indra, for instance, was often bloody and violent. The Gathas include verses such as these directed to followers of what he termed the *Druj* (the Lie):

> *Let none of you, therefore, give ear to the unholy incantations and evil doctrines of the Follower of the Druj, for in truth he will sacrifice the home, the town, the province and the country to destruction and death.* [7]

Heaven and hell

At death, Zoroastrians believe, each of us is judged according to the total goodness or evilness of our thoughts, words, and deeds. The greater the goodness, the wider the bridge to heaven, the House of Heavenly Song, the Kingdom of Light where the souls of the righteous reside. The greater the accumulated evil, the narrower the bridge, until it is so narrow that souls cannot cross. They fall into hell, the House of the Lie, a murky, woeful place.

Some Zoroastrians interpret this scenario allegorically and feel that it applies to this life as well as the next. Tehmurasp Rustamji Sethna, for instance, explains that:

> *When a man's actions are good he has self confidence and usually people say he has nothing to worry, his road is clear. On the other hand, if a man's actions are bad, it is usually said he is following a precarious path and any moment he will fall.* [8]

Those who cross the bridge to arrive at the gates of heaven are met by the light and truth of Ahura Mazda, symbolically represented as angels. Once the soul's evil actions are weighed against the good ones, it is conducted to the appropriate grade of heaven by a young woman whose beauty corresponds to the degree of one's goodness. She

Ahura Mazda is symbolically represented as a human-like figure with the wings of a great bird, holding a ring representing authority with one hand and giving blessings with the other. The same image is often used to indicate humanity's spiritual nature.

represents the sum of one's actions. It is not Ahura Mazda who judges and metes out reward or punishment. By the natural law, Asha, good deeds bring their own reward and evil deeds their just punishment. This doctrine is similar to that of karma in Hinduism and Buddhism, but rather than shifting the effects of one's life to reincarnation in another life, Zoroastrians feel that the effects of their actions will be felt in the present and in an after-life.

The final resurrection

There is no eternal hell in Zoroastrianism, for good is ultimately victorious. With the help of all individuals who choose goodness over evil, the world will gradually reach a state of perfection in which all souls, living or dead, are liberated forever from evil. This time is the *Frashokereti*, the "refreshment" of the world in which all of creation is resurrected into perfected immortality. Thenceforth the world will:

> *never grow old and never die, never decay and never perish, ever live and ever increase,*
> *and be master over its wish, when the dead will rise, when life and immortality will come,*
> *and the world will be restored.* [9]

This refreshment of the world is not the work of a single savior; it requires the contributions of many, many people. Zoroastrianism therefore places great emphasis on the moral responsibility of each person, for the good of the whole.

Spiritual practices

Zoroastrians do not have an ascetic tradition. They are called to work in the world to increase goodness, to hasten the Frashokereti. It is not sufficient to be good oneself. A Zoroastrian must actively resist evil and try to guide others toward good thoughts, words, and deeds, as Zarathushtra did, though not necessarily to convert them to the Zoroastrian religion. In the pure tradition, sincere efforts to perfect oneself and promote good in the world are more important than ritual.

Over time, however, rituals did develop. One that is particularly important is the act of tying the sacred cord (*kusti*) around one's mid-section, traditionally performed five times a day. Symbolically, the faithful are girding themselves as soldiers for Ahura Mazda. The kusti is worn by both males and females, in contrast with the male-only Hindu tradition of the sacred thread, for women and men are treated equally in many ways within Zoroastrianism.

While tying the kusti, the faithful recite a prayer to keep evil at bay, and also chant the most ancient and powerful of Mazdayasnan prayers: the *Ahuna-Vairya*. It is thought to pre-date Zarathushtra, and according to legend, the prophet himself recited it to protect himself from the temptations of Angra Mainyu. One translator renders it thus:

> *Just as a Ruler is all-powerful among men, so too is the Spiritual Teacher, even by reason*
> *of His Asha; the gifts of Good Mind are for those working for the Lord of Life; and the*
> *Strength of Ahura is granted unto him who to his poor brothers giveth help.* [10]

In addition to dedication to the good and protection from evil, Zoroastrian rituals emphasize purification. Menstruating women are considered impure and cannot

Zoroastrians tie the sacred cord, or kusti, around themselves for protection against evil.

participate. Water is venerated as a symbol of purification, and the devout will often dip their fingers into water, apply it to their eyes and forehead, and raise their hands in prayer to Ahura Mazda. Parsis in Bombay do this with ocean water at the beaches; Zoroastrians living inland honor springs and even wells. It is a great sin to pollute water or to place anything dead in it.

LIVING ZOROASTRIANISM
An interview with Tina Mehta

Tina Mehta, mother of two grown children, grew up in Calcutta in a Zoroastrian family but only later began to understand the deeper meanings of her religion. In London, she taught Zoroastrian Studies and worked as a counselor to AIDS patients and drug addicts. She and her husband are now living in Kuwait.

"As children, we were taken once a year to the river to worship and pray to the waters. There is an angel for the waters; we pray to the water spirit. There's an angel for the plants, so we pray to the plant spirit. Each of God's seven creations – the sky, the waters, the earth, the plants, the animals, man, and fire – each has a fravashi (eternal spirit). They also have specific angelic spiritual aspects. And all together, they make up the realm of Ahura Mazda. We see them through God's creations.

Because we are brought up praying to these spirits of various creations, we are very reluctant to pollute them, because we would then be polluting the angels, and therefore God. When I went swimming with my other friends who were non-Zoroastrians and they wanted to have a pee in the water, I couldn't because I was brought up believing that I shouldn't pollute the water. It was a joke to them: 'How is your pee going to destroy the whole river?' But I had been brought here to worship and I knew it just wasn't right somehow.

I used to resent being taken to the river to pray and worship. I thought, 'This is ridiculous.' And yet now I am very grateful I did that, because now I can understand when they are talking about environmental issues how important it is to actually worship the river because we would be less likely to pollute it. The same with the air and the plants. There are prayers where we apologize to animals and plants when we actually use them for food or for rituals. We do have to eat, but we eat with respect for the animal or plant that is giving its life to us.

As in the old days, we recognize that there are lots of creatures outside that could do you harm. Zoroastrian homes today still put lime powder – or things like Ajax – in little designs near the doorstep, to remind us that anything that is hurtful to the body, mind, or spirit should stay away and that whatever enters should enter with a good thought. When we've had a bad day, say at work, we see this marking and we remember that when we enter the home we don't bring that bad thought and bad feeling inside.

Sounds are also very important to us. That is why prayers in the Zoroastrian tradition are recited aloud. If there have been any bad sounds we overcome them with good sounds. If we have had a row in the house, then we counteract that aura of the row with good thoughts and good words. The mantric words act as a deterrent to evil sounds that have been uttered.

I think the work that is going on now (studying the historic links between Zoroastrianism and Judaism, Christianity, and Islam) will unify people. We have to realize that our antecedent is really one. Somehow that hasn't got through – we are in a state of considering each one as being different and separate. It's like three brothers just looking the other way. It must be very painful to the Father."

As of old, the other element emphasized in Zoroastrian rituals is fire. At fire temples, it is not the fire itself that is worshipped or even the god of fire, but rather the spiritual fire-quality. Dastur (High Priest) Framroze A. Bode explains:

Zarathushtra's followers are ordinarily known as fire-worshippers, but they do not worship the physical fire of wood. Athra-Fire is universal ethereal energy, breath, life, heat and radiance. It is the flame of consciousness which burns in each and every heart. It is the light of reason in every mind and the glow of the pure emotion of love. In the symbol of Fire is the reverence for all life. The outer symbol of Fire reminds one of the inner Divine Spark in the true temple of God in the human heart.[11]

When the physical body dies, Zoroastrians convey it to a Tower of Silence, a special circular building open at the top so that carrion-eating birds such as vultures can light on the corpses to pick the bones clean. This is done to avoid polluting the earth with decaying flesh, which the birds dispose of quickly. Once the bones are bleached clean by exposure to the sun, they are placed in a central pit with no monuments, no distinctions between rich and poor. But the survivors do pray for the departed and continue to observe death anniversaries at which the *fravashi*, or eternal principle and guide, of the deceased person is invoked. The fravashi is thought to continually evolve toward perfection and to help the living in their good works.

At seasonal festivals, the fravashis of all the great Zoroastrians of the past are honored by the community, and this continuing remembrance by the living is coveted as a kind of immortality. One of the most popular celebrations is the Festival of All Souls, when homes are cleaned for visits from the fravashis and the people celebrate both the birth and the revelation of Zarathushtra.

In a fire temple, a Zoroastrian priest performs rites over a sacred fire, revered since ancient times, and wears a mask to avoid contaminating it with his breath.

Zoroastrianism today

Few followers remain of this ancient way of combating evil with goodness. There are thought to be only about 130,000 living Zoroastrians. Conversion to the faith is not encouraged, partly because of the ancient pledge to India not to attract followers from other religions and partly because of a desire not to dilute the teachings. This issue is often debated, and there is some agreement that it is all right for outsiders to "accept" the Zoroastrian faith, if not to convert to it. In Iran, there is little incentive to do either,

Towers of Silence are open to the sky so that carrion-eating birds can clean the bones of the dead to avoid polluting the earth with decaying flesh.

for Zoroastrians, like Jews and Christians (all "People of the Book" – of revealed scriptures), are tolerated but limited in their privileges under Muslim rule. A form of Mazdayasna that does accept converts is the International Mazdayasnan Order, centered in Eugene, Oregon.

During the twentieth century, there has been a significant migration of Zoroastrians out of both India and Iran to other countries. London, New York, Chicago, Boston, Los Angeles, and Vancouver are now home to groups of Zoroastrians who mingle socially and professionally with people of other religions but do not inter-marry with them. Training is still available in Iran and India for the hereditary line of Zoroastrian priests, and there is considerable interest in preserving and understanding the tradition.

When the Parsis were influenced by Westernization and Protestant missionary activity, they became somewhat embarrassed about the mystical aspects of their faith. Some began reciting their prayers in English rather than the dead Avestan language, and interpreting what they were doing as talking to God rather than uttering powerful sacred mantras. They tended to de-emphasize rituals and beliefs in an evil spirit and the end of the temporal world in favor of the more abstract philosophy and ethical standards of the Gathas.

The pendulum now seems to be swinging in the other direction. Twentieth-century religious historians, metaphysicians, and linguists have attempted to translate the ancient language, uncover the deeper significance behind the rituals, and sift out the origins of the tradition from the thousands of years of later accretions. Such efforts have brought a renewed sense of pride and appreciation within Zoroastrianism. It now appears unlikely that the religion will soon disappear from the face of the earth it has so long tried to serve.

Suggested reading

Bode, Dastur Framroze Ardeshir, and Nanavutty, Piloo, *Songs of Zarathustra: The Gathas*, translated from the Avesta, London: George Allen and Unwin, 1952. Of the various translations of the Gathas available in English, this seems the most spiritually sensitive.

Boyce, Mary, *Zoroastrians: Their Religious Beliefs and Practices*, London: Routledge and Kegan Paul, 1985. Detailed historical information, beginning with the pre-Zarathushtran roots of the tradition.

Hinnells, John R., *Zoroastrianism and the Parsis*, London: Ward Lock International, 1981. A readable, straightforward portrayal of Zoroastrian history, beliefs, and practices, with illustrations.

Mehr, Farhang, *The Zoroastrian Tradition: An Introduction to the Ancient Wisdom of Zarathustra*, New York: Amity House, 1989. Good discussion of the principles of the Gathic and Pahlavi texts.

Sethna, Tehmurasp Rustamji, *Book of Instructions on Zoroastrian Religion*, Karachi: Informal Religious Meetings Trust Fund, 1980. A catechism of the faith, including prayers in both Avestan and English.

Taraporewala, I.J.S., *The Religion of Zarathushtra*, Madras, India: Theosophical Publishing House, 1926. A mystical, poetic explanation of the insides of Zoroastrianism.

9 JUDAISM

Wrestling with the one God

Judaism has no single founder, no central leader or group making theological decisions; Judaism is a people, a very old family. This family can be defined either as a religious group or a national group.

In religious terms, Jews are those who experience their long and often difficult history as a continuing dialogue with God. According to one tradition, God offered to share the divine law with seventy nations, but the semi-nomadic tribes of Israel were the only people in the world to answer God's call, to enter into a living covenant with their creator. This call is still available to all peoples, Jews feel. In a religious sense, "Israel" refers to all those who answer the call, who acknowledge and strive to obey the monotheistic God, through the *Torah*, or "teaching," given to the patriarchs, Moses, and the prophets.

As a nation, "Israel" is a people who have been repeatedly dispersed and oppressed. After the horrors of the Holocaust, they founded a homeland in Palestine where their ancestors had once walked. This creation of a Jewish state has in turn conflicted with the claims of the Palestinians, creating a tense situation in the Middle East.

In this chapter we will focus on Judaism as that which Mordecai Kaplan calls "an evolving religious civilization," first by taking an overview of the history of the Jewish people and then by examining the religious concepts and practices that generally characterize the followers of Torah today.

A history of Israel

The Jewish sense of history begins with the stories recounted in the Jewish Bible or *Tanakh* (which Christians call "the Old Testament"). Biblical history begins with the creation of the world by a supreme male deity, or God, and progresses through the patriarchs and Moses who spoke with God and led the people according to God's commandments, and the prophets who heard God's warnings to the faithless. But Jewish history does not end where the stories of the *Tanakh* end, about the second century BCE. After the holy center of Judaism, the Temple of Jerusalem, was captured and destroyed by the Romans in 70 CE, Jewish history is that of a dispersed people, finding unity in their evolving teachings and traditional practices.

Biblical history

Although knowledge of the early history of the children of Israel is based largely on the

The Tanakh, or Jewish Scriptures, consists of the Torah (or Pentateuch), the Prophets, and the Writings. These books date roughly from the 12th to the 2nd century BCE, and were written mostly in classical Hebrew.

TORAH	The Five Books of Moses	**NEVI'IM**	The Prophets
בראשית	GENESIS	יהושע	JOSHUA
שמות	EXODUS	שופטים	JUDGES
ויקרא	LEVITICUS	שמואל א	I SAMUEL
במדבר	NUMBERS	שמואל ב	II SAMUEL
דברים	DEUTERONOMY	מלכים א	I KINGS
		מלכים ב	II KINGS
		ישעיה	ISIAH
		ירמיה	JEREMIAH
		יחזקאל	EZEKIEL

KETHUVIM	The Writings		The Twelve Minor Prophets
תהילים	PSALMS		
משלי	PROVERBS	הושע	HOSEA
איוב	JOB	יואל	JOEL
שיר השירים	THE SONG OF SONGS	עמוס	AMOS
רות	RUTH	עבדיה	OBADIAH
איכה	LAMENTATIONS	יונה	JONAH
קהלת	ECCLESIASTES	מיכה	MICAH
אסתר	ESTHER	נחום	NAHUM
דניאל	DANIEL	חבקוק	HABAKKUK
עזרא	EZRA	צפניה	ZEPHANIAH
נחמיה	NEHEMIAH	חגי	HAGGAI
דברי הימים א	I CHRONICLES	זכריה	ZECHARIAH
דברי הימים ב	II CHRONICLES	מלאכי	MALACHI

Tanakh, scholars are uncertain of the historical accuracy of the accounts. Some of the people, events, and genealogies set forth cannot be verified by other evidence, such as archaeological findings or references to the Israelites in the writings of neighboring peoples. It may be that the Israelites were too small and loosely organized a group to be noted by historians of other cultures. No mention of Israel appears in other sources until about 1230 BCE, but biblical narratives and genealogies place Abraham, said to be the first patriarch of the Israelites, at about 1700 to 1900 BCE.

Jews hold the *Pentateuch*, the "five books of Moses" which appear at the beginning of the Tanakh, as the most sacred part of the scriptures. Traditionalists believe that, with the exception of verses describing the death of Moses, these books were divinely revealed to Moses and written down by him as a single document. Contemporary biblical researchers disagree. On the basis of clues such as the use of variant names for God, they speculate that these books were oral traditions reworked and set down later by several different sources with the intent of interpreting the formation of Israel from a religious point of view.

Some of the stories in the Pentateuch, such as the Creation, the Garden of Eden, the great flood, and the Tower of Babel, are similar to earlier Mesopotamian legends, though with a less friendly relationship between humans and the divine. In the narratives of

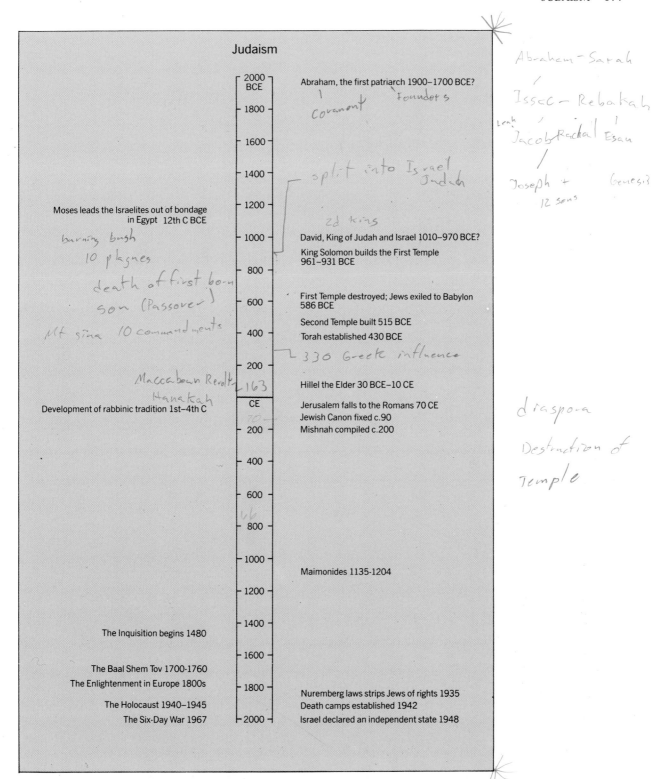

Judaism

Abraham, the first patriarch 1900–1700 BCE?

Covenant *Founders*

split into Israel Judah

2d king

Moses leads the Israelites out of bondage in Egypt 12th C BCE

burning bush

10 plagues

death of first born son (Passover)

Mt sina 10 commandments

David, King of Judah and Israel 1010–970 BCE?

King Solomon builds the First Temple 961–931 BCE

First Temple destroyed; Jews exiled to Babylon 586 BCE

Second Temple built 515 BCE

Torah established 430 BCE

330 Greek influence

Maccabean Revolt 163

Hanakah

Development of rabbinic tradition 1st–4th C

Hillel the Elder 30 BCE–10 CE

Jerusalem falls to the Romans 70 CE
Jewish Canon fixed c.90
Mishnah compiled c.200

Maimonides 1135-1204

The Inquisition begins 1480

The Baal Shem Tov 1700-1760
The Enlightenment in Europe 1800s

Nuremberg laws strips Jews of rights 1935
Death camps established 1942
The Holocaust 1940–1945
The Six-Day War 1967
Israel declared an independent state 1948

Timeline markers (BCE/CE)

2000 BCE, 1800, 1600, 1400, 1200, 1000, 800, 600, 400, 200, CE, 200, 400, 600, 800, 1000, 1200, 1400, 1600, 1800, 2000

Abraham – Sarah

Issac – Rebakah

Leah Jacob Rachal Esau

Joseph + 12 sons   Genesis

diaspora

Destruction of Temple

the continuing history of the Israelites, only the last four books (First and Second Samuel and First and Second Kings) are thought to be edited directly from contemporary sources. Although the accuracy of many of the stories has not yet been independently documented, they are of great spiritual significance in Christianity and Islam as well as Judaism. They are also politically important, for they later gave a scattered people a special sense of group identity.

FROM CREATION TO THE GOD OF ABRAHAM   The Tanakh begins with a sweeping poetic account of the creation of heaven and earth by God in six days, from the time of "the earth being unformed and void, with darkness over the surface of the deep and a wind from (or: the spirit of) God sweeping over the water."[1] After creating the material universe, God created man and woman in the "image" or "likeness" of Himself, placing them as masters of the earth, rulers of "the fish of the sea, the birds of the sky, and all the living things that creep on the earth."[2] This account of creation is attributed to the "priestly source," thought to be editors writing after the exile of the Jews to Babylon in 586 BCE.

A second, probably earlier, version of the creation story follows. It is thought to be a contribution from the "Yahwist source," which used the word transliterated as Yahweh for the supreme male deity. Instead of presenting woman as the equal to man, it portrays her as an offshoot of Adam, the first man; she was formed from one of his ribs to keep him company. This version also blames woman for the troubles of humanity. According to this legend, originally God placed the first two humans in a garden paradise. The woman Eve ("mother of all the living") was tempted by a serpent (a symbol of the older Goddess tradition) to taste the fruit of the tree of knowledge. She encouraged Adam to do likewise, against God's command. According to the legend, this ended their innocence. God knew that they had disobeyed because they were trying to cover their nakedness, to which their eyes were now open. God cursed the snake to be the lowliest of all animals, crawling on its belly, eating dust, and being the hated enemy of humans. He placed on woman the curse of painful childbirth, on man the curse of having to till recalcitrant soil for food, and banished the humans from the garden so that they no longer had access to the tree of life:

> And the Lord God said, "Now that the man has become like one of us, knowing good and bad, what if he should stretch out his hand and take also from the tree of life and eat, and live forever!"[3]

The theme of exile reappears continually in the Tanakh, and in later Jewish history, in which the people are rendered homeless again and again. The biblical narratives emphasize that the people are banished from their land and risk God's displeasure every time they stray from God's commands. They are repeatedly exiled from their spiritual home and continually seek to return to it.

Again and again, however, the people disobey God's will. One of the famous legends recounted concerns Noah, the sole righteous man of his generation. According to the narrator, who attributes thoughts and emotions to God, God despairs of the general wickedness of humans, regrets having created them, and sends a great flood "to destroy all flesh under the sky."[4] But with Noah, God establishes a covenant and gives directions for the building of an ark which saves Noah's family and two of each of God's creatures. God promises never again to destroy the created world, with the rainbow as a sign of

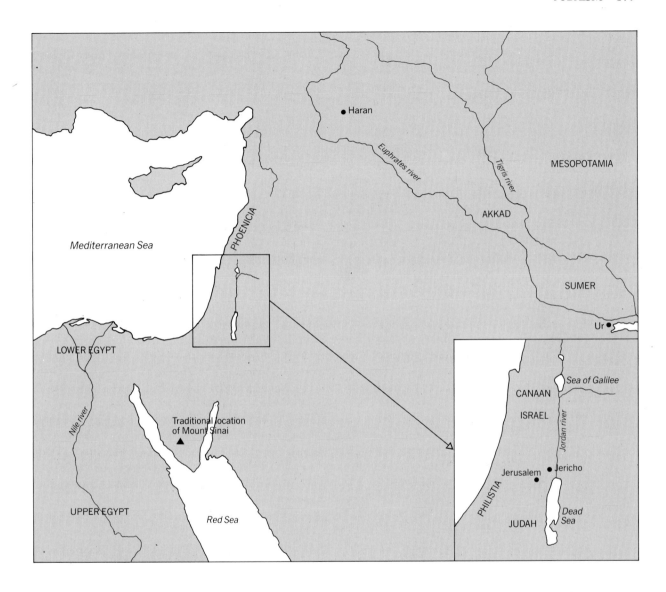

this covenant "between me and all flesh that is on earth."[5]

God does, however, continue to intervene in history, according to the narrators. Many generations after Noah, for instance, the people are becoming so strong and ambitious that, according to the legend of the Tower of Babel, God limits their power by confounding their speech and scattering them across the earth.

After this legendary scattering, the narrative focuses on Abraham, Isaac, and Jacob (the "patriarchs"), forefathers of the Israelites, who seem to have lived as semi-nomadic pastoralists within a relatively small area of what is now called the Middle East. Abraham was called by God to leave his home in Ur and then in Haran, Mesopotamian trading centers, to journey with his wife Sarah to Canaan. He left the land of his father and also the religion of his father, whom oral tradition describes as not only a

The Israelites identify themselves as a people whose ancestor Abraham moved from Ur and Haran in Mesopotamia to Canaan; Abraham's grandson Jacob, called "Israel," resettled his large family in Egypt, where the Israelites were eventually treated as slaves.

The settled agricultural peoples of Canaan paid homage to a high male god, called El, and an earlier Great Mother Goddess (Ishtar, disguised as his consort). The Goddess (shown here), associated with vegetation, agricultural knowledge, and abundance, was worshipped at asherahs, sacred tree-symbol altar poles, which the Israelites destroyed.

worshipper of the old gods but also a maker of statues devoted to them.

Abraham is held up as an example of obedience to God's commands. Without hesitation, he undergoes *circumcision* (cutting away of the foreskin of the penis) as an initiatory sacrifice, a sign of the covenant in which God agrees to be the divine protector of Abraham and his descendants, with all males to be likewise circumcised on the eighth day after birth. His first descendant is Ishmael, son of the Egyptian slave woman Hagar. His second is Isaac, son of Sarah, who jealously insists that Ishmael and Hagar be banished to the wilderness. God supports this demand, assuring Abraham that he will be father of two nations – one line through Isaac (to become the Israelites) and one through Ishmael (whom Muslims consider their ancestor).

God then tests Abraham by asking him to sacrifice his son Isaac. The patriarch prepares to comply, when the Lord stops him, satisfied that "now I know that you fear God."[6] The Hebrew word *yirah*, usually translated as "fear" of God, also means "awe of God's greatness," or what Rabbi Lawrence Kushner calls "trembling in the presence of ultimate holiness."[7] Yirah is the central attitude stressed in the Torah.

Scholars disagree on whether pure monotheism – the worship of a single God of the universe, exclusive of any other divine beings – was encouraged by the early patriarchs, or "fathers," as they are simply called in Hebrew. Many names for divinity are used in the early scriptures, and some researchers consider them names of separate gods. It is known that the religion of the Canaanites had some influence on that of the Israelites. The Canaanites were polytheistic, with highly developed mythology and ritual directed largely to agricultural fertility. They worshipped a pantheon of perhaps 70 rather lustful gods, headed by the high god El and his wife Asherah, counselor of the gods. Their son, the storm and rain god Baal, is a prominent actor in the divine mythology.

"El" was also the generic Canaanite term for divinity. This word appears frequently in the Hebrew Bible, often in the plural, as "Elohim." The authors' interpretations of God's "thinking" are also often expressed in the plural (e.g., "Let us make man in our image."[8]). Many scholars interpret the plural form as a way of indicating majesty rather than a group of gods. "El Shaddai" is usually translated as "God Almighty"; the name could refer to the highest god in a pantheon of lesser gods.

Sooner or later, however, the Israelites saw themselves as having been chosen by a single divine Patron. In their patriarchal culture, this God was perceived as a male in a close relationship to the people, like a father to his children, or a lord to his vassals. At first he may have been perceived as a private tribal god; later he was known as the supreme and only deity of the universe.

ISRAEL'S BIRTH IN STRUGGLE   It is also unclear who the people of the biblical narratives were. Some scholars think the word "Hebrew" is derived from the generic term *habiru*, used for the low-class landless people who lived as outlaws and were often hired as mercenaries. Others point to *Ibri* as the biblical word for Hebrew, meaning "children of Eber," an ethnic term. But because of frequent moving and inter-marrying, the Israelites were actually of mixed ethnic stock, including Hebrew, Aramean, and Canaanite. The word *Semite* is a general racial and linguistic term applied to Jews, Arabs, and others of eastern Mediterranean origin.

According to the genealogies set forth in the Pentateuch, the people who became known as Israelites were the offspring of Israel (first called Jacob), grandson of Abraham. Jacob received the new name after wrestling all night with a being who turned out to be an angel of God. "Israel" means "the one who struggled with God."

This story in which a human being struggles and finally is reborn at a higher level of spirituality has been taken as a metaphor for the spiritual evolution of the people Israel. As a result of the struggle, Israel the patriarch receives not only a new name but also the promise that many nations will be born from him. Some Jewish scholars have therefore extended understanding of the word Israel to mean the whole of humanity which struggles to grow toward God, and gradually does so. The nation Israel – "the smallest of peoples"[9] – is perceived as the spiritual center for this growth. This is its destiny, though Jews do not feel that it has yet been fulfilled.

EGYPT: BONDAGE AND EXODUS   Jacob is said to have had one daughter and twelve sons by four women. The twelve boys became the heads of the twelve tribes of Israel. The whole group left Canaan for Goshen in Egypt during a famine. At first they were well treated, but their numbers multiplied as prophesied, and the Egyptian Pharaohs are said to have become worried that they might pose an internal political threat. To keep them from becoming too powerful, the reigning Pharaoh ordered that they be turned into slaves for massive construction projects. To further curb the population, the Pharaoh ordered midwives to kill all boy babies born to the Israelite women.

One who escaped this fate was Moses, who was raised in the palace by the Pharaoh's own daughter. He is said to have fled the country after killing an Egyptian overseer who was beating an Israelite worker. While he lived in exile in Midian, the oppression of the Israelites in Egypt grew worse and worse.

According to the scriptural book of Exodus, Moses was chosen by God to defy the Pharaoh and lead the people out of bondage, out of Egypt. While he was tending his father-in-law's flocks on Mount Sinai, an angel of God appeared to him as a bush blazing with fire but not consumed by it. God called to him out of the bush and yet cautioned, "Do not come closer. Remove your sandals from your feet, for the place on which you stand is holy ground."[10] When God told Moses to go rescue "My people, the Israelite, from Egypt,"[11] Moses demurred, but God insisted, "I will be with you."[12] And when Moses asked how to explain to the Israelites who sent him to rescue them, God said:

> Thus you shall say to the Israelites, ''Ehyeh [I Am] sent me to you. ... The Lord, the God of your fathers, the God of Abraham, the God of Isaac, and the God of Jacob, has sent me to you.''[13]

The word given in this translation of the Tanakh as "Lord" (Adonai) is considered too sacred to be pronounced. In the ancient scriptures it is rendered only in consonants as YHWH or YHVH; the pronunciation of the vowels is not known. According to the scriptures, this ineffable name and this identity were first revealed to Moses.

With his brother Aaron to act as spokesperson, Moses did indeed return to Egypt. Many chapters of Exodus recount miracles used to convince the stubborn Pharaoh to let the people go into the wilderness to worship their God. These signs included a rod that turned into a serpent, plagues of locusts, flies and frogs, animal diseases, a terrible storm, lasting darkness, and finally, the killing by the Lord of all firstborn children and creatures. The Israelites were spared this fate, marking their doors with the blood of a slaughtered lamb so that the Destroyer would pass over them. At this, the Pharaoh at last let the Israelites go.

No mention of this exodus occurs in the writings of the Egyptians, who were excellent record-keepers and guarded their borders closely. But the presence of authentic historical descriptions in the midst of what some scholars believe is legendary material gives some support to the important belief in the Exodus from Egypt. The redemption from bondage by the special protection of the Lord has served ever since as a central theme in Judaism.

According to the scriptural account, the Lord's presence led the Israelites, manifesting as a pillar of cloud by day and a pillar of fire by night. The armies of the deceitful Pharaoh pursued them until the famous scene in which Moses stretched his rod toward the sea and God caused an east wind to blow all night, dividing the waters so that the Israelites could pass through safely on a dry seabed. As the Egyptians tried to follow, God told Moses again to hold out his arm over the sea, and the walls of water came crashing down on them, drowning every one.

FROM THE WILDERNESS TO CANAAN   According to the Tanakh, God told Moses that he would lead the people back to Canaan. First, however, it was necessary to travel to the holy Mount Sinai to re-establish the covenant between God and the people. The Lord is said to have descended to its summit in a terrifying show of lightning, thunder, fire, smoke, and trumpeting. God is said to have then given the people through Moses a set of rules for righteous living, later called the *Torah*. Among them are the Ten Commandments: God forbade the people to worship any other gods or anything in the

According to the legend of Exodus, God empowered Moses to hold back the waters of the Red Sea to let the children of Israel pass through, and then drown the pursuing Egyptians in the returning waters.

natural world or to create sculptured images of them; to swear falsely in the name of God; to work on the seventh day of the week (in honor of the day that God rested after creating heaven and earth); or to murder, commit adultery, steal, bear false witness, or covet anything belonging to others; and commanded them to honor their parents. God also gave a set of social norms, prescribed religious feasts, and detailed instructions for the construction of a portable tabernacle with a holy ark, *The Ark of the Covenant*, in which to keep the stone tablets on which God inscribed the commandments.

During the forty-day period while Moses was on the mountain receiving these instructions, the people who had just agreed to a holy covenant with God became impatient. The legend says that under Aaron's reluctant supervision, they melted down their gold jewelry and cast it into the form of a golden calf, happily reverting to what the authors of the biblical narratives considered idol-worship, which had been explicitly forbidden by God. Moses is said to have been so outraged by their revelry and idolatry that he smashed the stone tablets and destroyed the idol. He ordered the only people still siding with YHWH, the Levites, to slay three thousand of those who had strayed.

After another forty-day meeting with God on the summit of Mount Sinai, Moses again returned with stone tablets on which God had inscribed the commandments. Moses's face was said to be so radiant from his encounter with God that he had to veil his face. Aaron and his sons were invested as priests, the tabernacle was constructed as directed, and the people set off for the land of Canaan, with the Presence of the Lord filling the tabernacle.

Even with the powerful presence of the Ark they carried, the Israelites had to wander forty years through the desert before they could re-enter the promised land, fertile Canaan, which at that time belonged to other peoples. The long sojourn in the wilderness is a familiar metaphor in the spiritual search. One must pass through a difficult testing ground of not-knowing, of having no home base, before one finally finds a permanent home in the divine. But even in the wilderness, the Israelite's God did not forsake them. Every day they found their daily bread scattered on the ground, in the form of an unknown food which they named *manna* (What is it?).

Through the miraculous help of God, they at last captured the walled city of Jericho and fought many battles against the kings and tribes of Canaan. Archaeological evidence indicates that every Canaanite town was destroyed from one to four times between the thirteenth and eleventh centuries BCE. At Sinai, God had vowed to oust the inhabitants of the lands into which the Israelites advanced, warning them against adopting the local spiritual practices: "No, you must tear down their altars, smash their pillars, and cut down their sacred posts."[14] The editors of the scriptures clearly considered the "heathen" religions of other people spiritually invalid and morally inferior to their own. But the Israelites' attention to their God was not absolute. According to the scriptures, whenever they turned away from Adonai, forgetting or worshipping other gods, surrounding peoples found them easy prey.

THE FIRST AND SECOND TEMPLES OF JERUSALEM   The Ark was brought to Jerusalem (former home of the old high god El) by David, Israel's greatest king. As an obscure shepherd, he was chosen by the prophet Samuel to be anointed on the forehead with oil, for thus were future kings found and acknowledged in those times. Composer and singer of many famous Psalms, he was summoned to the court of the reigning king, Saul, to play soothing music and bear the king's arms. When Saul and his son were

God's presence abided with the Israelites, wandering or stationary, in the portable Ark of the Covenant, which was said to house the tablets of Moses. This painting from the Dura Europos Synagogue shows the Ark leaving the land of the Philistines. They had captured the Ark but sent it back after being cursed by bubonic plague.

killed in battle, David was made king. By defeating surrounding hostile nations, David created the beginnings of a secure, prosperous Israelite empire. He made the captured city of Jerusalem its capital.

Under the reign of King Solomon (son of David), a great Temple was built in Jerusalem. It was to be a permanent home for the Ark of the Covenant, housed in the innermost sanctum, and a place for making the burnt offerings of animals, grain, and oil to the divine. But Solomon also accumulated great personal wealth, at the expense of the people, and built altars to the gods of his wives, who came from other nations. This so angered the Lord, according to the scriptures, that he divided the kingdom after Solomon's death into Judah, with Jerusalem its capital, and Israel, to the north of Judah, with no permanent capital. Divided, neither prospered, and war became commonplace.

Under Ahab, a king of Israel who made his capital in Samaria, the situation became particularly grim, from the point of view of the scriptures. Ahab married the Phoenician princess Jezebel, an ardent worshipper of the Canaanite god Baal, and built altars to Baal and other Canaanite gods around the land. Jezebel herself is said to have destroyed altars to the God of Israel and to have attempted to slaughter all those who were faithful to this God.

At that point, the prophet Elijah appeared to demonstrate the supreme power of the Lord YHWH and to warn the people against worshipping other gods. The message from God that the people should worship him and end their evil ways was repeated by many prophets over the centuries. These prophets were men and women who had undergone transformational ordeals which made them instruments for the word of God. The "early prophets" such as Elijah focused on the sin of idolatry; the "later prophets" warned that social injustice and moral corruption would be the ruin of the Jewish state.

By the reign of King Hoshea of Israel, the kingdom was so corrupt and idolatrous that, in the scriptural interpretation, God permitted the strong kingdom of Assyria to overtake what was left of the small country. To sustain the population needs for its empire-building and keep Israel from rising again as a nation, Assyria carted off most of the Israelites to exile among the *Gentiles* (non-Jewish People, from the Hebrew word for "heathen"). Most of the Israelites became dispersed within Assyria; these people who thenceforth had no distinct tribal identity are known as the "Ten Lost Tribes of Israel."

Judah maintained its independence, declining and continually warned of impending doom by its prophets, until King Nebuchadnezzar of Babylonia (which by then had taken over the Assyrian empire) captured Jerusalem. In 586 BCE the great walls of the holy city were battered down, and its buildings put to the torch by the Babylonians. The Temple was emptied of its sacred treasures, the altar dismantled, and the building destroyed. Many Judeans were taken to exile in Babylonia, where they were thenceforth known as "Jews," since they were from Judah.

The prophets interpreted these events as reasonable punishment by God for Judah's wickedness. Nevertheless, Isaiah and a later anonymous prophet (known to historians as "Second Isaiah" or "Deutero-Isaiah") prophesied that God would soon usher in a new era of peace and justice among all peoples, from his holy temple in Jerusalem.

> *I never could forget you.*
> *See, I have engraved you*
> *On the palms of My hands . . .*   Isaiah 49: 15-16

After fifty years of exile in Babylon, the Jews were indeed allowed to return to their holy city by the Persian King Cyrus. Second Isaiah called him the Messiah ("anointed one"). Cyrus authorized the rebuilding of the Temple, and it was completed in 515 BCE. He returned the thousands of vessels of silver and gold that Nebuchadnezzar had earlier stripped from the First Temple and these sacred treasures were used to adorn the Second Temple.

The final years in Jerusalem

The Temple became the symbol of a scattered Jewish nation, many of whom did not return to Jerusalem (and were thenceforth said to be living in the *Diaspora*, from the Greek word for "disperse"). A new emphasis on Temple rites developed, with an hereditary priesthood tracing its ancestry to Aaron.

The priestly class also undertook to revise, or redact, the stories of the people, editing history to reveal the hand of God. Some scholars think that it was priestly editors who wrote the book of Genesis, glorifying the greatness and omnipotence of their God as creator of the universe. Nothing was attributed to chance or natural law; God's influence was seen in all historical events.

The Torah was established as the spiritual and secular foundation of the dispersed nation. In approximately 430 BCE, Ezra the scribe set the precedent of reading for hours from the Torah scrolls in a public square. These "five books of Moses" were accepted as a

*A model of the Second
Temple after enlargements
by Herod, shortly before its
destruction by the Romans.
Once it was destroyed,
images of the temple's
facade expressed the
messianic hope of the
restoration of the
holy land.*

sacred covenant, and prophecy was declared ended. Divine revelation gave way to interpretation of what had already been revealed.

Although the Jews lived under foreign rule – Persian, Greek, Parthian, and then Roman – the institutions of the priestly rites and the Torah tended to minimize cross-cultural religious borrowings in Judaism. Concepts of Satan, the angelic hierarchy, bodily resurrection, and the Day of Judgement are thought by some scholars to have made their way into Jewish belief from Zoroastrianism but were not uniformly accepted. The rationalism and humanism of the Greeks were quite attractive to some Jews.

Tension between traditionalists and those embracing Greek ways came to a head when Antiochus "the mad man" inherited the throne. He tried to force Greek ways on all Judea by abolishing the Torah as the Jewish constitution, burning copies of the Torah, killing families who circumcised their sons, building an altar to Zeus in the Temple in Jerusalem, and sacrificing a hog on it (in defiance of the Mosaic law against eating or touching dead pigs as unclean). A revolt led by the Hasmon family, the Maccabean rebellion, won a degree of independence for Judea in 140 BCE, but the establishment of the kingdom of God on earth remained a dream.

Under the Hasmonean kings three main groups of Jews stood out in Judea. One was the *Sadducees*, priests and wealthy businesspeople, conservatives intent on preserving the letter of the law. The *Pharisees* were more liberal citizens from all classes who sought to study the applications of Torah to everyday life. A third group, uncompromising in their piety and their disgust with what they considered a corrupted priesthood, retreated to the wilderness next to the Dead Sea, where they joined or formed the *Essene* Brotherhood. Their leader was "The Teacher of Righteousness," a priest, reformer, and mystic whose name was not uttered. Scrolls discovered in Qumran at the northwest end of the Dead Sea in 1947 reveal that the Essenes emphasized monastic discipline, communal living, obedience, study, and spiritual preparation for the Day of Judgement they anticipated, the New Age when the "sons of light" would be victorious over the "sons of darkness." The concepts seem directly related to Zoroastrianism, and were never adopted by mainstream Judaism.

Eventually the disagreements between the Sadducees and the Pharisees erupted into civil war. The Roman general Pompey was called in from Syria to arbitrate the dispute, but he took over the country instead. There followed a period of oppressive Roman rule of Palestine (which Canaan had been renamed), with the colonized people heavily taxed. Finally the Jews rose up in armed rebellion and after heroic resistance were slaughtered in the holy walled city of Jerusalem in 70 CE.

Jerusalem, including the second Temple, was reduced to ruins, along with all Judean towns. Those remaining Jews who had not been executed were forbidden to read Torah, observe the Sabbath, or circumcise their sons. None were allowed to enter Jerusalem when it was rebuilt as the Roman city Aelia Capitolina, except on the anniversary of the destruction of the Temple, when they could pay to lean against all that remained of it – the western wall – and lament the loss of their sacred home. Judaism no longer had a physical heart or a geographic center.

Dispersal and the Talmud

Judaism could have died then, as its people scattered throughout the Mediterranean countries. Two of the groups who survived the destruction of Judea were the heretics called Christians, and the rabbis, inheritors of the Pharisee tradition. Between them they have kept the teachings of the Tanakh vibrantly alive in Western civilization.

THE CHRISTIAN OFFSHOOT   Little is known of how Jews responded to the life and teachings of Jesus during his lifetime. He was a Jew and frequently referred to biblical stories and points of view. The Christian Gospels portray him as a follower of the Jewish commandments; he taught in synagogues and in the Temple of Jerusalem. His followers called him the Messiah (meaning "anointed," and therefore "king"). The Roman-occupation Jews used this term for a charismatic leader whom they longed for to cast off the yoke of foreign oppression and restore the kingdom of Israel to the heights it had known under King David.

The person most often considered a potential candidate for this role was Bar Kokhba, who led a brave but abortive attempt to free Judea after the destruction of the Sacred Temple. Jews were not looking for a savior in the sense that Christians pictured Jesus: as a suffering servant who was ushering in the spiritual kingdom of God. For the Jews, life was still as bad as before, and it got even worse. The messianic age of a new heaven and a new earth is yet to come, according to Judaism.

As time went on, the Christian tradition diverged farther and farther from its parent, which also continued to evolve separately, just as Buddhism diverged from Hinduism. Jews and Christians today disagree on many fundametal points of theology, despite their common origin. Whereas many Christians inappropriately assume that Judaism is Christianity minus Jesus, Leo Trepp points out eleven major ways in which Jewish belief contradicts Christian belief:

1 The God that Jews know is One (not three, as in the Christian Trinity).

2   God is formless and will never assume form. He could not have taken the form of a human, as Jesus.

3   No human will ever be divine.

4   No human will ever be perfect. Even the patriarchs and Moses are described in the Tanakh as having human limitations.

5   Jews believe that everyone has direct access to God. They do not believe in any intermediary between humans and God.

6   Jews believe that the soul comes to us morally neutral, with free will to choose between good and evil (in contrast to the Christian doctrine of original sin traced to Adam and Eve's transgression).

7   Judaism insists on obedience to the God-given commandments in Torah and on our personal responsibility to be co-workers of God on earth (in contrast to the Christian doctrine that faith in Jesus is the basis of salvation).

8   Judaism does not have sacraments.

9   Jews believe that "all the righteous peoples of the world have a share in the world to come" (Joshua ben Hanania, Tosefta Sanhedrin 13:2), in contrast to the exclusive Christian principle that only Jesus saves.

10   To Jews, Christian ethics are no more advanced than their own, and many speeches attributed to Jesus, such as the Sermon on the Mount, are merely restatements of traditional Jewish teachings. Christians consider Judaism an earlier, less evolved form of their own religion, the "Old Testament," as compared to the "New Testament" of Jesus.

11   To Jews, the New Testament is not divinely revealed. It was written after Jesus died and is thought to have been laced with anti-Jewish statements that were added by the authors to help distinguish Christianity from Judaism (a possibility to which we return in the next chapter).[15]

Despite these theological differences, Jews and Christians do share a common heritage. The great Jewish thinker Martin Buber (1878–1965), speaking to Christians, reminds them that they worship the same God celebrated in the Tanakh:

To you the book is a forecourt; to us it is the sanctuary. But in this place we can dwell together, and together listen to the voice that speaks there.[16]

The rabbinical tradition

The other group that survived the loss of Jerusalem was the heirs to the Pharisain tradition: the *rabbis*, who were teachers, religious decision-makers, and creators of liturgical prayer. No longer were there priests or Temple for offering sacrifices. The new temple was that of the human mind, ever groping toward God, and the substitute for animal sacrifice was liturgical prayer. The people met in *synagogues*, which simply means "meeting places," to read the Torah and to worship communally, praying simply and directly to God, with little ceremony. Worship was democratic; unlike the priesthood, the rabbis did not have special access to God's attention. A *minyan* – a quorum of ten adult males – had to be present for community worship.

Everyone was taught the basics of Torah as a matter of course, but many men also occupied themselves with deep study of the scriptures, from the age of five or six. Women were excluded from formal Torah study, because of notions of men's and women's different roles. Women's family responsibilities at home were considered primary for them; elsewhere they were to be subordinate to men. Literacy was highly valued for men, and this characteristic persisted through the centuries even in the midst of largely illiterate societies. It is said that in the afterlife one can see the Jewish sages still bent over their books studying. This is Paradise.

The revealed scriptures were closed; what remained was to interpret them as indications of God's word and will in history. This process continues to the present, giving Judaism a continually evolving quality in tandem with unalterable roots in the ancient books of Moses. Centering the religion in books and teachings rather than in a geographical location or a politically vulnerable priesthood has enabled the dispersed community to retain a sense of unity across time and space.

The giving of the Torah is seen as an expression of God's love for Israel, a divine guide for life, and the people therefore have deep love for the Torah. This feeling is related by Joshua Loth Liebman:

> *The Torah is our people's guarantee of immortality. It is as large and as deep as the world; it towers into the blue secrets of heaven.*
>
> *Sunrise and sunset, promise and fulfillment, birth and death, the drama of humanity – all are contained in this scroll...*

The Essenes lived communally and ascetically, awaiting the final judgement in settlements such as this one excavated at Qumran, where ancient biblical scrolls were found hidden in caves.

Throughout the ages, we Jews found in this Book of Books our encouragement and strength.

Though nations rose and fell, though empires conquered and decayed, Israel preserved its vitality and nobility through its allegiance to the lessons of Torah. [17]

The rabbis set themselves two tasks, collectively known as *midrash* – biblical exegesis and mystical interpretation of Torah. One was to interpret the mysteries in the written Torah. It was felt that the Torah was not merely a set of social laws and historical events; hidden within it were the universal laws and all knowledge about the nature of heaven and earth. To unearth the latter, one had to read between the lines.

For instance, in the text "And God said, 'Let us make man in our image'" (Genesis 1:26) the question arose, "Who is 'us'?" A succession of rabbis have used legal decisions (called *halakhah*, "the way to walk") and varied bits called *haggadah* (folklore, sociological and historical knowledge, theological arguments, ritual traditions, and their own inner understanding) to deduce the answers to such questions.

In addition to delving into the mysteries of the written Torah, the rabbis undertook to apply the biblical teachings to their contemporary lives, in very different cultural circumstances than those of the ancients, and to interpret scripture in ways acceptable to contemporary values. The model for this delicate task of living interpretation had been set by Hillel the Elder, who lived from about 30 BCE to 10 CE, probably overlapping with the life of Jesus. He was known as a humble and pious scholar who stressed loving relationships, good deeds, and charity toward the less-advantaged. He also established a valuable set of rules for flexible interpretation of Torah.

What is hateful to you, do not do to your neighbor:
that is the entire Torah;
the rest is commentary;
go and learn it.

Hillel the Elder [18]

This process of midrash yielded a vast body of legal and spiritual literature. The second task of the rabbis concerned the oral Torah. According to rabbinical tradition, God gave Moses two versions of the Torah at Sinai: the written Torah, which appears in the five books of Moses, and the oral Torah, a larger set of teachings which was memorized and passed down through the generations all the way to the early rabbis. After the fixing of the Jewish canon – the scriptures admitted to the Tanakh, in about 90 CE – the rabbinical schools set out to systematize all the commentaries and the oral tradition, which was continually evolving on the basis of expanded and updated understandings of the original oral Torah. In about 200 CE, Judah the Prince completed a terse edition of the oral Torah which was thenceforth known as the *Mishnah*. It is related to passages from the written Torah. Several centuries later, the Mishnah plus rabbis' commentaries on it were organized into the *Talmud* (meaning "study").

Midrash is still open-ended, for significant commentaries and commentaries upon commentaries have continued to arise over the centuries. No single voice has dominated this continual study of the Torah and its interpretations. Rabbis often disagreed in their interpretations. These disagreements, sometimes between rabbis from different centuries, are presented together. This continual interweaving of historical commentaries, as if all Jewry were present at a single marathon Torah-study event, has been a significant unifying factor for the far-flung, often persecuted Jewish population of the world.

In the hearty process of exegesis, the rabbis have actually introduced new ideas into Judaism, while claiming that they were merely revealing what already existed in the scriptures. Notions of the soul are not found in the Tanakh, but they do appear in the Talmud and Midrash. The way in which God is referred to and perceived also changes. In the early biblical narratives, Adonai appears to the patriarchs and Moses in dramatic forms, such as the burning bush and the smoking mountain. Later, the prophets are visited by angelic messengers and sometimes hear a divine inner voice speaking to them. In the rabbinical tradition God is presented in even more transcendent, less anthropomorphic ways. God's presence in the world, in relationship to the people, is called the *Shekhinah*.

According to midrash, the Shekhinah came to the earth at creation but as a result of human wickedness it withdrew to the heavens, to be brought down by human acts of faithfulness, charity, and loving-kindness. God spoke to Moses from a burning thorn-bush, rather than some more lofty object, to demonstrate that there is no place where the Shekhinah cannot dwell. Sometimes the loving protection of the Shekhinah is depicted as a radiant, winged presence.

Persecution

Jews of the time lived in the shadow of other politically dominant religions. At first they enjoyed a rather hospitable relationship with the Zoroastrian Persians in Mesopotamia, and the city of Babylon was a major center of Jewish intellectual activity. But by the third century CE, religious tolerance had begun to wane. Under the influence of the Magis, there was some destruction of Jewish synagogues and burial grounds (thought to be polluting by the Zoroastrians, who disposed of their dead in Towers of Silence).

In 468 CE, the situation worsened for Jews in Mesopotamia. The Jewish community living in the Persian capital of Ispahan was charged with flogging two Magi to death. In retaliation, half of the Jews were killed and children were captured to be raised as Zoroastrians. The violence reached Babylonia. There the Exilarch (Jewish leader of the Diaspora) was put to death along with many rabbis. Synagogues were razed and Torah study classes prohibited. Never again did the Jewish community in Babylonia regain its prosperous, influential position.

In the meantime, Palestine was increasingly Christianized as part of the Roman Empire, which by the fifth century CE had forbidden all "heathen" rites and established Christianity as the state religion. Jews were not grouped with heathens but they were legally treated as second class citizens, encouraged to convert to Christianity, and forbidden to hold public office. A 439 CE edict asserted, "Indeed, we believe it sinful that the enemies of the heavenly majesty and of the Roman laws should become the executors of our laws ... and have the power to judge or decide as they wish against Christians."[19]

Christians had been forbidden to lend money to anybody with interest; the Jewish scriptures forbade usury only in loans among fellow Jews. Jews often therefore became hated money-lenders to Christians, and were often disliked because of their perceived wealth. Their theology was treated as a heresy, for teaching that the Messiah had not yet come, and Jews were historically accused of killing the Christian Messiah. Jewish sages could not teach, and the Torah could only be read in its Greek translation, the Septuagint. To retain some degree of religious freedom, the Jews revived the Hebrew language and used it to sing subversive hymns about their continuing messianic hopes. In Spain the Visigoth Christian kings became so anti-Semitic that Jews were flogged, killed, or forcibly baptized as Christians, only to continue practicing their own faith secretly.

When Palestine and Syria fell in the seventh century CE and Spain in the eighth century CE to Muslim Arabs, Jews in the captured territories experienced a reprieve of sorts. There had long been Jewish tribes in Arab lands, and Muhammad perceived his religion as founded on the monotheistic faith of Abraham. Jews were generally left alone as fellow "People of the Book" though they had no political power.

In Spain, Muslim fundamentalists came to power in the eleventh century CE, massacring and threatening Jews. Many fled to other countries, including the great scholar and doctor Maimonides, whose family eventually settled in Cairo.

Maimonides, considered one of the greatest of all Jewish intellectuals, is particularly famous for his synthesis between reason and faith. In writings such as his *Guide of the Perplexed* he spoke on behalf of the rationality that had characterized Jewish intelligentsia since the dawning of the rabbinic age, but did so within the context of faith:

> What is man's singular function here on earth? It is, simply, to contemplate abstract
> intellectual matters and to discover truth . . . And the highest intellectual contemplation
> that man can develop is the knowledge of God and His unity. [20]

Despite the beauty of such theology, Jews' detractors were closing in on them. Spain had completely thrown off Muslim rule, and the Christian victors were increasingly vigorous in promoting their own faith. The dreaded Inquisition was established in 1480 to root out all perceived heretics within the Catholic Church. These included *conversos* (also called *marranos*, or "pigs") – Jews who had been forcibly converted to Christianity but continued to practice their own religion in private. Family members were forced to inform on each other, with "evidence" such as the discreet refusal to drink from the same cup as one who had eaten pork. The Inquisition ultimately claimed 375,000 victims, many of them killed by burning at the stake as the nobility watched. The luckier conversos got life imprisonment, heavy fines, or a life of severe economic restriction wearing garments of sackcloth with yellow crosses. The Inquisitors were appointed directly by King Ferdinand and led by the Dominican prior who was confessor to Queen Isabella.

After years of these horrors, the crown tried to put an end to the Jewish presence in Spain by an Edict of Expulsion, giving Jews the option of immediate conversion to Christianity or physical ejection from the country. Expulsions were also ordered in many Western European countries, forcing those who clung to their dishonored status as Jews to become "wandering Jews" or to resettle in the less developed countries of Eastern Europe. In many cities, they were segregated into *ghettos*, special Jewish-only quarters, often walled in and locked at night and during Christian holy days, to limit mixing between Christians and Jews. Despite the constriction and crowding within ghettos, they did at least permit a preservation of Judaic culture.

Poland became one of the major centers of Jewish culture until the revolt of the

Cossacks. Associating Jewry with the previous regime, the Cossacks led terrible massacres against the Jews, followed by even more killing as the country continually changed hands. Penurious Polish Jewish refugees became a common sight throughout Europe.

As anti-Semitism increased, Jews were heavily and arbitrarily taxed and treated as pariahs. Their longing for deliverance from danger, poverty, and oppression fueled the old messianic dream. Among the "pseudo-Messiahs" who rose to the occasion, the most famous was Shabbatai Tzevi (1626–1676) of Smyrna, the Turkish port now called Izmir. A rather unstable personality, he became convinced that it was his calling to be the Messiah. A young man named Nathan, who became his enthusiastic prophet, sent letters to Jews throughout Europe, Asia, and Africa announcing that the Messiah had at last appeared in his master. Many believed him and made provisions for their return to the Holy Land. However, when Tzevi entered the Ottoman Empire, he was arrested and put in jail. Given the choice of converting to Islam or being executed, he chose conversion and was given a government position.

The shock to his supporters was terrible. But some groups, labeled "believing fools" by the others, did not give up hope. They found biblical, talmudic, and mystical references predicting his conversion and felt that it was all part of his plan to gather as many "holy sparks" as possible into the coming kingdom. When he died ten years later, some still held out hope that he would return someday to redeem the Jews.

Enlightenment

The eighteenth-century European movement called the Enlightenment brought better conditions for Jews. It played down tradition and authority in favor of tolerance, reason, and material progress. In such an intellectual atmosphere, restrictions on Jews decreased. The French Revolution brought equality for the masses, including Jews living in France, and this trend spread to other European countries. Ghettos were torn down, and Jews ascended to positions of prominence in society. The Rothschild family, for instance, became international financiers, benefactors, and patrons of the arts.

In the midst of modernizing influences, worship changed in liberal congregations. No longer was knowledge of the Talmud of central interest, and more Christian-like stately rituals and sermons tended to replace Talmudic discussion in synagogue services. Reform leaders saw Judaism as continually evolving and harmonizing with the times, and felt that rather than holding to the messianic ideal of return to the land of Israel, Jews could better accomplish "the mission of Israel" dispersed throughout the world.

Hasidism and Kabbalah

Jewish mystics remained hidden for some years after the Shabbatai Tzevi disaster. But the fervent experience of and love for God had been an undercurrent in Judaism since perhaps the time of the Second Temple. The rabbinical movement incorporated some of this mysticism into the Talmud. However, mystical writings were excluded from the biblical canon and form the separate books known as the *Apocrypha*.

The apocryphal Book of Enoch describes the ascent to God as a journey through seven heavenly spheres to an audience with the King of the celestial court. The core mystical experience was the encounter with unspeakable holiness. "*Kadosh, Kadosh, Kadosh*" ("Holy, Holy, Holy") is still chanted daily when there is a minyan.

Ways of drawing near to the holy Presence were carried secretly as oral tradition until the twelfth and thirteenth centuries, when some of them were put into writing. The most important of these books is *The Zohar* ("Way of Splendor") by Moses de Leon, who said it was actually the work of a second-century mystic. Whoever wrote it, the Zohar is a massive and complex offering of stories, explanations of the esoteric levels of the Torah, and descriptions of visionary practice and experiences. It depicts the world we perceive with our senses as but a lower reflection of a splendid higher world. Mystics held the Tanakh in great esteem, but felt that it was not to be interpreted literally.

Jewish mysticism, known as *Kabbalah* ("tradition") from the eleventh century on, was never a single tradition, since the Jews were decentralized. One school emphasized esoteric meditations on the letters of the Torah; another focused on ethical practices. During the sixteenth century Kabbalah's most influential leader was Isaac Luria. He explained creation as the beaming of the divine light into ten special vessels, some of which were shattered by the impact because they contained lower forces that could not bear the intensity of the light. The breaking of the vessels spewed forth particles of evil as well as fragments of light into the world. According to Lurianic teachings, only the coming of the Messiah will bring *tikkun* ("correction" or "repair" of this situation), ending chaos and evil in the world. Although only God will decide when this will happen, humans have a great responsibility to prepare by regathering the "sparks of holiness" in the unclean realms to repair the holy vessels. To this end, Luria asked his followers to follow strict ascetic purification practices, prayer, observance of the mitzvot of the Torah, and chanting of sacred formulas.

Shabbatai Tzevi was a Lurianic Kabbalist. After the collapse of his pseudo-Messiahship, Kabbalah quietly went underground, to resurface in a very different form

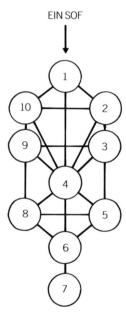

EIN SOF

1 KETHER (Crown)
2 HOKHMAH (Wisdom)
3 HESED (Love)
4 TIFERETH (Beauty)
5 NETSAH (Endurance)
6 YESOD (Foundation)
7 MALKUTH (Kingdom)
8 HOD (Splendor)
9 DIN (Judgement)
10 BINAH (Understanding)

A central Kabbalistic image is the Tree of God, a representation of the emanation of the qualities of the infinite Ein Sof into revealed aspects, the sephiroth.

in the eighteenth century as *Hasidism*, the path of ecstatic piety. It developed in Poland, where Jews were poverty-stricken and fearing for their lives. The rabbis had little to offer them, retreating into academic debates about legal aspects of the Torah.

Into this grim setting came the Baal Shem Tov (1700–1760), a beloved healer and Hasidic teacher offering a joyful version of Jewish holiness. To him, Torah study and obedience to the letter of the law were no better than deep-felt, pure-hearted prayer; everyone is capable of the highest enlightenment. He asserted that the divine could be found everywhere, in the present, thereby de-emphasizing the perennial waiting for a future Messiah. "Leave sorrow and sadness," he cried; "man must live in joy and contentment, always rejoicing in his lot."[21] Followers of the Baal Shem Tov worshipped through joyous songs and ecstatic, swaying prayer, and found God in the midst of the ghetto.

God can be found everywhere, emphasizes the Baal Shem Tov, but can only be seen by those who are not taken in by surface appearances and who really want to find him. God is here in the midst of even the most mundane everyday activities; if carried out in remembrance of God, even eating, drinking, and working become holy acts. It is through the ups and downs of everyday life that the soul advances toward God. The highest goal is *devekut*, "cleaving" to God, free of the egotism and vanity that separate humans from the Holy One.

> As the hand held before the eye conceals the greatest mountain, so the little earthly life hides from the glance the enormous lights and mysteries of which the world is full, and he who can draw it away from before his eyes, as one draws away a hand, beholds the great shining of the inner worlds.
>
> *attributed to Reb Nachman of Bratzlav*

Soon an estimated half of all Eastern European Jews were followers of the Hasidic path. Spread of the teachings is credited to Dov Ber, who emphasized the importance of the *tzaddik*, or enlightened saint and teacher, called *rebbe* (or Reb) when ordained as a Hasidic spiritual guide. Ber urged Hasidim to take spiritual shelter with a tzaddik, whose prayers and wisdom would be more powerful than their own because of the tzaddik's personal relationship with God. In time the position of tzaddik became hereditary and subject to exploitation by less-than-holy lineage carriers. Nevertheless, the religious fervor associated with Hasidism continued as an influence within Judaism.

Holocaust

The fervent love for God in good and bad times may have helped European Jews withstand poverty and humiliation. But how could anything prepare them for what was to follow? The world is still trying to understand what happened.

There had been a partial improvement in social conditions for Jews during the eighteenth and early nineteenth centuries. But reactionary anti-Semitism resurfaced late in the nineteenth century in Russia and Eastern Europe, where Jews formed a sizeable minority of the population. Their growing wealth and presence in higher education circles were often targets of distrust and envy.

Western powers led by statesmen such as Benjamin Disraeli, the Jewish Prime Minister of England, and Woodrow Wilson of the United States emphasized the rights of

Jews throughout Europe to full citizenship. But Jews were increasingly associated with left-wing movements pushing for change, even though many socialists were non-observant Jews who did not identify personally with Judaism or even with the Jewish nation. Leon Trotsky, for example, was religiously indifferent but of Jewish blood. His leadership in the violent Bolshevik Revolution and the Red Army led to terrible reprisals, called *pogroms*, against Jewish communities by the White Russians in the civil war. In a thousand separate incidents, up to seventy thousand Jews were killed by unrestrained rioting mobs. The slogan of the mobs was "Beat the Jews, save Russia." Even after the Bolshevik Revolution, continuing social chaos in Russia led to massacres of an estimated quarter-of-a-million Jews.

News of Bolshevik atrocities, coupled with anti-Semitic literature, led the United States to reverse its previous policy of welcoming Jewish immigrants fleeing persecution elsewhere. Quotas were severely limited. Even in England, long a tolerant home for Jewish immigrants, an anti-Bolshevik newspaper correspondent to Russia submitted a piece that reflected widespread suspicion of Jewish motives – a distorted interpretation of the messianic ideal:

> The essence of Judaism . . . is above all a racial pride, a belief in their superiority, faith in their final victory, the conviction that the Jewish brain is superior to the Christian brain, in short, an attitude corresponding to the innate conviction that the Jews are the Chosen People, fated to become one day the rulers and legislators of mankind. [22]

The situation was most dangerous in Germany. Adolf Hitler's Nazi Party bolstered its popular support by blaming the Jews for every problem facing the country in the wake of World War I. Germany could not regain its health until all Jews were stripped of their power or driven out of the country, Hitler maintained. Racist theories that those of "pure" Nordic blood were genetically ideal, while Jews were a dangerous "mongrel" race that should be eliminated for the sake of "racial hygiene," were openly circulated. Seeing the handwriting on the wall, many Jews, including eminent professionals, managed to emigrate, leaving their homes, their livelihood, and most of their possessions behind. Others stayed, hoping that the terrifying signs would be short-lived.

Beginning in 1935, German Jews were deprived of their legal and economic rights by the Nuremberg Laws, and when Hitler invaded Austria in 1938, Austrian Jews fell under the same laws. Jewish businesses were forcibly taken over by "Aryans." Polish Jews living in Germany were rounded up into trucks and conveyed to the Polish border, where Polish officials refused to take them in.

Among those who waited on the border, cold and hungry, during the interminable diplomatic maneuverings, were an old couple named Grynszpan. When their seventeen-year-old son Herschel shot a Secretary of the German Embassy in Paris in crazed protest, all pretext of legality was dropped. Within two days Storm Troopers began a ferocious attack on the German Jewish community, destroying almost every synagogue and Jewish place of business, raiding homes, and deporting Jews to concentration camps.

Terrorized and under heavy pressure from the Gestapo, over 150,000 Jews left Germany and 100,000 left Austria. Few countries, however, would allow them to enter. The United States government's attempts to arrange for systematic emigration were abandoned when Germany invaded Poland and then in rapid succession Denmark,

Norway, Belgium, Holland, and France, thereby placing several million more Jews under Nazi control.

In Poland, systematic oppression began with orders to all Jews to move into the towns, where walled ghettos were then created to confine them. They had to wear a yellow or white badge with the Star of David on it to reveal their stigmatized status, and since all other jobs were taken away from them, they could do only menial labor.

Along the Russian front, special groups (*Einsatzgruppen*, or "Action Groups") were assigned to slaughter Jews, gypsies, and commissars as the German troops advanced and to incite the local militia to do the same. The Einsatzgruppen would locate the presiding rabbi and leaders of the Jewish intelligentsia in each town, tell them to round up all their people for relocation in a "Jewish region," and then herd them outside of town to ravines or dugouts and machine-gun them all down. Sometimes the people were drowned instead, or gassed by poison in traveling vans. The Jews were unsuspecting, for news of this activity was forbidden. One cannot comprehend the numbers of men, women, and children killed in these mass murders — 34,000 at Babi Yar, 26,000 at Odessa, 32,000 at Vilna — probably totalling hundreds of thousands.

In the Eastern European ghettos, Jewish Councils (*Judenrats*) were set up as intermediaries between the Jewish people and the Nazis. By 1942 large-scale death camps had been set up by the Nazis to facilitate the "Final Solution" — total extermination of all Jews in Europe, a population the Nazis estimated at eleven million.

A young Jewish man wears a star of David armband for identification in Nazi Germany.

The Judenrat in Warsaw, the largest of the ghettos, was ordered to select 6000 Jews a day to be "resettled" (exterminated). After two days of this, the head of the Judenrat committed suicide, but the mass round-ups continued. In 1943 there was a heroic resistance effort in the Warsaw ghetto, with defenders holding out for five weeks until every Jewish fighter was killed.

In addition to forced marches which few survived, or unique situations such as the burning alive of 20,000 to 30,000 Jews in four Odessa warehouses, Jews were transported by cattle cars (in which many suffocated to death) from all over Europe to concentration camps. There they were starved, worked to death as slaves, tortured, "experimented" on, and/or shipped to extermination camps. The industrial-scale gas chambers were found to be the most efficient means of killing and also an impersonal way to get around the increasing unwillingness of Germans to kill so many Jewish men, women, and children.

Efficiency became an issue as it became apparent that Germany would lose the war, for Hitler was determined to complete his Final Solution. Even when trains were needed for military purposes near the end, the Nazis continued to use them for transporting Jews to death camps. A current theory among historians is that extermination of the Jews was Hitler's chief motive for World War II, rather than territorial expansion per se.

Hitler was not the only one responsible for the genocide, however. There were a tremendous number of people in Germany, Austria, Rumania, and even France whose active or passive participation was needed in carrying out the killings. In Germany alone there were 700,000 members of the SS, in addition to over a million who worked for the railways and an uncounted supporting cast of other workers.

Citizens and governments of some occupied countries, such as Denmark, Finland, Italy, Belgium, Greece, and Bulgaria, refused to cooperate and did what they could to hide Jews and help them escape. But there was little outcry from the outside world. The Vatican was silent, though it sheltered 477 Jews and several thousand more found refuge in monasteries and convents. The Allies took no special action to save the Jews during the war. Bombing the gas chambers was militarily feasible and urged by Winston Churchill, who called the killing "probably the greatest and most horrible crime ever committed in the whole history of the world." But he had no support from his own government or from the United States. In the United States, the government even asked Jewish organizations not to publicize the exterminations, to avoid interference with the war effort — and lest the country be besieged with Jewish refugees. Reversing its policy in 1943 through pressure and financial support from American Jews, the United States managed to save 200,000 Jews. In hindsight, many historians have concluded that Hitler's hideous policy could have been slowed by determined resistance from free Allied countries.

> *If we bear all this suffering and if there are still Jews left, when it is over, then Jews, instead of being doomed, will be held up as an example. Who knows, it might even be our religion from which the world and all peoples learn good, and for that reason and reason only do we have to suffer now.* *from the Diary of Anne Frank*

From 1939 to the end of the war, some six million Jews were exterminated. This was over a third of the Jewish people in the world and half of all Jews in Europe. Those who

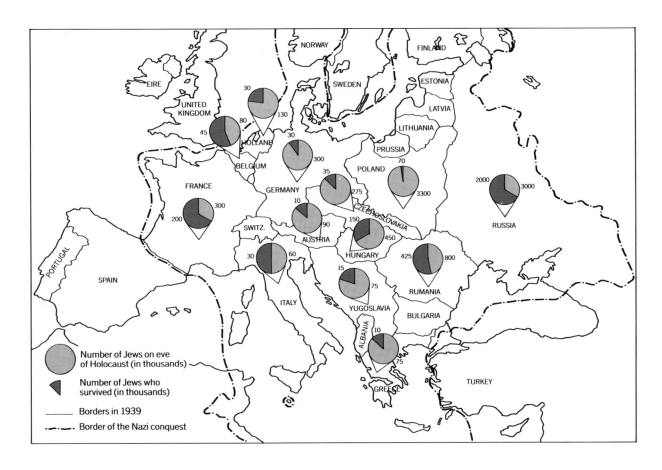

Hitler's Final Solution was to herd Jews into concentration camps throughout Nazi-occupied Europe and then ship the survivors east into extermination camps in Poland. The pie charts show the number of Jews in each country who were left after the holocaust, relative to their previous populations.

had endured the horrors, had watched their spouses, parents, and children killed, and had somehow survived themselves, were psychologically and physically devastated. They found it impossible to speak of their experiences. How could anyone understand? The death camps, they said, were "not of this world."[23] It came to be called the *Holocaust,* "the whole burnt offering."

The world had never before witnessed systematic evil of this magnitude. Jews were not merely killed; they were deliberately and diabolically turned into subhuman creatures before being dispassionately destroyed. One small example of the dehumanizing tactics of the killers: When "work permits" were issued to those Jewish men who were still healthy enough to be useful if kept alive temporarily rather than killed at once, sometimes a second permit was also issued, to be given to the family member of the man's choice. The Nazis refused to make the decision, forcing the man to select which among his loved ones would be killed. He could not give away his own work permit.

Under such brutalizing circumstances, how could the people maintain their ethical commandments? How could they interpret their situation as the divine will? Why would God allow this horror to happen to his chosen people? Could religious Jews continue believing as they did before? According to a survey of 708 holocaust survivors in Israel, over half said the experience had altered their relationship to the Divine. Of these, three out of four either turned away from faith in a personal God or shifted to belief in an impersonal God. Rabbi Eliezer Berkovits points out, however, that the amazing thing is that so many kept and were strengthened by their Jewish faith. Even those who questioned "Why?" often continued to ask this question of God.

> *I believe in the sun even when it is not shining.*
> *I believe in love even when not feeling it.*
> *I believe in God even when He is silent.*
> > *Inscription on the wall of a cellar in Cologne where Jews hid*

Elie Wiesel, an eminent Holocaust survivor, says that we cannot turn away from the questions about how it could happen. We must ask why the free governments of the world did not take strong action to stop the genocide, for smaller-scale actions are being undertaken against other minority groups even today. As Wiesel points out:

> *According to Jewish tradition, the death of one innocent person tarnishes the cosmos. Other people's tragedies are our tragedies. We must study the past, the horrors of the past and the melancholy of the past, if we are to be sensitive in the present. [In this] there are eternities of distress – the terrifying power of evil over innocence – but also some strength in the resolve of the victim never to become a killer.*[24]

Zionism

After the unprecedented horrors of the Holocaust, many Jews found it important to claim their heritage openly, rather than make empty martyrs of the six million. A central way of doing so was to establish a Jewish state, a spiritual and secular homeland for the dispersed Jewish nation. This trend is called Zionism, a historical reference to the building of the First Temple on Mount Zion in Jerusalem, from which Jews had been barred since the Second Temple fell to the Romans in 70 CE.

The possibility of returning to Zion after centuries of exile had its supporters and opponents in Jewish communities. Reform Jews wanted nothing to do with the establishment of a Jewish state. The new destiny of Jews was to be lived out among the Gentiles, where the Enlightenment had fueled hopes of a freer future and where Jews hoped they could be recognized as legitimate citizens of the countries where they were born. Much support for Zionism came from traditional Orthodox Jews, but not all Orthodox embraced the idea. Some of them felt it was up to God to end the exile, for it was God who punished the people for their unfaithfulness by sending them away from the promised land.

Zionism began as an organized movement in the nineteenth century. One of its first proponents was Moses Hess. He had argued that a spiritual center was needed to inspire the whole Diaspora. This idea was taken up later by the mystical Isaac Kook, European Chief Rabbi. Kook held that life's central purpose is to raise the profanities of existence to a state of holiness; Jews could best do so if they were revitalized by actual contact with nature in the land which God had chosen for them.

In addition to spiritual reasons for Zionism, there was the political agenda of creating a place where Jews could be free of anti-Semitism and oppression. In sympathy with

Much of the Promised Land to which the Jews wanted to return was a desert, occupied by Palestinians. This group is celebrating the founding of Tel Aviv, now a modern city, on sand dunes in 1909.

this Jewish cause, pressed by the Viennese Theodor Herzl, Britain issued the Balfour Declaration. It arranged for limited Jewish settlement in Palestine at the end of World War I. The land had belonged to Turkey, who entered the war late on the losing side. Hebrew was adopted as one of the official languages of the country and a Jew was sent to govern it. The Arabs living in the area were understandably incensed, and the British, who still wanted to maintain an alliance with Arab countries in the Middle East, endeavored to strictly limit Jewish immigration to the token state. They continued to do so after World War II ended, leaving large numbers of survivors of the Holocaust in Displaced Persons camps with no place to settle. One shipload of survivors trying to enter Palestine was sent back to Germany by the British Navy.

In 1947, the United Nations suggested a partition of Palestine into two areas, one to be governed by Jews and the other by Arabs, with Jerusalem (a holy city to Christianity and Islam as well as Judaism) run by an international agency. The Arabs had not agreed to this plan, nor had England, but it was put into effect. Previously patient and submissive under centuries of foreign rule and persecution, Zionists proved surprisingly effective in establishing and defending their new state. They were so strong, in fact, that the United Nations called for an armistice to end the fighting between the new state of Israel and her Arab neighbors. Israel was allowed to keep some areas that were supposed to have been Arab under the original partition plan, and also to occupy the suburbs of Jerusalem. Jewish settlers from around the world were welcomed.

Arabs emigrated from the Jewish territories in great numbers, but they stayed in the Old City of Jerusalem. And the surrounding Arab states continued military resistance to the fact of a Jewish state. In a series of stunning successes, Israel proved itself militarily defendable during the Six-Day War in 1967, in response to Egyptian attempts to bar shipping through the Suez Canal. It also recaptured the old walled city of Jerusalem, the sacred prize from which it had been excluded since the Roman takeover. Jews around the world, including those who had not been Zionists, took great pride in this military

Members of a Kibbutz at Kfar Rupin, Israel, wait with soldiers from a nearby army camp in an underground shelter. A four hour artillery battle takes place overhead between Israel and Jordan (April 26th, 1969).

success, and financial contributions to help support the country increased.

Israel has established itself as a sovereign state in the Middle East, on the land promised to Abraham, thus satisfying its political agenda. Its spiritual agenda, the mission of serving as a vital center for the Jewish faith, was placed somewhat in the background in the face of its urgent needs to farm the desert, create self-sufficient communities, and defend itself. Within a remarkably short time, these needs were met. Nevertheless, in the face of continuing resistance from surrounding countries, Israel is ironically one of the most dangerous places in the world for a Jew to live.

Torah

It is difficult to outline the tenets of the Jewish faith. As we have seen, Jewish spiritual understandings have changed repeatedly through history. Rationalists and mystics have often disagreed. Since the nineteenth century, there has been an open split between liberal and fundamentalist Jews, to be discussed at the end of the chapter.

Despite these internal differences, there are certain major themes that can be extricated from the vast history and literature of Judaism. These are Torah, which literally means "the Guidance, the Teachings." In its narrowest sense, Torah refers to the Five Books of Moses. On the next level, it means the entire Tanakh and the Talmud, the written and the oral law. For some, it is all sacred Jewish literature. At the highest level, Torah is God's will, God's wisdom.

The One God

The central Jewish belief is monotheism. It has been stated in different ways in response to different cultural settings (emphasizing the divine Unity when Christians developed the concept of the Holy Trinity; emphasizing that God is formless and ultimate holiness in opposition to the earthy heathen gods; de-emphasizing the willful deliverer-of-all-suffering aspect of God after the Holocaust). But the central theme is God's oneness. This metaphysical understanding is difficult to explain in linear language, which refers to the individuated objects perceived by the senses. As the eleventh-century Spanish mystic Ibn Gabirol put it, "None can penetrate ... the mystery of Thy unfathomable unity."[25]

One of the most elegant attempts to "explain" God's oneness has been offered by the great twentieth-century Polish/American Hasidic scholar, Abraham Joshua Heschel. Unity is in a sense another word for "eternity," Heschel says. "One" also refers to the state of perfection, which is the sole reality, and toward which all existence is drawn. "One" also means "the same," the unity of all qualities which appear to be opposites on the earth plane. God is both immanent and transcendent, both loving and powerful, both known and hidden, both personal Father and impersonal Eternal. God is revealed in nature – the heavens and earth glorify God (although Heschel sadly notes that "the awareness of grandeur and the sublime is all but gone from the modern mind"[26]). But God is not the same as nature; God is its creator. "The earth is our sister, not our mother,"[27] Heschel states.

> Plurality is incompatible with the sense of the ineffable. You cannot ask in regard to the divine: Which one? There is only one synonym for God: One.
>
> Abraham Joshua Heschel[28]

God is everywhere, even in the darkness, as David the psalmist sings:

Where can I escape from Your spirit?
Where can I flee from your presence?
If I ascend to Heaven, You are there:
*   if I descend to Sheol [the underworld],*
*   You are there too.*

If I take wing with the dawn
*   to come to rest on the western horizon,*
*   even there Your hand will be guiding me,*
*   Your right hand will be holding me fast.*
                                    Psalm 139:7–14

In patriarchal Judaism, God is often perceived as a loving Father who is nonetheless infinitely majestic and sometimes reveals his power when his children need chastising.

Love for God

The essential commandment to humans is to love God. The central prayer in any Jewish religious service and the inscription on the *mezuza* at the doorpost of every traditional Jewish home is the *Shema Israel*:

> *Hear, O Israel! The Lord is our God, the Lord alone. You shall love the Lord your God with all your heart and with all your soul and with all your might. Take to heart these instructions with which I charge you this day. Impress them upon your children. Recite them when you stay at home and when you are away, when you lie down and when you get up. Bind them as a sign on your hand and let them serve as a symbol on your forehead; inscribe them on the doorposts of your house and on your gates.*
>
> Deuteronomy 6:4–9

Even Maimonides, the great proponent of reason and study, asserted the primacy of love for God. He emphasized that one should not love God from selfish or fearful motivations, such as receiving earthly blessings or avoiding problems in the life after death. One should study Torah and fulfill the commandments out of sheer love of God.

The sacredness of human life

Humans are the pinacle of creation, created in the "image" of God. Scholarly Jews do not take this passage from Genesis to mean that God literally looks like a human. It is often interpreted in an ethical sense: that humans are so wonderfully endowed that they can mirror God's qualities, such as justice, wisdom, righteousness, and love.

Jewish theology has been shaped by the most compelling thinkers of each era. In the twentieth century, Martin Buber described the cherished human-divine encounter as an I-Thou relationship, in which one loses self-awareness but is totally present.

All people are potentially equal; they are said to be common descendants of the first man and woman. But they are also potentially perfectable, and in raising themselves they uplift the world. God limited the divine power by giving humans free will, involving them in the responsibility for the world's condition, and for their own. If we are suffering, according to the Talmud, we should examine our own deeds.

Martin Buber describes the relationship between God and humans as reciprocal:

> *You know always in your heart that you need God more than everything; but do you not know too that God needs you – in the fulness of His eternity needs you? How would man exist, how would you exist, if God did not need him, did not need you? You need God, in order to be – and God needs you, for the very meaning of your life . . . There is divine meaning in the life of the world . . . of human persons, of you and of me . . . We take part in creation, meet the Creator, reach out to Him, helpers and companions.* [29]

Human life is sacred, rather than lowly and loathsome. Judaism celebrates the body. Sexuality within marriage is holy, and the body is honored as the instrument through which the soul is manifested on earth.

> *I praise You, for I am awesomely, wondrously made.*
>
> Psalm 139:14

Law

Because of the great responsibility of humankind, Jews give thanks that God has revealed in the written and oral Torah the laws by which they can be faithful to the divine will and bring the divine order to earth. To the extent that they act according to these laws, they are upholding their part of the ancient covenant with God. The Hebrew word for transgression or sin means literally to "miss the mark"; the word for righteousness literally means "straight," not deviating from the right path because of stress or desire.

The Torah is said to contain 613 commandments, or *mitzvot* (singular: *mitzvah*). Judaism makes no distinction between spirit and matter, sacred and secular life, so these include general ethical guidelines such as the Ten Commandments and the famous saying in Leviticus 29:18 – "Love your fellow as yourself" – plus detailed laws concerning all aspects of life, such as land ownership, purchase of women (who were considered possessions in biblical times), loans, family offenses, sacred observances, diet, and ritual slaughter. A Sabbath prayer, "Ahavat Olam," thanks the Lord for this guidance, a token of the divine love:

> With everlasting love You have loved Your people Israel. You have taught us the Torah and its Mitzvot. You have instructed us in its laws and judgements.
>
> Therefore, O Lord our God, when we lie down and when we rise up we shall speak of Your commandments and rejoice in Your Torah and Mitzvot.
>
> For they are our life and the length of our days; on them we will meditate day and night.[30]

Suffering and faith

The Tanakh depicts the universe as being governed by an all-powerful, personal God who intervenes in history to reward the righteous and punish the unjust. Within this context, Jews have had considerable difficulty in answering the eternal question: Why must the innocent suffer?

The Tanakh itself brings up the issue with the challenging parable of Job, a blameless, God-fearing, and wealthy man. The story involves Satan, whom Jews see as an angel beneath God, who creates both darkness and light; Satan is the loyal opposition within the fold rather than an external opponent. In a conversation with God, the Adversary predicts that Job will surely drop his faith and blaspheme the Lord if he is stripped of all his possessions. With God's assent, the Adversary creates a test, fomenting incidents that destroy everything, including Job's children. On hearing the news:

> Job arose, tore his robe, cut off his hair, and threw himself on the ground and worshipped. He said, "Naked came I out of my mother's womb, and naked shall I return there; the Lord has given, and the Lord has taken away, blessed be the name of the Lord."[31]

With an itchy inflammation covering him from head to foot, Job begins to curse his life and to question God's justice. In the end, Job acknowledges not only God's power to control the world but also his inscrutable wisdom, which is beyond human understanding. God then rewards him with long life and even greater riches than he had before the test.

Simhat Torah is a joyous celebration of the Torah, with everyone joining in the dancing and singing. This one is taking place at the western ''Wailing Wall,'' where for nearly two thousand years Jews have made pilgrimages to pray.

Debate over the meanings of this story, which came from the esoteric wisdom tradition, has continued over the centuries. One rabbinical interpretation is that Satan was cooperating with God in helping Job grow from fear of God to love of God. Another is that faith in God will finally be rewarded in this life, no matter how severe the temporary trials. Another is that those who truly desire to grow toward God will be asked to suffer more, that their sins will be expiated in this life so they can enjoy the divine bliss in the life to come. Such interpretations assume a personal, all-powerful, loving God doing what is best for his people, even when they cannot understand his ways.

One of the modern interpretations of the problem of suffering is that God is loving but is not all-powerful and cannot intervene in history on the side of the good, disrupting natural laws. This position is taken by Harold Kushner, a rabbi for whom the problem is not an academic question. His first son, a bright and happy child, had a disease that caused him to age rapidly. The Kushners were told by a doctor that Aaron would never grow more than three feet tall, would be hairless, would look like an old man, and would die as a teenager, which he did. Kushner wonders why God has done this to him, and worse, to Aaron:

> *Why should he have to suffer physical and psychological pain every day of his life? Why should he have to be stared at, pointed at, wherever he went? Why should he be condemned to grow into adolescence, see other boys and girls beginning to date, and realize that he would never know marriage or fatherhood?*[32]

The only way that Kushner could answer his questions without losing faith in God was to change his concept of God, to understand that pain and misfortune are part of life, not sent by God. From this point of view, the best one can do is try to make them meaningful by taking positive action – as some Jews did by establishing the state of Israel after the Holocaust – and to turn to God for strength in enduring the pain.

It is this turning to God, this closeness to God, that is important in the Jewish faith, no matter how one interprets the reasons for suffering. God is always available like a shepherd caring for his sheep, no matter how dark the outer circumstances.

> *Though I walk through a valley of deepest darkness,*
> *I fear no harm, for You are with me;*
> *Your rod and Your staff – they comfort me.*
>
> *Psalm 23:4*

Repairing creation

A final theme running throughout Judaism is the recognition that the world is imperfect and that Jews have a special responsibility for raising it up. Their long history of exile and homelessness is often given the broader metaphorical meaning of existing in an imperfect world, cut off from the Creator. Israel would only find its way home when all of creation was lifted up, or "repaired."

In the rabbinical tradition, the way out of exile is found through wisdom and righteous living. Ethical commandments have their origin in God and if followed, will lead humanity back to its Source. Another way home is mystical communion with God, without losing contact with humanity. Kabbalist Perle Epstein explains the challenge:

> *With Moses as his model, the Jewish mystic must concentrate on God in his every daily act, with his every breath; but he must always come down from the ''high place'' and live among the people as well. By ''yoking'' himself to God he develops a power of love so great that he brings the godly influx into this imperfect world of men.* [33]

Sacred practices

The ideal is to remember God in everything one does, through prayer and keeping the commandments. These commandments are not other-worldly. Many are rooted in the body, and spiritual practices often engage all the senses in awareness of God.

Boys are ritually circumcised when they are eight days old, to honor the seal of God's commandment to Abraham. Women are considered ritually unclean during their menstrual periods and for seven days afterwards. They are not to have sexual intercourse with their husbands and at the end of this forbidden period observant Jewish women undertake complete immersion in a *mikva*, a special deep bath structure. Marital sex is sacred, with the Sabbath night the holiest time for making love. By contrast, adultery – defined as sexual relations between a married woman and a man who is not her husband – is strictly forbidden as one of the worst sins against God. The Mosaic laws had presented femal adultery as a serious property offense because a woman was thought to belong to her father or her husband.

What one eats is also of cosmic significance, for according to Torah, some foods are definitely unclean. For example, the only ritually acceptable, or *kosher*, meats, are those from warmblooded animals with cloven hoofs who chew their cuds, such as cows, goats, and sheep. Poultry is kosher, except for birds of prey, but shellfish are not. Meat is also kosher only if it has been butchered in the traditional humane way by an authorized Jewish slaughterer. He or she cuts the arteries of the throat in a single painless motion of an extremely sharp, smooth knife with no nicks in it. Great pains are taken to avoid eating blood; meat must be soaked in water and then drained on a salted board before cooking. Meat and milk cannot be eaten together, and separate dishes are maintained for their preparation and serving. In modern interpretation, these commandments are important guides to being in spiritual harmony with the universe.

For traditional Jews, the morning begins with a prayer before opening one's eyes, thanking God for restoring one's soul. The hands must then be washed before reciting blessings and, for all traditional Jews, putting a special fringed rectangle of cloth around the neck. It is usually worn under the clothes as a reminder of the privilege of being given divine commandments. For weekday morning prayers men also put on *t'fillin*, or phylacteries, small leather boxes containing biblical verses about the covenant with God, including the "Shema." One is tied on the forehead and the other on the upper arm, held against the heart, in fulfillment of the commandments. Traditional Jewish men also wear a fringed prayer shawl (*talit*), and keep their heads covered at all times, if possible.

Specific prayers are recited morning, afternoon, evening, and at bedtime. Men are supposed to say them in Hebrew, and preferably with a minyan (quorum of ten) in a synagogue. Women can say them also, but they are excused from rigid schedules because their household responsibilities are considered important.

Jews are also expected to give thanks continually. One should recite a hundred benedictions to God every day. To this end, there is a blessing to be said every time one takes a drink of water. There is even a blessing to be recited after using the toilet:

> *Blessed art thou, Lord our God, King of the universe, who hast formed man in wisdom, and created in him a system of ducts and tubes. It is well known before thy glorious throne that if but one of these be opened, or if one of those be closed, it would be impossible to exist in thy presence. Blessed art thou, O Lord, who healest all creatures and doest wonders.* [34]

The Jewish Sabbath runs from sunset Friday night to sunset Saturday night, because the Jewish "day" begins with nightfall. The Friday night service welcomes the Sabbath as a bride and is often considered an opportunity to drop away the cares of the previous week so as to be in a peaceful state for the day of rest. The Saturday morning service incorporates public and private prayers, singing, and the reading of passages from the Torah. Torah scrolls are kept in a curtained ark on the wall facing Jerusalem. They are hand-lettered in Hebrew and are treated with great reverence. It is a great honor to be "called up" to read from the Torah.

More liberal congregations dispense with some of the ritual surrounding the reading of the Torah and place emphasis instead on an in-depth discussion of the passage read. Often it is examined not only from an abstract philosophical perspective but also from the point of its relevance to political events and everyday attempts to live a just and humane life. Torah study, and study of all Jewish literature, is highly valued, and synagogues usually have libraries for this purpose, sometimes in the same space that is used for worship.

In Hasidic congregations, the emphasis falls on the intensity of praying, or *davening*, even in saying fixed prayers from the prayer book. Some sway their bodies to induce the self-forgetful state of ecstatic communion with the Loved One. Others quietly shift their attention from earthly concerns to "cleave to God." The rabbinical tradition states the ideal in prayer: "A person should always see himself as if the Shekhinah is confronting him."[35]

In addition to or instead of going to a Sabbath service, observant families usually begin the Sabbath with a special Friday night dinner. The mother lights candles to bring in the Sabbath light; the father recites a blessing over the wine. Special braided bread, *challah*, is shared as a symbol of the double portions of manna in the desert. The rituals help to set a different tone for the day of rest, as do commandments against working, handling money, traveling except by foot, lighting a fire, cooking, and the like. The Sabbath is set aside as a day for prayer, study, thought, friendship, and family closeness, with the hope that this renewed life of the spirit will then carry through the week to come. At the end of the Sabbath day, there is a ceremony, the *havdala* ("separation"), to mark the shift back from holy to secular time.

It is customary to recognize coming of age, at thirteen, in Jewish boys by the *Bar Mitzvah* ("son of the commandment") ceremony. The boy has presumably undertaken some religious instruction, including learning to pronounce Hebrew, if not to understand it. He is called up to read a portion from the Torah scroll and recite a passage from one of the books of the prophets, in Hebrew, and then perhaps to give a short teaching about a topic from the reading. Afterwards there may be a simple *kiddush*, a celebration with blessing of wine and sweet bread or cake, but a big party is more likely. This custom of welcoming the boy to adult responsibilities has been extended to girls in non-Orthodox congregations in the *Bat Mitzvah* ("daughter of the commandment").

Left *Before praying, traditional Jewish men bind t'fillin to their arm and forehead in remembrance of their covenant with God.*
Right *Rosh Hashanah brings the blowing of the shofar in three ways: a note of alarm, three wails, and nine sobbing blasts of contrition.*

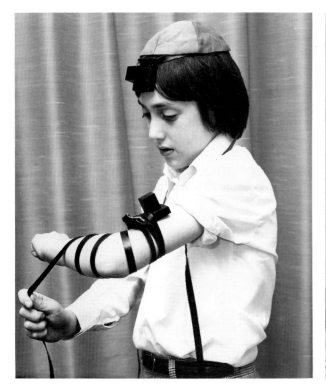

Holy days

Like other peoples, Jews honor the circle of the seasons with special ceremonies. For Jews, many of these times are also linked to special events in history.

The spiritual year begins with the High Holy Days of Rosh Hashanah and Yom Kippur. *Rosh Hashanah*, a time of spiritual renewal, is celebrated on the first day of the seventh month (around the fall equinox). For thirty days prior to Rosh Hashanah, each morning brings blowing of the *shofar* (a ram's horn that produces an eery, unearthly blast) to remind the people that they stand before God. At an evening Rosh Hashanah service, a prayer is recited asking that all humanity will remember what God has done, that there will be honor and joy for God's people, and that righteousness will triumph while "all wickedness vanishes like smoke."[36]

Yom Kippur follows ten days later. It honors and renews the sacred covenant of the Jewish people with God, but does so in the spirit of atonement. Historically, this was the only time when the high priest entered the Holy of Holies in the Temple of Jerusalem, and the only time that he would pronounce the sacred name of the Lord, YHWH, in order to ask for forgiveness of the people's sins. Today, there is an attempt at personal inner cleansing. Congregations confess their sins, ask that their negligence be forgiven, and pray for their reconciliation to God in a new year of divine pardon and grace.

Sukkot is a fall harvest festival. A simple outdoor booth is built and decorated as a dwelling place of sorts for seven days. The fragile home reminds the faithful that their real home is in God, who sheltered their ancestors on the way from Egypt to the promised land of Canaan. Some contemporary groups also pray for peace amid our vulnerability to nuclear war. Participants hold the *lulav* (a bundle made of a palm branch, myrtle twigs, and willow twigs) in one hand and the *etrog* (a citrus fruit) in the other and wave them together toward the four compass directions, earth and sky, praising God and acknowledging him as the unmoving center of creation. There is an offering of water, precious in the desert lands of the patriarchs, and great merrymaking. During the Second Temple days, the ecstatic celebration even included burning of the priests' old underclothes. The last day of the seven-day Sukkot festival is *Simhat Torah* ("Joy in Torah"), ending the yearly cycle of Torah readings, from Creation to the death of Moses, and beginning again.

Near the winter solstice, the darkest time of the year, comes *Hanukkah*, the Feast of Dedication. Each night for eight nights, another candle is lit on a special candle holder. The amount of light gradually increases like the lengthening of sunlight. Historically, Hanukkah was a celebration of the victory of the Maccabean Rebellion against the attempt by Antiochus to force non-Jewish practices on the Jewish people. According to rabbinical tradition, when the Jews regained access to the Temple, they found only one jar of oil left undefiled, still sealed by the high priest. It was only enough to stay alight for one day, but by a miracle, the oil stayed burning for eight days. Many Jewish families also observe the time by nightly gift-giving, as rewards for Torah study. The children have their own special Hanukkah pastimes, such as "gambling" for nuts with the *dreidel*. It is a top with four letters as an abbreviation of the sentence "A great miracle happened there."

As the winter rainy season begins to diminish in Israel, the people celebrate the reawakening of nature on *Tu B'shvat*. Observances lavish appreciation on a variety of

fruits and plants. In Israel, the time is now marked by planting of trees to help restore life to the desert.

On the full moon of the month before spring comes *Purim*. It theoretically commemorates the legend of Esther, queen of Persia, and Mordecai, who saved their fellow Jews from destruction by the evil viceroy Haman. It has been linked to Mesopotamian mythology about the goddess Ishtar, whose spring return brings joy and fertility. Purim is a bawdy time of mocking life's seriousness, and the jokes frequently poke fun at sacred Jewish practices. As the story of Esther is read from an ornate scroll, the congregation responds with noisy stomping, rattles, horns, and whistles whenever Haman's name is read.

The next major festival is *Pesach*, or *Passover*, which celebrates the liberation from bondage in Egypt. It was the tenth plague, death to all first-born sons of the Egyptians, which finally brought the Pharaoh to relent. The Israelites were warned to slaughter a lamb for each family and mark their doors with its blood so that the angel of death would pass over them. They were to roast the lamb and eat it with unleavened bread and bitter herbs. So quickly did they depart that they didn't even have time to bake the bread, which is said to have baked in the sun as they carried it on their heads. The beginning of Pesach is still marked by a *Seder* dinner with the eating of unleavened bread *(matzah)*, to remember the urgency of the departure, and bitter herbs as a reminder of slavery, so that they would never impose it on other peoples. Also on the

table are *charoset* (a sweet fruit and nut mixture, a reminder that slavery can appear sweet) and salt water (a reminder of the tears of the slaves) into which parsley or some other plant (a reminder of spring life) is dipped and eaten. Children ask ritual questions about why these things are done, as basic religious instruction.

Several new holidays have been set aside in the period that follows. One is Holocaust Memorial Day, *Yom Mashoah,* in April or May. Observances often include the singing in Yiddish (the language of European Jews) of a song from the Jewish Resistance Movement. In part:

> *Never say that you are*
> *going your last way,*
> *though leaden skies*
> *blot out the blue of day.*
> *The hour for which we*
> *long will certainly appear.*[37]

Another is Israel Independence Day, *Yom Haatzma-ut*, honoring May 14, 1948, when Israel was affirmed as a sovereign state.

Summer brings *Shavuot,* traditionally identified with the giving of the Torah to Moses at Mount Sinai and the people's hearing of the voice of God. It is likely that Shavuot was initially a harvest festival that later was linked with the revelation of the Torah. In Israeli kibbutzim the old practice of bringing the first fruits to God has been revived. Elsewhere, the focus is on reading of the Ten Commandments and on presenting the Torah as a marriage contract between God and Israel.

Then come three weeks of mourning for the Temples, both of which were destroyed on the ninth day of the month of Av (July or August), *Tisha Be-Av*. This is traditionally a time of fasting and avoidance of joyous activities. Some feel that there is no longer cause for mourning because even though the temple has not been rebuilt, the old city of Jerusalem has been recaptured. Others feel that we are all still in exile from the state of perfection.

Contemporary Judaism

Within the extended family of Judaism, there are many groups, many different focuses, and many areas of disagreement. Issues include the full participation of women, the role of Israel, the use of Hebrew, conversion to Judaism, ritualism, and adherence to Torah and Talmud. But in general, it can be said that a spirit of Jewish renewal is developing; the issues are signs of rejuvenation rather than decay of Judaism. The renewal is a shift from a recent pattern in which large numbers of people who were born Jewish did not observe their spiritual traditions, or did so only rarely, or followed the forms without understanding them.

> The more our age refuses to see the full face of the universe and restricts itself to the sight of a tiny fraction of its skin, the more anxious I become when I consider the universe in its eternal rhythm, and the more I wish to oppose the general current.   Marc Chagall[38]

Judaism, like all modern religions, has struggled to meet the challenge of secularization: the idealization of science, rationalism, industrialization, and materialism. The response of the *Orthodox* has been to stand by the Pentateuch as the revealed word of God and the Talmud as the legitimate oral law. Orthodox Jews feel that they are bound by the traditional rabbinical halakhah, as a way of closeness to God. But within this framework there are great individual differences, with no central authority figure or governing body. Orthodoxy includes mystics and rationalists, Zionists and anti-Zionists. The Orthodox also differ in their tolerance for other Jewish groups and in their degree of accommodation of the surrounding secular environment. Converts to Judaism are allowed, with the notion that they are actually Jewish souls that happened to get born into Gentile bodies. To liberate one's soul into Judaism, the would-be convert must undergo total immersion in a mikva, after a period of religious training and convincing evidence that the person finds biblical teachings appealing and challenging.

Contemporary *Hasidism* is cleaving to traditional piety, but sometimes with new language and new understandings. Women have made the point that to see the Divine as "King" or "Father" is not only male chauvinistic but also gives the impression of a feudal, patronizing authority figure.

Hasidism has always embraced the dual male-female, active-passive aspects of the divine and emphasized the cosmic unification of these poles. The Lubavich Hasidim,

LIVING JUDAISM:

An interview with Marc and Meryl Kronisch

Marc is a physical education teacher, Meryl a family therapist. As members of P'Nai Or ("Faces of Light"), a neo-Hasidic group founded by Reb Zalman Schachter-Shalomi, they offer Sabbath services in their home for people of all faiths. Marc leads the service; Meryl supervises the potluck dinner and makes sure that everyone is comfortable. They have a young daughter, Sarah Rivka.

Meryl: I grew up in a very Jewish neighborhood, but my family went to services only on high holidays. Even now, Marc is more religious than I am. There are some things that if I weren't married to Marc I wouldn't do. I wouldn't keep a kosher house, for instance. But I think it's important for Sarah to learn about these things when she's young and understand them, unlike me, so that she will have a choice and make a choice knowledgeably.

Marc: I grew up in a conservative Jewish community. I went to Hebrew school since I was six years old, and then Hebrew high school and Bar Mitzvah classes. We celebrated the holidays conservatively, but saying the words without knowing the meaning behind them.

When I went away to college, I didn't really think Judaism was meaningful for me and I started exploring alternatives. Once I went to an ecumenical yoga retreat with representatives from many different paths. Reb Zalman was there, and I got really turned on because I knew all the chants he was doing. It all came back to me – I had never experienced the meaning like I did then. I started to explode into Judaism again and discovered the beauty of the path I was born into.

I observe the Sabbath every week. To me the most important thing is to be receptive, to put down the active week. The Sabbath is a bridge of time – time becomes meaningless. That's the biggest challenge: to put down all the active modes, including your thoughts about all the things you did and all the things that aren't getting done. The rituals help you to do that. I try to sleep a little bit more, take naps, go for quiet walks in the woods, that kind of thing. The Sabbath is also an emotional rest, so Meryl and I try to do some emotional release on Friday afternoon. On the spiritual level, the Sabbath is for really trying to let God's energy come in and be open to the light. Lighting the candles helps. We say special blessings over the wine and the bread and try to eat very consciously to really turn the physical into the spiritual. I think that's what Judaism does: It elevates the physical acts into the spirit as well as pulls down the spirit. It's like Jacob's Ladder – the angels not only ascended but also descended; it's a two-way experience.

Sometimes just being with my daughter is so prayerful that I don't even have to say a word of tradition. I could just sit there with my mouth open looking at this miracle and feeling connected. The Jewish word for prayer – *davening* – means connection.

originally from Lithuania with strong communities in many countries, are leaders in joining kabbalistic mysticism with rabbinical learning. It is the Lubavich who have been especially instrumental in keeping Judaism alive, albeit hidden, in the Soviet Union during the decades that it was forbidden there. Inspired by this tradition is *Neo-Hasidism*, a popular "New Age" trend using emotional songs, stories, and prayer to draw people into charismatic experience of the presence of God. It tends to use non-exclusive, universal language.

The *Reform* movement, the extreme opposite of Orthodoxy, began in eighteenth-century Germany as an attempt to help modern Jews appreciate their religion rather than regarding it as antiquated, meaningless, or even repugnant. In imitation of Christian churches, synagogues were redefined as places for spiritual elevation, with choirs added for effect, and the Sabbath service was shortened and translated into the vernacular. The liturgy was also changed to eliminate references to the hope of return to Zion and animal sacrifices in the Temple. Halakhic observance was de-emphasized, and Judaism was studied as an evolving, open-ended religion rather than one fixed forever by the revealed Torah. Reform congregations now exist in the United States, too, where they are continually engaged in a "creative confrontation with modernity." Rather than exclusivism, Reform rabbis cultivate a sense of the universalism of Jewish values. Converts are accepted, largely through mixed marriages performed by Reform rabbis, with the promise of raising the children as Jews. It is felt that only by making Judaism palatable to modern tastes and modern minds can it survive. Reform Judaism is not fully accepted in Israel; fundamentalist Israeli religious officials are reluctant to acknowledge Reform converts as true Jews who can be Israeli citizens.

Fundamentalist objections notwithstanding, the liberalization process has also given birth to other groups with intermediate positions. *Conservative* Judaism is the largest Jewish movement in the United States (which now has the world's largest Jewish population). Conservatives feel they are totally dedicated to traditional rabbinical Judaism and are at the same time restating and restructuring it in modern terms so that it is not perceived as a dead historical religion. To appeal to intelligent would-be believers, Conservatives have sponsored critical studies of Jewish texts from all periods in history. They believe that Jews have always searched and added to their laws, liturgy,

Some branches of Judaism accept women as rabbis. Shown here is Rabbi Julia Neuberger of a Jewish Liberal synagogue in London.

midrash, and beliefs to keep them relevant and meaningful in changing times. Some of the changes introduced are acceptance of riding to a synagogue for Sabbath services and acceptance of women into rabbinical schools as candidates for ordination as rabbis. These changes are not forced on local congregations, which have the right to accept or reject them.

Rabbi Mordecai Kaplan, a highly influential American thinker who died in 1983, branched off from Conservativism (which initially rejected his ideas as too radical), and founded a movement called *Reconstructionism.* Kaplan held that the Enlightenment had changed everything and that strong measures were needed to preserve Judaism in the face of rationalism. Kaplan asserted that "as long as Jews adhered to the traditional conception of Torah as supernaturally revealed, they would not be amenable to any constructive adjustment of Judaism that was needed to render it viable in a non-Jewish environment."[39] He defined Judaism as an "evolving religious civilization," both cultural and spiritual, and asserted that the Jewish people are the heart of Judaism. The traditions exist for the people, and not vice versa, he said. Kaplan denied that the Jewish people were specially chosen by God, an exclusivist idea. Rather, they had chosen to try to become a people of God. Kaplan created a new prayer book, deleting traditional portions he and others found offensive, such as derogatory references to women and Gentiles, references to physical resurrection of the body, and passages describing God as rewarding or punishing Israel by manipulating natural phenomena such as rain. Women were accepted fully into synagogue participation.

There are also numerous small *havurot,* or communities of Jews, who are not affiliated with any formal group but get together on a regular basis to worship and celebrate the traditions. They favor a democratic organization and personal experience, and are often engaged in trying to determine what parts of the traditions to use and how. Some incorporate study groups continuing the ancient intellectual tradition of grappling with the ethical, philosophical, and spiritual meanings of the texts.

Now that Israel has become a state, the former dissension between Zionists and non-Zionists has given way to approval and disapproval over how Israel is comporting itself. There are those who expected it to exercise spiritual leadership in the world, in fulfillment of the ancient messianic longings. It has not yet played this role, intent on establishing its right to exist rather than be destroyed by its hostile neighbors. The respected historian Gershom Scholem even maintains that this role was not an authentic, God-given one. He feels that Jews invented it long ago "as a kind of spiritual recompense, a lame justification for the existence of Judaism in the Diaspora."[40] He feels that it is to the credit of Israel that it has not announced itself a country created to save the world.

Another issue that many Jews both inside and outside Israel have with the current Israeli government is its seeming lack of compassion toward the subject Palestinian population in its midst. Now that Israel has clearly established itself as a formidable power on the world stage, there is a growing movement urging it to be more peaceful, particularly toward its Muslim cousins. Reconstructionist Arthur Waskow proposes an additional set of questions to be read on Pesach that reminds Jews to draw from their own history the lesson of compassion for other oppressed peoples:

"Why is this Pesach night different from every other Pesach night?"
Because on every other Pesach night, we call out to another people, "Let our people go!"

– and tonight another people calls out to us: ''Let our people go!''
  Tonight the children of Hagar and Ishmael and the children of Sarah and Isaac call out
to each other:
  ''We too are children of Abraham!
  We are cousins, you and we!...''

''Why do we dip herbs twice, once in salt water and once in sweet charoset?''
For the tears of two peoples, Israeli and Palestinian; for the sweetness of two peoples,
Palestinian and Israeli; for the future of both peoples, who must learn not to repeat the
sorrows of the past but to create the joys of the future. [41]

Suggested reading

Band, Arnold J., trans., *Nahman of Bratslav: The Tales*, New York: Paulist Press, 1978. Challenging, difficult, fascinating parables told by the Hasidic master, Reb Nachman of Bratzlav.

Ben-Sasson, H. H., ed., *A History of the Jewish People*, Cambridge, Massachusetts: Harvard University Press, 1976. Leading scholars of the Hebrew University in Jerusalem offer a comprehensive, scholarly analysis of Jewish history which assumes some knowledge of the tradition.

Cohen, Arthur A. and Mendes-Flohr, Paul, eds., *Contemporary Jewish Religious Thought*, New York: Charles Scribner's Sons, 1987. Brief essays on all aspects of Jewish belief, from Aesthetics to Zionism, by writers from all Jewish schools.

Encyclopedia Judaica, Jerusalem: Keter Publishing House Jerusalem Ltd., 1972. The authoritative, multi-volume reference on all aspects of Judaism, as seen from a broad spectrum of points of view.

Epstein, Perle, *Kabbalah: The Way of the Jewish Mystic*, Boston and London: Shambhala, 1988. A highly readable introduction to the life and practices of the Kabbalists, whose ways are of interest to contemporary mystics.

Glatzer, Nahum N., ed., *The Judaic Tradition*, Boston: Beacon Press, 1969. A useful compilation of writings from all periods of Jewish history.

Heschel, Abraham J., *Between God and Man: An Interpretation of Judaism*, ed. Fritz A. Rothschild, New York: The Free Press, 1959. An intimate exploration of the relevance of traditional Judaism for today's world, by a great twentieth-century theologian.

Schachter-Shalomi, Zalman, with Donald Gropman, *The First Step: A Guide for the New Jewish Spirit*, New York: Bantam Books, 1983. A modern explanation of the essence of Judaism, of special interest to non-observant Jews who want to find their way back into the faith.

Schneider, Susan Weidman, *Jewish and Female: Choices and Changes in our Lives Today*, New York: Simon and Schuster, 1984. A guide to contemporary Judaism from a woman's point of view, with extensive resources at the end.

Scholem, Gershom G., *Major Trends in Jewish Mysticism*, New York: Schocken Books, 1974. The classic scholarly work on the development of mystical Judaism.

Silver, Daniel Jeremy (vol. 1), and Martin Bernard, (vol. 2), *A History of Judaism*, New York: Basic Books, 1974. A perceptive spiritual as well as secular history of the Jewish nation.

Tanakh: The Holy Scriptures, The New JPS Translation according to the Traditional Hebrew Text, Philadelphia: The Jewish Publication Society, 1988. The preferred translation of the Hebrew Scriptures, in graceful and spiritually sensitive modern English.

10 CHRISTIANITY

"Jesus Christ is Lord"

Christianity is a faith based on the life, teachings, death, and resurrection of Jesus. He was born as a Jew about two thousand years ago in Roman-occupied Palestine. He taught for fewer than three years and was killed on charges of blasphemy. Nothing was written about him at the time; some years after his death attempts were made to record what he had said and done. Yet his birth is now celebrated around the world and used as the major point from which time is measured in the West, and the religion centered around him has more followers than any other.

In studying Christianity we will first examine what can be said about the life and teachings of Jesus, based on accounts in the Bible and historians' knowledge of the period. We will then follow the evolution of the religion as it spread to all continents and became theologically and liturgically more complex. This process continues in the present, in which there are not one but many different versions of Christianity.

The evidence of the Bible

The Christian Bible consists of the Jewish Tanakh (called the "Old Testament") plus the twenty-seven books of the "New Testament" written after Jesus's earthly mission. What we know about Jesus's life and teachings is derived largely from the first four books of the New Testament. They are called the *gospels* ("good news"). On the whole, they seem to have been originally written about forty to fifty years after Jesus's death. They are based on oral transmission of the stories and discourses, which may have been influenced by the growing split between Christians and Jews.

The gospels were first written down in Greek and perhaps Aramaic, the common spoken languages of the day, and then copied and translated in many different ways over the centuries. They offer a composite picture of Jesus as seen through the eyes of the Christian community. Eighteenth- to twentieth-century scholars tried to analyze them for clues to the "historical Jesus." But now the Biblical scholars' emphasis is on trying to understand why certain stories were told — what deep meanings they were intended to suggest.

Three of the gospels, Matthew, Mark, and Luke, are so similar that they are called the *synoptic* gospels, referring to the fact that they can be "seen together" as presenting rather similar views of Jesus's career, though they are organized somewhat differently. Most historians think that they draw from a single basic source, most likely an early version of the short gospel called Mark. It is probably a compilation of oral traditions, circulated anonymously at first. Its intended audience may have been non-Palestinian Christians who were converts from pagan faiths.

The other two synoptic gospels often parallel Mark quite closely but add additional material. The gospel attributed to Matthew (one of Jesus's original disciples, a tax collector) is sometimes called a Jewish Christian gospel. It represents Jesus as a second Moses as well as the Messiah ushering in the kingdom of heaven, with frequent references back to the Old Testament. Matthew's stories emphasize that the Gentiles accept Jesus, whereas the Jews reject him as savior.

Luke, to whom the third gospel is attributed, is traditionally thought to have been a physician referred to by Paul the apostle. He seems to have written with a Gentile (non-Jewish) Christian audience in mind. Luke presents Jesus's mission in universal rather than exclusively Jewish terms and accentuates the importance of his ministry to the underprivileged and lower classes.

The Gospel of John, traditionally thought to have been written by "the disciple Jesus loved," is of a very different nature than the other three. It concerns itself less with following the life of Jesus than with seeing Jesus as the eternal Son of God, the incarnation of God on earth.

Other gospels circulating in the early Christian church were not included in the official canon of the Bible. They include magical stories of Jesus's infancy, such as an account of his making clay birds and then bringing them to life. The Gospel According to Thomas, one of the long-hidden manuscripts discovered in 1945 by a peasant in a cave near Nag Hammadi, Egypt, is of particular interest. Some scholars feel that it may have been written as early or even earlier than the canonical gospels. It contains many sayings in common with the other gospels but places the accent on mystical concepts of Jesus:

No one now knows what Jesus, the founder of the world's largest religion, looked like. Rembrandt used a young European Jewish man as his model for this sensitive "portrait" of Jesus.

> *Jesus said: I am the Light that is above*
> *them all, I am the All,*
> *the All came forth from me and the All*
> *attained to me. Cleave a (piece of) wood, I*
> *am there; lift up the stone and you will*
> *find Me there.* [1]

The life of Jesus

It is not possible to reconstruct from the gospels a single chronology of Jesus's life or to account for much of what happened before he began his ministry.

Birth

Historians think Jesus was probably born several years before or after the first year of what is now called the Common Era. When sixth-century Christian monks began figuring time in relationship to the life of Jesus, they may have miscalculated slightly. Traditionally, Christians have believed that Jesus was born in Bethlehem. This detail fulfills the rabbinic interpretation of the Old Testament prophecies that the Messiah would be born in Bethlehem, the city of David the great king, and in the lineage of David. Both Matthew and Luke offer genealogies tracing Jesus to David, but the people in their lists are different. Some scholars suggest that Jesus was actually born in or near Nazareth, his home town in Galilee. This region, whose name meant "Ring of the

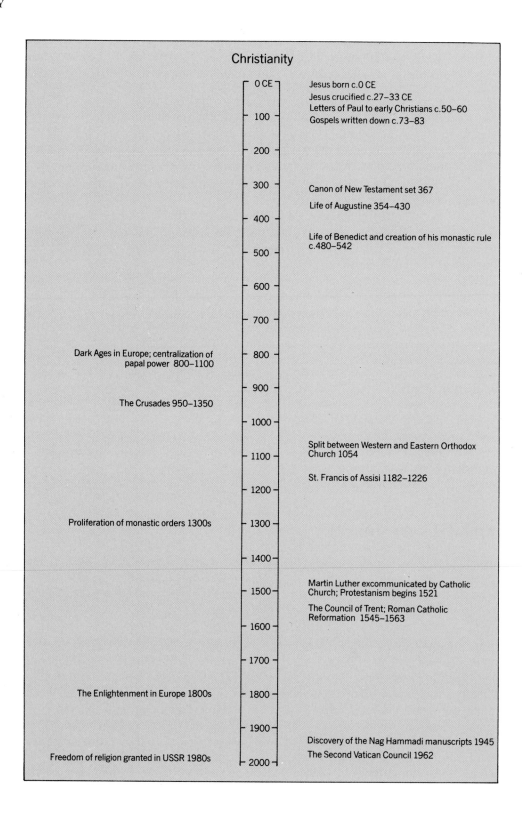

Christianity

0 CE		Jesus born c.0 CE
		Jesus crucified c.27–33 CE
		Letters of Paul to early Christians c.50–60
100		Gospels written down c.73–83
200		
300		Canon of New Testament set 367
		Life of Augustine 354–430
400		
		Life of Benedict and creation of his monastic rule c.480–542
500		
600		
700		
800	Dark Ages in Europe; centralization of papal power 800–1100	
900	The Crusades 950–1350	
1000		
1100		Split between Western and Eastern Orthodox Church 1054
		St. Francis of Assisi 1182–1226
1200		
1300	Proliferation of monastic orders 1300s	
1400		
1500		Martin Luther excommunicated by Catholic Church; Protestanism begins 1521
1600		The Council of Trent; Roman Catholic Reformation 1545–1563
1700		
1800	The Enlightenment in Europe 1800s	
1900		
		Discovery of the Nag Hammadi manuscripts 1945
2000	Freedom of religion granted in USSR 1980s	The Second Vatican Council 1962

Gentiles," was not fully Jewish; it was also scorned as somewhat countrified by the rabbinic orthodoxy of Judaea. Both Judaea and Galilee held allegiance to Rome at the time.

According to the gospels Jesus's mother was Mary, who was a virgin when she conceived him by the Holy Spirit; his father was Joseph, a carpenter from Bethlehem. Luke states that they had to go to Bethlehem to satisfy a Roman ruling that everyone should travel to their ancestral cities for a census. When they had made the difficult journey, there was no room for them in the inn, so the baby Jesus was born in a manger in the animals' quarters. He was named Jesus, which means "God saves." This birth legend is greatly loved, for it exemplifies the humility that Jesus taught. The kingdom of which he spoke was the antithesis of earthly power and riches.

According to Luke, those who came to pay their respects were poor shepherds to whom a host of angels had appeared with the glad tidings that a Savior had been born to the people. Matthew tells instead of Zoroastrian Magi from "the east" who followed a star to find the Christ child, bringing him symbolic gifts of gold and frankincense and myrrh. This story affirms his kingship and his adoration by Gentiles, in contrast to the suspicion with which the Jewish rulership under King Herod were later said to regard him.

Jesus is often pictured as a divine child, born in a humble stable, and forced to flee on a donkey with his parents. (Monastere Benedictin de Keur Moussa, Senegal, Fuite en Egypte.)

Preparation

No other details are given about Jesus's childhood in Nazareth until at twelve he came of age and accompanied his parents on their yearly trip to Jerusalem for Passover. Left behind by mistake, he was said to have been discovered by his parents in the Temple discussing the Torah with the rabbis; "all who heard him were amazed at his understanding and his answers." When scolded, he reportedly replied, "Did you not know that I must be in my Father's house?"[2] This story is used to demonstrate his sense of mission even as a boy, his knowledge of Jewish tradition, and the close personal connection between Jesus and God. In later accounts of his prayers, he spoke to God as "Abba," a very familiar word for father.

The years of Jesus's young manhood are a mystery. He may have been a student in the school of Hillel, the love-emphasizing Jewish scholar who lived about the same time, and he could have been influenced by the Essenes, the ascetic Jewish sect that had retreated to the Dead Sea wilderness to prepare for the apocalypse. What is described, however, is the ministry of John the Baptist, a prophet citing Isaiah's prophecies of the coming kingdom of God. He called Jews to repent of their sins and receive baptism in the Jordan River in preparation for the Kingdom. Apocalyptic expectations were running high at the time, with Israel chafing under Roman taxation and rule.

According to all four gospels, at the age of about thirty Jesus appeared before John to be baptized. It was the custom for Jews to baptize Gentile converts to Judaism. John the Baptist radically extended baptism to Jews themselves. By accepting such a ritual of spiritual cleansing for himself, Jesus is thought to have identified completely with his people as sinners. Then, says the gospel-writer:

When he came up out of the water, immediately he saw the heavens opened and the Spirit descending upon him like a dove; and a voice came from heaven, "Thou art my beloved Son; with thee I am well pleased."[3]

At some point, Jesus reportedly undertook a forty day retreat in the desert wilderness, fasting. During this retreat, he was allegedly tempted by Satan (whom some modern writers see as a symbol of the self-centered ego) to use his spiritual power for secular ends, but he refused.

Ministry

In John's gospel, Jesus's baptism by John the Baptist was followed by his gathering of the first disciples, the fisherman Simon (called Peter), Andrew (his brother), James, and John (brother of James), who recognized him as the Messiah. As he traveled, speaking, he is said to have performed many miracles, such as turning water into wine, healing the sick, restoring the dead to life, walking on water, casting devils out of the possessed, and turning a few loaves and fish into enough food to feed a crowd of thousands, with copious leftovers.

Jesus reportedly performed these miracles quietly and compassionately; John's gospel interpreted them as signs of the coming kingdom of God. The stories also have symbolic meanings taken from the entire Jewish and early Christian traditions. In the sharing of the loaves and fishes, for instance, it may have been more than physical bread that Luke was talking about when he said, "and all ate and were satisfied."[4] The people came to Jesus out of spiritual hunger, and he fed them all, profligate with his love. Bread often signified life-giving sustenance. Jesus was later to offer himself as "the bread of life."[5]

On another level of interpretation, the story may prefigure the Last Supper of Jesus with his disciples, with both stories alluding to the Jewish tradition of the Great Banquet, the heavenly feast of God, as a symbol of the messianic age. The fish were a symbol of Christ to the early Christians; what he fed them was the indiscriminate gift of himself.

Theological interpretations of the biblical stories are based on the evidence of the Bible itself, but people also bring their own experiences to them. To William, a twentieth-century Nicaraguan peasant, the miracle was not the multiplication of the loaves but the sharing: "The miracle was to persuade the owners of the bread to share it, that it was absurd for them to keep it all while the people were going hungry."[6]

Everywhere he went, Jesus reportedly told people that the kingdom of God for which they had been waiting had already started to appear. "The time is fulfilled, and the kingdom of God is at hand; repent, and believe in the gospel"[7]; "I must preach the good news of the kingdom of God ... for I was sent for this purpose."[8] He taught them to pray for the advent of this kingdom: "Thy kingdom come, Thy will be done on earth as it is in heaven."[9]

True to the apocalyptic Jewish writings of the time, Jesus said that things would get much worse right before the end. But:

> then will appear the sign of the Son of man in heaven, and then all the tribes of the earth will mourn, and they will see the Son of man coming on the clouds of heaven with power and great glory; and he will send out his angels with a loud trumpet call, and they will gather his elect from the four winds, from one end of heaven to the other.[10]

It was his mission, he said, to gather together those who could be saved as the "elect" in this general resurrection of the righteous.

John the Baptist is said to have baptized Jesus only reluctantly, saying that he was unworthy even to unfasten Jesus's shoes. When he did so, the Spirit allegedly descended upon Jesus as a dove. (Painting by Esperanza Guevara, Solentiname, Nicaragua.)

> *Every one who drinks of this water will thirst again, but whoever drinks of the water that I shall give him will never thirst; the water that I shall give him will become in him a spring of water welling up to eternal life.*
>
> *Jesus, as quoted in The Gospel of John, 4:13-14*

When Jesus asked his disciples, "Who do you say that I am?" Peter answered, "You are the Christ."[11] "Christ" is Greek for "anointed one," which in Aramaic (*M'shekha* or *Messiah*) also means "perfected" or "enlightened one." Jesus warned his disciples not to tell anyone that he was the Christ. He also warned that he would suffer and be killed but then rise from the grave.

Perhaps as a foreshadowing of his resurrection and a confirmation of his divinity, there followed a spectacular event allegedly witnessed by three disciples. It has been called "The Transfiguration." Jesus had climbed a mountain to pray, and as he did:

> *He was transfigured before them, and his face shone like the sun, and his garments became white as light. And behold, there appeared to them Moses and Elijah, talking with him . . . When lo, a bright cloud overshadowed them, and a voice from the cloud said, "This is my beloved Son, with whom I am well pleased; listen to him."*[12]

The presence of Moses and Elijah (who in Jewish apocalyptic tradition were expected to return at the end of the world) places Jewish law and prophecy behind the claim that Jesus is the Christ. They are representatives of the old covenant; Jesus brings a new dispensation of grace.

The resurrected Jesus always displays his wounds, symbolizing the ongoing wounding of God by human actions. At the same time that God confronts humans with their sins, He also offers total forgiveness, according to some Christian theologians. (Grunewald, The Isenheim Altarpiece, c. 1510–15.)

Challenges to the authorities

As Jesus traveled through Galilee, his fame spread and many people were brought to him to be healed. His popularity and the miracle-working were disturbing to the Jewish authorities. Herod Antipas, ruler of Galilee, had already executed John the Baptist and may have been concerned that Jesus might also be a trouble-maker. Jesus therefore moved outside Herod's jurisdiction for a while, to carry on his work in Tyre and Sidon.

According to the gospels, the Jewish authorities came to regard Jesus as a law-breaker, if not a blasphemer. He seems to have honored the Jewish traditions but to have at times stretched interpretation of the rules in order to gain a deeper understanding of divine law. One sabbath he and his disciples picked ears of grain to eat as they were passing through a field. The Pharisees accompanying them reportedly asked if this were not against Jewish laws forbidding work on the sabbath. Jesus referred them to an obscure sabbath event in the life of David and then remarked, "The sabbath was made for man, not man for the sabbath; so the Son of man is lord even of the sabbath."[13] On the other hand, Jesus said that it was important not only to abide by the Jewish laws but even to exceed them in righteousness.

Jesus dismissed as "blind guides" the Pharisees and scribes (legal experts the Jews continually referred to in the gospels as opposing Jesus on religious legal grounds). He also confronted commercial interests in the Temple in Jerusalem:

> *In the temple he found those who were selling oxen and sheep and pigeons, and the money-changers at their business. And making a whip of cords, he drove them all, with the sheep and oxen, out of the temple; and he poured out the coins of the money-changers and overturned their tables. And he told those who sold the pigeons, ''Take these things away; you shall not make my Father's house a house of trade.''*[14]

According to the gospel accounts, Jesus appropriated to himself the messianic prophecies of Second Isaiah. Jesus claimed that John the Baptist was Elijah reincarnated, observing that in Jewish tradition Elijah would reappear to announce the apocalypse and restore creation. The authorities had killed John the Baptist and, Jesus prophesied, they would attack him, too, not recognizing who he was. John's gospel is particularly intent on portraying him as the *Christ*. John quotes Jesus as saying things like "My teaching is not mine, but his who sent me"; "I am the light of the world"; "You are from below, I am from above; you are of this world, I am not of this world"; and "Before Abraham was, I am."[15]

According to the gospels, Jesus used the term "Son of man" as an indirect way of referring to himself. At the time, it was a common term for the messiah who would bring the divine judgement and salvation when the apocalypse occurred. Some researchers suggest another meaning: The Son of man is the model of perfected humanity, the exemplar of what we can all be if our lives become centered in the divine.

Crucifixion

The anti-institutional tenor of Jesus's teachings and his seemingly blasphemous claim to be equal with God did not endear him to those in power. Jewish public opinion was divided, according to the gospels.

The distrustful ones prevailed, as Jesus had reportedly foreseen. He knew that to return to Jerusalem would be politically dangerous. But eventually he did so, at Passover. He entered the town on a donkey, accompanied by multitudes who cried:

> *''Hosanna! Blessed be he who comes in the name of the Lord! Blessed be the kingdom of our father David that is coming! Hosanna in the highest!''*[16]

However, Jesus warned his disciples that his end was near and that they, too, would be in danger as they continued his work. At a meal during the Passover season, he gave them instructions for a ceremony with bread and wine to be performed thenceforth to maintain a mystical communion with him. The offering of his body and blood was a new covenant between God and the faithful. However, one of the disciples would betray him to the hostile Jewish authorities, he said. This one, Judas, had already done so, selling information leading to Jesus's entrapment for thirty pieces of silver.

Jesus took three of his followers to a garden called Gethsemane, on the mount of Olives, where he is said to have prayed intensely that the cup of suffering would pass away from him, if it be God's will, "yet not what I will, but what thou wilt."[17] A crowd led by Judas, and reportedly sent by the Jewish authorities, approached with swords and clubs; they led Jesus away to be questioned by the chief priest, elders and scribes.

Then followed several trials of sorts. The high priest, Caiaphas, asked Jesus several questions to establish that he was a blasphemer. One concerned the claim that he was the Son of God. Jesus answered:

> *You have said so. But I tell you, hereafter you will see the Son of man seated at the right hand of Power, and coming on the clouds of heaven.* [18]

Caiaphas pronounced this statement blasphemy, and they took him to Pilate, the Roman governor, for sentencing. To Pilate's leading question, "Are you King of the Jews?" Jesus again answered, "You have said so."[19] He refused to defend himself against the charges of the Jewish authorities. Pilate's wife warned him against harming Jesus, because of a dream she had. According to Luke's account, Pilate tried shifting the burden to Herod, for Jesus was a Galilean under Herod's jurisdiction, but Jesus would say nothing to Herod, who sent him back.

It was Pilate's custom to release one prisoner every year at Passover, so he offered to the people the release either of Jesus or of Barabbas, a political prisoner. Allegedly stirred up by the chief priests and elders, the crowds chose Barabbas and asked for Jesus's death by crucifixion.

They took Jesus to a hill called Golgotha and nailed him to a cross, as was the Roman executionary custom. The accusation – "This is Jesus, King of the Jews" – was set over his head, and two robbers were crucified alongside him. The authorities, the people, and even the robbers mocked him for saying that he could save others when he could not even save himself.

Jesus hung there for hours until he reportedly cried out, "My God, my God, why hast thou forsaken me?"[20] and died. This event is thought to have happened on a Friday some time between 27 and 33 CE. A wealthy Jewish disciple called Joseph of Arimathea asked Pilate for Jesus's body, which he wrapped in a linen shroud and placed in his own tomb, with a large stone against the door. A guard was placed at the tomb to make sure that no followers would steal the body and claim that Jesus had risen from the dead.

Resurrection

That seemed to be the end of it. Jesus had prophesied the end of the world and the coming of the kingdom of God, but he had died instead. His disciples were terrified, so they hid, mourning and disheartened. The whole religious movement could have died out, as did Shabbatai Tzevi's Jewish messiahship centuries later. However, what happened next seemed to change everything. Some of the women who had been close to Jesus visited the tomb on Sunday and found it empty, with the stone rolled away. Radiant angels then appeared and told them that Jesus had risen from death. The women ran and brought two of the male disciples, who witnessed the empty tomb with the shrouds folded.

Then followed numerous alleged appearances of the risen Christ himself to various disciples. He dispelled their doubts about his physical resurrection, having them touch his wounds and even eating a fish with them, which no ghost would do. He said to them:

Jesus's crucifixion was interpreted by many later Christians as the sacrifice of an innocent lamb as atonement for the sins of humanity. A different interpretation was that God gave ''himself'' in love, drawing the world into a loving relationship with the divine. (Rembrandt van Rijn, The Three Crosses, 1653.)

All authority in heaven and on earth has been given to me. Go therefore and make disciples of all nations, baptizing them in the name of the Father and of the Son and of the Holy Spirit, teaching them to observe all that I have commanded you; and lo, I am with you always, to the close of the age.[21]

Although the reported details of the reappearances of the resurrected Jesus differ considerably from gospel to gospel, some scholars think that to have women as the first witnesses to the empty tomb suggests authenticity, for no one trying to build a case would have rested it on the testimony of women, who had little status in a patriarchal society.

It was the resurrection that presumably turned defeat into victory for Jesus, and discouragement into powerful action for his followers. As the impact of all they had seen set in, the followers came to believe that Jesus had been God in human form, walking among them, leading them to the goal of eternal life.

The teachings of Jesus

Many of the sayings attributed to Jesus take the form of parables. He told his disciples that he gave parables to the multitudes and explained their meanings only to his inner circle. He often used the statement "He who has ears, let him hear" to suggest that he was speaking in parables.

The coming of the kingdom

The central theme in Jesus's teachings is the coming of the kingdom of God (also called the kingdom of heaven). From the gospels, it is not clear whether Jesus said it would soon come, had already begun with his appearance, or both. Critical opinion is also divided on whether the ethics Jesus commanded were just meant as preparation for the imminent kingdom or whether they are timeless.

Another area of confusion concerns the nature of the kingdom: Is the reign of God an inner state of spiritual transformation? Luke quotes Jesus as saying:

The kingdom of God is not coming with signs to be observed; nor will they say, "Lo, here it is!" or "There!" for behold, the kingdom of God is in the midst of you.[22]

Or is the kingdom of heaven a total remaking of the outer world? The book of Revelation, placed at the end of the New Testament and attributed to a follower named John, describes an apocalyptic vision of the total conversion of heaven and earth. The vision culminates in the creation of a holy city, inhabited only by the pure and illuminated only by the glory of God.

Jesus spoke of the kingdom largely through metaphors and parables. He described the kingdom as like a pearl of such value that a merchant sells all that he has in order to buy it, or like a mustard seed which begins tiny but grows into such a tall tree that birds can nest in its branches, or like fishermen separating the good fish from the undesirable fish. Is he also speaking metaphorically when he says:

So it will be at the close of the age. The Son of man will send his angels, and they will gather out of his kingdom all causes of sin and all evildoers, and throw them into the furnace of fire; there men will weep and gnash their teeth. Then the righteous will shine like the sun in the kingdom of their Father. He who has ears, let him hear.[23]

The transformation of earthly life

Whatever the kingdom is, how does one prepare for it? The first step Jesus required of his disciples was that they leave all their possessions and human attachments to follow him – to pay more attention to the life of the spirit than to physical comfort and wealth. He said that it was extremely difficult for the wealthy to enter the kingdom of heaven. God would take care of physical needs, which were relatively unimportant anyway:

Is not life more than food, and the body more than clothing? Look at the birds of the air; they neither sow nor reap nor gather into barns, and yet your heavenly Father feeds them. Are you not of more value than they? And which of you by being anxious can add one cubit to his span of life?[24]

Jesus taught that his followers should concentrate on laying up spiritual treasures in heaven, rather than material treasures on earth, which are short-lived. Because God is a generous father, those who love him and want to follow the path of righteousness should pray to him for help, in private: "Ask, and it will be given you; seek, and you will find; knock, and it will be opened to you."[25]

Jesus called people to spiritual liberation by asking them to follow his guidance and abide in his presence:

Take my yoke upon you, and learn from me; for I am gentle and lowly in heart, and you will find rest for your souls. For my yoke is easy, and my burden is light. [26]

Nevertheless, he preached a radical system of ethics. He said that to follow this system fully was more difficult than to live by the more elaborate code of Jewish laws: "You have heard that it was said to the men of old," Jesus began, "You shall not kill; and whoever kills shall be liable to judgement. But I say to you that every one who is angry with his brother shall be liable to judgement …"[27] Not only should a man not commit adultery; it is wrong even to look at a woman lustfully. Rather than revenging an eye for an eye, a tooth for a tooth, do not resist evil. If a person strikes you on one cheek, turn the other cheek to be struck also. If anyone tries to rob you of your coat, give him your cloak as well. And not only should you love your neighbor, Jesus says:

Love your enemies and pray for those who persecute you, so that you may be sons of your Father who is in heaven; for he makes his sun rise on the evil and on the good, and sends rain on the just and on the unjust. [28]

The central ethic Jesus taught was love. He stated that to love God and to "love your neighbor as yourself"[29] were the two great commandments in Judaism, upon which everything else rested. To love God meant placing God first in one's life, rather than concentrating on the things of the earth. To love one's neighbor meant selfless service, even to those despised by the rest of society. Jesus often horrified the religious authorities by talking to prostitutes, tax-collectors, and the poorest and lowliest of people. In the kingdom, he said, the first will be last and the last will be first. He set an example of loving service by washing his disciples' feet. This kind of love, he said, should be the mark of his followers, and at the last judgement, when the Son of man judges the people of all time, he will grant eternal life in the kingdom to the "sheep" who loved and served him in all:

Then the righteous will answer him, "Lord, when did we see thee hungry and feed thee, or thirsty and give thee drink? And when did we see thee a stranger and welcome thee, or naked and clothe thee? And when did we see thee sick or in prison and visit thee?" And the King will answer them, "Truly, I say to you, as you did it to one of the least of these my brethren, you did it to me." [30]

Salvation

Jesus indicated that God had given him the authority not only to judge but also to save those who honestly repented of their past errors.

The virtues stressed for followers are those of humility, of mutual love, and of appealing to Jesus with faith in his ability to care, heal, and save. As for Jesus, he characterized himself as a good shepherd who is willing to lay down his life for his sheep. Foreshadowing the crucifixion, he said he would offer his own flesh and blood as a sacrifice for the sake of humanity. His coming death would mark a "new covenant" in

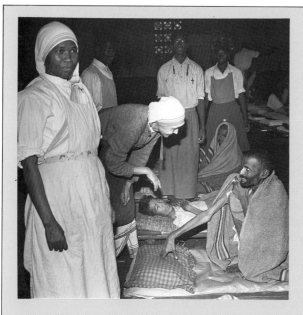

Mother Teresa and the Missionaries of Charity minister to the poorest of the poor around the world. Here on the outskirts of Calcutta they cheerfully tend to the needs of lepers, seeing in all people the Jesus whom they love.

CHRISTIAN LOVE IN ACTION:
Mother Teresa's Missionaries of Charity

The love of which Christ spoke is not an intellectual abstraction. According to the diminutive nun loved around the world as Mother Teresa, love must be put into action.

Mother Teresa was born in 1910 in Albania, to a wealthy family which lost all its money when her father died. She entered a convent of the Loretto Sisters when she was eighteen and never saw her mother and sisters again before their deaths. She felt called to India, where she initially taught at a girls' school in Calcutta. Then came an even more difficult inner calling "to be God's love in action to the poorest of the poor." At a time when India was in turmoil after the shooting of Gandhi and the separation into Hindu and Muslim states, Calcutta was crowded with refugees. With no resources, Mother Teresa simply walked through the streets, with only loving care to give to those who had been abandoned by society, beggars, lepers, the dying. She wanted to live and serve the poor like Jesus, claiming nothing for herself, not even the security of knowing where she would sleep. She said: "Poverty is not created by God. It is made by you and me. We are responsible because we do not share."[31]

To assist in this work, Mother Teresa eventually received permission to found a new order, the Missionaries of Charity. Some of the first sisters were her former pupils. They wore simple white saris with blue stripes, the colors of the Virgin Mary and the garment of Indian women; they lived in poverty, without possessions or grand institutions, to help them understand the poor. In training them to work without the assurance of financial backing or physical safety, Mother Teresa emphasized that the most important thing is to pray and pray and pray; divine providence will always give what is needed.

As her work has expanded around the globe to 230 houses on all continents, the results of her faith have been demonstrated again and again. There is no plan, no fundraising organization (although the Missionaries of Charity do accept individual donations). Wherever the sisters go, they try to help the poorest of the poor in whatever ways are needed. In each person they care for, they see the face of Jesus. In Calcutta, the Missionaries have picked up 42,000 sick, starving, and dying people from the streets and given them tender personal care, hand-feeding them a special formula made from soybeans. In New York City, they feed the homeless, shop and clean for the elderly poor, and care for those with AIDS.

During a period of intense mortar-bombing between Christian and Muslim militia in Beirut, Mother Teresa learned that a home for sixty spastic children had been stranded without caretakers on the Muslim side of the battle lines. When she insisted on crossing the lines to get them, the local clergy assured her that it was impossible. With utter faith, she said that she had asked the Virgin to arrange a cease-fire, which did indeed happen the next day, giving her time to rescue the terrified, helpless children. Within a day, the children were smiling. Mother Teresa says: "The Missionaries do small things with great love. It is not how much we do, but how much love we put into doing it. To God there is nothing small. The moment we have given it to God, it becomes infinite."

For creating this grassroots vehicle for "the joy of loving," Mother Teresa has been awarded the world's highest honors, including a Nobel Peace prize. In 1990 she announced her intention to retire, but the loving work will continue.

which his blood would be "poured out for many for the forgiveness of sins."[32] Near the end, John's gospel quotes him as saying to his disciples:

> Let not your hearts be troubled; believe in God, believe also in me. In my Father's house are many rooms . . . And when I go and prepare a place for you, I will come again and will take you to myself, that where I am you may be also . . . I am the way, and the truth, and the life; no one comes to the Father, but by me. [33]

Jesus called people to be reborn as children of God. Indeed, he said, it was only as children that they could enter the kingdom of heaven, surrendered to simple, unswerving faith and pure-hearted living. In a famous series of statements about supreme happiness called the *Beatitudes*, Jesus is quoted as having promised blessings for the "poor in spirit,"[34] the mourners, the meek, the seekers of righteousness, the pure in heart, the merciful, the peacemakers, and those who are persecuted for the sake of righteousness and of spreading the gospel.

The Early Church

Persecution did become the lot of Jesus's followers. But within three hundred years, despite strong opposition, Christianity had become the official religion of the vast Roman Empire. As it became the establishment, rather than a tiny, disorganized handful of heretics within Judaism, Christianity began to define and organize itself.

From persecution to empire

The earliest years of what became the mainstream of Christianity are described in the New Testament books that follow the gospel accounts of the life of Jesus. "The Acts of the Apostles" was presumably written by the same person who wrote the gospel of Luke, for the language is the same, both books are addressed to the same person named Theophilus, and Acts refers back to the gospel of Luke as an earlier part of a single history of the rise of Chrisitanity. Acts is followed by letters to some of the early groups of Christians, most of them apparently written by Paul, a major organizer and teacher, about 50 to 60 CE.

An event called *Pentecost* galvanized the early Christians into action. At a meeting of the disciples, something that sounded like a great wind came down from the sky, and what looked like tongues of fire swirled around to touch each one's head. It is believed that they all began speaking in languages they had never studied. Some mocked them, saying they were drunk, but Peter declared that they had been filled with the Spirit of God, as the Old Testament prophet Joel had prophesied would happen in the last days before the onset of the kingdom of God. He testified that the Jesus whom the people had crucified had been raised up by God, who had made him "both Lord and Christ."[35] Reportedly, three thousand people were so convinced that they took baptism that day.

One of the persecutors of Christians was Saul. He was a Pharisee tentmaker who lived during the time of Jesus but never met him. Instead, after Jesus died, he helped to throw many of his followers into prison and sentence them to death. On the way to Damascus in search of more heretics, he and his companions allegedly saw a light brighter than the sun and heard the voice of Jesus asking why Saul was persecuting him. This resistance was useless, said the vision of Jesus, who then appointed him to do the opposite: to go to both Jews and Gentiles:

> *to open their eyes, that they may turn from darkness to light and from the power of Satan to God, that they may receive forgiveness of sins and a place among those who are sanctified by faith in me.* [36]

Saul was baptized and immediately began promoting the Christian message under his new name, Paul. His indefatigable work in traveling about the Mediterranean world was of great importance in shaping and expanding the early Christian church. He was shipwrecked, stoned, imprisoned, and beaten, and probably died as a martyr in Rome, but nothing short of death deterred him from his new mission.

Paul tried to convince Jews that Jesus's birth, death, and resurrection had been predicted by the Old Testament prophets. This was the messiah they had been waiting for, and now, risen from death, he presided as the cosmic Christ, offering God's forgiveness and grace to those who trust in God rather than in themselves. Some Jews were converted to this belief, but the Jewish authorities repeatedly accused Paul of leading people away from Jewish law and tradition.

He also tried to sway Gentiles: worshippers of the old gods whose religion was in decline, supporters of the emperor as deity, ecstatic initiates of mystery cults, and followers of dualistic Greco-Roman philosophers who regarded matter as evil and tried to emancipate the soul from its corrupting influence. He taught them that God did not reside in any idol but yet was not far from them, "For in him we live and move and have our being." [37] To make it easier for Gentiles to embrace Christianity, Paul and others argued that the Jewish tradition of circumcision should not be required of them; the important thing was for the Holy Spirit to cleanse one's heart and for people to be saved by repentant faith in the Lord Jesus's grace.

Christianity spread rapidly. Soon it departed from its status as one of many unorthodox Jewish sects and became largely non-Jewish in membership. By 200 CE, it had spread throughout the Roman Empire and into Mesopotamia, despite sometimes fierce opposition. Christians were generally discriminated against by respectable citizens and were subject to imprisonment, torture, and confiscation of property. Persecution did not sway the most ardent of Christians, for it united them intimately to the passion and death of Christ.

With the rise of Constantine to the imperial throne early in the fourth century CE, opposition lapsed and then turned to official embracing of Christianity. Constantine said that God showed him a vision of a cross to be used as a standard in battle. After he used it and won, he instituted tolerance of Christianity alongside paganism, for which he was the chief priest of the state cult. Just before his death, Constantine was baptized as a Christian. This delayed baptism was not uncommon at that time, for there was a belief that it would wash away all of one's sins but could not be repeated.

By the end of the fourth century CE, pagans were stripped of all rights, and ordered into Christian churches to be baptized. Some paid outward service to Christianity but remained inwardly faithful to their old traditions. As Christianity became the favored religion, many converted to the faith for secular reasons, such as political power.

By the end of the fifth century CE, Christianity was the faith claimed by the majority of people in the vast Roman Empire. It also spread beyond the empire, from Ireland on the west to perhaps India and Ceylon on the east, with a partial, tense presence in Mesopotamia, where Zoroastrianism prevailed.

Evolving organization and theology

During its phenomenal growth from persecuted sect to state religion throughout much of the ancient world, Christianity was developing organizationally and theologically. By the end of the first century CE it had a bureaucratic structure which carried on the rites of the church and attempted to define true Christianity.

One form that was judged to be outside the mainstream was Gnostic Christianity. It now appears that *gnosticism* (direct comprehension of reality) preceded Jesus; Christian Gnosticism was an adaptation of this mystical way to the appearance of Jesus. The Nag Hammadi library found in Egypt presents Jesus as a great Gnostic teacher. His words are interpreted as the secret teachings given only to initiates. "He who is near to me is near to the fire," he says in the Gospel According to Thomas.[38] The gnostics held that only spiritually mature individuals could apprehend Jesus's real teaching: that the kingdom of heaven is a present reality experienced through personal realization of the Light.

When the New Testament canon of twenty-seven officially sanctioned texts was set and translated into Latin in the fourth century, the Gnostic Gospels were not included. Instead, the Church treated possession of Gnostic texts as a crime. The Nag Hammadi texts survived only because they were hidden.

What became mainstream Christianity is based not only on the life and teachings of Jesus, as set forth in the gospels selected for the New Testament, but also on the ways that they have been interpreted over the centuries. One of the first and most important interpreters was Paul. His central contribution – which was as influential as the four gospels in shaping Christianity – was his interpretation of Jesus's death and resurrection. This came to him directly as a revelation from the risen Christ, he said.

Paul made *agape* – altruistic, self-giving love – the center of the Christian ideal. He

The Nag Hammadi manuscripts found in Egypt were buried about 400 CE, but contain copies and translations of early Christian texts condemned as heretical by the Church.

placed it ahead of adherence to law, thereby departing from rabbinical Judaism. He also placed it ahead of spiritual wisdom, asceticism, faith, and supernatural "gifts of the Spirit," such as the ability to heal, prophesy, or spontaneously speak in unknown tongues:

> *Let all that you do be done in love.*
>
> The First Letter of Paul to the Corinthians, 16:14.

Love was applied not only to one's neighbors but also to one's relationship with the divine. It was love plus gnosis – knowledge of God, permeated with love – that became the basis of contemplative Christianity, as it was shaped by the "Fathers" of the first centuries.

The cross, with or without Jesus crucified on it, became a central symbol of Christianity. It marked the path of suffering service, rather than political domination, as the way of conquering evil and experiencing union with a compassionate God. To participate in Jesus's sacrifice, Christians could repent of their sins, be baptized, and be reborn to new life in Christ. Descriptions of this process are offered in the early fifth century CE "Confessions" of the bishop Augustine, one of the most influential theologians in the history of Christianity:

> *Where I was angry within myself in my chamber, where I was inwardly pricked, where I had sacrificed, slaying my old man and commencing the purpose of a new life, putting my trust in Thee – there hadst Thou begun to grow sweet unto me and ''hadst put gladness in my heart.''* [39]

Twentieth-century theologian Rowan Williams explains this repentance and spiritual resurrection as:

> *the refusal to accept that lostness is the final human truth. Like a growing thing beneath the earth, we protest at the darkness and push blindly up in search of light, truth, home – the place, the relation where we are not lost, where we can live from deep roots in assurance. ''Because I live, you will live also.''*
>
> (John 14:18–19) [40]

The expectation of the coming of God's Kingdom, so prevalent in Jesus's time, began to wane as time went by. The kingdom of God was shifted to the indefinite future, with emphasis placed on a preliminary judgement at one's death. There was nevertheless the continuing expectation that Christ would return in glory to judge the living and the dead and bring to fulfillment the "new creation." This belief in the *Second Coming* of Christ is still an article of faith today.

Another early development was the doctrine of the *Holy Trinity*. Whereas Jews had insisted on the oneness of God, Christians believed that God had become immanent in the person of Jesus. Furthermore, after his physical death Jesus promised to send the Holy Spirit to his followers. This makes three aspects of God, or three "persons" within the one divine being: Father, Son, and Holy Spirit. Elaborate explanations were used to reconcile threeness with oneness, for Christian theologians believed that the mystery of God was one, expressed in three ways. The Father is envisioned as the almighty male creator of heaven and earth. The Son is the Word of the Father, the divine in human form, who returned at the ascension to live with the Father in glory, though he remains fully present in and to his "mystical body" on earth – the community of believers. The Holy Spirit of God is sent by the Father to constitute the Church and vitalize its members. Although this belief is set forth rather baldly here, it is sometimes understood as a spiritual mystery that cannot be grasped intellectually.

Although Jesus had spoken in parables with several levels of meaning, according to one's spiritual understanding, the evolving Church found it necessary to articulate some of its beliefs more clearly. A number of *creeds*, or professions of faith, were composed for use in religious instruction, baptism, liturgy, and exorcism, and as clear stands against the challenge of various heresies. Many are still in use today in various branches of the Church.

Early monasticism

Alongside the development of doctrine and the consolidation of church structure, another trend was developing. Some Christians were turning away from the world to live in solitary communion with God, as ascetics. There had been a certain amount of asceticism in Paul's writings. He himself was celibate, as he believed avoiding family entanglements helped one to concentrate on the Lord.

The Holy Trinity, depicted as three angels in a famous icon by Rublev, is a distinctively Christian view of God. God is One as a communal plurality, an endless circle sharing the love intrinsic to the godhead, inviting all to be healed and saved by this love.

By the fourth century CE, there were Christian monks living simply in caves in the Egyptian desert with little regard for the things of the world. They had no central organization but tended to learn from the examples of sincere monks. Avoiding emphasis on the supernatural powers that often accompany the ascetic life, they told stories demonstrating the virtues they valued, such as humility, submission, and the sharing of food. For example, an earnest young man was said to have visited one of the desert fathers and asked him how he was faring. The old man sighed and said, "Very badly, my child." Asked why, he said, "I have been here forty years doing nothing other than cursing my own self each day, inasmuch as in the prayers I offer, I say to God, 'Accursed are those who deviate from Your commandments.'"[41] The young seeker was moved by such humility and made it his model.

> *The carefree man, who has tasted the sweetness of having no personal possessions, feels that even the cassock which he wears and the jug of water in his cell are a useless burden, because these things, too, sometimes distract his mind.*
>
> A Desert Father [42]

The desert monks were left to their own devices at first. In Christian humility, they avoided judging or trying to teach each other and attempted to be, at best, harmless. But by the fifth century CE, the monastic life shifted from solitary, unguided practice, to formal spiritual supervision. Group monasteries and structures for guidance by an abbot were set up and rules devised to help monks persevere in their calling. The Rule of St. Benedict became a model for all later monastic orders. Patient obedience to such rules and one's superiors became central aspects of monasticism.

The Eastern Orthodox Church

Christianity's history has been marked by internal feuds and divisions. One of the deepest schisms occurred in 1054, when the Western Church and the Eastern Orthodox Church split apart.

The history of the Orthodox Church

Late in the third century CE, the Roman Empire had been divided into an eastern and a western section. In the fourth century CE, Constantine established a second imperial seat in the east, in Constantinople (now Istanbul, Turkey). It was considered a "second Rome," especially after Rome fell to the Goths in 410. The two halves of the Christian world grew apart from each other, divided by language (Latin in the west, Greek in the east), culture, and religious differences.

In the western half, religious power was becoming more and more centralized in the Roman pope and other high officials; after the barbarian invasions, the clergy were often the only educated people. The Byzantine east was more democratic, with less distinction between clergy and laypeople; it had no single leader of its own and did not recognize the Roman pope's claim to universal authority in the Church. By the early Middle Ages, there were also doctrinal disagreements. In its version of the Nicene Creed,

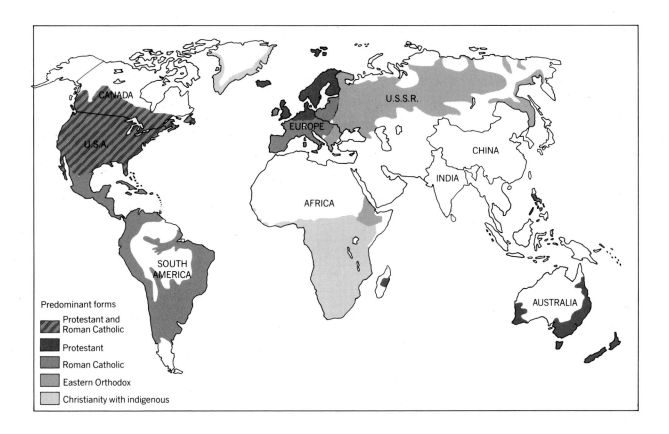

the western church professed that the Holy Spirit came from both the Father and the Son; the eastern church retained what it considered the original understanding, that the Holy Spirit proceeds only from the Father.

Map showing the approximate distribution of Protestants, Roman Catholics and Eastern Orthodox Christians in the world today.

In 1054, leaders of the eastern and western factions excommunicated each other over the disagreement about the Holy Spirit, and also over the papal claim, celibacy for priests (not required in the eastern church), and whether the Eucharistic bread should be leavened or unleavened. To the eastern church, the last straw was its treatment by Crusaders.

From 950 to 1350, loosely organized waves of Christians poured out of Europe in what were presented as "holy Crusades" to recapture the holy land of Palestine from Muslims, to defend the Byzantine Empire against Muslim Turks, and in general wipe out the enemies of Christianity. It was a tragic and bloody time. One of the many casualties was the already tenuous relationship between the eastern and western churches. When Crusaders entered Constantinople in 1204, they tried to intervene in local politics. Rebuffed, they were so furious that they ravaged the city. They destroyed the altar and sacred icons in Hagia Sophia, the awesome Church of the Holy Wisdom (later taken over as a Muslim mosque), and placed prostitutes on the throne reserved for the Patriarch of the region. Horrified by such profanity, the Orthodox Church ended its dialogue with Rome and proceeded on its own, claiming to be the true descendant of the apostolic church. Despite periodic attempts at reconciliation, the eastern and western churches are still separate.

When the Ottoman Turks took Constantinople in the fifteenth century, Russia became more prominent in the Orthodox Church, calling itself the "third Rome." The Orthodox Church had spread throughout the Slavic and eastern Mediterranean countries, each having its own leader, known as patriarch, metropolitan, or archbishop. There are now fifteen self-governing Orthodox Churches worldwide, including the Orthodox Church in America. This last was granted its independence in 1970 and claims over four million members. The older Eastern ethnic groups also have archdioceses in the New World, such as the New York-based Archdiocese of the Greek Orthodox Church in North and South America. The official center of the Orthodox Church remains in Constantinople (Istanbul), even though Turkey is Muslim.

The Russian Orthodox Church was severely repressed by the Soviet government during the twentieth century. As the oppressive old order was overturned, it was assumed that the church would die with it. Persecution increased this possibility. Large numbers of monasteries and cathedrals were closed or converted to museums or warehouses, so that the faithful had to travel great distances to worship together. It was not politically safe to worship in any religion after Stalin's anti-religious campaign. But the Orthodox Church did not die, for it was deeply rooted in the lives and hearts of the people; in the mid-1980's the Russian Orthodox Church had an estimated fifty million members. Most of those who dared to worship publicly were the *babushkas* – the old women who were apparently not regarded as politically dangerous.

Late in the 1980s, the new trend of *perestroika* brought renewed freedom of religious observance in the Soviet Union. Usurped buildings were turned back to religious purposes. Some 1700 churches were reopened in 1988 and 1989, and each was immediately filled with worshippers again. Seminaries where new clergy are trained report a great increase in enrollment. Late in 1989, Soviet President Mikhail Gorbachev ended seven decades of suppression of religion, pronouncing the right of the Soviet faithful to "satisfy their spiritual needs."[43]

Almost 85 per cent of Orthodox Christians live in communist countries. Another set of communities exists as a religious minority in Muslim countries. In Cyprus and Greece, Orthodoxy is the state religion. And in the West, Orthodox are minorities in nations where Roman Catholicism and Protestantism are the predominant forms of Christianity.

Over the centuries, the individual Orthodox Churches have probably changed less than have the many descendants of the early western church. There is a strong conservative tradition, attempting to preserve the pattern of early Christianity. Even though hierarchs can make local adaptations suited to their region and people, they are united in doctrine and sacramental observances. Any change that will affect all churches is decided by a *synod* – a council of officials, trying to reach common agreements as did the early church. Although women are important in local church affairs, they cannot be ordained as priests or serve in hierarchical capacities.

Distinctive features of Orthodox spirituality

In addition to the Bible, Orthodox Christians honor the writings of the saints of the Church. Particularly important is a collection called *The Philokalia*. It consists of texts written by Orthodox masters between the fourth and fifteenth centuries. "Philokalia" means love of the exalted, excellent, and beautiful, in other words, the transcendent divine source of life and truth.

The Philokalia is essentially a Christian guide to the contemplative life for monks but also for laypeople. A central practice is called "unceasing prayer"; the continual remembrance of Jesus or God, often through repetition of a verbal formula that gradually impresses itself on the heart. The most common phrase is the "Jesus prayer": "Lord Jesus Christ, Son of God, have mercy on me, a sinner." The repetition of the name of Jesus brings purification of heart and singularity of desire. To call upon Jesus is to experience his presence in oneself and in all things.

The Orthodox Church has affirmed that humans can approach God directly. Some may even see the light of God and be utterly transformed by it:

> *He who participates in the divine energy, himself becomes, to some extent, light; he is*
> *united to the light, and by that light he sees in full awareness all that remains hidden to*
> *those who have not this grace; . . . for the pure in heart see God . . . who, being Light,*
> *dwells in them and reveals Himself to those who love Him, to His beloved.* [44]

Another distinctive feature of Orthodox Christianity is its veneration of *icons*. These are stylized paintings of Jesus, his mother Mary, and the saints. They are created by artists who prepare for their work by prayer and ascetical training. There is no attempt at earthly realism, for icons are representations of the reality of the divine world. They are beloved as windows to the eternal. In addition to their devotional and instructional functions, some icons are reported to have great spiritual powers, heal illnesses, and transmit the holy presence. Believers enter into the grace of this power by kissing the icon reverently and praying before it.

Most icon painters, such as this monk at Mt. Athos, Greece, use the ancient Byzantine style in creating sacred icons, which represent Christian stories and open windows to the divine.

Some of the major icons in an Orthodox church are placed on an *iconostasis*. This is a screen separating the floor area for the congregation from the Holy of Holies, the sanctuary which can be entered only by the clergy. On either side of the opening to the altar are icons of the Virgin Mary ("Mother of God") and Jesus, symbols of the descent of the divine into earthly human life.

Orthodox choirs sing the liturgy in many-part harmony, producing an ethereal and uplifting effect as the sounds echo and re-echo around each other. Everything strives toward that beauty to which the Philokalia refers. Archimandrite Nathaniel of the Russian Orthodox Pskovo-Pechorsky Monastery, which has been a place of uninterrupted prayer for almost six hundred years despite eight hundred attacks on its walls and numerous sieges, speaks of the ideal of beauty in Orthodox Christianity:

> *The understanding of God is the understanding of beauty. Beauty is at the heart of our monastic life. The life of prayer is a constant well of beauty. We have the beauty of music in the Holy Liturgy. The great beauty of monastic life is communal life in Christ. Living together in love, living without enmity, as peaceful with each other as one dead body is peaceful with another dead body. We are dead to enmity.* [45]

Medieval Roman Catholicism

In the west, the old Roman Empire gradually fell to pagan invaders from the sixth to tenth centuries CE. Islam also made spectacular advances in areas previously converted to Christianity. Arabs took Palestine, Syria, Mesopotamia, Egypt, North Africa, and most of Spain. However, the Angle and Saxon invaders of England were new converts to Christianity, with whole tribes joining the faith at the behest of their chiefs. By the fourteenth century, most of central and western Europe was claimed for Christianity, and missionaries spread the faith to isolated areas of Asia.

Western Europe became de-centralized into feudal kingdoms, with the Christian Church the major force uniting Europe. The chief forces sustaining Christianity through these chaotic centuries were its centralized organization and the periodic refreshing of its spiritual wellsprings through monasticism and mysticism.

Papal power

As secular power became diffused among warring feudal lords, the Church became a rock of relative stability in which many of the powerless sought refuge. By the beginning of the second century CE after Jesus died, a consolidation of spiritual power had begun with the designation of specific people to serve as clergy and bishops (superintendents) to administer the church affairs of each city or region. The bishops of the chief cities of the Roman Empire had the greatest responsibilities and authority, with the greatest prestige being held by the Bishop of Rome, eventually known as the *pope*. By the fifth century CE, Pope Leo I argued that all popes were apostolic successors to Peter, the "rock" on which Jesus reportedly said he would found his church. On Leo's behalf, the Roman Emperor passed an edict requiring all Christians to submit to the authority of the Bishop of Rome, the successor to Peter.

The strongest of administrators during these early centuries was Gregory I ("the Great"), who died in 604 CE. Wealthy by birth but ascetic by choice, he devoted his

Christians light candles around a Christmas tree in Bucharest, December 25, 1989.

personal fortune to founding monasteries and feeding the poor. Suffering from health problems and longing for the quiet life of a monk, he was reluctantly convinced to be pope at a time of pestilence, floods, and military invasions. In this setting, he managed to provide for the physical needs of the poor, promote the discipline of the clergy (including the western ideal that priests should be celibate), revamp the liturgy (Gregorian chanting is named after him), and to re-establish the Church as a decent, just institution carrying high spiritual values.

The papacy began to wield tremendous secular power. Beginning in the eighth century, the approval of the papacy was sought as conferring divine sanction on kings. In the ninth century the Church produced documents old and new establishing the hierarchical authority of the papacy over the Church, and the Church over society, as the proper means of transmitting inspiration from the divine to humanity. Those who disagreed could be threatened with *excommunication*. This was a dread ban cutting a person off from the redemption of the church (blocking one's entrance to heaven in the afterlife), as well as from the benefits of the Church's secular power. Crusades were launched under the auspices of the Church, with war used ostensibly in defense of the faith, with no humane restraints on treatment of the "infidel."

Late in the eleventh century, Pope Gregory VII set forth an unprecedented set of claims for the papacy. The pope, he asserted, was divinely appointed and therefore could be ruled by no human. The Roman Church he ruled had never made a mistake and never would. The pope had the right to depose emperors; the princes of the world should kiss his feet.

This centralization of power became a major unifying element as Europe entered its "Dark Ages." Kingdoms broke up between 800 and 1100 as Vikings invaded from the north and Magyars from the east. For the sake of military protection, peasants gave up

The young Catherine of Siena, ''mother of thousands of souls,'' had a vision in which Christ, in the company of the Virgin Mary and other saints, gave her a wedding ring, the sign of the mystical marriage.

their freedom to feudal lords. The feudal lords in turn began to war among themselves. In the midst of the ensuing chaos, people looked to the pope as an orderly wielder of power.

Church and states were at times locked in a mutual struggle for dominance, with popes alternately supporting, dominating, and being deposed by secular rulers. The power of the papacy was also somewhat limited by the requirement that the pope be elected by a council of cardinals. The position could not become hereditary. But it was nonetheless open to intrigue, scandal, and power-mongering.

The thirteenth century saw the power of the papacy placed behind the *Inquisition.* This instrument of terror was based on Augustine's concept that heretics should be controlled for the sake of their own eternal salvation, out of love for their souls. But whereas Augustine saw fines and imprisonment as reasonable coercion to help people change their minds, the medieval Inquisitors had them tortured and burned to deter others from dangerous views.

Though strong, the papacy was often embroiled in its own political strife. During the fourteenth century, the popes left their traditional seat in turbulent Rome for the more peaceful climate of Avignon, France. There they built up an elaborate administrative structure, increasingly involved in worldly affairs. After the papacy was persuaded to return to Rome, a would-be reformer, Pope Urban, turned to terror tactics to get his way. At one point he had five cardinals tortured and killed. Many people refused to follow him; for a while they followed an "anti-pope" they established in Avignon.

Intellectual revival and monasticism

Although the papacy was subject to abuses, mirrored on a lesser scale by the clergy (not a few of whom lived with concubines), Christian spirituality was vigorously revived in other quarters of medieval society. During the twelfth and thirteenth centuries great universities developed in Europe, often from cathedral schools. Theology was considered the greatest of the sciences, with Church ideals permeating the study of all areas of life. Heightened intellectual sensitivity led to a keen sense of human sinfulness, in the midst of the lustiness of medieval life. Romantic, chivalrous conduct became idealized. Gothic cathedrals were built as soaring reflections of the feeling that humans had to aspire very high above their earthly lives to approach the heavenly throne of God.

Although the Roman Catholic Pope wields enormous power, he is also expected to carry out a rite of humility dating from the 7th century or earlier: lovingly washing the feet of the less powerful, as Jesus did for his disciples.

The yearning for spiritual purity was particularly pronounced in monasticism. It was largely through monks and nuns that Christian spirituality survived and spread. Monasteries also became bulwarks of western civilization. In Ireland, particularly, they were the centers of larger communities of laypeople, and places of learning within illiterate societies.

During the twelfth century many new monastic orders appeared in the midst of a massive popular re-invigoration of spiritual activity. A major influence was a new community in Cluny, France. Its monks specialized in liturgical elaborations and prayer, leaving agricultural work to serfs. They were ascetics, but they did not turn away from the world, as had followers of St. Benedict's Rule. Instead, they sought to permeate worldly matters with spirituality, to integrate monasticism with society.

An alternative direction was taken by the Cistercians, Gregorians, and Carthusians. They returned to St. Benedict's Rule of combining manual work and prayer; "to labor is to pray," said the monks. The Carthusians lived cloistered lives as hermits, meeting each other only for worship and business matters. Despite such austere practices, people of all classes flocked to monastic life as a pious refuge from decadent society.

> *It is not only prayer that gives God glory but work. . . . He is so great that all things give Him glory if you mean they should.*
>
> *Gerard Manley Hopkins* [46]

In contrast to monks and nuns living cloistered lives, mendicant friars, or brothers, worked among the people. The Dominican Order was instituted primarily to teach and refute heresies. A famous Dominican scholar, Thomas Aquinas, created a monumental work, *Summa Theologica*, in which rational sciences and spiritual revelations were joined in an immense, consistent theological system. It is now thought to be the most complete statement of the Roman Catholic faith.

Franciscans, following the lead of the beloved St. Francis of Assisi, wandered about without personal property or established buildings, telling people about God's love and accepting charity for their meager needs. The mendicant Dominicans and Franciscans, still noted as missionaries today, became one of the major features of medieval Christianity.

In addition to organized orders of nuns, there was a grassroots movement among thirteenth-century German women to take private vows of chastity and voluntary simplicity. These women, who were called *beguines*, lived frugally by their own work. Because they were not organized into a religious order, they chose their own lifestyles, with their chief intention being simply to live "religiously." At times persecuted because it did not fit into any traditionally sanctioned pattern, the movement persisted, drawing tens of thousands of women. Eventually they built small convents for themselves; by the end of the fourteenth century, there were 169 beguine convents in Cologne, the heart of the movement. They lasted into the eighteenth century.

Medieval mysticism

Mysticism also flowered during the middle ages, renewing the spiritual heart of the Church. Many of these mystics were women, beginning with Hildegard of Bingen

(1098–1179). She was a German abbess and seer. From childhood, she had inner experiences of light and divine visions of the meanings of the scriptures.

In thirteenth-century Italy, there was the endearing figure of St. Francis of Assisi (1182–1226). The careless, dashing son of a merchant, he underwent a spiritual transformation while recovering from a battle wound. He traded his fine clothes for simple garb and "left the world"[47] for a life of radical poverty, caring for lepers and rebuilding dilapidated churches. A mystical communication from Christ, his model, revealed to him that his real mission was to rebuild the Church by re-emphasizing the Gospel and its commands of love and poverty. A band of brothers and then of sisters, led by the saintly Clare, gathered around him. Together they preached, worked, begged, tended lepers, and lived a simple life of penance and prayer in the woods. Everything was done in mystical joy, one of St. Francis's hallmarks. He was also known for his rapport with wild animals and is often pictured with birds resting lovingly on his shoulders. It is said that he disapproved of the Crusades and personally crossed the battle line, demanding to see the sultan. The Muslim ruler and the Christian monk reportedly spent three days together, after which the sultan gave Francis a seal that is still honored, allowing Franciscans to go into Muslim holy places that are otherwise closed to outsiders.

Francis stressed obedience to the authority of the Church, even while trying to reform it. Two years before his death, he received what Catholics considered the grace of the *stigmata*. These were replicas on his own body of the crucifixion wounds of Jesus. This miracle was interpreted as a sign of the saint's union with Christ by suffering, prayer, holiness, and love.

St. Francis statues often show birds perched on him, representing his kinship with the natural world.

The flowering of English mysticism during the fourteenth century included Julian of Norwich. As a girl, she had prayed that when she reached the age of thirty (the age at which Jesus began his public mission) she would have an illness that would bring her an understanding of his *Passion* (the sufferings of his final days). As requested, she did indeed become so ill when she was thirty that she almost died. During this crisis, she had visions and conversations with Christ which revealed the boundless love with which he continually offers himself for humanity. Her writings delve into the perennial problem of reconciling the existence of evil with the experience of a loving God.

An anonymous fourteenth-century English writer contributed a volume entitled *The Cloud of Unknowing*. Christianity then and now largely follows what is called the *affirmative way*, with art, liturgy, scriptures, and imagery to aid devotion. But the author of The Cloud spoke to those who were prepared to undertake the *negative way* of abiding in sheer love for God, with no thoughts. God cannot be known through ideas or physical images; "a naked intent toward God, a desire for him alone, is enough."[48] In the silence of wordless prayer, the light of God may pierce the cloud of human unknowing that obscures the divine from the seeker.

Fourteenth-century Italy witnessed a period of unprecedented degradation among the clergy, while the papacy occupied itself with organizational matters in Avignon. In this spiritual vacuum, laypeople gathered around saintly individuals to imbibe their atmosphere of genuine devotion. One of the most celebrated of these was the young Catherine of Siena. In her persistent efforts to restore spiritual purity and religious discipline to the Church, she gained the ear of Pope Gregory XI, helping to convince him to return to Rome. She was called "mother of thousands of souls," and people were said to be converted just by seeing her face.

The Protestant Reformation

Despite the genuine piety of individuals within the Catholic Church, some who clashed with its authority claimed that those in power seemed often to have lost touch with their own spiritual tradition. With the rise of literacy and printing in the late fifteenth century, many Christians were rediscovering early Christianity and comparing it unfavorably with what the Roman Catholic Church had made of it. Roman Catholic fund-raising or church-building financial activities were particularly criticized. These included *indulgences* (services or payments for official absolution of sin by the clergy), the sale of relics, purchases of masses for the dead, spiritual pilgrimages, and the earning of spiritual "merit" by donating to the Church.

Leadership of the reform movement fell into the hands of Martin Luther. Luther was a monk and priest who lectured at the University of Wittenberg. He struggled personally with the question of how one's sins could ever be totally atoned by one's own actions. The Roman Catholic Church's position was that to be forgiven of post-baptismal sins, people should repent and then confess their sins to a priest and be pardoned. In addition, the punishment due to sins could be remitted either for the performance of prescribed penances, or if these were impossible, through granting of an indulgence. Indulgences could even be procured to make sure that the dead were freed from *Purgatory* (the intermediate place of purifying suffering for those who died in a state of repentance and grace but who were not yet sufficiently stainless to enter heaven). To this end, the Cathedral Church at Wittenberg housed an immense collection of relics, including hairs from the Virgin Mary and a thorn from the "crown" of thorns placed on Jesus's head before he was crucified. This relic collection was said to be so powerful and extensive that those who viewed them on the proper day and contributed sufficiently to the church could receive indulgences from the pope freeing themselves or their loved ones from almost two million years in Purgatory.

By intense study of certain writings of the early Church fathers, Luther discovered an entirely different approach. Both Paul and St. Augustine could be interpreted as saying that God, through Jesus, offered salvation to sinners in spite of their sins. This salvation was offered by the "Uncreated Grace" of God and claimed through the conviction of sinfulness and absolute faith in salvation, rather than through the "created graces" offered by the Church. The "good works" prescribed by Catholics to earn merit in heaven were not the original Christian way to salvation, Luther argued. Salvation from sin comes from faith in God, which itself comes from God, by grace. This gift of faith brings "*justification*" (being found righteous in God's sight) and then flowers as unselfish good works, which characterize the true Christian:

> *From faith flows love and joy in the Lord, and from love a joyful, willing and free mind that serves one's neighbor willingly and takes no account of gratitude or ingratitude, of praise or blame, of gain or loss. . . . As our heavenly father has in Christ freely come to our help, we also ought freely to help our neighbor through our body and its works, and each should become as it were a Christ to the other.* [49]

In 1517 Luther invited the university community to debate this issue with him, by the established custom of nailing his theses to the door of the church. He apparently had no intention of splitting with the entire Church. But in 1521 the Roman Catholic Church chose to excommunicate him. By this time, Luther had decided that the hierarchy of the

Martin Luther's political influence and prolific writings led to a deep split in the western church, severing Protestant Reformers from the Roman Catholic Church. (Lucas Cranach the Elder, Martin Luther, 1533.)

Church was simply a human institution.

Cut off from Rome, Luther sought support from the secular princes of Germany. For reasons sometimes more political than spiritual, many came over to his side and helped to enforce his ideas. Although there were some attempts at compromise by followers of both Luther and Rome, disinterest at the top on both sides led to collapse of conciliatory efforts.

Another major reformer who eventually broke with Rome was the Swiss priest Huldreich Zwingli (1484–1531). He rejected practices not mentioned in the Bible, such as abstaining from meat during Lent (the season mourning the crucifixion of Jesus), adoration of relics and saints, religious pilgrimages, and celibacy for monks and priests. He even questioned the spiritual efficacy of rituals such as masses for the dead and confession of one's sins to a priest:

> *The truly sacred writings know of no other confession than that by which a man comes to know himself and to throw himself upon the mercy of God. . . . As, therefore, it is God alone who remits sins and puts the heart at rest, so to Him alone ought we to ascribe the healing of our wounds, to Him alone display them to be healed.* [50]

The ideals of these reformists were adopted by many Christians. The freedom of scriptural interpretation which they opened turned out to be a Pandora's box. *Protestantism,* as the new branch of Christianity came to be called, was never as monolithic as the Roman Catholic Church had been in the west. Branches began springing up immediately.

A major seat of Protestantism developed in Geneva, under John Calvin (1509–1564). He shared the reform principles of salvation by faith alone, the authority of the Bible, and "the priesthood of all believers." But Calvin carried the doctrine of salvation by faith to a new conclusion. To him, the appropriate response to God was a zealous piety and awe-struck reverence in which one "dreads to offend him more than to die."[51] Human actions were of no eternal significance because God had already decided the destiny of each person. By grace, some were to be saved; for God's own reasons, others were predestined to be damned eternally. Although there was therefore nothing that people could do about it, their behavior would reveal which fate awaited them. Calvin therefore set up ways of policing people's behaviors to see who was acting in ways revealing damnation. The damned were to be excommunicated to keep the society of the "elect" pure. He was a forceful organizer, and used the power of the government to exile or kill heretics who objected.

Calvin's version of Christianity made its followers feel that they should fear no one except God. Convinced that they were predestined to do God's will, they were impervious to worldly obstacles to the spread of their faith. Calvinism became the state religion of Scotland and also had a following in England.

Concurrently, the Church of England separated from the Church of Rome when Henry VIII separated from the Church of Rome in order to have a marriage annulled which had produced him no sons.

As this Protestant Reformation progressed, political entities in Europe chose specific forms of Christianity as their official religion. Spain, France, and Italy remained largely Roman Catholic. Germany was largely Lutheran. Ireland split between Catholicism and Protestantism, leading to wars that continue today. The Calvinist Church of Scotland called itself Presbyterian, a reference to its form of organization. Some Polish and

Hungarian communities adopted a form of Unitarianism, which rejected the ideas of original sin, the Trinity, and Jesus's divinity, in favor of a simple theism and imitation of Jesus.

Some Protestant groups that were outlawed by the Church of England emigrated to new colonies in North America that espoused the ideal of religious freedom. These offshoots included such *denominations* (organized groups of congregations) as Baptists, Congregationalists, Quakers, and Methodists. Mainstream Anglicans (members of the Church of England) were called Episcopalians in the New World after the American Revolution. During the nineteenth century, yet more Protestant churches sprang up in the United States. Mormonism, for instance, was founded on the visions of Joseph Smith and the gold plates he said he found, comprising the Book of Mormon, an account of ancient New World civilizations that had come from Mesopotamia. Evangelical churches – those emphasizing salvation by explicit, personal faith in Jesus, personal conversion, the importance of the Bible, and preaching instead of ritual – have proliferated in North America. Fundamentalist evangelical sects are also gaining strongholds in South America, which. had been solidly Roman Catholic ever since its indigenous religions were repressed by Spanish conquerors. Protestant missionaries also carried the gospel to Asia and Africa.

Despite the great diversity among Protestant denominations, most share certain characteristics that distinguish them from Roman Catholicism. First, they place their emphasis on the Bible rather than on the authority of the Church, though they differ in how the Bible should be interpreted. Second, they emphasize individual relationship to Jesus and God rather than the mediation of God's grace through the Church. Third, they see the Church as a community of believers rather than the Catholic "mystical body of Christ," in which Jesus continues to be present through the *sacraments* (sacred

The emotional quality of worship services at this Baptist church in Indianapolis is joyful intimacy with Jesus.

rituals). The "high churches" (Lutheran and Anglican) tend to be closer to Catholicism on several of these counts than are the younger denominations. The latter may observe the central sacrament of Holy Communion, but those who are historically farther from Catholicism tend to see Communion as a memorial of Jesus's death and resurrection rather than a vehicle of his mystical presence.

Instead of priests, most Protestant churches have ministers, whose main function is to preach and build up the community rather than to act as vehicles of God's grace. The Quakers have gone even farther in rejecting human spiritual authority. They follow the example of George Fox (1624–1691), who experienced in the inner light the certainty of the divine; these "Children of the Light" utterly rejected any outer religious forms and instead simply sit in the silence, surrendered to God.

The Roman Catholic Reformation

As the Protestant reformers were defining their positions, so was the Roman Catholic Church. Because reform pressures were underway in Catholicism before Luther, Catholics refer to the movement as the Catholic Reformation, rather than the "Counter-Reformation," as Protestants call it. However, the Protestant phenomena provoked the Roman Catholic Church to clarify its own position, largely through the Council of Trent (1545 to 1563). It attempted to legislate moral reform among the clergy, to deny wonder-working powers of images, to tighten the church bureaucracy, and to recognize officially the absolute authority of the pope as the earthly vicar of God and Jesus Christ. The Council also took historic stands on a number of issues, emphasizing that its positions were *dogmas*, or authoritative truths.

Faith alone is not enough for salvation, the Council ruled. What is needed is "faith cooperating with good works." These works include works of mercy, veneration of the saints, relics, and sacred images, and participation in the sacraments. In the sacrament of the Eucharist, the Council reiterated the doctrine of *transubstantiation*: what appear to be ordinary bread and wine are mysteriously transformed into the body and blood of Christ.

In addition to the actions of the Council of Trent, the Roman Catholic Church gradually chose more virtuous popes than in the past, and several new monastic orders grew out of the desires for reform. The Jesuits offered themselves as an army for God at the service of the pope. The Society of Jesus, as the order was formally called, was begun by Ignatius Loyola in the sixteenth century. His *Spiritual Exercises* is still regarded as an excellent guide to meditation and spiritual discernment. However, it was as activists and educators in the everyday world that Jesuits were highly influential in the Reformation, and they pioneered in carrying Roman Catholicism to East Asia.

Roman Catholicism was also carried to the western hemisphere and the Philippines by Spanish conquistadores. At home, Spain was host to a number of outstanding mystics during the sixteenth and seventeenth centuries. St. Teresa of Avila (1515–1582), a Carmelite nun, became at mid-life a dynamo of spiritual activity, founding a new order of ascetic Reformed (or Discalced) Carmelite nuns and monks. Discalced Carmelites usually pray much, and eat and sleep little. Despite her organizational activity, St. Teresa was able to maintain a calm sense of deep inner communion with God. In her masterpiece entitled *Interior Castle*, she described the state of "spiritual marriage":

> *Here it is like rain falling from the heavens into a river or a spring; there is nothing but*
> *water there and it is impossible to divide or separate the water belonging to the river from*
> *that which fell from the heavens.* [52]

St. Teresa's great influence fell onto a young friend, now known as St. John of the Cross. He became a member of one of the Carmelite houses for men; when imprisoned by other Carmelites who opposed the reforms, he experienced visions and wrote profound spiritual poetry. For John, the most important step for the soul longing to be filled with God is to surrender all vestiges of the self. He rejected even the spiritual joys experienced by mystics, welcoming the "dark night of the soul" and spiritually "dry" periods because they lessened the satisfaction with self, which stood in the way of the infusion of one's being with God.

Aside from mystical infusions, true "reforms" in the Roman Catholic Church came centuries later, with the convening in 1962 of the Second Vatican Council.

The impact of the Enlightenment

Major potential threats to Christianity arose during the eighteenth-century "Enlighten-ment" in Europe. Intellectual circles embraced human reason and rejected what they considered superstition, including the miracles and revelations of the Bible. Nineteenth-century scientific advances suggested a certain skepticism about the biblical version of the creation of the world.

Such views spread rapidly, with particular impact in Protestantism. Many Protestant theologians tried to support the tenets of their faith in "rational" terms, but with an emphasis on "reasonableness" and usefulness, and an aversion to dogmatic insistence on orthodox conformity in religious belief. Individuals were encouraged to judge religious beliefs by their own experience.

Undaunted, and in some cases invigorated, by these challenges to traditional faith, Protestantism developed a strong missionary spirit, joining Roman Catholic efforts to spread Christianity to every country, along with colonialism. John Wesley, the founder of Methodism, explained:

> *I looked upon all the world as my parish; . . . that in whatever part of it I am, I judge it*
> *meet, right, and my bounden duty to declare unto all that are willing to hear, the glad*
> *tidings of salvation.* [53]

The "social gospel" movement brought Protestant churches to the forefront of efforts at social and moral reform. Women, long excluded from important positions in the church, played major roles in church-related missionary and reform efforts, such as abolition of slavery; they cited certain biblical passages as supporting equality of the sexes. When Sarah Grimke and other women were criticized by their Congregational church for speaking publicly against slavery, Grimke asserted, "All I ask of my brethren is that they will take their feet from off our necks and permit us to stand upright on that ground which God has designed us to occupy."[54]

Liberal trends in Protestant theology led to biblical criticism – that is, to efforts to analyze the Bible as literature. What, for instance, were the earliest texts? Who wrote them? How did they relate to each other? Such questions would have been unthinkable to generations raised to regard the Bible as the revealed work of God.

Vatican Councils I and II

In the meantime, the Roman Catholic and Eastern Orthodox Churches had continued to defend tradition against the changes of modern life. A general council of the Roman Catholic hierarchs was held in 1868. It found itself embroiled chiefly in the question of papal infallibility, a doctrine which it upheld. The Pope, proclaimed the bishops of the council, can never err when he speaks *ex cathedra*, from the seat of authority.

In 1962 Pope John XXIII, known for his holiness and friendliness, convened the Second Vatican Council for the express purposes of updating and energizing the Church and making it serve the people better. When questioned about his intentions, he demonstrated by opening a window to let in fresh air. With progressives and traditionalists often at odds, the majority nevertheless voted for major shifts in the Church's mission.

Many of the changes involved the conduct of the *mass*, or the Eucharist. Rather than celebrate it in Latin, which most people did not understand, much of the liturgy was to be translated into the local languages. Rites were to be simplified. As in Protestant churches, priests were instructed to deliver homilies, or sermons, during Sunday and

The large and august Second Vatican Council convened by Pope John XXIII in 1962 came to historic conclusions. Their recommendations turned Catholicism in a new direction, bringing the hierarchy closer to the common people in a compassionate partnership.

holy day masses. Greater use of sacred music was encouraged, and not just formal organ and choir offerings. For the first time the laity were to be invited to participate actively. After Vatican II thus unleashed creativity and simplicity in public worship, entirely new forms appeared, such as informal folk masses – with spiritual folk songs sung to guitar accompaniment.

Another major change was the new emphasis on *ecumenism*, in the sense of rapprochement among all branches of Christianity. The Roman Catholic Church acknowledged that the Holy Spirit is active in all Christian churches, including Protestant denominations and the Eastern Orthodox churches. It pressed for a restoration of unity among all Christians, with each preserving its traditions intact. It also extended the hope of dialogue with Jews, with whom Christians share "spiritual patrimony"[55] and with Muslims, upon whom the Church "looks with esteem," for they "adore one God" and honor Jesus as a prophet.

Appreciative mention was also made of other world religions as ways of approaching the same One whom Christians call God. Specifically described were Hinduism ("through which men contemplate the divine mystery") and Buddhism (which acknowledges the radical insufficiency of this shifting world").[56]

Vatican II clearly marked major new directions in Catholicism. Its relatively liberal, pacificistic characteristics are still meeting with some opposition within the Church decades later. In the 1980s, conservative elements in the Vatican seemed to be reversing the direction taken by Vatican II to some extent, to the dismay of liberal Catholics. In the final section of this chapter, concerning current trends in Christianity, we will note several ways in which the renewed conservatism in the Vatican is being expressed.

Sacred practices

Christianity, like other religions, offers both private and public ways of experiencing the divine. They include devotion to Mary and the saints, contemplation and prayer, receiving the sacraments, and public worship services. Forms and understanding of these practices vary among the various branches of Christendom.

> *The basic thrust of Jesus' message is to invite us into divine union, which is the sole remedy for the human predicament.*
> *Father Thomas Keating*[57]

Devotions to Mary

Thus far in this chapter, little has been said about Mary, the mother of Jesus, for she has not been in the forefront of historical theological disputes. Veneration of Mary has come more from the grassroots than from the top. Drawings of her were found in the catacombs in which the early Christians met; explicit devotion to her was well developed by the third or fourth century CE. Despite the absence of detailed historical information, she serves as a potent and much-loved spiritual symbol. She is particularly venerated by Roman Catholics, Eastern Orthodoxy, and Anglicans; Protestants have for the most part relegated Mary to a supporting role and have avoided the cult surrounding her.

Some researchers feel that devotion to Mary is derived from earlier worship of the

Mother Goddess. They see her as representing the feminine aspect of the Godhead. She is associated with the crescent moon, representing the receptive willingness to be filled with the Spirit. In the story of the *Annunciation* – the appearance of an angel who told her she would have a child conceived by the Holy Spirit – her reported response was "Behold, I am the handmaid of the Lord; let it be to me according to your word."[58] This receptivity is not seen as utter powerlessness, however. Mary, like Christ, embodies the basic Christian paradox: that power is found in "weakness."

Whether or not devotion to Mary is linked to earlier Mother Goddess worship, oral Christian traditions have given her new symbolic roles. One links her with Israel, referred to as the daughter of Zion or daughter of Jerusalem in Old Testament passages. God comes to her as the overshadowing of the Holy Spirit, and from this love between YHWH and Israel, Jesus is born to save the people Israel.

Mary is also called the New Eve. The legendary first Eve disobeyed God and was cast out of the garden of Eden; Mary's willing submission to God allows birth of the new creation, in which Christ is in all. Mary is therefore everyone's loving mother. In the Orthodox and Catholic traditions, she is referred to as the Mother of God.

Another symbolic role ascribed to Mary is that of the immaculate virgin. According to the gospels of Matthew and Luke, she conceived Jesus by heavenly intervention rather than human biology. Roman Catholicism asserts that at the Immaculate Conception, she was freed by God from all the "original sin" traced back to Adam and Eve's disobedience. Even in giving birth to Jesus, she remained a virgin. Orthodoxy does not insist on these doctrines, nor on the Catholic dogma that Mary ascended bodily to heaven after her physical death. The emphasis on virginity is a spiritual sign of being dedicated to God alone, rather than to any temporal attachments.

According to the faithful, Mary is not just a symbol but a living presence, like Christ. She is appealed to in prayer and is honored in countless paintings, statues, shrines, and churches dedicated to her name. Catholics are enjoined to repeat the "Hail Mary" prayer:

> *Hail; Mary, full of grace, the Lord is with thee. Blessed art thou among women, and blessed is the fruit of thy womb, Jesus. Holy Mary, Mother of God, pray for us sinners, now and at the hour of our death.*

Theologians are careful to point out, however, that veneration of Mary is really directed toward God; Mary is not worshiped in herself but as the mother of Christ, reflecting his glory. If this were not so, Christians could be accused of idolatry.

Be this as it may, Mary has been said to appear to believers in many places around the world. At Lourdes, in France, it is claimed that she appeared repeatedly to a young peasant girl named Bernadette in the nineteenth century. A spring found where she indicated has been the source of hundreds of medically authenticated healings from seemingly incurable diseases. In 1531, in Guadalupe (within what is now Mexico City), Mary appeared to a converted Aztec, Juan Diego. She asked him to have the bishop build a church on the spot. To convince the skeptical bishop, Juan filled his cloak with the out-of-season roses to which she directed him. When he opened the cloak before the bishop, the petals fell away to reveal a large and vivid image of Mary, with Indian features. The picture is now enshrined in a large new church with moving walkways to handle the crowds who come to see it, and the Virgin of Guadalupe has been declared Celestial Patroness of the New World.

Veneration of saints and angels

Roman Catholics and Orthodox Christians honor their spiritual heroes as *saints*. These are men and women who are recognized as so holy that the divine life of Christ is particularly evident in them. After their death, they are carefully judged by the Church for proofs of exalted Christian virtue, such as tolerance under extreme provocation, and of miraculous power. Those who are *canonized* by this process are subject to great veneration.

> *Each saint is a unique event, a victory over the force of evil. So many blessings can pour from God into the world through one life.*
>
> Father Germann, Vladimir, U.S.S.R. [59]

Orthodox Christians are given the name of a saint when they are baptized. Each keeps an icon of this *patron saint* in his or her room and prays to the saint daily. Icons of many saints fill an Orthodox Church, helping to make them familiar presences rather than names in history books. Saints are often known as having special areas of concern and power. For instance, St. Anthony of Padua is invoked for help in finding lost things. *Relics*, usually parts of the body or clothes of saints, are felt to radiate the holiness of the saints' communion with God. They are treasured and displayed for veneration in Catholic and Orthodox churches.

Roman Catholics and Orthodox Christians also pray to the angels for protection. *Angels* are understood as spiritual beings who serve as messengers from and adoring servants of God. They are usually pictured as humans with wings, for they are thought to be able to move very quickly, but they are said to have no bodies. In popular piety, each person is thought to have a guardian angel for individual protection and spiritual help.

Contemplative prayer

The contemplative tradition within Christianity has re-emerged during the twentieth century. The hectic pace and rapid change of modern life make periods of quietness essential, if only for stress relief. Many Christians, not aware of a contemplative way within their own church, turned to Eastern religions for instruction in meditation.

One of the most influential twentieth-century Christian contemplatives was the late Thomas Merton (1915–1968). He was a Trappist monk who received a special dispensation to live as a hermit in the woods near his abbey in Kentucky. Merton lived simply in nature, finding joy in the commonplace, experienced attentively in silence. He studied and tried to practice the great contemplative traditions of earlier Christianity and reintroduced them to a contemporary audience through his writings. In meditative "prayer of the heart," or "contemplative prayer," he wrote:

> *We seek first of all the deepest ground of our identity in God. We do not reason about dogmas of faith, or ''the mysteries.'' We seek rather to gain a direct existential grasp, a personal experience of the deepest truths of life and faith, finding ourselves in God's truths. . . . Prayer then means yearning for the simple presence of God, for a personal understanding of his word, for knowledge of his will and for capacity to hear and obey him.* [60]

The Christian monk Thomas Merton and the Tibetan Buddhist Dalai Lama, two great ecumenical figures of the 20th century, met right before Merton died during his trip to visit monks of the eastern traditions.

Before he became a Christian monk, Merton had studied eastern mysticism, assuming that Christianity had no mystical tradition. He became friends with a Hindu monk who advised him to read St. Augustine's *Confessions* and *The Imitation of Christ* (written anonymously during the fourteenth century but often ascribed to Thomas a Kempis, who may have edited it). These classical works led Merton toward a deep appreciation of the potential of the Christian inner life, aligned with a continuing openness to learn from eastern monasticism. He died by accident while visiting Buddhist and Hindu monastics.

Even though Merton's life was cut short, an opening had been created. Today western Christians, particularly in the United States, are flocking to retreat centers to learn how to meditate in Christian fashion and to experience spiritual renewal through inner silence. In Catholic churches, believers are also encouraged to follow the plaques or paintings called *Stations of the Cross*, each depicting scenes from the last days of Jesus, in order to identify with his Passion, humble the self, and draw near to the Christ.

In Orthodoxy, the central contemplative practice is repetition of the Jesus Prayer. Eventually its meaning imbeds itself in the heart and one lives in a state of unceasing prayer.

The sacraments

The word *sacrament* can also be translated as "mystery." In Christianity, the sacraments are the sacred rites that are thought capable of transmitting the mystery of Christ to worshippers.

The first to be administered is *baptism*. Externally, it involves either immersing the person in water or, more commonly, pouring sanctified water (representing purification) on the candidate's head, while invoking the Holy Trinity. In a recent ecumenical document, the World Council of Churches defined the general meaning of the practice:

> *By baptism, Christians are immersed in the liberating death of Christ where their sins are buried, where the ''old Adam'' is crucified with Christ, and where the power of sin is broken . . . They are raised here and now to a new life in the power of the resurrection of Jesus Christ.* [61]

Aside from adult converts to Christianity or one of its branches, the rite is usually performed on infants, with parents taking vows on their behalf. There are arguments that infant baptism has little basis in the Bible and that a baby cannot make the conscious repentance of sin and "conversion of heart" implied in the ceremony. Baptists and several other Protestant groups therefore reserve baptism for adults.

A second ceremony is often offered in early adolescence – *confirmation*. After a period of religious instruction, a group of young people are allowed to make a conscious and personal commitment to the Christian life.

In Roman Catholic, Anglican, and Orthodox Chrisitanity, the central sacrament available to those who have been baptized and perhaps confirmed into the church is the *Holy Eucharist* (also called Holy Communion). It is a mystery through which the invisible Christ is thought to grant communion with himself. Believers are given a bit of bread to eat, which is received as the body of Christ, and a sip of wine or grape juice, understood as his blood. Jesus set the pattern for doing so at what is called The Last Supper, the meal he shared with his inner circle before his capture by the authorities in Jerusalem.

The body and blood of Christ are seen as the spiritual nourishment of the faithful, that which gives them eternal life in the midst of earthly life.

Mother Julia Gatta, Anglican priest, describes this sacred experience from the point of view of the clergy who preside at the liturgy:

> *To be the celebrant of Eucharist is, I think, the most wonderful experience on earth. In a sense, you experience the energy flowing both ways. . . . One experiences the Spirit in them offering their prayer through Christ to the Father. But at the same time, you experience God's love flowing back into them. When I give communion to people, I am aware that I am caught in that circle of love.* [62]

The partaking of sacred bread and wine is the climax of a longer liturgy of Holy Communion. The Communion service, often called a *mass* in Catholicism, begins with liturgical prayers, praise, and confession of sinfulness. A group confession chanted by some Lutheran congregations enumerates these flaws:

> *Most merciful God, we have sinned against you in thought, word, and deed, by what we have done and by what we have left undone. We have not loved you with our whole heart; we have not loved our neighbors as ourselves.* [63]

Catholics were traditionally encouraged to confess their sins privately to a priest before taking communion, in the sacrament of *penance*, or "reconciliation." In the Eastern Church, the confession is heard in the open, with the priest standing to the side to make it clear that it is God, rather than the priest, who judges. After hearing the confession,

The sacrament of Eucharist, celebrated here in the Philippines, engages believers in a communal mystical encounter with the presence of Christ.

the priest pronounces forgiveness and blessing over the penitent, or perhaps prescribes a penance.

Orthodox Christians were also traditionally expected to spend several days in contrition and fasting before taking communion, but this tradition has declined in favor of more frequent participation in communion. The reason for the emphasis on purification, for dropping away earthly burdens and failings, is that during the service, the church itself is perceived as the kingdom of God, in which everything is whole and holy. In Orthodox services, the clergy walk around the perimeter of the church, swinging a censer filled with incense to set apart the area as a sacred space, as well as to lift the prayers of the congregants to God.

In all Christian churches, passages from the Old and New Testaments may be read and the congregation may sing several *hymns*, songs of praise or thanksgiving to God. The congregation may be asked to recite a credal statement of Christian beliefs, and to make money offerings. There may be an address by the priest or minister (called a sermon or a homily) on the readings for the day. These parts of the liturgy constitute the Liturgy of the Word, in which Christ is thought to be present as the living Word addressing the people through scripture and preaching. Then the priest or minister may consecrate the bread and wine in ritual fashion and share them among the people. In Roman Catholic or Orthodox masses, the cup of wine and the bread are usually held up to be mystically transformed by the Holy Spirit into the blood and body of Christ. They are treated with profound reverence. In sharing the communion "meal" together, the people are united with each other as well as with Christ. The traditional ideal was to take communion every day and certainly every Sunday (the day set aside as the Sabbath).

In Protestant churches, the Liturgy of the Word is often used by itself, without the communion service. When communion is offered, it is treated as a memorial service, in remembrance of Jesus.

In both Protestantism and Roman Catholicism, there are now attempts at updating the liturgy to make it more meaningful and personally relevant for twentieth-century Christians. One innovation that seems to have taken hold everywhere is the "sharing of the peace." Partway through the worship service, congregants turn to everyone around them to hug or shake hands and say, "The Peace of Christ" — "and also with you."

The liturgical year

Just as Christians repeatedly enact their union with Christ through participation in the Eucharist, the Church every year celebrates a cycle of celebrations leading the worshipper through the life of Jesus and the gift of the Spirit. As the faithful repeat this cycle year after year, they hope to enter more deeply into the mystery of God in Christ, and the whole body of believers in Christ theoretically grows toward the kingdom of God.

CHRISTMAS AND EPIPHANY   There are three major events in the church calendar, each associated with a series of preparatory celebrations. The first is the season of light: Christmas and Epiphany. *Christmas* is the celebration of Jesus's incarnation on earth, born in a manger. *Epiphany* (called Theophany in the Eastern Church) means "manifestation" or "showing forth." It celebrates the recognition of Jesus's spiritual kingship by the three Magi (in the Western Church), his acknowledgement as the Messiah and the beloved Son of God when he is baptized by John the Baptist, and his first recognized miracle: the turning of water into wine at the wedding in Cana.

In early Christianity, Epiphany was more important than the celebration of Jesus's birth. The actual birth date is unknown. The setting of the date near the winter solstice allowed Christianity to take over the older "pagan" rites celebrating the return of longer periods of daylight at the darkest time of year. In the gospel of John, Jesus is "the true light that enlightens every man,"[64] the light of the divine appearing amid the darkness of human ignorance.

The month preceding Christmas is supposed to be a time of joyous anticipation. In industrialized countries, it is more likely a time of frenzied marketing and buying of gifts, symbolizing God's gift to the world in the person of Jesus. Attempts are being made to sidestep the extreme commercialization of the season and to return to simpler, more sacred ways of honoring the birth of the Christ child.

Young children re-enact the Christmas story in many countries throughout the world.

Many churches stage pageants re-enacting the birth story, with people taking the parts of Mary, Joseph, the innkeeper who has no room, the shepherds, and the three Magi. It is traditional to cut or buy an evergreen tree (symbol of eternal life, perhaps borrowed from pagan ceremonies) and erect it in one's house, decorated with lights and ornaments. On Christmas Eve some Christians gather for a candlelit "watch-night" service, welcoming the turn from midnight to a new day in which Christ has come into the world. On Christmas Day, children are sometimes told that presents have been magically brought by St. Nicholas, a fourth-century bishop noted for his great generosity. Exchange of gifts may be followed by a great feast.

The Virgin of Guadalupe, who reportedly appeared in the 16th century to an indigenous convert to Catholicism, speaking the native language Nahuatl, has been embraced as patron saint of the Americas.

EASTER   The second major focus of the liturgical year is *Easter*. This is the commemoration of Jesus's death (on "Good Friday") and Resurrection (on Easter Sunday, which falls in the spring but is celebrated at different times by the eastern and western churches). Like Christmas, Easter is a continuation of earlier rites – those associated with the spring solstice, celebrating the regeneration of plant life and the return of warm weather after the cold death of winter. It is also related to Pesach, the Hebrew Passover, the Jewish spring feast of deliverance.

Liturgically, Easter is preceded by a forty-day period of repentance and fasting, called Lent. Many Christians are called to acts of asceticism, prayer, and charity, to join in Jesus's greater sacrifice. Lent begins with Ash Wednesday, when many Christians have

ash smudges placed on their foreheads by a priest who says, "Remember, man, thou art dust and unto dust thou shalt return." On the Sunday before Easter, Jesus's triumphal entry into Jerusalem is honored by the waving of palm branches in churches and the proclaiming of Hosannas. His death is mourned on "Good Friday." The mourning is jubilantly ended on Easter Sunday, with shouts of "Christ is risen!"

In Russia, the Great Vigil welcoming Easter morning lasts from midnight until dawn, with the people standing the entire time. Jim Forest describes such a service in a church in Kiev, with two thousand people crowding into the building and as many more standing outside:

> *The dean went out the royal doors into the congregation and sang out, "Christos Voskresye!" [Christ is risen!] Everyone responded in one voice, "Veyeastino voskresye!" [Truly he is risen!] It is impossible to put on paper how this sounds in the dead of night in a church overheated by crowds of people and hundreds of candles. It is like a shudder in the earth, the cracking open of the tomb. Then there was an explosion of ringing bells.* [65]

PENTECOST   Fifty days after the Jewish Passover (which Jesus is thought to have been celebrating at the Last Supper with his disciples) comes the Jewish harvest celebration, Shavuot (which may in turn have been an adaptation of an earlier Canaanite agricultural celebration). Jews nicknamed it *Pentecost*, which is Greek for "fiftieth." Christians took over the holiday season but gave it an entirely different meaning.

In Christianity, Pentecost commemorates the occasion described in Acts when the Holy Spirit descended upon the disciples after Jesus's death and resurrection, filling them with the Spirit's own life and power, and enabling them to speak in foreign tongues they had not known. In early Christianity, Pentecost was an occasion for baptisms of those who had been preparing for admission to the church.

The TV control center at the Crystal Cathedral, California.

THE TRANSFIGURATION AND ASSUMPTION Some Christian churches also emphasize two other special feast days. On August 6, the people honor the Transfiguration of Jesus on the mountain, revealing his supernatural radiance. On August 15, they celebrate the Assumption of Mary, known as "The Falling Asleep of the Mother of God." These feasts are prominent in the Eastern Church, which generally places more emphasis on the ability of humanity to break out of its earthly bonds and rise into the light, than on the heaviness and darkness of sin.

Contemporary trends

Christianity is gaining membership and enthusiastic participation in some quarters and losing ground in others. In Egypt, Orthodox Coptic Christians, heirs to the ancient tradition of the Desert Fathers, have long been submerged under Muslim rule, but the monasteries have begun to flourish again. In the Soviet Union, a growing spirit of openness has allowed Christians to worship more freely.

Roman Catholicism is torn by divisions between conservatives and liberals. After the liberal tendencies of Vatican II, Pope John Paul II reaffirmed certain traditional stands and strengthened the position of the right wing of the Church. Bishops in the United States have increasingly opposed this conservatism. They see a dwindling priesthood (it is estimated that by the year 2000, there will be only half as many active Catholic priests in the United States as there were in 1966, partly because of the requirement that priests be celibate). They also see other trends such as increased interest in participation by women (who are not allowed by the Vatican to be priests), and widespread disregard of papal prohibitions on effective birth control, abortion, test-tube conception, surrogate motherhood, genetic experimentation, divorce, and homosexuality.

As the Vatican responds to these trends by insisting on tradition and authority, many American Catholic leaders are concerned that, in the words of Father Frank McNulty of Newark, New Jersey, "people often do not perceive the church as proclaiming integral truth and divine mercy, but rather as sounding harsh, demanding."[66] Acting as a group, Roman Catholic bishops in the United States have issued statements deploring sexism as a "sin" (recommending that spiritual positions of responsibility and authority be opened to women and that non-sexist language be used in liturgy), supporting peace efforts, insisting on the morality of economic social justice, and questioning the morality of spending for "Star Wars" (the Strategic Defense Initiative begun under President Reagan). A 1987 poll by ABC News revealed that forty per cent of Catholics in the United States favored a break with the Vatican, creating an independent American Catholic Church with only symbolic ties with Rome.

In Protestantism, traditional denominations in Europe and the United States are declining in membership. According to a Gallup poll, only a minority of the "unchurched" actually disagree with their denomination's teachings. They are more likely to drop away because of apathy, a lack of services, or a lack of welcome on the part of the minister. The numbers of women in the ministry are increasing, however; the National Council of Churches predicts that by the year 2000 some twenty-five per cent of all Protestant clergy in the United States will be women. Gender-inclusive language is increasingly common in theological documents.

trends are taking vigorous root. These include evangelical and charismatic groups, non-Western Christian churches, liberation theology, creation-centered Christianity, and the ecumenical movement.

Evangelicalism

To evangelize is to preach the Christian gospel and convert people to Christianity. A 1936 Southern Baptist book entitled *Winning Others to Christ* declared, "Christian service offers no more exalted possibility than that of winning a person from a life of sin to a life in Christ."[67] In the face of liberalizing, materialistic, rationalistic trends in industrial society, this approach receded to the background. But late in the twentieth century it has reasserted itself so strongly that by the late 1980s, forty-five per cent of Protestants in the United States could be considered evangelicals.

Although evangelicals vary from arch-fundamentalists to those of more liberal persuasion, this trans-denominational grouping has certain characteristics in common. According to historian George Marsden, in the broadest sense evangelicals are Christians who emphasize five things:
1 The final authority of Scripture.
2 The real, historical character of God's saving work recorded in Scripture.
3 Eternal salvation only through personal trust in Christ.
4 The importance of evangelism and missions.
5 The importance of a spiritually transformed life.[68]

Evangelicals study the Bible together, value being "born again" in Christ, and resist certain modern intellectual traditions. For instance, they oppose Charles Darwin's evolutionary theory of natural selection, believing instead that God created everything on earth as described in the biblical book of Genesis. Their message has become particularly visible and effective through books sold in exclusively Christian bookstores and through the medium of television.

Television evangelism, with its accompanying pleas for continuing financial donations to the cause, has suffered a number of scandals as certain top evangelists have been exposed for sexual and financial transgressions. Howard Cleinbell, a theology professor, speaks of this indulgence in the forbidden as "pedestalitis" (inadvertently assuming that the clergy consists only of males):

> *The person who is in the clergy has to deny his shadow side. He's put on a pedestal by followers, and as such he puts himself on a pedestal. So when his gutsy, earthy, sensual side is denied or hidden, the pressure builds up on a subconscious level, which often results in acting out in secret ways.* [69]

Despite some disillusionment with evangelical Christianity in North America, the movement is making great strides in South America. There it is threatening the ascendency of the Roman Catholic church, which in turn overpowered indigenous traditions centuries ago.

Charismatics

Overlapping somewhat with the evangelical surge, there is a rising emphasis on

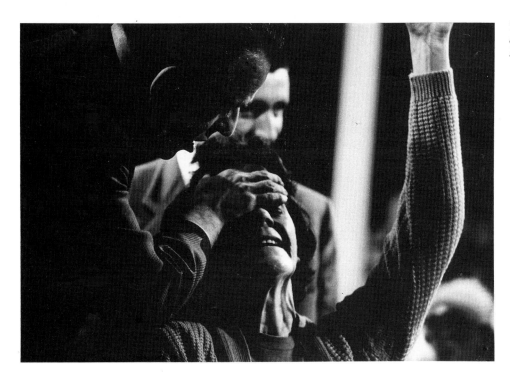

The laying on of hands at a charismatic service in Manchester, England.

charismatic experience – that is, divinely inspired powers – among Christians of all classes and nations. While Christian fundamentalists stress the historical Jesus, charismatics feel they have also been touched by the "third person" of the Trinity, the Holy Spirit. These include members of Pentecostal churches but also Roman Catholics and members of mainline Protestant sects. Under the influence of the Spirit, they speak in tongues, pray and utter praises spontaneously, heal by the laying on of hands and prayer, and bear witness to spiritual miracles. Dogma and religious authority are usually less important in these groups than personal spiritual experience.

Mainstream Christian churches, which have often rejected emotional spiritual experience in favor of a more orderly piety, are gradually becoming more tolerant of it. The movement is often called "Charismatic Renewal," for it claims to bring true life in the Spirit back to Christianity. Because it transcends ecclesiastical forms, the charismatic movement has helped to bring Protestant and Catholics back into spiritual fellowship.

Cultural broadening

Although contemporary Christianity was largely shaped in Europe and its North American colonies, a large percentage of the Christian Church lies outside these areas. It has great numerical strength and vigor in Africa, Latin America, and parts of Asia.

As missionaries spread Christianity to these regions, they often assumed that European ways were culturally superior to indigenous ways and peoples. But some of these newer Christians have come to different conclusions. Theologians of the African Independent Churches, for instance, reject the historical missionary efforts to divorce them from their traditions of honoring their ancestors. This effort tore apart their social structure, they feel, with no scriptural justification:

> As we became more acquainted with the Bible, we began to realise that there was nothing at all in the Bible about the European customs and Western traditions that we had been taught. What, then was so holy and sacred about this culture and this so-called civilisation that had been imposed upon us and was now destroying us? Why could we not maintain our African customs and be perfectly good Christians at the same time? . . .
>
> We have learnt to make a very clear distinction between culture and religion . . . [For instance], the natural customs of any particular nation or race must never be confused with the grace of Jesus Christ our Saviour, Redeemer and Liberator. [70]

Theologians from non-Western countries are proposing that their people's traditional values could enrich Christianity if taken seriously in their own right. Because many are poor Third World countries, they recall Christians to Jesus's radical ethics of poverty, humility, and service.

Liberation theology

Although many Christians make a distinction between the sacred and the secular, some have involved themselves deeply with social issues as an expression of their Christian faith. For instance, the late Baptist preacher, Martin Luther King, became a great civil rights leader, declaring, "It was Jesus of Nazareth that stirred the Negroes to protest with the creative weapon of love."[71] This trend is now called *liberation theology* – a faith that stresses the needs for concrete political action to help the poor. Beginning in the 1960s with Vatican II, Roman Catholic priests and nuns serving in Latin America began to make conscious, voluntary efforts to understand and side with the poor in their

For liberation theologians, the message of the gospel often entails down-to-earth physical help to the poor. Maryknoll lay sisters Norma Jejia, Julia Mamani, and Delia Gamboa are here lending a hand to the families of a Peruvian barrio.

struggles for social justice. The Peruvian theologian Gustavo Gutierrez, who coined the expression "theology of liberation," explains the choice of voluntary poverty as:

> *a commitment of solidarity with the poor, with those who suffer misery and injustice . . . It is not a question of idealizing poverty, but rather of taking it on as it is – an evil – to protest against it and to struggle to abolish it.* [72]

For their sympathetic siding with those who are oppressed, Catholic clergy have been murdered by political authorities in countries such as Guatemala. They have also been strongly criticized by conservatives within the Vatican. Cardinal Ratzinger, who heads the Congregation for the Doctrine of the Faith, has decried liberation theology. He characterizes it as Marxist and says that it inappropriately emphasizes liberation from material poverty rather than liberation from sin. The movement has nevertheless spread to all areas where there is social injustice. Bakole Wa Ilunga, Archbishop of Kananga, Zaire, reminds Christians that Jesus warned the rich and powerful that it would be very difficult for them to enter the kingdom of heaven. By contrast, writes Ilunga:

> *Jesus liberates the poor from the feeling that they are somehow less than fully human; he makes them aware of their dignity and gives them motives for strugggling against their lot and for taking control of their own lives.* [73]

Creation-centered Christianity

Another current trend in Christianity is an attempt to develop and deepen its respect for nature. In the Judeo-Christian tradition, humans are thought to have been given dominion over all the things of the earth. Sometimes this "dominion" was interpreted as the right to exploit, rather than the duty to care for, the earth. This view contrasts with indigenous beliefs that the divine resides everywhere, that everything is sacred, and that humans are only part of the great circle of life. Some Christians now feel that the notion of having a God-given right to control has allowed humans to nearly destroy the planet. In some cases, they are turning to indigenous spiritual leaders for help in extricating the planet from ecological destruction as we will see in Chapter 13. Historian and passionate earth-advocate Father Thomas Berry feels that "we need to put the Bible on the shelf for twenty years until we learn to read the scripture of life."[74]

A Christianity that would accord greater honor to the created world would also tend to emphasize the miracle that is creation, thus helping to unite science and religion. Creation-centered Christians – such as the late Jesuit father and paleontologist Teilhard de Chardin – see the mind of God in the perfect, intricate balances of chemistry, biology, and physics that allow life as we know it to exist. This rejoicing in all of life as divine has been carried by Dominican scholar Matthew Fox to conclusions that the Vatican found unacceptable. They forced on him a year of public silence beginning in December, 1988. Fox's teachings include appreciation of the feminine aspect of the divine and celebration of the human body as blessed.

Ecumenical movement

In spite of the great and growing diversity among Christians, there is at the same time an increasing attempt to unify all Christians around some point of agreement or at least fellowship.

LIVING CHRISTIANITY
An interview with John Blazo, Maryknoll Lay Brother

In contrast to their earlier cultural chauvinism, Western Christian missionaries now often recognize that they can learn and grow through their experiences in other cultures. Maryknoll, a missionary institution within the Roman Catholic Church, has developed a form of liberation theology based on strengthening leadership among the poor. Brother John Blazo served in Nicaragua for a year and in Guatemala for five years, sometimes with his life in danger from militarists opposing church help to the poor.

"In both of these places, the church has been focusing on local leadership. We encourage people in basic leadership skills – how to be self-supporting, how to make more decisions independently of us. When I first got to Nicaragua, the people's first response was always 'Tell us,' but I said, 'I'm not here to tell you what to do. I don't speak Spanish that well. This is your church, this is your village. I just got out of language school and I don't know what the customs are. You know that; you know what has happened in the past. You know what you want to do. I'm just asking you the questions to see if you want to do this or not.' It was a very slow process.

The idea is for the group to help itself to see what are their living situations, what is their reality, and then compare that to 'What does the Lord say about this?' and 'What does our Catholic church say about this?' Then they can make the necessary changes to bring about something else. The famous text we always use is Moses and the Red Sea – with the community and with the help of the almighty God, they put down their oppressor, they went through the armies and the Red Sea to a new light. But it took time to do all that. God is with those people who are suffering, who are trying to work and trying to improve their life; that's God's will. Some of the political structures are set up to keep people down – to provide cheap labor or cheap resources, to control. That's what humans did; that's certainly not God's will.

There's another element: evangelization, looking for people who aren't sacramentalized, who aren't Catholic. When Maryknoll was founded in 1911, the sense was that it was important to get them into your church. In the changing church, there are still elements of that. I'd love more people to come into the Catholic church, but I'm not going to try to bend people's necks, saying that things are perfect in the Catholic church and we have the only way. We certainly don't do that.

This work has helped me to be a broader person and to go deeper in my own religion. My constant question is 'What is basic Christianity and what is a cultural expression?' The cultural expression can always change, but the basics theoretically can't. There is the belief in one God, and I think the other thing we have to be really pushing is the idea of reconciliation amongst people. Those are basics which are obviously not limited to Christianity. There is also belief in the afterlife – belief in heaven and hell, belief in Jesus as God. Jesus died for us, Jesus showed a way of working, of having ways of forgiving our sins, so let's emphasize the positive, let's struggle toward doing better. You see people struggling to do good, especially the very poor people, and you say, 'The last thing I want to do is focus on what possible wrong they might be doing which might not even be wrong. It's just a different cultural way of doing something. You're making the effort – I can tell, because I know you.' "

Vatican II asserted that the Roman Catholic Church is the one church of Christ but opened the way to dialogue with other branches of Christianity by declaring that the Holy Spirit was active in them as well. The Orthodox Church likewise believes that it is the "one, holy, Catholic, and Apostolic Church." Although it desires reunion of all Christians and denies any greed for organizational power, it insists on uniformity in matters of faith. Orthodox and Roman Catholic Churches therefore do not share Holy

Communion with those outside their respective disciplines. Some Protestant denominations have branches that also refuse to acknowledge each other's validity.

There are, however, attempts to restore some bonds among all Christian churches. There are dozens of official ecumenical dialogues going on among them. The World Council of Churches, centered in Geneva, was founded in 1948 as an organizational body allowing Christian churches to cooperate on service projects even in the midst of their theological disagreements. Its Faith and Order Commission links three hundred culturally, linguistically, and politically, not to mention theologically, different Christian churches in working out the problems of Christian unity.

As the Lambeth Conference of Anglican Bishops in 1988 put it:

The ultimate goal is not simply the unity of the Church . . . It is the perfect reign of God over a reconciled, restored and transformed creation.[75]

Barbara Harris became the first female bishop in the history of the Anglican Church, February 11, 1988, at a ceremony in Boston.

Suggested reading

Abbott, Walter M., ed., *The Documents of Vatican II*, New York: The America Press, 1966. Landmark conclusions of the Council Fathers, with special emphasis on the poor, religious unity and social justice.

Dillenberger, John and Welch, Claude, *Protestant Christianity Interpreted through its Development*, New York: Charles Scribner's Sons, 1954. The classic history and interpretation of Protestantism.

Forest, Jim, *Pilgrim to the Russian Church*, New York: Crossroad, 1988. A highly readable, moving account of a Western journalist's experiences within contemporary Russian Orthodoxy.

Fosdick, Harry Emerson, ed., *Great Voices of the Reformation*, New York: Random House, 1952. Extensive quotations, with commentary, from major early Protestant leaders.

Keating, Thomas, *The Mystery of Christ: The Liturgy as Spiritual Experience*, New York: Amity House, 1987. The life and presence of Jesus, as experienced through the liturgical cycle.

Lossky, Vladimir, *The Mystical Theology of the Eastern Church*, Crestwood, New York: St. Vladimir's Seminary Press, 1976. A brilliant introduction to the inner meanings of Orthodox Christianity.

Matura, Thadee, *Gospel Radicalism*, Maryknoll, New York: Orbis Books, 1984. The "hard sayings" of Jesus about renunciation, discipleship, humility, and love, as they might be applied in contemporary life.

The Holy Bible. Respected contemporary translations: The Revised Standard Version, The New English Bible, and the New Jerusalem Bible.

Price, James L., *Interpreting the New Testament*, second edition, New York: Holt, Rinehart and Winston, 1971. Excellent survey of the literature and interpretation of the New Testament.

Ware, Timothy, *The Orthodox Church*, Middlesex, England and Baltimore, Maryland: Penguin Books, 1984. An excellent overview of the history, beliefs, and practices of the Eastern Church.

Robinson, James M., ed., *The Nag Hammadi Library*, San Francisco: Harper and Row, 1977. A fascinating collection of early scriptures that are not included in the Christian canon.

Tugwell, Simon, *Ways of Imperfection*, London: Darton, Longman and Todd, 1984, and Springfield, Illinois: Templegate Publishers, 1985. Spirituality as a whole vision of life, as seen by a series of great Christian practitioners.

Walker, Williston, and Norris, Richard A., Lotz, David W., and Handy, Robert T., *A History of the Christian Church*, fourth edition, New York: Charles Scribner's Sons, 1985, and Edinburgh: T&T Clark, 1986. A classic history of Christianity, authoritatively updated.

11 ISLAM

"There is no god but God"

In about 570 CE, a new prophet was born. This man, Muhammad, is considered by Muslims to be the last of a continuing spiral of prophets who have come to restore the true religion. They regard the way that he founded, Islam, as the final stage in the evolution of the Judeo-Christian-Islamic tradition.

After carrying the torch of civilization in the West while Europe was in its Dark Ages, Islam is undergoing a great resurgence in the twentieth century. It is now the religion of an estimated one-quarter of the world's people. Its monothesistic creed is very simple: "There is no god but God, and Muhammad is his Messenger." Its requirements of the faithful are straightforward, if demanding. But beneath the simplicities of outward conformity to the teachings – and aggressive interpretations of them in some quarters – lie profundities and subtleties of which non-Muslims are largely unaware. Glimmers of appreciation for the faith are just beginning to appear in Western media, partly as sincere Muslims attempt to counteract negative media portrayals of the faithful as mysterious, violent "Arab fanatics."

The Prophet Muhammad

Islam, like Christianity and Judaism, traces its ancestry to the patriarch Abraham. Ishmael was said to be the son of Abraham and an Egyptian slave, Hagar. When Abraham's wife Sarah also bore him a son (Isaac), Abraham took Ishmael and Hagar to the desert valley of Becca (Mecca) in Arabia to spare them Sarah's jealousy.

The sacred book of Islam, the Holy Qur'an, received as a revelation to Muhammad, relates that Abraham and Ishmael together built the holiest sanctuary in Islam, the Ka'bah. It was thought to be the site of Adam's original dwelling place; it also contained a venerated black meteorite. According to the Qur'an, God told Abraham that the Ka'bah should be a place of pilgrimage. It was regarded as a holy place by the Arabic tribes. The chief deity worshipped there seems to have been Allah (El), the Creator and Father and King of other deities, and there is also evidence of the worship of goddesses associated with the power of the Black Stone.

According to Muslim tradition, the region sank into historical oblivion, "the Age of Ignorance," as it turned away from Abraham's monotheism. For many centuries, the events of the rest of the world passed it by, aside from contact through trading caravans. Then into a poor clan of the most powerful of the tribes in the area was born a child named Muhammad ("the praised one"). His father died before he was born; his mother

Left *The Black Stone in Mecca has been a Muslim center of worship since Abraham and Ishmael first built the Ka'bah next to it, according to the Qur'an. The meteorite is considered a symbol of the primordial covenant between God and humans.*

Below *Muhammad allegedly undertook spiritual retreats in this cave on Mt. Hira outside Mecca. It was here that he received the revelations of the Qur'an.*

Although representations of humans, including himself, were forbidden by the Prophet to avoid idolatry, Persian artists later gave imaginative expression to Muslim stories, such as the Miraj, or Ascension, of the Prophet.

died during his infancy. He was nursed by a woman of another tribe and raised among them as a shepherd.

Allah (God) is *the* focus in Islam, the sole authority, not Muhammad. But Muhammad's life story is important to Muslims, for his example is considered a key that opens the door to the Divine Presence. The stories of Muhammad's life and his sayings are preserved in a vast literature called the *Hadith* (tradition) which reports on the Prophet's *Sunnah* (model pattern of behavior). They indicate that the Prophet-to-be returned to live and travel with his uncle as a young teenager. On a trip to Syria, he was noticed by a Christian monk who recognized his deep spirituality. Another who appreciated his fine qualities was the allegedly beautiful, intelligent, and wealthy Khadijah, his employer. When she was forty and Muhammad twenty-five, she offered

to marry him. Khadijah became Muhammad's strongest supporter during the difficult and discouraging years of his early mission.

With Khadijah's understanding of his spiritual propensities, Muhammad began to spend periods of time in solitary retreat. These retreats were not uncommon in his lineage. They were opportunities to turn within, away from the world, and to immerse oneself in the divine presence. Some accounts say that the rocks and trees around his favorite retreat cave on Mount Hira outside Mecca greeted him and wished him peace.

When Muhammad was forty years old, he made a spiritual retreat during the month called Ramadan. An angel in human-like form, Gabriel, reportedly came to him and insisted that he recite. Three times Muhammad demurred that he could not, for he was unlettered, and three times the angel embraced him. After the third time, Muhammad

was able to recite the first words of what became the Qur'an, repeating them as the
angel dictated:

> Proclaim! (or Read!)
> In the name
> Of thy Lord and Cherisher,
> Who created –
> Created man, out of
> A (mere) clot
> Of congealed blood:
> Proclaim! And thy Lord
> Is Most Bountiful, –
> He Who taught
> (The use of) the Pen, –
> Taught man that
> Which he knew not.

Muhammad returned home, deeply shaken. Khadijah comforted him and encouraged
him to overcome his fear of the responsibilities and ridicule of prophethood. The
revelations continued intermittently, asserting the theme that it was the One God who
spoke and who called people to *Islam* (which means complete trusting surrender to
God). According to tradition, Muhammad described the form of these revelations thus:

> *Revelation sometimes comes like the sound of a bell; that is the most painful way. When it
> ceases I have remembered what was said. Sometimes it is an angel who talks to me like a
> human, and I remember what he says.* [2]

The Prophet shared these revelations with the few people who believed him: his wife Khadijah, his young cousin 'Ali, his friend the trader Abu Bakr, and the freed slave Zayd.

After three years, Muhammad began to preach publicly. He was ridiculed and stoned by the Qurayshites, the aristocrats of his tribe who operated the Ka'bah as a pilgrimage center and organized profitable trading caravans through Mecca. Finally, according to some accounts, Muhammad and his followers were banished for three years to a desolate place where they struggled to survive by eating wild foods such as tree leaves.

The band of Muslims were asked to return to Mecca, but their persecution by the Qurayshites continued. Muhammad's fiftieth year, the "Year of Sorrows," was the worst of all: he lost his beloved wife Khadijah and his protective uncle. With his strongest backers gone, persecution of the Prophet increased.

According to tradition, at the height of his trials, Muhammad experienced the Night of Ascension. He is said to have ascended through the seven heavens to the far limits of the cosmos, and thence into the Divine Proximity. There he met former prophets and teachers from Adam to Jesus, saw paradise and hell, and received the great blessings of the Divine Presence. He was proclaimed the synthesis of all the previous prophets.

Pilgrims to Mecca from Yathrib, an oasis to the north, recognized Muhammad as a prophet. They invited him to come to their city to help solve its social and political problems. Still despised in Mecca as a potential threat by the Qurayshites, Muhammad and his followers left Mecca secretly. Their move to Yathrib, later called al-Medina ("The City [of the Prophet]"), was not easy. The Prophet left last, accompanied (according to some traditions) by his old friend Abu Bakr. To hide from the pursuing Meccans, it is said that they took refuge in a cave, where the Prophet taught his friend the secret practice of the silent remembrance of God.

The *Hegira* ("leaving") from Mecca took place in June 622 CE. The Muslim era is calculated from the beginning of the year in which this event took place, for it marked the change from persecution to appreciation of the Prophet's message. In Medina, he drew up a plan for solving community tensions that later served as a model for Muslim social administration. In a battle between the young community and Meccans at Badr near Medina, the small group of Muslims was victorious. In Muslim legend, it was a handful of pebbles thrown at the Meccans by Muhammad that decided the outcome, for the hand that threw was really God's hand. The Meccans repeatedly tried to attack the Medinans, but the latter held fast. They were inspired by revelations to Muhammad about the battle against oppression.

The Quranic revelations to Muhammad emphasize the basic unity of Jews, Christians, and Muslims, members of the same monotheistic tradition of Abraham. But Jews refused to accept Islam since it recognized Jesus and claimed to complete the Torah. In addition, they were politically allied to the Qurayshites who opposed the Prophet. Eventually their farms were appropriated by increasing numbers of Muslim converts; some Jews were killed as political opponents. The Qur'an taught that the Jews and Christians had distorted the pure monotheism of Abraham; Muhammad had been sent to restore and supplement the teachings of the apostles and prophets. He was instructed to have the people face Mecca rather than Jerusalem during their prayers.

In 630 CE the Prophet returned triumphant to Mecca with such a large band of followers that the Meccans did not resist. The Ka'bah was purged of its idols, and from that time to the present it has been the center of Muslim piety. Acquiescing to Muhammad's political power and the Quranic warnings about the dire fate of those

Islam

CE

Birth of Muhammad c.570 CE

— 600

Revelation of the Qur'an to Muhammad begins c.610

Rapid spread of Islam begins 633

The Hegira ("leaving") from Mecca 622

Umayyad dynasty 661–750

Muhammad's triumphant return to Mecca 630

Factional schisms lead to Sunni-Shi'ite split c.682

— 700

Death of Muhammad, election of Abu Bakr as first caliph 632

Written text of Qur'an established 650

European advance of Islam stopped at Battle of Tours 732

— 800

Islam reaches its cultural peak under Abbasid caliphs 750–1258

— 900

al-Hallaj killed 922

— 1000

al-Ghazali 1058–1111

— 1100

Salah-al-Din recaptures Jerusalem from Crusaders 1171

— 1200

Christians take Spain, institute Inquisition 1300s

— 1300

— 1400

Turks conquer Constantinople, renaming it Istanbul 1453

— 1500

Akbar becomes Mughal emperor in India 1556

— 1600

— 1700

Muslim areas fall under European domination 1800s–1900s

— 1800

— 1900

Oil-rich Muslim states join OPEC and Muslim resurgence begins 1970s

Partition of Muslim Pakistan from Hindu India 1947

— 2000

who tried to thwart God's prophets, many Meccans converted to Islam. Former opponents were reportedly treated leniently.

The Prophet then returned to Medina, which he kept as the spiritual and political center of Islam. From there, campaigns were undertaken to spread the faith, making peace with or suppressing dissident groups. In addition to northern Africa, the Persian states of Yemen, Oman, and Bahrain came into the fold. As the multi-cultural, multi-racial embrace of Islam evolved, the Prophet declared that the community of the faithful was more important than the older tribal identities that had divided people. The new ideal was a global family, under God. In his "Farewell Sermon," Muhammad stated, "You must know that a Muslim is the brother of a Muslim and the Muslims are one brotherhood."[3]

In the eleventh year of the Muslim era Muhammad made a final pilgrimage to the Ka'bah to demonstrate the rites that were to be followed thenceforth. Then he became very ill. As he recognized that the end was near, he gave final instructions to his followers, promising to meet them at "the Fountain" in the next life. But he left no clear instructions as to who should succeed him. In the confusion that followed, his steadfast friend Abu Bakr was elected the first *caliph* (successor to the Prophet). Another possible successor, the trustworthy and courageous 'Ali (the Prophet's cousin and husband of his favorite daughter, Fatima), was busy with funeral arrangements and took no part in the voting. The Shi'ite faction would later claim him as the legitimate heir. In foreign relations, Abu Bakr's leadership was not widely accepted, so he and Umar, who became the second caliph at his death, put military pressure on the Byzantine and Persian Empires. Soon, Persia, Egypt, and the Fertile Crescent were within the Muslim fold.

The Qur'an

The heart of Islam is not the Prophet but the revelations he received. Collectively they are called the *Qur'an* ("reading" or "reciting"). He received the messages over a period of twenty-three years, with some later messages replacing earlier ones. At first they were striking affirmations of the unity of God and the woe of those who did not heed God's message. Later messages also addressed the organizational needs and social lives of the Muslim community.

As Muhammad heard the revelations, he committed them to memory and then taught his followers to memorize them. The tradition was originally oral, said to be carefully safeguarded against changes and omissions. Recited, the passages have a musical beauty and power that Muslims believe to be unsurpassed; these qualities cannot be translated. The recitation is to be rendered in what is sometimes described as a sad, subdued tone, because the messages concern God's sadness at the waywardness of the people. Muhammad said, "Weep, therefore, when you recite it."[4]

Recitation of the Qur'an is thought to have a healing, soothing effect, but can also bring protection, miraculous signs, knowledge, and destruction, according to Muslim tradition. It is critical that one recite the Qur'an only in a purified state, for the words are so powerful that the one who recites it takes on a great responsibility. Ideally, one learns the Qur'an as a child, when memorization is easiest and when the power of the words will help to shape one's life.

During the life of the Prophet, there was also an attempt to write down the oral tradition as an additional way of safeguarding it from loss. The early caliphs continued this effort until a council was convened by the third caliph around 650 CE to establish a single authoritative written text. This is the one still used. It is divided into 114 *suras* (chapters). The first is the *Fatiha*, the opening sura which has been called the essence of the Qur'an:

> *In the name of God, Most Gracious, Most Merciful.*
> *Praise be to God,*
> *The Cherisher and Sustainer of the Worlds;*
> *Most Gracious, Most Merciful;*
> *Master of the Day of Judgment.*
> *Thee do we worship,*
> *And Thine aid we seek.*
> *Show us the straight way,*
> *The way of those on whom*
> *Thou hast bestowed Thy Grace,*
> *Those whose portion*
> *Is not wrath,*
> *And, who go not astray.* [5]

The verses of the Qur'an are terse, but are thought to have multiple levels of meaning. Translator and commentator Abdullah Yusuf Ali notes that in the mystical early passages there are often three layers: **1** a reference to a particular person or situation, **2** a spiritual lesson, and **3** a deeper mystical significance. He offers interpretation of these three levels in the first two verses of Sura 74 ("O thou wrapped up / [In a mantle]! / Arise and deliver thy warning!"):

> *As to **1**, the Prophet was now past the stage of personal contemplation, lying down or sitting in his mantle; he was now to go forth boldly to deliver his Message and publicly proclaim the Lord ... As to **2**, similar stages arise in a minor degree in the life of every good man, for which the Prophet's life is to be a universal pattern. As to **3**, the Sufis understand, by the mantle and outward wrappings, the circumstances of our phenomenal existence, which are necessary to our physical comfort up to a certain stage; but we soon outgrow them, and our inner nature should then boldly proclaim itself. ...* [6]

The Qur'an makes frequent mention of figures from Jewish and Christian history, all of which is considered part of the fabric of Islam by Muslims. In the story of the conception and birth of Jesus (Isa), the same angel, Gabriel, brings the message of the conception to Mary who later brought the Qur'an to Muhammad. Some people have compared Muhammad to Mary, a receptive vehicle for the Divine Word, "virgin" in the sense of being unlettered as well as pure. Some also liken him to Jesus, who as an infant announces to Mary's amazed relatives:

> *I am indeed*
> *A servant of God:*
> *He hath given me*
> *Revelation and made me*
> *A prophet*
>
> *And He hath made me*
> *Blessed wheresoever I be,*
> *And hath enjoined on me*
> *Prayer and Charity as long*
> *As I live.* [7]

LIVING ISLAM
An Interview with Khaled aly Khaled

Trained as a doctor of pharmacy, Khaled aly Khaled of Egypt did not appreciate his Muslim heritage when he was a child. He explains that his faith grew slowly as he became aware of the scientific accuracy and literary genius of the Qur'an.

"For a very long time in Egypt, we had the idea that it is better for you not to stick to a religion. If you stuck to a religion, people looked at you as just a fool. They thought there is a correlation between the success in the real life and the religion. If you have success in the real world, you didn't have to do these things that were religious. If you pray and fast and talk about Qur'an, the people start to think that you are not having any success.

Ten years ago I could not even read Qur'an. So I started from the very end, very far from religion, but I am getting back to it. For me, maybe the most important thing is scientific interpretation of the Qur'an. I can just believe what I can see, what I can feel, and just try to make interpretation of what I can collect from data. I started to read about the planets and their movement, from the scientific point of view. It is hard to believe these kind of things come just from blind nature. But a Big Mind behind this system? I could not believe that. That's against the science. But it cannot come as an accident. If you change one part out of one hundred million parts, the whole universe will collapse. So you cannot be accurate unless you have some mind or some knowledge to control the whole thing.

Now I'm sure that someone is behind the universe, is creating it, is creating me. You cannot feel the miracle of the universe unless you work in science. The human body cannot come from a primary cell reacting to another primary cell to create a creature from two cells and construct the body. It is beyond probability. Some supreme power created everything.

Some of the statements in the Qur'an had no meaning at that time, 1400 years ago, but they have meaning now. For example, 'We have created this universe and we have made it expanding.' 'We have made the earth look like an egg.' Such statements cannot come from just an average person living 1400 years ago. Among ancient Egyptians, ancient Syrians, we cannot find this information. I started to believe that someone was giving the knowledge to Muhammad. I'm not a very good believer – don't ask me to believe just because there is a book. But this information cannot come from any source except One Source.

As for the language of the Qur'an, scholars who speak Arabic have tried to write just one statement similar to this book in beauty. They could not. One computer scientist did a computer analysis of the Qur'an. He found that the number of chapters, the number of statements, and the number of times each letter is used are all multiples of 19 (which is the number of angels in the Hellfire). Then he tried to see if he could write a book about any subject, using multiple numbers of any figure. No one could do it. The beauty of the Qur'an is pure, supreme.

If you compare the speech of Muhammad to the Qur'an, there is a big difference in beauty. He himself cannot make even one statement like that. He cannot write, he doesn't have knowledge, he just was taking care for the sheep. From this, I started to believe that there is a God."

The Qur'an offers a further commentary on the earlier Jewish and Christian scriptures, using them to teach spiritual lessons. Sometimes the details of the stories are changed; in some cases, stories are cited that do not now appear in the official canons of those traditions (such as the one of the young Jesus and the clay birds that came to life). Non-believers think Muhammad simply borrowed from the earlier stories, confusing their details, and from Arabic indigenous traditions as well. By contrast, Muslims deeply believe in the Qur'an as the revealed word of God. It represents the truth, which they feel has been distorted over time by followers of Judaism and Christianity. As Abdullah Yusuf Ali explains the Quranic stories of Jesus, "The original Gospel was not the various stories written afterwards by disciples, but the real Message taught direct by Jesus."[8]

The central teachings

On the surface, Islam is a very straightforward religion. Its teachings can be summed up very simply, as in this statement by the Islamic Society of North America:

> Islam is an Arabic word which means peace, purity, acceptance and commitment. As a religion, Islam calls for complete acceptance of the teachings and guidance of God.
>   A Muslim is one who freely and willingly accepts the supreme power of God and strives to organize his life in total accord with the teachings of God. He also works for building social institutions which reflect the guidance of God.[9]

This brief statement can be broken down into a number of articles of faith.

The Oneness of God

The first sentence chanted in the ear of a traditional Muslim infant is the Shahadah — "La ilaha illa 'llah." Literally, it means "There is no god but God." Exoterically, the phrase supports absolute monotheism. In the minority mystical view, it means that ultimately there is only one Absolute Reality; the underlying essence of life is eternal unity rather than the apparent separateness of things in the physical world. Muslims feel that the Oneness of God is the primordial religion taught by all prophets of all faiths. Muhammad merely served to remind people of it.

It has been estimated that over ninety per cent of Muslim theology deals with the implications of Unity. God, while One, is called by ninety-nine names in the Qur'an. These are each considered attributes of the One Being, such as al-Ali ("The Most High") and ar-Raqib ("The Watchful"). Allah is the name of God that encompasses all the attributes. There are actually three thousand names of God, according to Muslim oral tradition. One thousand are known only to angels, one thousand only by prophets. Three hundred are in the Torah, three hundred in the Psalms of David, three hundred in the New Testament. The Ninety-Nine Most Beautiful Names are in the Qur'an, and the last, the greatest name, is hidden in the whole Qur'an. Each of the names refers to the totality, the One Being.

Unity applies not only to the conceptualization of Allah (God), but also to every aspect of life. In the life of the individual, every thought and action should spring from a heart and mind intimately integrated with the divine. Islam theoretically rejects any divisions within itself; all Muslims around the globe are supposed to embrace as one family. All humans, for that matter, are a global family; there is no one "chosen people," for all are invited into a direct relationship with God. Science, art, and politics are not separate from religion in Islam; there is not even a word for "secular" in Islamic languages. Individuals should never forget Allah; the Oneness should permeate their thoughts and actions. Abu Hashim Madani, an Indian Sufi sage, is said to have taught, "There is only one thing to be gained in life, and that is to remember God with each breath; and there is only one loss in life, and that is the breath drawn without the remembrance of God."[10]

> "The 'remembrance of God' is like breathing deeply in the solitude of high mountains: here the morning air, filled with purity of the eternal snows, dilates the breast; it becomes space and heaven enters our heart."
>
> *Frithjof Schuon*[11]

Muslims express their belief in the Oneness of the divine by saying the Shahada ("There is no god but God"), the sentence emblazoned on this Turkish plaque.

Prophethood and the compass of Islam

Devout Muslims feel that Islam encompasses all religions. Islam honors all prophets as messengers from the one God:

> Say ye: We believe
> In God, and the revelation
> Given to us, and to Abraham,
> Isma'il, Isaac, Jacob,
> And the Tribes, and that given
> To Moses and Jesus, and that given
> To (all) Prophets from their Lord:
> We make no difference
> Between one and another of them:
> And we bow to God (in Islam).[12]

Muslims believe that the original religion was monotheism, but that God sent prophets from time to time as religions decayed into polytheism. Each prophet came to renew the message, in a way specifically designed for his or her culture and time. Muhammad, however, received messages meant for all people, all times. The Quranic revelations declared him to be the "Seal of the Prophets," the last and ultimate authority in the continuing prophetic tradition. The prophets are mere humans; none of them are divine, for there is only one Divinity.

Islam is thought to be the universal religion in its pure form. All scriptures of all traditions are also honored, but only the Qur'an is considered fully authentic, because it is the direct, unchanged, untranslated word of God. Whatever exists in other religions that agrees with the Qur'an is divine truth.

Human relationship to the divine

In Muslim belief, God is all-knowing and has created everything for a divine purpose. We humans are unique in creation. According to Islam, we are created in the form of God, with the ability to develop qualities of the divine in ourselves. We are born free of sin, naturally more good than bad, and are capable of noble achievements. We have the free will to act with integrity and the power of intelligence to distinguish between the true and the false. With God's help we can defy the petty tendencies of the ego and clothe ourselves in the divine attributes.

> We are nearer to him than his jugular vein.
>
> *The Holy Qur'an, Sura 50:16*

Islam emphasizes that our faith in God must be based on intelligent personal conviction, rather than blind conformity to religious norms. *Muslim* means one who has accepted through free choice to conform his or her personal will to the Divine Will, as revealed through the prophets.

To Muslims, our covenant with God is that in return for God's blessings and the gifts of being human, we are to remember that our real nature is divine and act accordingly. The goal of human perfection is the actualization of the Names of God. They must be developed in balance, for every quality can become a defect if not tempered by other qualities. To manifest *al-Haqq* (The Truth) without aspects such as *al-Rahim* (The Divine Compassion) leads to unhealthy imbalances in the personality.

In Islamic mysticism, forgetfulness of the divine is the most serious sin. As Professor Seyyed Hossein Nasr explains:

> *It is a going to sleep and creating a dream world around us which makes us forget who we really are and what we should be doing in this world. Revelation is there to awaken man from this dream and remind him what it really means to be man.* [13]

The veils that separate us from realizing God come from us, not from God; Muslims feel that it is ours to remove the veils by seeking God and acknowledging the omnipresence, omniscience, and omnipotence of the Divine. For the orthodox, the appropriate stance is a combination of love and fear of God. Aware that God knows everything and is all-powerful, one wants to do everything one can to please God, out of both love and fear. This paradox was given dramatic expression by the caliph 'Umar ibn al-Khatab:

> *If God declared on the Day of Judgment that all people would go to paradise except one unfortunate person, out of His fear I would think that I am that person. And if God declared that all people would go to hell except one fortunate person, out of my hope in His Mercy I would think that I am that fortunate person.* [14]

The unseen life

Muslims believe that our senses do not reveal all of reality. In particular, they believe in the angels of God. These are nonphysical beings who serve God day and night. They are numerous, and each has a specific responsibility. The created world itself is woven of the invisible ether, which is the vehicle of the divine Word. Sun, moon, planets, stars, trees, flowers, mountains, animals, humans – all of us are created of the same invisible substance. All worship God continually, each in its own tongue.

The Last Judgement

Like Zoroastrians, Jews, and Christians, Muslims believe in a final judgement, described in great detail in the Qur'an. At some unknown time, the world will end cataclysmically. As the Day of Reckoning approaches, the Gog and Magog (wild, lawless people) will swarm across the earth, devouring its fruits and waters, and a beast shall rise from the ground and speak to the people. The Anti-Christ will rule temporarily but then be vanquished by a spiritual representative called the Mahdi. After this conclusive battle, all humans will die, to be gathered into the general bodily resurrection:

According to Muslim belief, angels are everywhere; they come to our help in every thought and action. A group of angels are here shown helping the 8th-century Sufi ascetic, Ibrahim ibn Adham.

*Does man think that We
Cannot assemble his bones?
Nay, We are able to put
Together in perfect order
The very tips of his fingers.*[15]

After the general upraising, all will be judged according to their former thoughts and actions. They will be weighed in the Balance of Justice, exposed in "The Book," questioned as to why they acted thus, and sent across the path. It is a bridge over hell, wide for those who have been faithful, sharp as a blade for those who have not believed.

The good will enter paradise; the infidel (nonbelievers) will suffer in hell.

This final judgement is prefigured by the state one enters after death. It is called the *barzakh*, the "isthmus" between this life and eternity. The situations in the Lesser Resurrection into the barzakh and the Greater Resurrection at the end of the world are similar; they differ mostly in intensity.

Basically, Islam says that what we experience in the afterlife is a revealing of our tendencies in this life. Our thoughts, actions, and moral qualities are turned into our outer reality. We awaken to our true nature, for it is displayed before us. For the just and merciful, barzakh is a Garden of Bliss. Those who say, "Our Lord is God . . . shall have all that your souls shall desire . . . A hospitable gift from One Oft-Forgiving, Most Merciful!"[16] The desire of the purified souls will be for closeness to God, and their spirits will live in different levels of this closeness. For them, there will be castles, couches, fruits, sweetmeats, honey, houris (beautiful virgin women), and immortal youths serving from goblets and golden platters. Such delights promised by the Qur'an are interpreted metaphorically by some mystics as reminders to the soul that Paradise is an extremely appealing state.

> *People are asleep, but when they die, they wake up.*
> Hadith of the Prophet Muhammad

By contrast, infidels, or unbelievers, will experience the torments of Hell, fire fueled by humans, boiling water, pus, chains, searing winds, food that chokes, and so forth. It is they who condemn themselves; their very bodies turn against them "on the Day when their tongues, their hands, and their feet will bear witness against them as to their actions."[17] The great medieval mystic Al-Ghazzali speaks of spiritual torments of the soul as well: the agony of being separated from worldly desires, burning shame at seeing one's life projected, and terrible regret at being barred from the vision of God. Muslims do not believe that hell can last forever for any believer, though. Only the unbelievers will be left there; the others will eventually be lifted to paradise, for God is far more merciful than wrathful.

The Sunni-Shi'ite Split

The preceding pages describe beliefs of all Muslims, but factions within Islam differ somewhat on other issues. Fifty years after Muhammad's death, resentments over the issue of his succession divided the unity of the Muslim community into factions. The two main opposing groups have come to be known as the *Sunni*, who now comprise about eighty per cent of all Muslims worldwide, and the *Shi'ite*.

As discussed earlier, a series of caliphs was elected to lead the Muslim community after Muhammad's death. The fourth caliph was 'Ali, the Prophet's cousin and son-in-law. He was reportedly known for his holy and chivalrous qualities, and was the first of the Prophet's relatives to hold the position of caliph. But the opposition party, the Umayyads, never accepted him as their leader, and he was assassinated by a fanatic from a sect within his own party. His son Husayn, grandson of the Prophet, challenged the authority of the next Umayyad caliph and in return was massacred along with many of his relatives and supporters. This horror unified Shi'ite opposition to the elected successors and they broke away, claiming their own legitimate line of succession through the direct descendants of the Prophet, beginning with 'Ali. Nearly fourteen hundred years later the two groups are still separate, though there is in some circles a definite trend toward re-establishing a bond of sorts.

Sunnis

Those who follow the elected caliphs are "the people of the Sunnah." They consider themselves traditionalists who emphasize the authority of the Qur'an and the Hadith and Sunnah (the sayings and practices of the Prophet, as collected under the Sunni caliphs). They feel that the fact that all of Muhammad's sons died before he did is a sign of the Divine Wisdom, leaving the matter of successors to the *ummah*, the Muslim community. The caliph is not a replacement of the Prophet; he is the leader of worship and the administrator of the *Shari'ah*, the sacred law of Islam.

The *Shari'ah* consists of teachings and practices for everything in Muslim life, from how to conduct a war to how to pray. Like Torah for Jews, the Shari'ah sets the pattern for all individual actions and theoretically bonds them into a coherent, divinely regulated, peaceful community.

The Shari'ah is based chiefly on the Qur'an and the Hadith and Sunnah of Muhammad, who was the first to apply the generalizations of the Qur'an to specific life situations. The revelations of the Qur'an include not only human-divine relationships but also humans' relationships with each other. Religion is not a thing apart; all of life is

Only one hundred years after Muhammad's death, Islam had spread around the Mediterranean. Its diffusion continued for centuries and the numbers of converts are still increasing, making Islam the fastest-growing religion today. Of areas previously converted to Islam, all remain Muslim except for Spain and Sicily.

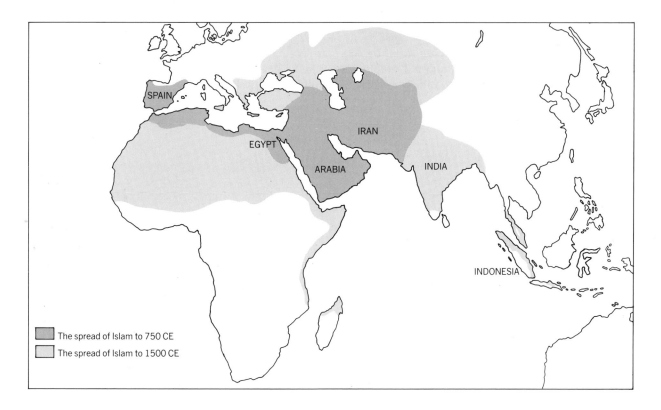

SPAIN

EGYPT

IRAN

ARABIA

INDIA

INDONESIA

The spread of Islam to 750 CE
The spread of Islam to 1500 CE

to be integrated into the spiritual unity which is the central principle of Islam. For example, the faithful are enjoined to be kind to their parents and kin, children and strangers, to protect orphans and women, to exercise justice and honesty in their relationships and business interactions, to stop killing infants, to manage their wealth carefully, and to avoid adultery and arrogance.

In the third century of Islam, the Abbasid dynasty replaced the Umayyads, who had placed more emphasis on empire-building and administration than on spirituality. At this point, there was a great concern for purifying and regulating social and political life in accord with Islamic spiritual tradition. Mechanisms for establishing the Shari'ah were developed. Since then, Sunnis have felt that as life circumstances change, laws in the Qur'an, Hadith, and Sunnah should be continually interpreted by a consensus of opinion and the wisdom of learned men and jurists. For example, the twentieth-century Muslim faces new ethical questions not specifically addressed in the Qur'an and Hadith, such as whether or not test-tube fertilization is acceptable (some think yes, on condition that the sperm is the father's and the egg the mother's).

Shi'ites

The tone of Shi'ite Islam is more passionate and the authority to interpret the Shari'ah more concentrated in one person. Shi'ites are ardently devoted to the memory of Muhammad's close relatives: 'Ali, Fatima (the Prophet's beloved daughter), and their sons Hasan and Husayn. The martyrdom of Husayn in his protest against the alleged tyranny, oppression, and injustice of the Umayyad caliphs is held up as a symbol of the struggle against human oppression. It is commemorated yearly, with participants in mourning processions crying and beating their chests.

Rather than recognize the Sunni caliphs, Shi'ites pay their allegiance to a string of seven or twelve *Imams* ("leaders," "guides"). The first three were 'Ali, Hasan, and Husayn. According to a saying of the Prophet acknowledged by both Sunni and Shi'a:

> *I leave two great and precious things among you: the Book of Allah and my Household. If you keep hold of both of them, you will never go astray after me.*[18]

"Twelver" Shi'ites believe that there were a total of twelve Imams, legitimate hereditary successors to Muhammad. The twelfth Imam, they believe, was commanded by God to go into an occult hidden state in 940 CE, to continue to guide the people and return publicly at the Day of Resurrection as the Mahdi. A minority of Shi'ites, the Isma'ilis and "Seveners" recognize a different person as the seventh and last Imam, and believe that it is he who is hidden and still living. There must always be an Imam. As Muhammad Rida al-Muzaffar explains:

> *The Imamate must continue uninterrupted, although the Imam may live hidden among mankind until Allah wills that he reappear on a certain day, a Divine mystery known only to Him. The fact that he has lived for such a long time is a miracle granted to him by Allah ... Even though medical science is not yet able to prolong human life as much as possible, ... Allah can, for He is All-Powerful and Omnipotent. For the Qur'an states that Nuh [Noah] lived to a very old age, and that 'Isa [Jesus] is alive now, and once one has accepted Islam, there can be no denying what the Qur'an says.*[19]

Unlike the Sunni Caliph, the Imam combines political leadership (if possible) with

Islamic Iranians flagellate themselves on the 40th day of mourning after the anniversary of the Martyrdom of Imam Husayn, the prophet Muhammad's grandson.

continuing the transmission of Divine Guidance. This esoteric religious knowledge was given by God to Muhammad, from him to 'Ali, and thence from each Imam to the successor he designated from 'Ali's lineage. It includes both the outer and inner meanings of the Qur'an. The Shari'ah is therefore interpreted for each generation by the Imam, for he is closest to the divine knowledge. When the Imam is not in a position to assert political power, those in positions of authority are expected to carry out his decisions. This assumption of spiritual authority has at times been carried to autocratic, violent extremes by Isma'ilis in power.

Aside from the issue of succession to Muhammad, Sunnis and Shi'ites are in general agreement on most issues of faith. Shi'ites follow the same essential practices as Sunnis, but, as discussed in a later section on spiritual practices, add several that express their ardent commitment to re-establishing what they see as the true spirit of Islam in a corrupt, unjust world.

Sufism

In addition to these two main groups within Islam, there is also an esoteric tradition which is said to date back to the time of the Prophet. He himself was at once a political leader and a contemplative with a deep prayer life. He reportedly said that every verse of the Qur'an has both an outside and an inside. Around him were gathered a group of about seventy people. They lived in his Medina mosque in voluntary poverty, detached from worldly concerns, praying night and day. After the time of the first four caliphs,

Muslims of this deep faith and piety, both Sunni and Shi'ite, were distressed by the increasingly secular, dynastic, wealth-oriented characteristics of Muhammad's Umayyad successors. The mystical inner tradition of Islam, called *Sufism* (Arabic: *tasawwuf*), also involved resistance to the legalistic, intellectual trends within Islam in its early development.

Sufis have typically understood their way as a corrective supplement to orthodoxy. They consider their way a path to God that is motivated by longing for the One. In addition to studying the Qur'an, Sufis examine their own hearts and the world around them. They feel that the world is a book filled with "signs" – divine symbols and elements of beauty that speak to those who understand. The intense personal journeys of Sufis and the insights that have resulted from their truth-seeking have periodically refreshed Islam from within. Much of the allegorical interpretation of the Qur'an and devotional literature of Islam is derived from Sufism.

The early Sufis turned to asceticism as a way of deepening their piety. In this, they may have been influenced by ascetics from other traditions with which they came into contact, particularly Christianity. The Christian ascetics were following Jesus's advice not to worry about material life because God would take care of their physical needs; the Prophet had said something very similar to his followers: "If ye had trust in God as ye ought He would feed you even as He feeds the birds."[20] Muhammad himself had lived in poverty, reportedly gladly so. Complete trust in and surrender to God became an essential step in the journey. *Dervishes* (poor mendicant mystics) with no possessions, no attachments in the world, were considered holy people like Hindu sannyasins. But Sufi asceticism is based more on inner detachment than on withdrawal from the world; the ideal is to live with feet on the ground, head in the heavens.

To this early asceticism was added fervent, selfless love. Its greatest exponent was Rabi'a, the eighth-century saint. All her attention was placed on her Beloved, which became a favorite Sufi name for God. Rabi'a emphasized disinterested love, with no selfish motives of hope for paradise or fear of hell. "I have served Him only for the love of Him and desire for Him."[21] Any other motivation is a veil between lover and Beloved. When no veils of self exist, the mystic dissolves into the One she loves.

Sufi dervishes enter a state of ecstatic unity with the divine by repeating the Shahadah.

> *The Beloved is all, the lover just a veil.*
> *The Beloved is living, the lover a dead thing.*
>
> *Jelaluddin Rumi*[22]

In absolute devotion, the lover desires *fana*, total annihilation in the Beloved. This Sufi ideal was articulated in the ninth century CE by the Persian Abu Yazid Bistami. He is said to have fainted while saying the Muslim call to prayer. When he awoke, he observed that it is a wonder that some people do not die when saying it, overwhelmed by pronouncing the name Allah with the awe that is due to the One. In his desire to be annihilated in God, Bistami so lost himself that he is said to have uttered pronouncements such as "Under my garment there is nothing but God,"[23] and "Glory be to Me! How great is My Majesty!"

The authorities were understandably disturbed by such potentially blasphemous statements. Sufis themselves knew the dangers of egotistical delusions inherent in the mystical path. There was strict insistence on testing and training by a sufficiently trained, tested, and illumined *murshid* ("teacher") or *shaykh*. Advanced practices were taught only to higher initiates. It was through the shaykh that the *barakah* ("blessing," sacred power) was passed down, from the shaykh of the shaykh, and so on, in a chain reaching back to Muhammad, who is said to have transmitted the barakah to 'Ali.

A number of esoteric orders evolved, most of which traced their spiritual lineage back to Junayd. He taught the need for constant purification, a continual serious examination of one's motives and actions. He also knew that it was dangerous to speak openly of one's mystical understandings; the exoteric-minded might find them blasphemous, and those who had not had such experiences would only interpret them literally and thus mistakenly. He counseled veiled speech, and much Sufi literature after his time is couched in metaphors accessible only to mystics.

Despite such warnings, the God-intoxicated cared little for their physical safety and exposed themselves and Sufism to opposition. The most famous case is that of Mansur al-Hallaj. After undergoing severe ascetic practices, he is said to have visited Junayd. When the master asked, "Who is there?", his disciple answered, *"ana'l-Haqq"* ("I am the Absolute Truth," i.e., "I am God"). After Junayd denounced him, al-Hallaj traveled to India and throughout the Middle East, trying to open hearts to God. He wrote of the greatness of the Prophet Muhammad, and introduced into the poetry of divine love the simile of the moth that flies ecstatic into the flame and, as it is burned up, realizes Reality.

Political maneuverings made a possible spiritual revival a threat to authorities back home, and they imprisoned and finally killed al-Hallaj in 922 CE for his *"ana'l-Haqq."* His hands and feet were hacked off, and then his head. Now, however al-Hallaj is considered by many to be one of the greatest Muslim saints, for it is understood that he was not speaking in his limited person. Like the Prophet, who had reportedly said, "Die before ye die,"[24] al-Hallaj had already died to himself so that nothing remained but the One.

> *What's in your head – toss it away! What's in your hand – give it up! Whatever happens – don't turn away from it . . . Sufism is the heart standing with God, with nothing in between.*
>
> *Abu Sa'id Abel-Khayr*[25]

A more moderate Sufism began to make its way into Sunni orthodoxy through Abu Hamid al-Ghazzali. He had been a prominent theologian but felt compelled to leave his prestigious position for a life of spiritual devotion. Turning within, he discovered mystical truths which saved him from his growing scepticism about the validity of religion. His persuasive writings combined accepted Muslim theology with the assertion that Sufism is needed to keep the mystical heart alive within the tradition. By the fourteenth century, three sciences of religion were generally accepted by the orthodoxy: jurisprudence, theology, and mysticism.

Over the centuries, other elements have been added to Sufism. Some Sufis have embraced teachings from various religions, emphasizing that the Qur'an clearly states that the same Voice has spoken through all prophets. Shihabuddin Suhrawardi (1153–1191 CE), for instance, combined many currents of Islam with spiritual ideas from the Zoroastrians of ancient Iran and the Hermetic tradition from ancient Egypt. His writings are full of references to the divine light and hierarchies of angels. We humans have descended from the angels and realms of light, he wrote; we are in exile here on earth, longing for our true home, searching for that radiant purity, dimly remembered, in this dark world of matter.

Although Sufi teachings and practices have been somewhat systematized over time, they resist doctrinal, linear specification. They come from the heart of mystical experiences which defy ordinary logic. Paradox, metaphor, the world of creative imagination, of an expanded sense of reality – these characteristics of Sufi thought are better expressed through poetry and stories. A favorite character in Sufi teaching tales is Mulla Nasrudin, the wise fool. An example, as told by Idries Shah:

> One day Nasrudin entered a teahouse and declaimed, ''The moon is more useful than the sun.'' Someone asked him why. ''Because at night we need the light more.''[26]

These "jokes" boggle the mind, revealing the limitations of ordinary thinking at the same time that they offer flashes of metaphysical illumination for those who ponder their deeper significances.

Poetry has been used by Sufis as a vehicle for expressing the profundities and perplexities of relationship with the divine. Jalal al-Din Rumi, the thirteenth-century founder of the Mevlevi Dervish Order in Turkey (famous for its "Whirling Dervishes" whose dances lead to transcendent rapture), was also a master of mystical poetry. He tells the story of a devotee whose cries of "O Allah!" were finally answered by God:

> Was it not I that summoned thee to service?
> Did not I make thee busy with My name?
> Thy calling ''Allah!'' was My ''Here am I,''
> Thy yearning pain My messenger to thee.
> Of all those tears and cries and supplications
> I was the magnet, and I gave them wings.[27]

The aim of Sufism is to become so purified of self that one is a perfect mirror for the divine attributes. The central practice is called *dhikr*, or "remembrance." It consists of stirring the heart and piercing the solar plexus, seat of the ego, by movements of the head, while continually repeating *la ilaha illa 'llah*, which Sufis understand in its esoteric sense: There is nothing except God. Nothing in this ephemeral world is real except the Creator; nothing else will last. As the seventy thousand veils of self – illusion, expectation, attachment, resentment, egocentrism, discontent, arrogance – drop away over the years, this becomes one's truth, and only God is left to experience it.

The Five Pillars and jihad

While Sufism carries the inner practice of Islam, the outer practice is set forth in the *Shari'ah*, the straight path of the Divine Law. It specifies patterns for worship (known as *The Five Pillars of Islam*) as well as detailed prescriptions for social conduct, to bring remembrance of God into every aspect of daily life and practical ethics into the fabric of society. These prescriptions include injunctions against drinking intoxicating beverages, eating certain meats (including pork, rodents, predatory animals and birds, and improperly slaughtered animals), gambling and vain sports, sexual relations outside of marriage, and sexually provocative dress, talk, or actions. They also include positive measures, commanding justice, kindness, and charity. Women are given many legal rights, including the right to own property, to divorce, to inherit, and to make a will. These rights divinely decreed during the time of the Prophet, fourteen hundred years ago, were not available to western women until the nineteenth century. Polygamy is allowed for men who have the means to support several wives, to bring all women under the protection of a husband.

The Shari'ah is said to have had a transformative effect on Muhammad's community. Before Muhammad, the people's highest loyalty was to their tribe. Tribes made war on each other with no restraints. Women were possessions like animals. Children were often killed at birth either because of poverty or because they were females in a male-dominated culture. People differed widely in wealth. Drunkenness and gambling were commonplace. Within a short time, Islam made great inroads into these traditions, shaping tribes into a spiritual and political unity with a high sense of ethics.

A Muslim must obey the Five Pillars because they are considered God's commandments.

Belief and witness

The first pillar of Islam (the *Shahada*) is believing and professing the unity of God and the messengership of Muhammad: "There is no god but God, and Muhammad is his Messenger." The Qur'an requires the faithful to tell others of Islam, so that they will have the information they need to make an intelligent choice. It rules out the use of coercion in spreading the message:

> *Let there be [or: There is] no compulsion*
> *In religion: Truth stands out*
> *Clear from Error: whoever*
> *Rejects Evil and believes*
> *In God hath grasped*
> *The most trustworthy*
> *Hand-hold, that never breaks.* [28]

Muslims do feel they have an obligation to preach goodness to others and forbid them from evil actions.

Daily prayers

The second pillar is the performance of a continual round of prayers. Five times a day, the faithful are to perform ritual ablutions with water (or sand or dirt if necessary), face Mecca, and recite a series of prayers and passages from the Qur'an, bowing and kneeling. Around the world, this joint facing of Mecca for prayer unites all Muslims into a single world family. When the prayers are recited by a congregation, all stand and bow shoulder to shoulder, with no distinctions of social standing. In a mosque, women and men pray in separate groups, with the women behind a screen, to avoid sexual distractions. There may be an *imam*, or prayer-leader, but no priest stands between the worshipper and Allah. On Friday afternoon, there is usually a special prayer service in the mosque, but Muslims observe no sabbath day. Remembrance of God is an everyday obligation; invoking the Name of Allah continually polishes the rust from the heart.

Repeating the prayers is thought to strengthen one's belief in God's existence and goodness and to carry this belief into the depths of the heart and every aspect of external life. Praying thus is also expected to purify the heart, develop the mind and the conscience, comfort the soul, encourage the good and suppress the evil in the person, and awaken in the believer the innate sense of higher morality and higher aspirations. The words of praise and the bowing express continual gratefulness and submission to the One. At the end, one turns to one's neighbors to say the traditional Muslim greeting – "*Assalamu Alaykum*" ("Peace be on you") – and another phrase adding the blessing, "and mercy of God."

While mouthing the words and performing the outer actions, one should be concentrating on the inner prayer of the heart. The Prophet reportedly said, "Prayer without the Presence of the Lord in the heart is not prayer at all."[29] Internal prayer of the heart should actually continue at all times, keeping it pure of negativity, humbled to God, and growing in realization of the One.

Fasting

The third pillar is fasting. Frequent fasts are recommended to Muslims, but the only one that is generally obligatory is the fast during Ramadan, commemorating the first revelations of the Qur'an to Muhammad. For all who are beyond puberty, but not infirm or menstruating or nursing children, a dawn-to-sunset abstention from food, drink, sexual intercourse, and smoking is required for the whole month of Ramadan.

Because Muslims use a lunar calendar of 354 days, the month of Ramadan gradually moves through all the seasons. When it falls in the summer, the period of fasting is much longer than in the shortest days of winter. The hardship of abstaining even from drinking water during these long and hot days is an unselfish surrender to God's commandment and an assertion of control over the lower desires. The knowledge that Muslims all over the world are making these sacrifices at the same time builds a special bond among the faithful and helps bolster their self-discipline. Fasting also bridges the gap between haves and have-nots, helping the haves to experience what it is to be hungry, to share in the condition of the poor. Those who have are encouraged to be especially generous in their almsgiving during Ramadan.

Fasting is expected to allow the body to burn up impurities and provide one with "a Transparent Soul to transcend, a Clear Mind to think and a Light Body to move and act."[30] People do become more sensitive than usual. At the same time that this sensitivity makes one more spiritually awake, it also tends to increase irritability. Esoterically, it is believed that the external fast is prescribed to help people grow in internal fasting. That is, control of the body's desires also builds the mastery needed to control the lower emotions, such as anger and jealousy. The irritability bred by Ramadan fasting is a particular challenge to this emotional mastery.

An ultimate form of year-round fasting is the abstention from any thought or action that draws a veil between the lover and the Beloved. For the very devout, closeness to God is the only aim in life.

Zakat

The fourth pillar is *zakat*, or spiritual tithing and alms-giving. At the end of the year, all Muslims must donate at least two and a half per cent of their income (after basic expenses) to needy Muslims. This provision is designed to help even out inequalities in wealth and to prevent personal greed. Its literal meaning is "purity," for it purifies the distribution of money, helping to keep it in healthy circulation.

Pilgrims to Mecca circumambulate the Ka'bah, like angels rotating around the One.

In addition to zakat, Shi'ites are obligated to give one-fifth of their income to the Imam. Because the Imam is now hidden, half of this now goes to the deputy of the Imam to be used however he thinks appropriate; the other half goes to descendants of the Prophet as a gift of love and honor, to spare them the humiliation of poverty.

Hajj

The fifth pillar is *hajj*, the pilgrimage to Mecca. All Muslims who can possibly do so are expected to make the pilgrimage at least once in their lifetime. It involves a series of symbolic rituals designed to bring the faithful as close as possible to God. Pilgrims wrap themselves in a special garment of unsewn cloths, rendering them all alike, with no class distinctions. The garment is like a burial shroud, for by dying to their earthly life they can devote all their attention to God. It is a time for *dhikr*, the constant repetition of the Shahada, the remembrance that there is no god but God.

The Ka'bah is considered the site of the first house of God built on the earth, originally established by Abraham and Ishmael. Pilgrims walk around it seven times, like the continual rotation around the One by the angels and all of creation, to the seventh heaven. Their hearts should be filled only with remembrance of Allah.

Another sacred site on the pilgrimage is the field of 'Arafat. It is said to be the place where Adam and Eve were taught that humans are created solely for the worship of God. Here pilgrims pray to be forgiven of anything that has separated them from the Beloved. After symbolic gestures of sacrifice and defiance of Satan, they then circumambulate the Ka'bah again. If they have been truly purified and centered in the devotion of the heart, they now draw even nearer to the Throne of God. This closeness is symbolized by drinking water from the holy well of Zamzam, the spring which God is said to have provided for Hagar when she and Ishmael were left alone in the desert.

Hajj draws Muslims from all corners of the earth together for this intense spiritual experience. Because Islam is practiced on every continent, it is truly an international gathering. The crowds are enormous. During the month of Dhu'l-hijjah, the time for the pilgrimage, an estimated two million pilgrims converge upon Mecca. To help handle the crowds, the Saudi government has built the immense King Abdul Aziz International Airport near Jedda, with a special terminal just for hajj pilgrims. The journey was once so hazardous that many people and camels died trying to cross the desert in fulfillment of their sacred obligation.

Throughout Muslim history, hajj has brought widely diverse people together, consolidating the center of Islam, spreading information and ideas across cultures, and sending pilgrims back into their communities with fresh inspiration.

Jihad

In addition to these Five Pillars of Islam, there is another important injunction: *jihad*. Commonly mistranslated as "holy war," it means "striving," resisting evil both individually and as a community. The Greater Jihad, Muhammad said, is the struggle against the lower self. It is the internal fight between wrong and right, error and truth, selfishness and selflessness, hardness of heart and an all-embracing love. As Seyyed Hossein Nasr explains, the inner jihad is:

an inner battle against that which the soul has become, in order to transform it into that which it "is" and has never ceased to be if only it were to become aware of its own nature . . . . Through inner jihad, the spiritual man dies in this life in order to cease all dreaming, in order to awaken to that Reality which is the original of all realities, in order to behold that Beauty of which all earthly beauty is but a pale reflection, in order to attain that Peace which all men seek but which can in fact be found only through this practice. [31]

The Greater Jihad is often personified as a battle against Shaitan (Satan), understood as the lowly impulses in oneself.

Whatever good, (O man!)
Happens to thee, is from God
But whatever evil happens
To thee, is from thy (own) soul

The Holy Qur'an, Sura 4:79

On the external level, the Lesser Jihad is exerting effort to protect the Way of God against the forces of evil. The Qur'an supports fighting to defend the faith, but only when it is attacked:

To those against whom
War is made, permission
Is given (to fight), because
They are wronged; – and verily,
God is Most Powerful
For their aid;

(They are) those who have
Been expelled from their homes
In defiance of right,
(For no cause) except
That they say, "Our Lord
Is God" [32]

This revelation seems to date from the Medina period when the faithful were being attacked by Meccans. The Qur'an gives permission to fight back under such circumstances, but also gives detailed limitations on the conduct of war, to prevent atrocities.

Muhammad is the prototype of the true *mujahid*, or fighter in the Way of God, one who values the Way more than life, wealth, or family. He is thought to have had no desire for worldly power, wealth, or prestige. By fasting and prayer, he continually exerted himself toward the One, in the Greater Jihad. In defending the Medina community of the faithful against the attacking Meccans, he was acting from the purest of motives. It is believed that a true mujahid who dies in defense of the faith goes straight to paradise, for he has already fought the Greater Jihad, killing his ego.

The absolute conviction which characterizes jihad derives from recognition of the vast disparity between evil and the spiritual ideal, both in oneself and in society. Continual exertion is thought necessary in order to maintain a peaceful equilibrium in the midst of changing circumstances. Traditionalists and radicals have differed in how this exertion should be exercised in society. Revolutionary social justice movements have at times interpreted the Lesser Jihad as "holy war," and it is this interpretation which is most associated with Islam by non-Muslims. The Lesser Jihad is not emphasized in the Qur'an, and many Muslims are not in sympathy with its interpretation as divinely sanctioned war. The goal and meaning of Islam, and of Jihad, is peace through devoted surrender to God. The peaceful society is like paradise. Sri Lankan Sufi Shaikh M. R. Bawa Muhaiyaddeen observes:

> *If one knows the true meaning of Islam, there will be no wars. All that will be heard are the sounds of prayer and the greetings of peace. Only the resonance of God will be heard. That is the ocean of Islam. That is unity. That is our wealth and our true weapon. Not the sword in your hand.* [33]

The spread of Islam

In the time of Muhammad, Islam combined spiritual and secular power under one ruler. This tradition, which helped to unify the warring tribes of the area, was continued under his successors. Islam expanded phenomenally during the centuries after the Prophet's death, contributing to the rise of many great civilizations. The *Ummah* became a family that spread from Africa to Indonesia. Non-Muslims have the impression that it was spread by the sword, but this does not seem to be the general case. The Qur'an forbids coercion in religion, recommending instead that Muslims invite others to the Way by their wisdom, beautiful teaching, and personal example. Islam spread mostly by personal contacts: trade, attraction to charismatic Sufi saints, appeals to Muslims from those feeling oppressed by Roman and Persian rule, unforced conversions. There were some military battles conducted by Muslims over the centuries, but they were not necessarily for the purpose of spreading Islam, and many Muslims feel that wars of aggression violate Muslim principles. Citizens of newly-entered territories were asked to pay a poll tax entitling them to Muslim defense against enemies and exempting them from military service.

Muhammad's non-violent takeover of Mecca occurred only two years before he died. It was under his successors that Islam spread through the Arab world and far beyond. Only a year after he died, a newly-converted Qurayshite, Khalid ibn al-Walid, began a series of campaigns that within seven years had claimed the entire Arabian peninsula and Syria as well for Islam. Another group of converts quickly swept through the elegant Persian Empire, which had stood for twelve centuries. Within ten years of the Prophet's death, a mere four thousand horsemen commanded by Amr ibn al-As took the major cities of Egypt, centers of the brilliant Byzantine Empire. Another wave of Islamicization soon penetrated into Turkey and Central Asia, North Africa, and north through Spain, to be stopped in 732 CE in France at the battle of Tours. At this point, only a hundred years after Muhammad died, the Muslim Ummah under the Umayyad caliphs was larger than the Roman Empire had ever been.

Muslims cite the power of the divine will to establish a peaceful, God-conscious society as the reason why this happened. By contrast with their strong convictions, the populations they approached were often demoralized by border fighting among themselves and by grievances against their rulers. Many welcomed them without a fight. For example, Syrian Christians at Shayzar under Byzantine rule reportedly went out to meet the Muslim commander and accompanied him to their city, singing and playing tambourines. In Spain, Visigoth rule and taxation had been oppressive; the persecuted Jews were especially glad to help Islam take over. Both Christians and Jews often converted to Islam.

The Alhambra, built in Granada, Spain, from 1354 to 1391, is one of the masterpieces of Islamic architecture. The "stalactite" traceries bordering the archways symbolize the light that descends to the earth from higher realms.

Some historians cite economics as an underlying motive for Arabs' expansion beyond their original territory. Although Arabic civilization did become quite opulent, the central leadership did not always support the far-reaching adventures. The conquered peoples were generally dealt with in the humane ways specified in the Qur'an and modeled by Muhammad in his negotiations with tribes newly subjected to Muslim authority. The terms offered by Khalid to the besieged Damascus were these:

> *In the name of God, the merciful, the compassionate. This is what Khalid would grant the inhabitants of Damascus when he enters it. He shall grant them security for their lives, properties and churches. Their city wall shall not be demolished, neither shall any Moslem be quartered in their homes. Thereunto we give them the pact of God and the protection (dhimmah) of His Messenger, upon whom be God's blessing and peace, the caliphs and the Believers. So long as they pay poll-tax nothing but good shall befall them.* [34]

Monotheistic followers of revealed traditions, Christians and Jews, who like Muslims were "people of the book," were treated as *dhimmis*, or protected people. They were allowed to maintain their own faith, but not to try to convert others to it. The Dome of the Rock was built on the site of the old Temple of the Jews in Jerusalem, honoring Abraham as well as Muhammad in the city that is still sacred to three faiths: Judaism, Christianity, and Islam.

The Umayyad caliphs had their hands full administering this huge Ummah from Damascus, which they had made its capital. They tended to focus more on organizational matters than on the spiritual life. Some were also quite worldly, such as Walid II, who is said to have enjoyed a pool filled with wine so that he could swim and drink at the same time. In 750 CE a rival to the caliphate is said to have invited eighty of the princes of the line to a banquet, where he had them all killed. Four years after "the bloodshedder," a new series of caliphs took over: the Abbasids. They held power until 1258 CE.

Under the Abbasids, Muslim rule became more Persian and cosmopolitan and Islamic civilization reached its peak. The capital was moved to the new city of Baghdad. No more territories were brought under centralized rule, and merchants, scholars, and artists became the cultural heros. A great House of Wisdom was built, with an observatory, a famous library, and an educational institution where Greek and Syriac manuscripts on subjects such as medicine, astronomy, logic, mathematics, and philosophy were translated into Arabic. In Cairo, Muslims built in 972 CE a great university and mosque, Al-Azhar, which is still the center of Muslim scholarship.

In its great cities, Islam went through a period of intense intellectual and artistic activity, absorbing and transmitting the highest from other cultures. For instance, from Persia, which became a Shi'ite stronghold, it adopted a thousand-year-old tradition of exquisite art and poetry. To these avid cultural borrowings Islam added its own innovations. The new system of nine Arabic numerals and the zero revolutionized mathematics by liberating it from the clumsiness of Roman numerals. Muslim philosophers were highly interested in Aristotelian and Neo-Platonic thought, but in their unique synthesis these intellectual ways were harmonized with revealed religion. Muslim scholars' research into geography, history, astronomy, literature, and medicine lifted these disciplines to unprecedented heights.

Although Baghdad was the capital of the Abbasids, independent caliphates were declared in Spain and Egypt. Muslim Spain was led by successors to the Umayyads and

became a great cultural center. Cordova, the capital, had seven hundred mosques, seventy libraries, three hundred public baths, and paved streets. Europe, by contrast, was in its Dark Ages; Paris and London were only mazes of muddy alleys.

Tunisia and Egypt comprised a third center of Islamic power: the Shi'ite Fatimid imamate (so-named because they claimed to be descendants of Muhammad's daughter Fatima). Under the deranged Fatimid caliph Al-Hakim, the Fatimids broke with Islamic tradition and persecuted dhimmis; they also destroyed the Church of the Holy Sepulchre in Jerusalem, provoking European Christian crusades to try to recapture the Holy Lands. In Spain, zealous Spanish converts to Islam also failed to protect the dhimmis, and both Christians and Jews became martyrs to their faith. During the thirteenth century, Christians took Spain and instituted the dread Inquisition against those not practicing Christianity. By the beginning of the sixteenth century, an estimated three million Spanish Muslims had either been killed or had left the country.

Crusading Christians also fought their way down to Jerusalem, which they placed under a month-long seige in 1099. When the small Fatimid garrison surrendered, the Crusaders slaughtered the inhabitants of the holy city. Severed hands and feet were piled

Left   *At a Muslim mosque, there are no social distinctions, as all worshippers line up shoulder to shoulder to pray together.*
Right   *Whereas non-Muslims tend to think of Islam as a religion carried by the sword, Muslims believe their faith spread by its innate appeal and its reputation for humane, just government. The inhabitants of a besieged city are depicted welcoming the Muslim conquerors.*

A Muslim mosque hugs the earth, for Islam attempts to establish just, godly societies in this world and conceives of God as being everywhere. Al-Azhar, a venerable institution in Cairo, combines a mosque with a major university.

everywhere. Anti-Crusading Muslims led by the famous Salah-al-Din' (known in the West as Saladin) retook Jerusalem in 1171 and treated its Christian population with the generous leniency of Islam's highest ideals for the conduct of war. But widespread destruction remained in the wake of the crusaders, and a reservoir of ill-will against Christians lingered, to be exacerbated centuries later by European colonialism in Muslim lands.

Its advance stopped in Europe, Islam carried its vitality to the north, east, and south. Although Mongolian invasions threatened from Central Asia, the Mongols were converted to Islam; so were the Turks. The Mongolian invasions were so destructive, however, that agricultural recovery is even now incomplete.

In 1453, the Turks conquered Constantinople, the heart of the old Byzantine Empire, and renamed it Istanbul; Hagia Sophia was turned into a mosque even though it did not face Mecca. At its height, the Turkish Ottoman Empire dominated the eastern Mediterranean as well as the area around the Black Sea.

Farther east, Islam was carried into northern India, where Muslims destroyed Hindu Idols but allowed the Hindu majority a protected dhimmi status. Under the Muslim Mughals, the arts and learning flourished in India. The Emperor Akbar, who rose to the Mughal throne in 1556, made yearly pilgrimages to the shrine of the Sufi saint, Moinuddin Chishti. In his ecumenical spiritual curiosity, he created a house of worship where representatives from many traditions – Hindu, Zoroastrian, Jain, Christian – were invited to the world's first interfaith dialogues. Eventually he devised a new religion that was a synthesis of Islam and all these other religions, with himself as its supposedly enlightened head, but it died with him and Muslim orthodoxy returned.

Under British colonization of India, tensions between Hindus and Muslims were inflamed, reportedly so that England could divide and rule. India gained its independence under Gandhi, who was unable to end the enmity between the two faiths. In 1947, West and East Pakistan (now the independent nation of Bangladesh) were partitioned off to be Muslim-ruled and predominantly populated by Muslims, while India was to be run by Hindus. Millions are said to have lost their lives trying to cross the borders, and the strife between the two faiths continues.

The greatest concentration of Muslims developed even farther east, in Indonesia, where Muslim traders and missionaries may have first landed as early as the tenth century CE. Many centuries later, large segments of the population embraced Islam, at least partly to shore up their defense against European colonialism. As practiced in Indonesia, Islam has clear Indian and animistic influences. Although eighty per cent of the people are now Muslim, the government refuses to establish Islam as a state religion; President Suharto stated in 1989, "We want each and all religions existing and developing in our country to achieve progress in an atmosphere of unity and mutual respect."[35]

To the south, Islam spread into Africa along lines of trade — salt from the north for gold and slaves from the south. In competition with Christianity, Islam sought the hearts of Africans and eventually won in many areas. Many converted to Islam; many others maintained some of their indigenous ways in combination with Islam. The prosperous Mali empire was headed by a Muslim, who made an awesome pilgrimage to Mecca with a gold-laden retinue of eight thousand in 1324. As the spread of Islam encompassed an increasing diversity of cultures, hajj became important not only for individuals but also for the religion as a whole, holding its center in Mecca in the midst of worldwide variations.

Relationships with the West

Although Islam honors the prophets of all traditions, its own religion and prophet were denounced by medieval Christian Europe. Christianity had considered itself the ultimate religion and had launched its efforts to bring the whole world under its wings. Islam felt the same way about its own mission. Northern Christians were aghast as the Mediterranean area where Christianity began converted to Islam instead. In the struggle for souls, the Church depicted Muhammad as an idol-worshipper, an anti-Christ, the Prince of Darkness. Islam was falsely portrayed as a religion of many deities, in which Muhammad himself was worshipped as a god (thus the inaccurate label "Muhammadanism"). Europeans watched in horror as the Holy Lands became Muslim and the "infidel" advanced into Spain. Even though it was Muslim scholars and artists who preserved, shared, and advanced the classic civilizations while Europe was benighted, the voluptuous wealth of Arabic culture was interpreted in a negative light.

By the nineteenth century, Western scholars began to study the Arabic classics, but the ingrained fear and loathing of Muhammad and Muslims remained. The ignorance about, and negative stereotyping of, Muslims continues today. Western cartoonists, for instance, inevitably draw Muslims as wild-eyed radicals dressed in desert robes and brandishing scimitars. Annemarie Schimmel, Professor of Indo-Muslim Culture, Harvard University, explains:

The idea that the Muslims conquered everything with fire and sword was unfortunately deeply ingrained in the medieval mind. All these misconceptions about Islam as a religion and the legends and lies that were told about it are really unbelievable. I have often the feeling that this medieval image of Islam as it was perpetuated in ever so many books and even scholarly works is part of our subconscious. When someone comes and says, ''But real Islam is something completely different,'' people just will not believe it because they have been indoctrinated for almost fourteen hundred years with the image of Islam as something fierce and something immoral. Unfortunately, some of the events of our century, and in the last decade particularly where much bloodshed was indeed to be witnessed, have revived this medieval concept of Islam. [36]

Borrow the Beloved's eyes. Look through them and you'll see the Beloved's face everywhere. . . .
Let that happen, and things you have hated will become helpers.

Jalal al-Din Rumi [37]

Although it had enjoyed great heights of culture and political power, the Muslim world fell into decline. Muslim scholars have different interpretations as to how this happened. It seems that the Mongol invasions were at least partly responsible, for they eradicated irrigation systems and libraries and killed scholars and scientists, erasing much of the civilization that had been built up over five hundred years. Some today feel that spiritual laxness was the primary reason that some of the previously glorious civilizations became impoverished third world countries. Another theory is that Muslim culture was no longer dynamic. As it rigidified and stagnated, it was overwhelmed by cultures both less civilized than itself (the Mongols in the thirteenth century) and more civilized (the Europeans, who were becoming major world powers on the strength of their industrialization and colonizing navies).

During the late eighteenth and early nineteenth centuries, many Muslim populations fell under European domination. They did not emerge from foreign rule until the mid-twentieth century (with the exception of 31,000,000 Muslims living in the Soviet Union and millions more under secular rule in China). They gained their independence as states that had adopted certain Western ideals and practices. In many cases, they had let go of their Muslim heritage, considering it a relic that prevented them from success in the modern world. Arabic was treated as an unimportant language; Western codes of law had replaced the Shari'ah in social organization. But yet they were not totally Westernized, and they resumed local rule with little training for twentieth-century self-government and participation in a world economy dominated by industrial nations.

Before the colonial forces moved out, foreign powers led by England helped to introduce a Jewish state in the midst of the Middle East. Some allege that their chief motivation was to protect European interests. Lord Palmerston of England suggested that a wealthy Jewish population transplanted to Palestine, and highly motivated to protect itself, would prop up the decaying Ottoman Empire so that it could serve as a bulwark against Russian imperialism; the new Jewish presence in Palestine would also serve as a check against the attempts of the Egyptian leader Mehemet Ali to create a pan-Islamic state encompassing Egypt, Syria, and the Arabian peninsula. The influential

Lord Shaftesbury had a further dream: returning the Jews to Palestine would help to implement the Christian ideal of the Second Coming of Christ by fulfilling part of the prophecy. For Arabic Muslims, military defeat at the hands of the small new state of Israel was the final humiliation.

Muslim resurgence

The Muslim world was generally helpless against manipulations by foreign nations until it found its power in oil. In the 1970s, oil-rich nations found that by banding together they could control the price and availability of oil. OPEC (The Organization of Petroleum Exporting Countries) brought greatly increased revenues into previously impoverished countries and strengthened their self-image as well as their importance in the global balance of power. Of the thirteen OPEC nations, most are predominantly Muslim (Algeria, Libya, Saudi Arabia, Kuwait, Qatar, the United Arab Emirates, Iraq, Iran, Indonesia, and half-Muslim Nigeria). Other predominantly Muslim oil-exporting countries who are not members of OPEC (Egypt, Tunisia, Syria, Malaya, Oman, Bahrain, and Brunei) have also benefited from oil price controls.

As the wealth suddenly poured in, it disrupted established living patterns. Analysts feel that people may have turned back to Islam in an effort to restore a personal sense of familiarity and stability amid the chaos of changing modern life; the increase in literacy, urbanization, and communications helped to spread revived interest in Islam. There was also the hope that Islam would provide the blueprint for enlightened rule, bringing the spiritual values into community and politics just as Muhammad had done in Medina.

Veiling of Muslim women is a complex phenomenon, only partly associated with religious disapproval of revealing clothing. Some modern women choose to cover their hair in a return to traditional values; for others veiling is a sign of high social status.

The resurgence of Islam takes several forms. One is a call for return to Shari'ah rather than secular law derived from European codes. The feeling of the orthodox is that the world must conform to the divine law, rather than diluting the law to accommodate it to the material world. For example, Egypt has made it illegal for its Muslim citizens to drink alcoholic beverages in public. In Saudi Arabia, morality squads actively enforce the obligatory prayers. In post-Revolutionary Iran, an attempt has been made to shape every aspect of life according to Shari'ah. Malaysia, which is only fifty-three per cent Muslim, is considering establishing Shari'ah as civil law, including extreme punishments such as stoning of adulterers and amputation of the hands of thieves. Private behaviors are also becoming more traditional. In particular, to honor the nonspecific Quranic encouragement of physical modesty, many Muslim women have begun covering their bodies except for hands, face, and feet, as they have not done for decades.

The problem with trying to re-establish Shari'ah is that it has been locally adapted to various societies over the centuries; to attempt to restore its original form designed for Muhammad's time or any other form from another period is to deny the usefulness of its flexibility. Some customs thought to be Muslim are actually cultural practices not specified in the basic sources; they are the result of Islamic civilization's assimilation of many cultures in many places. The veiling and seclusion of women were not practiced in the time of Muhammad, who worked side-by-side with women; the Qur'an encourages equal participation of women in religion and in society. Veiling and seclusion were practices absorbed from conquered Persian and Byzantine cultures, particularly the upper classes; peasant women could not carry out their physical work under encumbering veils or in seclusion from public view. Pakistani journalist Ahmed Abdulla asserts:

> *The greatest bane of Muslim society today and also one of the causes of its problems and ailments is rigidity, refusal to open up, undue veneration of and misplaced attachment to customs and traditions which have nothing to do with Islam.*[38]

The global family of Islam is not a political unit; its unity under Arab rule broke up long ago. There is as yet no consensus among Muslim states about how to establish a peaceful, just modern society based on basic Muslim principles. But there is widespread recognition that there are problems associated with modern Western civilization that should be avoided, such as crime, drug abuse, and unstable family life.

> *Today everyone cries for peace but peace is never achieved, precisely because it is metaphysically absurd to expect a civilization that has forgotten God to possess peace.*
> *Seyyed Hossein Nasr*[39]

Another sign of Muslim resurgence is the increase in outreach, as Muslims become more confident of the value of their faith. Islam is the fastest-growing of all world religions, with one billion two hundred million followers. New mosques are going up everywhere, including a $25 million Islamic Cultural Center in the heart of Manhattan, with Kuwait, Saudi Arabia, and Libya as major contributors to the project. Muslims who constitute a minority in their countries are beginning to stand up for their rights to practice their religion. They no longer feel they have to be secretive about praying five times a day or apologetic about leaving work to attend Friday afternoon congregational worship.

A third sign of Muslim resurgence is the increasing attention being given to developing educational systems modeled on Islamic thought. Islam is not anti-scientific or anti-intellectual; on the contrary, it has historically bridged reason and faith and placed a high value on developing both in order to tap into the fullness of human potential. Western education has omitted the spiritual aspects of life, so Muslims consider it incomplete and imbalanced. The 1977 First World Conference on Muslim Education defined the goals of education thus:

Education should aim at the balanced growth of the total personality of Man through the training of Man's spirit, intellect, his rational self, feelings and bodily senses. Education should cater therefore for the growth of Man in all its aspects: spiritual, intellectual, imaginative, physical, scientific, linguistic, both individually and collectively and motivate all aspects toward goodness and the attainment of perfection. The ultimate aim of Muslim education lies in the realisation of complete submission to Allah on the level of the individual, the community and humanity at large. [40]

In secular societies where they are in the minority, some Muslims have set up their own schools for Qur'an-centered education to counter the mass culture's influence. This group is studying the Qur'an in Birmingham, England.

In addition to return to Shari'ah, numerical growth, and attention to Muslim-based education, governments are becoming Islamicized. There are more frequent references to Islam and Quranic statements by political leaders. Some use it to support the status quo and glorify Islam's past heights. Others use Muslim idealism to rally opposition to ruling elites who have ties to the West or who are perceived as corrupt. The situation in Iran has been most dramatic. Pahlavi Shahs of predominantly Shi'ite Iran had tried rapidly to modernize their country, turning it into a major military and industrial power. In the process, they eroded the authority of the *ulama*, who are clerics and expounders of the Shari'ah. A revolutionary leader emerged from this disempowered group, the Ayatollah Khomeini, and swept the Shah from power in 1979.

The Ayatollah insisted that the ulama were the legitimate heirs to the Twelfth Imam and must control the society until he returns. Once in power, however, the ulama had no clear program for reorganizing society according to Muslim principles. Shari'ah has never specified a single political or economic system as best. Attempts to redistribute wealth in revolutionary Iran have been muddled, and Khomeini made some drastic changes in Islam in order to justify violent revolutionary behavior.

The basic change was a shift away from Shi'ites' traditionally passive resignation to less-than-perfect rule until the Twelfth Imam reappears. The new conviction was that Shi'ites must actively and radically pursue social justice in order to pave the way for the Twelfth Imam's return. Sunni-led governments are automatically illegitimate from the Shi'ite point of view, and Khomeini considered Iran the only nation to follow the true Muslim way. In Khomeini's thinking, it was essential for all Muslim countries to cut ties with non-Muslim world powers:

> *I would like to warn the governments of the Islamic countries not to repeat their past mistakes, but extend the hand of brotherhood to each other. With humility toward God and relying on the power of Islam, they should cut the cruel hands of the oppressors and world-devouring plunderers, expecially the United States, from the region.* [41]

With this thinking, the Ayatollah attempted to export his revolution to other Muslim countries with Shi'ite populations that could carry on the work. He conducted a devastating war against "atheist" Iraq (where the fifty per cent of citizens who are Shi'ites are ruled by the forty-five per cent who are Sunni), continually denounced predominantly Sunni Saudi Arabia for its ties to the West, and inspired some Lebanese Shi'ites to see their political struggle against Christians and Jews as part of a great world battle between Islam and the satanic forces of Western imperialism and Zionism. Since Khomeini's call for governmental change was not heeded, radicals resorted to sabotage and terrorism as their most powerful weapons. Their surprise attacks on civilians have tended to turn world opinion against Islam, rather than promoting its ideals. Little is known of the clandestine radical groups; the Muslim governments they oppose control the media and have portrayed them as mindless fanatics, supporting Western fears and stereotyping of Islam.

In Khomeini's rhetoric, the major powers were responsible for the corruption and selfish materialism prevalent in the world; they were satanic forces. He saw Muslims as the righteous underdogs and urged them to "mobilize the oppressed and chained nations so the superpowers can be pushed out of the scene and the governments can be handed over to the oppressed." [42] In this great cause, he glorified martyrdom, inspiring soldiers to give their lives. Furthermore, Khomeini elevated himself to the position of

being the Supreme Guide for all Muslims, the temporal spokesman for the divine will.

The harshness of many of Khomeini's actions has confirmed non-Muslims' stereotypes of Islam as a religion of the sword, practiced by terrorists and fanatics. An unusual side-effect of this extremely negative publicity has been a widespread attempt by moderate Muslims to share positive information about their faith. Interest has grown rapidly: Muslim speakers are now in great demand by non-Muslim communities who want to understand and appreciate Islam, rather than remain ignorant about it. Jews are surprised to discover how closely it parallels their own faith; Christians are gradually undoing centuries of sensationalist misinformation about Islam bred by fear. In Iran less radical, more pragmatic forces have sought to take over since Khomeini's death; they are attempting a more conciliatory position in an attempt to salvage the economy.

Until recently, Muslims tended to point to their glorious past as proof of the value of their tradition. But the newest thought is forward-looking, exploring how Islam can help to shape a better world. Dr. A. K. Aboulmagd, a constitutional lawyer from Egypt's Al-Azhar, speaks for this growing sentiment:

> *I'm glad and proud I'm a Muslim. I carry on my shoulders a scale of values, a code of ethics that I genuinely believe is good for everybody. . . . I even venture sometimes to say that Islam was not meant to serve the early days of Islam when life was primitive and when social institutions were still stable and working. It was meant to be put in a freezer and to be taken out when it will be really needed. And I believe that time has come. But the challenge is great because not all Muslims are aware of this fact: That the mission of Islam lies not in the past but in the future.*[43]

Suggested reading

Abdalati, Hammudah, *Islam in Focus*, Indianapolis, Indiana: American Trust Publications, 1975. A thorough, non-sectarian explanation of Muslim ideals and practices.

Dessouki, Ali E. Hillal, ed., *Islamic Resurgence in the Arab World*, New York: Praeger Publishers, 1982. A scholarly study of the contemporary Islamic resurgence in specific Arab nations.

Esposito, John L., *Islam: The Straight Path*, New York, Oxford: Oxford University Press, 1988. A scholarly, clear introduction to historical and contemporary Islam.

The Holy Qur'an. Although the Qur'an is considered untranslatable, numerous translations from the Arabic have been attempted. Muslims' favorite English translation is by Abdullah Yusuf Ali, Durban, South Africa: Islamic Propagation Center International, 1946. It gives the Arabic, an English translation, introductions to each Sura, and helpful commentaries on the verses that reveal their deeper meanings.

Kramer, Martin, ed., *Shi'ism, Resistance, and Revolution*, Boulder, Colorado: Westview Press, 1987. Perceptive analyses of recent revolutionary developments in Shi'ism, in the context of Muslim tradition.

Lings, Martin, *What is Sufism?* Berkeley and Los Angeles: University of California Press, 1975 and London: Unwin Paperbacks, 1981. An excellent introduction to the inner experience of Islam.

Nasr, Seyyed Hossein, *Ideals and Realities of Islam*, second edition, London: Unwin Hyman Ltd., 1985. Thoughtful presentation of both esoteric and exoteric features of Islam.

Nasr, Seyyed Hossein, ed., *Islamic Spirituality I: Foundations*, New York: Crossroad Publishing Company, 1987 and London: SCM Press, 1989. Excellent chapters on key features of Muslim spirituality, from fasting to angels, with sections on Sunnism, Shi'ism, and Sufism.

Nasr, Seyyed Hossein, Dabashi, Hamid, and Nasr, Seyyed Vali Reza, *Shi'ism: Doctrines, Thought, and Spirituality*, Albany, New York: State University of New York Press, 1988. To balance the predominant media attention to Shi'ite politics, a set of thoughtful essays on aspects of Shi'ite spirituality.

Rumi, Jelaluddin, *We Are Three*, translations of Rumi poems by Coleman Barks, Athens, Georgia: Maypop Books, 1987. Free contemporary renderings of Rumi's startling, passionate poetry of the love between humans and the divine.

Schimmel, Annemarie, *Mystical Dimensions of Islam*, Chapel Hill, North Carolina: University of North Carolina Press, 1975. A classic survey of Sufi history, teachings, and saints.

Schuon, Frithjof, *Understanding Islam*, London: George Allen and Unwin, 1963. Profound and lyrical observations about the way of Islam.

12 SIKHISM

"By the guru's grace shalt thou worship Him"

Although Muhammad was declared the Seal of the Prophets, another prophet appeared in northern India in the fifteenth century. This was Guru Nanak, whose followers were called *Sikhs*, meaning "disciples, students, seekers of truth." They understand their path not as another sectarian religion but as a statement of the universal truth within, and transcending, all religions. Many of their beliefs are a synthesis of the Hindu and Muslim traditions of northern India, but Sikhism also has its own unique quality.

This spiritual essence of Sikhism is little known to the outside world, which instead equates the word "Sikh" with the military and political aspects of the Punjabis' struggle for independence. As awareness of Sikh spirituality spreads, Sikhism is becoming a global religion, although it does not actively seek converts.

The sant tradition

Before Guru Nanak, Hinduism and Islam had already begun to draw closer to one another in northern India. The foremost philosopher in this trend was the Hindu guru, Ramananda, who held theological arguments with teachers from both religions. But a deeper marriage occurred in the hearts of *sants*, or "holy people," particularly Sufi mystics such as Mirabi and Hindu bhaktas such as Sri Caitanya. They shared a common cause in emphasizing devotion to the Beloved above all else.

The most famous of the bridges between Hindu and Muslim is the fifteenth-century weaver Kabir (1440–1518). He was the son of Muslim parents and the disciple of the Hindu guru, Ramananda. Rather than taking the ascetic path, he remained at work at his loom, composing songs about union with the Divine that are at once earthy and sublime. He could easily transcend theological differences between religions, for he was opposed to outward forms, preferring ecstatic personal intimacy with God. Speaking for the One, he wrote:

Are you looking for me? I am in the next seat.
My shoulder is against yours.
You will not find me in stupas, not in Indian shrine rooms, nor
*   in synagogues, nor in cathedrals:*
not in masses, nor kirtans, not in legs winding around your
*   own neck, nor in eating nothing but vegetables.*
When you really look for me, you will see me instantly —
you will find me in the tiniest house of time.
Kabir says: Student, tell me, what is God?
He is the breath inside the breath. [1]

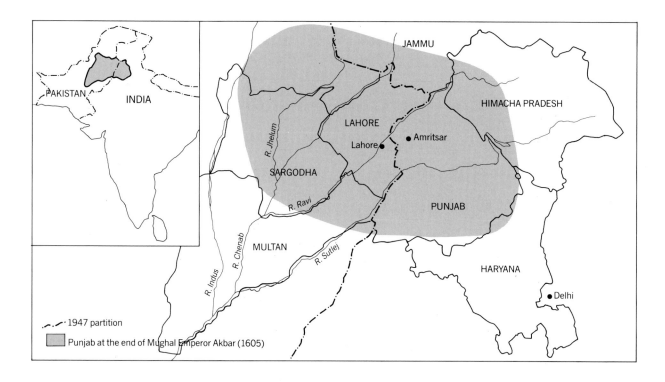

1947 partition

Punjab at the end of Mughal Emperor Akbar (1605)

The Punjab at the end of the reign of the Mughal Emperor Akbar. The 1947 partition of India left two-thirds of the Punjab, including many of its Sikh temples, inside Pakistan, a Muslim state.

Guru Nanak

When Guru Nanak was born in approximately 1469, the area of Northern India called the Punjab was half-Muslim, half-Hindu, and ruled by a weak Afghan dynasty. For centuries, the Punjab had been the lane through which outer powers had fought their way into India. In 1398, the Mongolian leader Tamerlane had slaughtered and sacked Punjabis on his way both to and from Delhi. Toward the end of Nanak's life, it was the Mughal Emperor Babur who invaded and claimed the Punjab. This casting of the Punjab as a perpetual battleground did not play an overt part in Nanak's spiritual mission, but it later became a crucial aspect of Sikhism.

Nanak was reportedly little concerned with things of the earth. As a child he was moody and mystical, resisting schooling and the appurtenances of his Hindu religion. Even after he was married, it is said that he roamed about in nature rather than working and gave away any money he had to the poor. At length he took a job as an accountant, but his heart was not in it.

When Nanak was thirty-six, his life was transformed by a late-night immersion in a river, from which it is said he did not emerge for three days. According to one account, he was taken into the presence of God, who gave him a bowl of milk to drink, saying that it was actually nectar (*amrit*) which would give him "power of prayer, love of worship, truth and contentment."[2] The Almighty charged him to go back into the tainted world to redeem it from *Kali yuga* (the darkest of ages) by teaching people to pray, give charitably, and live clean lives.

After his underwater experience, Nanak began traveling through India, the

Himalayas, Afghanistan, Sri Lanka, and Arabia, teaching in his own surprising way When people asked him whether he would follow the Hindu or Muslim path, he replied, "There is neither Hindu nor Mussulman [Muslim], so whose path shall I follow? I shall follow God's path. God is neither Hindu nor Mussulman …"³ Nanak mocked the Hindu tradition of throwing sacred river water east toward the rising sun in worship of their ancestors – he threw water to the west. If Hindus could throw water far enough to reach their ancestors thousands of miles away in heaven, he explained, he could certainly water his parched land several hundred miles distant in Lahore by throwing water in its direction. At another time he set his feet toward the Ka'bah when sleeping in a mosque; questioned about this rude conduct, he is said to have remarked, "Then turn my feet toward some direction where there is no God nor the Ka'bah."⁴ He espoused the inner rather than the outer path. In Muslim terms:

> *Make mercy your mosque and devotion your prayer mat,*
> *   righteousness of your Qur'an;*
> *Meekness your circumcising, goodness your fasting, for thus*
> *   the true Muslim expresses his faith.*
> *Make good works your Ka'bah, take truth as your pir, compassion*
> *   your creed and your prayer.*
> *Let service to God be the beads which you tell*
> *   and God will exalt you to glory.*⁵

Nanak's absolute faithfulness to truth, as opposed to external adherence to religious formalities, won him followers from both Hinduism and Islam. Before he died in 1539, they argued over who would bury him. He reportedly told Muslims to place flowers on one side of his body, Hindus on the other; the side whose flowers remained fresh the next day could bury him. The next day they raised the sheet that had covered his body and reportedly found nothing beneath it; all the flowers were still fresh, leaving only the fragrance of his being.

> *Listen, my heart: love God ceaselessly*
> *As the fish loveth water:*
> *The deeper the water*
> *The happier and more tranquil the fish.*
> *God alone knoweth the suffering*
> *Of fish separated from the waters.*
>
> *   Guru Nanak*⁶

The succession of gurus

Before Nanak's death, he appointed a spiritual successor, his devoted disciple Angad Dev. This second guru strengthened the new Sikh tradition and developed a script for setting down its memorized teachings, which had been given orally in the common language.

There were eventually a total of ten Sikh gurus. The fourth founded the holy city of Amritsar and built within it the religion's most sacred shrine, the Golden Temple. The fifth guru compiled the sacred scriptures of the Sikhs, the *Adi Granth* ("original holy book"), from devotional hymns composed by Guru Nanak, the other gurus, and Hindu

A painting of Guru Nanak adorns a wall at this Sikh gurdwara in Coventry, England.

and Muslim poets and saints, including Kabir. When a copy was sent to the Emperor Akbar, he was so pleased with its universalism that he offered a gift of gold to the Book. But apparently because of suspicions that the fifth guru supported a rival successor to Akbar's throne, he was executed by Akbar's son and successor, Jehangir, in 1606.

From that point on, Sikhism took measures to protect itself. The sixth guru built a Sikh army, carried two swords, and taught the people to defend their religion. The ninth guru was beheaded in 1675 rather than accepting forced conversion to Islam. It is said that he was acting on behalf of the principle of religious freedom for Hindus as well as Sikhs – for religious tolerance in general.

The Tenth Guru, Guru Gobind Singh, is as esteemed as the first, but for entirely different reasons. Whereas Nanak was an ardent devotee, a destroyer of empty ritual, Guru Gobind Singh created institutions that made Sikhism strong in the midst of political chaos. In 1699 he reportedly told an assembly of Sikhs that the times were so dangerous that he had developed a new plan to give the community strength and unity. Utter loyalty would be necessary, he said, asking for volunteers who would offer their heads for the cause. One at a time, five stepped forward. Each was escorted into the Guru's tent, from which the Tenth Guru emerged alone with a bloody sword. After this scene was repeated five times, the Guru brought all the men out of the tent, alive. Some say the blood was that of a goat, in a test of the people's loyalty; others say that Guru Gobind Singh had actually killed the men and brought them back to life. At any rate, their willingness to serve and bravely sacrifice themselves was dramatically proven, and the Five Beloved Ones became models for Sikhs.

Guru Gobind Singh instituted a special baptismal initiation using a double-edged sword dipped in nectar (*amrit*). After baptizing the Five Beloved Ones, he asked that they and thousands from all castes, including untouchables, baptize him – thus underscoring the principle of equality among all Sikhs. The baptized men were given the surname *Singh* ("lion"); the women were all given the name *Kaur* ("princess") and treated as equals. Together, they formed the *Khalsa* ("Pure Ones"), a fraternity pledged to a special code of discipline. They were sworn to wear five distinctive symbols of their dedication (unshorn hair, a comb, a steel bracelet, a sword, and short breeches). These symbols clearly distinguished Sikhs from Muslims and Hindus, supporting the assertion that they constituted a third path with its own right to spiritual sovereignty. All of these innovations were designed to turn the meek into warriors capable of shaking off Muslim rule; the distinctive dress made it impossible for the Khalsa to hide from their duty by blending with the general populace.

In addition to transforming the Sikh faithful into a martially-oriented, unified community, Guru Gobind Singh ended the line of succession to supreme guruship. As he was dying, he transferred his authority to the Adi Granth rather than to a human successor. Thenceforth, the Granth Sahib (another name for the Adi Granth, with Sahib an expression of veneration) was to be the *Guru Granth Sahib* – the living presence of the Guru embodied in the sacred scriptures, to be consulted intuitively by the Khalsa for spiritual guidance and decision-making.

As the Mughal Empire began to disintegrate and Afghans invaded India, the Sikhs seized the opportunity to fight for their own sovereignty. Under the eighteenth-century Maharaja Ranjit Singh, they formed a Sikh Empire that lasted half a century until the British took over in 1849. In the resulting struggle for Indian independence, Sikhs were renowned as ardent fighters, comprising a large portion of the resistance forces.

The Guru Granth Sahib consists of 1430 pages of hymns composed by Sikh gurus and also by Muslim and Hindu saints. The scripture is royally housed and is daily put to bed and awakened, rather like a Hindu deity.

Central beliefs

Although Guru Gobind Singh restructured the form of the Sikh community, its spiritual ideals originate with Guru Nanak, for the most part. The Guru Granth Sahib includes almost a thousand of his hymns.

Sikhism's major focus is that there is only one God, worshipped under many names around the world. God is beyond time and space, the only truth, the only reality. This concept is very clearly stated in the *Mool Mantra* ("basic sacred chant") which prefaces every Sikh prayer:

There is One God
His Name is Truth.
He is the Creator,
He is without fear and without hate.
He is beyond time Immortal,
His Spirit pervades the universe.

He is not born,
Nor does He die to be born again,
He is self-existent.
By the guru's grace shalt thou worship Him. [7]

Following Guru Nanak's lead, Sikhs often refer to God as *Sat* ("truth") or as *Ek Onkar*, the One Supreme Being. God is pure being, without attributes. The light of God shines fully through the Guru, the perfect prophet. There have been ten human gurus acting as conveyers of the enlightenment of God. The light of God is also present in the Guru Garanth Sahib, the Holy Word (*sabd*) of God, and in all of creation, in which the Holy Name (*nam*) of God dwells. God is separate from creation, but yet can be found within it, as the ninth guru wrote:

> *Why do you go to the forest to find God? He lives in all and yet remains distinct. He dwells in you as well, as fragrance resides in a flower or the reflection in a mirror. God abides in everything. See him, therefore, in your heart.* [8]

Sikhism does not claim to have the only path to God, nor does it try to convert others to its way. As Ralph Singh, founder of the Sikh community Gobind Saban in the United States explains, "When you have a beacon of light, those who are of that light see no divisions."[9] A Muslim, Said Mian Mir, was invited to lay the cornerstone of the Golden Temple in Amritsar. It was constructed with four doors, inviting people from all traditions to come in to worship. When Guru Gobind Singh created an army to resist Muslim Emperors and Hindu kings, he admonished Sikhs not to feel enmity toward those religions or their followers; the enemy, he emphasized, was oppression and corruption. Sikh soldier-saints are pledged to protect the freedom of all religions. Sikhism is, however, opposed to empty ritualism and other religions' claims to exclusiveness.

According to the Sikh ideal, the purpose of life is to realize God within the world, through the everyday practices of work, worship, and charity, of sacrificing love. All people are to be treated equally, for God's light dwells in all and pride is a major hindrance to God-realization. From Guru Nanak's time on, Sikhism has refused to acknowledge the traditional Indian caste system.

Like Hinduism, Sikhism conceives a series of lives, with karma (the effects of past actions on one's present life) governing transmigration of the soul into new bodies, be they human or animal. But the Sikh slant on this process is more optimistic than the Hindu. Heaven and hell are only states of mind; the ultimate goal of life is *sahaj*, or mystical union with the divine.

> *Separated from God through many deaths and births,*
> *I have now met Him and I by the Guru's grace,*
> *Though I was as the dry tree, am now green again.*
>
> *Guru Arjan, the Fifth Guru* [10]

Sacred practices

The heart of the Sikh community is those who have taken initiation into the Khalsa. They are the "saint-soldiers," the "army of the Lord," pledged to protect all in need. They let their hair grow long, a gift of God unshorn as a "spiritual crown," a source of strength. Men gather it into a turban and women place it under a veil (or in some cases, a turban), as a sign of respect – they bare their heads only to God. A comb is worn tucked into the turban so that the Khalsa can comb their hair twice a day, to keep it

LIVING SIKHISM
An interview with Professor Gurbachan Singh

Professor Singh was formerly the editor of the largest newspaper in the Punjab. He is now living in New York State, helping to found a Sikh community modeled on the Gobind Sadan community outside of Delhi.

"I am proud to be a Sikh! But we support all religions. Truth is always the same. Truth at the time of Moses is the same as it is now. Love at the time of Muhammad is the same as it is now. I have studied many books and many religions – I have studied Qur'an, I have studied the Gita. There is no problem – we should not hate each other. We should respect others' rights, and others' duties, whether low or high, without any distinction. We believe in power, energy, the right to protect ourselves and to act for the master on behalf of human rights. But a Sikh never attacks anybody. If you observe the 5 K's, God will be always with you and nobody can hurt you.

I was born into the Khalsa, and I kept it according to my ancestors. My forefathers became members of the Khalsa community in the time of the Ninth Guru in the seventeenth century. They were becoming a sect, and then at the time of Guru Gobind Singh in 1699, they converted into Khalsa because all the Sikhs did. Since then, from my forefathers until now, for more than a dozen generations, we have been Khalsa.

I have a living teacher, Baba Virsa Singh, even though our Guru is the Guru Granth Sahib. In the university, what do you receive? You receive knowledge. Your professor who is teaching you is not regarded as your knowledge. He is explaining his experience. I am telling my experience to you, and you are telling your experience to me. This is our mutual transformation of knowledge. To get knowledge from one's experience is not a crime. A man who gives knowledge cannot become a god, cannot become a prophet. Those who are giving this type of training, they are just like teachers.

Our gurdwaras are just like schools, colleges, universities where we can get our spiritual knowledge. And our feelings lift us to Almighty. When we love and praise God, he will give his qualities to us. A man who worships him, ultimately he mingles with him and he becomes like that. Because the Spirit which is in our body is a part of that God, but by doing perverted things, by the environment, it has become covered with dirt. If we remove this dirt by reciting the Name of the God, it will be very pure and we can achieve all the possible qualities.

In the lives of holy saints, there are so many miracles. Every holy man in the world has miracle events in his life. Why? In a real sense, they have become sons of that Almighty Power. He knows that this is my child, and what I possess, my child is the owner of that thing. Just as our children ultimately become the owners of our property."

orderly. The "uniform" also consists of a steel bracelet (a reminder of unity with God and of dedication to service), a sword worn at all times (a powerful sign of personal dignity and a readiness to fight in defense of oneself or those who are weak), and knee-length breeches (worn for modesty and continual preparedness to fight, even at night). These accoutrements are called the "5 K's," for the Punjabi name of each one begins with a "K." In addition to dress, the Khalsa are pledged to a strict code of conduct which forbids, among other things, the use of drugs, alcohol, or tobacco. There are also Sikhs who follow the Gurus but do not choose initiation into the Khalsa.

The Sikh gurus created several institutions to help erase caste distinctions. One is *langar*, the communal feeding of all who come, regardless of caste. This takes place at

Sikhs at the dedication of a new temple, with Khalsa members guarding the Guru Garanth Sahib.

Above *The Golden Temple in Amritsar, holiest of Sikh shrines. Like the religion itself, Sikh temples tend to be built in the Mughal style, which combines both Hindu and Muslim elements.*

Below *Langar, a free meal, is provided daily at some gurdwaras and all visitors are expected to partake. Rich and poor must sit side-by-side, with no distinction.*

the *gurdwara*, the building where the Guru Granth Sahib is enshrined and public worship takes place. During worship as well as langar, all kinds of people sit together, though men and women may sit on opposite sides. People of all ethnic origins, ideologies, and castes, including Untouchables, may bathe in the *sarowar* (a tank of water at a Sikh holy place). Sikh baptism does away with one's former caste and makes the person a chief. Many Sikh officials were originally Shudras, of the lowest caste in India.

The basic sacred practices are prayers and singing of hymns from the Guru Granth Sahib. The prescribed morning and evening prayers take about two hours a day. Most important of the prayers is the *Japji. Jap*, meaning "recitation," refers to the use of sound, the Name of God (*nam*), as the best way of approaching the divine and the remedy for all ills. Like combing the hair, hearing the sacred word combs all negative thoughts out of the mind. As one devotee puts it, the sounds are "vibrating into you ... clearing and opening your mind to God's grace."[11] Much of the Japji is devoted to the blessings of hearing the Word. For example:

Hearkening to the Name bestows
Truth, divine wisdom, contentment.
To bathe in the joy of the Name
Is to bathe in the holy places. [12]

Passages from the Guru Granth Sahib are chanted or sung as *ragas* (melodies), often with musical accompaniment. The tone is devotional, with the attunement established by Guru Nanak. But great discipline is required to attend these pre-dawn public services every day, and in contrast to the pride developed by Guru Gobind Singh in the Khalsa, worshippers humble themselves before the sacred scriptures. The Granth is escorted into the congregating room like a king and placed on an elevated platform with a canopy, with an attendant continually waving a fly-whisk over the sacred book. Worshippers bow to it, bring offerings, and then sit below, on the floor, with their bare feet tucked beneath them. Every morning and evening, the spirit of God reveals its guidance to the people as an officiant opens the scripture at random, intuitively guided, and reads a passage that is to be a special spiritual focus for the day. The scripture is also intuitively consulted as a guide to decision-making.

In addition to group chanting, singing, and listening to collective guidance from the Guru Granth Sahib, devout Sikhs are encouraged to begin the day with private meditations on the name of God. As one advances in this practice and abides in egoless love for God, one is said to receive guidance from the inner guru, the living word of God within each person.

Sikhism today

Despite its politically precarious position within India, Sikhism is still a vibrant religion and is becoming a global faith. The center of Sikhism remains the Punjab. The area of this territory, which is under Indian rule, was dramatically shrunk by the partition of India in 1947, for two-thirds of the Punjab was in the area thenceforth called Pakistan. The two million Sikhs living in that part migrated, many of them to Western countries and parts of India other than the Punjab. Emigration continued, and there are now large Sikh communities in England, western Canada, and the west coast of the United States.

At Sikh services, devotees first approach the Guru Granth Sahib to pay their respects before taking a seat on the floor.

In India, Sikhs and Hindus lived side-by-side in mutual tolerance until recent years, when violent clashes began between Sikh separatists and Hindus. The separatists want to establish an independent Sikh state, called Khalistan, in which they can establish a pure society, strong in its religious observances. Khalistan would also protect Sikhs from assimilation by the much larger Hindu community. In 1984, Prime Minister Indira Gandhi chose to attack the Golden Temple, Sikhism's holiest shrine, for Sikh separatists were using it as a shelter for their weapons. The attack seemed an outrageous desecration even to moderate Sikhs, and counter-violence increased. The Prime Minister herself was killed by her Sikh bodyguards in 1984. Pakistani-Indian antipathies are also interwoven into the crises, and Pakistan is believed by India to be abetting the Sikh terrorists. But internal support for the secessionists is waning as the people of the Punjab tire of the endless bloodshed.

In the United States, a California-based Sikh yoga teacher named Harbhajan Singh Puri (popularly known as "Yogi Bhajan") began in 1969 to initiate people into the Sikh faith. He originally called the group 3HO ("Healthy, Happy, Holy Organization"), a counter to the drug culture. Although there have been some allegations of malfeasance over the years, his many American Sikh converts often display the strong discipline and devotion of traditional Sikhism. Some rise well before dawn for an hour of yoga postures before morning prayers.

In contrast to the media reports of Sikh violence in India, there is an oasis of serenity outside of Delhi where a modern Sikh saint, Baba Virsa Singh, is drawing thousands of spiritual seekers, Sikh and non-Sikh. This community, Gobind Saban, is becoming globally renowned as a holy place of hard agricultural work (no donations are accepted), miracles, and ecumenical devotion. Shri Surendra Nath, a Member of the Union Public Service Commission in New Delhi, writes appreciatively of the dedication of the founder (known affectionately as "Babaji," like many Hindu saints) to relieving the sufferings of humanity and leading the people toward God-realization:

> *It is to this glorious path and to this beautiful journey that Babaji invites one and all to join in, irrespective of caste, creed or religion because different faiths and religious philosophies all have the common aim of God realisation just as innumerable streams and rivers ultimately lead to the same mighty ocean.* [13]

Suggested reading

Cole, W. Owen, and Sambhi, Piara Singh, *The Sikhs: Their Religious Beliefs and Practices*, London: Routledge and Kegan Paul, 1978. A clearly-written survey of the Sikh tradition

McLeod, W. H., trans. and ed., *Textual Sources for the Study of Sikhism*, Totowa, New Jersey: Barnes and Noble Books, 1984 and Manchester: Manchester University Press, 1984. Interesting compilation of Sikh literature, from selections from the Adi Granth to rules for the Khalsa initiation ceremony, all with explanatory comments.

Singh, Khushwant, trans., *Hymns of Guru Nanak*, New Delhi: Orient Longmans Ltd., 1969. Stories about Guru Nanak's life and selections from his sacred songs.

Singh, Ralph, *Sikhism: A Distinct, Universal Religion*, Central Square, New York: Gobind Sadan, U.S.A. A succinct pamphlet about central Sikh beliefs and practices.

Singh, Trilochan, Singh, Jodh, Singh, Kapur, Singh, Bawa Harkishen, and Singh, Khushwant, trans., *The Sacred Writings of the Sikhs*, New York: Samuel Weiser, 1973. Selections from the Adi Granth and other hymns by Guru Gobind Singh.

13 NEW RELIGIOUS MOVEMENTS

"To walk in the same direction"

The history of religions is one of continual change. Each religion changes over time, new religions appear, and some older traditions disappear. Times of rapid social change are particularly likely to spawn new religious movements, for people seek the security of the spiritual amidst worldly chaos. In the period since World War II, thousands of new religious groups sprang up around the world. In sub-Saharan Africa, there are now over five thousand different religions; every Nigerian town of several thousand people now has up to fifty or sixty different kinds of religion.[1] In Japan, an estimated thirty per cent of the population belongs to one of hundreds of new religious movements. Imported versions of ancient traditions, such as Hinduism and Buddhism, have made many new converts in countries such as the United States and Canada, where they are seen as "new religions." The United States seems a particularly fertile breeding ground for new religious movements, for there is a climate of religious freedom and many people are seeking alternatives to the spiritual emptiness of secular industrial life.

This proliferation of new religious movements has of course met with resistance from previously organized religions. As Hare Krishna devotees or Jain meditation groups move into old Christian church buildings, the newcomers are branded with labels such as "cults" or "sects." These words have specific, neutral meanings: a *cult* is a religion focusing on a single person or deity, such as Jesus, while a *sect* is a splinter group or a subgroup associated with a larger tradition, such as the Theravada sect within Buddhism. But these labels have been used pejoratively to distinguish new religions from older ones, each of which already claims to be the best or only way. The label *new religious movement* seems more neutral at this time and is becoming widely used.

In addition to negative reactions from previously organized religions, new religious movements meet with opposition from family members of those who join. In the United States, the "anti-cult" movement employs special agents who capture and "deprogram" followers of new religions, at the request of their parents. Mental health professionals warn about the psychological dangers of some of the new ways, but as indicated in Chapter 1 of this book, there are potential dangers associated with giving power over one's life to any religion, new or old.

In this chapter we will survey some representative examples of new religious movements that have developed in the nineteenth and twentieth centuries. All have some link with previous traditions but are sufficiently different to be studied independently of those traditions. Previous chapters included groups which are modern and perhaps exported versions of older ways with which they are still identified (such as the Hare Krishna movement, which is clearly allied with the sixteenth-century Hindu bhakti tradition of Sri Caitanya). The pages that follow will cover more distinct manifestations of the current burgeoning of spiritual vitality.

The phenomenal growth of the new religious movements is so new, and their diversity so great, that they defy easy categorization. Each considers itself a complete way of "retying" humans to the divine, rather than a category. But in order to provide a framework in which to understand them, we will divide them into nine categories based on their major focus. These are: **1** preparation for the millenium, **2** personal empowerment, **3** charismatic leadership, **4** group identification and personal dedication, **5** the occult, **6** mysticism, **7** metaphysical study, **8** nature worship, and **9** religious unity.

Millenarian movements

Throughout the history of religions, there have been prophecies of the *millenium* – a longed-for era of peace, abundance, and happiness. The term is taken from Revelation, the last book in the Christian Bible, which predicts a thousand-year period of special holiness in which Christ rules the earth. The Isaiahs of the Old Testament had foretold a new heaven and a new earth, an end to corruption and tyranny and the coming of the kingdom of God for the faithful. In the nineteenth and twentieth centuries, such messages have often been given to oppressed peoples, rallying them around a hopeful vision of extreme change and perhaps a return to the glorified past.

Latin American examples

In colonized Latin America, Indians held the myth of a return to the Land Without Evil; those under Portuguese influence dreamed of the return of Dom Sebastian (king of Portugal) to establish a new land where no one would have to work and everyone would be happy and wealthy. Such changes usually involve the dramatic destruction of the old order. Antonio the Counselor told the impoverished peasants of Brazil's *sertao* (the sparsely populated, dry interior):

> In 1896 we shall see the herds return to the sertao and the sertao will become the seaboard and the seaboard will become the sertao. . . . In 1899 the waters will turn to blood and the planet will appear in the East with the rays of the sun and the sun will crash into the sky and . . . from the waves of the sea will emerge Dom Sebastian with his whole army. [2]

Although 1896 passed without apocalyptic drama, millenarian expectations still run high among the poor of Brazil.

Rastafarianism

In Jamaica, millenarian expectations have been expressed as *Rastafarianism*. In 1895, Alexander Bedward of the Baptist Free Church prophesied a coming holocaust in which all the white people would be killed, leaving the blacks, "the true people," to celebrate the new world. He sat in his special robes as the predicted date came and went; eventually he was placed in an asylum for the insane. A more generalized hopeful vision was spread by Marcus Garvey, who saw a fundamental change in society that would be led by blacks. Garvey linked these dreams to the return of blacks to Africa, from which their ancestors had been taken as slaves; there they would rebuild a great civilization. A prophecy attributed to Garvey – "Look to Africa when a black king shall be crowned, for the day of deliverance is near"[3] – was thought to have been realized when Ras (Prince) Tafari of Ethiopia was crowned as Haile Selassie, Emperor of Ethiopia.

An elaborate mystique was built up around Haile Selassie as the living God. Hopeful lore was based on interpretations of his statements and of passages from the Old Testament and the New Testament book of Revelation. Poor Jamaicans (who likened themselves to the Jews in captivity in Babylon) repeatedly prepared to be given free passage back to Africa.

Haile Selassie's reign (until his death in 1974) did nothing to liberate Jamaican Africans, but young blacks in Jamaica have nevertheless developed a new religious movement around these ideals. They intend to revive the "Way of the Ancients," their concept of the lost civilization of pre-colonial Africa, and to free people of African extraction from subservience. "Babylon," the oppressor, is the United States, Britain (the former colonial power in Jamaica), the state of Jamaica, and the Christian Church. In protest against Babylon, Rastafarians wear their hair in long uncombed curls, called "dreadlocks," a symbol of the natural non-industrial life. Some give use of marijuana (*ganja*) ritual religious significance. A distinctive music, *reggae*, has evolved as an expression of black pride, social protest, and Rastafarian millenarian ideals.

The Rastafarian movement has spread beyond Jamaica to blacks elsewhere in the Caribbean, North America, Europe, Australia, and New Zealand. In Nigeria, as well, new religious movements are spreading the message that blacks have spiritual wealth that exceeds that of the white cultures which have dominated many of the world religions.

The Arcane School

In the white-dominated societies themselves, many people are concerned about the potential for world destruction, whether from nuclear war or accident, social disintegration, or environmental deterioration. A number of groups have formed explicitly to pray for the future of the planet. For example, the *Arcane School* founded in New York in 1923 by Alice Bailey encourages groups to meet each month on the full moon (when spiritual energies are thought to be highest) to enact rituals designed to encourage the return of the "Christ principle," either as a person or as a "New Age" of widespread illumination.

Jehovah's Witnesses

Another group, who call themselves *Jehovah's Witnesses*, foresee a new world in which people of all races (including many raised from the dead) will join hands in peace. They believe that this will happen only after ninety-nine per cent of humanity is destroyed for not obeying the Bible. In the understanding of Jehovah's Witnesses, God will not let anyone, including "false Christians," ruin the earth. Those who are of the true religion will be saved from the general destruction, reunited with their dead loved ones in a paradise on earth in which there is no pain, no food shortages, no sickness, no death.

The baptism of Jehovah's Witness followers in a portable pool during their International Convention.

The nineteenth-century founder of Jehovah's Witnesses, Charles Taze Russell, predicted that 1914 would be the date of this apocalypse. When 1914 passed, the prophecy was changed: 1914 was the date when Jesus began to rule in heaven, but his rule is not yet visible on earth. In the meantime, Jehovah's Witnesses go from door to door, trying to convert people to their program of studying the Bible as an announcement of the millenium. They encourage people to leave politics and "false religions." The latter include mainstream Christian churches, who, the Witnesses feel, began to deviate from Jesus's message in the second and third centuries by developing untrue doctrines: that God is a Trinity, that the soul is resurrected after death, and that the unrepentant wicked endure eternal torment (rather than the utter annihilation which the Witnesses predict for them). Emphasis on the immediacy of the millenium is waning as 1914 recedes, but there are now an estimated three million Jehovah's Witnesses at work in the world.

Personal spiritual empowerment

Rather than waiting for cataclysmic change in the world, many new religious movements empower people to change their own lives and enjoy happiness in the midst of a less-than-perfect society. In broader terms, the idea is that as people are transformed, one by one, the world will become a better place. The *personal growth movement* – in which people come to an understanding of their personality structure and life patterns and take them in hand to create the life they choose – is now strong in industrial nations but does not always have a spiritual character. In this section, we will look at a few personal empowerment movements that teach people to draw their personal strength from the divine power.

Syncretistic Nigerian movements

A number of new religions of this nature in Nigeria combine ritual elements of indigenous and Christian traditions. They take problems with the spirit world, such as retaliations from spirits who have not been treated respectfully, seriously and mix Christian prayers and incense with fetishes, talismans, divining, chanting, and drumming. This *syncretistic* mixture (a reconciliation of normally differing beliefs) gives a sense of power against evil spirits and is also applied to contemporary, this-worldly problems. These groups are most popular in urban areas, where they offer a refuge from unpleasant aspects of city life. An advertisement for *The Brotherhood of the Cross and Star* promises health, money, children, popularity, freedom from court cases, and power. Those who say they once felt like nobodies, alienated within modern impersonal culture, now feel recognized as important individuals within a loving group. The movements revive the traditional African community spirit as a stable support network within a changing society.

Transcendental Meditation

Beginning in the 1960s and 1970s, *Transcendental Meditation*, a technique taught by the Indian guru Maharishi Mahesh Yogi, claimed great benefits for practitioners. By simply spending twenty minutes each day repeating a secret mantra which they were given, TM followers were supposed to be able to work more efficiently, become more satisfied with their lives, be better athletes, be more creative, end drug addiction, and learn more effectively. TM research also indicated that crime rates declined in areas where groups were meditating strongly; meditation groups have therefore been rushed to troubled areas (such as places of rioting) to spread an atmosphere of peacefulness. Some have claimed that rather than being carefully chosen to harmonize with the person's energy vibrations (as initiates were told), the mantras were assigned according to the initiate's age. Nevertheless, many in the West, which was in the 1960s and 1970s just beginning to learn about meditation, have experienced greater peace in their lives from devoting some time to concentrating on a mantra. And those who chose to carry the training farther were introduced to the classics of Hindu sacred literature.

Soka Gakkai

A new offshoot of Nichiren Shoshu Buddhism, *Soka Gakkai*, now claims over seventeen million members around the world. Through the chanting of *Nam-myoho-renge-kyo*, which is said to invoke the principles of the Lotus Sutra, they reportedly become happier in an earthly sense. According to a pamphlet distributed by the group:

> *One who chants is able to gain the power and wisdom to live with confidence, overcome any problem, and develop a happy future. . . . Such benefits include better jobs, places to live and cars to drive. Buddhism maintains that all realms are essential to happiness.* [4]

This focus on material benefits may be a selective interpretation of classical Buddhism,

Rastafarian male musicians carry the message of reasserting black spiritual and social rights.

which seems to have emphasized detachment from earthly concerns. But Soka Gakkai's strategy is to help people gain earthly power first and then lead them toward higher goals. The leaders explain:

> *'When enough people passionately embrace the viewpoint that life is sacred and inviolable, peace will ensue.'* [5]

In Japan, Soka Gakkai has built a great modern temple (Taiseki-ji, "Home of Eternal Life") at the foot of Mt. Fuji and developed its own political party – the *Komeito* ("Clean Government Party") since the social welfare benefits it sought for the lower classes were not forthcoming. Rightists accuse the party of communist sympathies; leftists suspect it of using its political platform to advance religious fanaticism. Its literature cheerfully accentuates the positive.

New Thought

Emphasis on self-improvement through positive thinking has burgeoned in the United States into a number of new religious movements such as the *United Church of Religious Science*, the *Unity School of Christianity*, and the *Spiritual Frontiers Fellowship*, sometimes referred to collectively as "New Thought." Although they resemble Christianity in some aspects, these groups do not see God as separate from humans nor believe in humankind's innate sinfulness. Rather, they emphasize that our real inner selves are emanations of God – that we have access to the infinite divine potential if only we can learn to tap into it. We can create anything we choose and heal ourselves and others if we use the power of mind wisely. Many of these groups use daily affirmations to train the mind to remember its divine context. An affirmation by Ernest Holmes, founder of

In the syncretism of Santeria, the Yoruba river goddess Oshun is merged with the Christian Our Lady of La Caridad del Cobre, patron saint of Cuba.

The ''Mother Church'' of Christian Science, founded by Mary Baker Eddy in Boston in the 19th century. Eddy revealed the loving, maternal aspect of God as the Holy Comforter, referring to the motherhood as well as the fatherhood of the divine.

the United Church of Religious Science, illustrates the method:

> *I am energized by the vitality of the living Spirit. All the Power there is, with all the energy
> and vitality It has, is mind, and I experience enthusiasm for life, the glad expectation of the
> more yet to be, and give gratitude for what has been and now is. Every weight or burden
> of thought or feeling falls from me and I am lifted up into the atmosphere of that Divine
> Presence which knows only the vitality, the joy, and the strength of Its own being. I am
> one with all this.* [6]

New Thought groups are spinoffs of *Christian Science*, founded by Mary Baker Eddy in
the late nineteenth century. It differs significantly from New Thought in two major
ways: Christian Science is centered on the Bible and on Jesus (Mrs. Eddy sought to
reinstate what she considered "primitive Christianity"), and it maintains the conviction
that human sinfulness is what stands between humans and the loving God. When
humans abide in moral and spiritual sinfulness — including states such as hatred, fear,
selfishness, and envy — these qualities obscure the true reality. When one squarely faces
these manifestations of mental darkness and surrenders oneself prayerfully to the reality
which is God, Christian Scientists affirm that healing naturally takes place as one's true
being emerges. In their faith, Christian Scientists usually refuse medical treatment,
turning instead to prayer. Christian Scientist Tom Johnsen explains:

> *This is not positive thinking or psychological training, and it is not beseeching God. Prayer
> is so much more than that. It is a yielding of heart and being to God, to divine love. It
> affirms truth. When there is that yielding of the human mind to the divine, the body
> naturally manifests that reality, and healing takes place, as in the New Testament.
> Healing is not magical, not just an occasional lightning bolt from on high. Health is the
> natural and very normal result when one's whole being grasps and is grasped by one's
> relationship to God.* [7]

The Light of Truth Universal Shrine is a pastel vision rising from the hills of Virginia. It houses a meditation room, altars to all faiths, and spiritual artefacts from all religions, celebrating the Hindu motto, ''Truth is One, Paths are Many.''

Once branded as a movement of lunatics, Christian Science now publishes a newspaper (*The Christian Science Monitor*), a magazine (*World Monitor*), and a television news program ("World Monitor") that are respected for their intelligence and open-mindedness.

Charismatic teachers

Hinduism has long honored the tradition of guru-worship – of placing one's life at the feet of the guru, as a sort of father or mother figure whose authority over and concern for each chela are theoretically absolute. The West has not had this tradition in its major religions (with exceptions such as shaikhs in some Sufi orders, abbots in monasteries and mothers superior in convents). Family and friends of those who offer willing submission to a guru's guidance have sometimes been concerned that the devotees are doing the wrong thing. Nevertheless, many new religious movements have at their center a charismatic teacher around whom the faithful have gathered.

Radhasoami

One of the groups emphasizing charismatic leadership is the *Radhasoami* movement, a hybrid path from India. Its leaders often have Sikh backgrounds, but while orthodox Sikhs believe in a succession of masters that stopped with the Tenth Guru and was transferred to the holy scripture, Radhasoamis believe in a continuing succession of living masters. The first of the Radhasoami gurus was Shiv Dayal Singh. In 1861 he offered to serve as a spiritual savior, carrying devotees into Radhasoami, the ineffable Godhead. Some ten thousand took initiation under him. After his death, the movement eventually split into what are now thirty branches, each with its own living master, although there is theoretically only one of these at a time on the earth. The Punjabi branches are known collectively as *Sant Mat*, or Path of the Masters.

Radhasoami is primarily an esoteric path, without exoteric ceremonies. Initiates are taught a secret yoga practice of concentrating on the third eye with attention to the inner sound and inner light in order to commune with the all-pervading power of God, called the "Word," or *Naam*. The faithful are told that the experience must be both initiated and guided by a perfected being. Sant Mat masters teach respect for all earlier Perfect Masters, for they feel they are of the same continuing lineage that includes Buddha, Mahavira, Jesus, Muhammad, Kabir, and the Sikh saints.

The Radhasoami approach to the Godhead now claims an estimated 1.7 million initiates. Those in the Agra area of India have created whole spiritual suburbs who live and work as well as worship together. Outside of India, devotees gather in *satsangs* (spiritual congregations), who are supposed to support each other in the path. They are required to be vegetarians, to meditate every day, to forgo alcohol and if possible, tobacco, and to be employed. This requirement extends to the living master, who must support himself by outside work rather than by contributions from initiates. Rajinder Singh, a contemporary Sant Mat "god-man," is an engineer for AT&T.

Paramhansa Yogananda, author of The Autobiography of a Yogi, *taught that we become like that which occupies our thoughts. If the mind dwells on evil, we will become ugly; if the mind looks for the good, we will become beautiful.*

In the Radhasoami tradition, the living master is seen as one's beloved and essential guide to the divine. Master Sant Darshan Singh died in 1989; his position was filled by Rajinder Singh, who is standing in the background in this photograph.

Other Indian guru-worship groups

Most other contemporary examples of global guru-worship movements come from India, where devotees have long bowed to gurus as their spiritual parents. Paramhansa Yogananda (founder of *The Self-Realization Fellowship*), Swami Prabhupada (*International Society for Krishna Consciousness*), Sri Chinmoy (founder of 113 *Sri Chinmoy Centers* on five continents), Gurumayi Chidvilasanda (contemporary leader of the *Siddha Yoga Dham* movement), Maharaj Ji (the *Divine Light Mission*), Satya Sai Baba (who stays in his South Indian ashram, where thousands flock to see him, but is said to appear to people around the world when they need help), and Shree Rajneesh (the *Rajneesh Foundation*) all came from India. They have been accorded a certain respect by non-Indian seekers simply because of the spiritual mystique associated with Mother India – they typically wear long robes and look profound. But their appeal is not just superficial. In most cases, their own meditation practices have developed their magnetism and insight. Like the Sant Mat gurus, they have taught ancient ways of enlightenment adapted for contemporary life and for people who have not grown up as Hindus, Sikhs, or Jains.

Beyond these similarities, the Indian gurus who have started popular new religious movements abroad should not be categorized, praised, or castigated as a group, for their messages and styles differ considerably. At one extreme, Rajneesh (once respected for his lively insights into ancient tantric sutras) was forced to leave the United States in 1985 amid bizarre charges of violence, sexual improprieties, and manipulative political tactics at his Oregon ashram. He was the owner of a string of Rolls Royces contributed by his devotees (who gave their own wealth to the Foundation and lived as renunciates). By contrast, many of the gurus listed above have brought honor to their profession by serving unselfishly and encouraging the highest qualities in their devotees. As indicated in the chapter on Hinduism, worship for the guru is a tool to help people surrender the ego, that they may transcend the limited self and experience the Truth.

Rajneesh, an expounder of tantric texts, led a baffling career from philosophy professor to leader of a cult whose members were encouraged to alternate periods of silent meditation with twenty minutes of uninhibited emotion and activity.

Seek God for His own sake. The highest perception is to feel Him as Bliss, welling up from your infinite depths. Don't yearn for visions, spiritual phenomena, or thrilling experiences. The path to the Divine is not a circus!

Paramhansa Yogananda[8]

Group dedication

In addition to the security of giving control of one's life to a father or mother figure (the guru), certain new religious movements offer the gratifying feeling of belonging to an extended family that understands one's spiritual orientation and provides a framework for meaningful service. The group is also a safe refuge of sorts. Even though it may require spiritual discipline, and is therefore not an easy way of living, it provides a clearly spiritual reality that is distinctly different from the surrounding materialistic world.

Krishna Consciousness

After the death of their Indian founder, the Western Krishna-worshipping groups split into ISKON (International Society of Krishna Consciousness) and the League of Devotees, a more ecumenical group centered in New Vrindaban, West Virginia. The devotees there gather each day at 4 am for an hour of communal chanting of the names of God, a practice which seemingly nourishes them with the spiritual energy they need in order to maintain a harmonious, hard-working, God-centered community. They feel that maintenance of this sacred attunement to the group's ideals throughout the day is so important that they are proposing to build Cities of God around the world. These are towns for twelve thousand people of all faiths whose lives are dedicated to the divine.

Unification Church

Being surrounded by spiritually dedicated people as well as a spiritually inspiring environment is important to many who join the communally-oriented new religious movements. A study was recently made of British "Moonies" (members of the *Unification Church* founded in 1954 in Korea by the Reverend Sun Myung Moon). It showed that most were young adults from stable middle-class homes that emphasized responsibility, service, and religious faith. Among their peers, pre-Moonies felt lonely and isolated; they were uncomfortable with the moral dissolution of modern society and were searching for a way of "doing good." Reverend Moon's − "the spirit of sacrifice for the greater cause" − message therefore had a strong appeal.

Reverend Moon says he seeks to unite people of all religions in cooperating with God to prevent global catastrophe, which he sees as threatening the survival of humankind. He began by trying to draw Christians of all denominations together, for Christianity places a high value on service. Confucian ideals are also prominent in the moral way of life he advocates. His theology, called the Divine Principle, is centered on the "Three Blessings of God"[9] which will establish the Kingdom of Heaven on Earth: Individual Perfection, Divinity in the Family, and Human Dominion of Love over the earth.

The Unification Church has enhanced its perceived legitimacy by sponsoring world

One of the activities of the Unification Church is the Religious Youth Service, which brings together youth of all nations and all religions in service projects.

conferences of all Christian denominations, world assemblies of all religions, and technological and dietary aid to third-world nations. In order to finance these projects, Moon's followers are asked to give up unnecessary worldly possessions and devote themselves tirelessly to the cause by working at low pay in Unification businesses, such as its fishing industry. Marriages between Moonies are often arranged and blessed by Reverend Moon at mass marriage ceremonies, creating whole families of devotees within the larger family of the Unification Church, which in turn stresses identification with the entire global family of humanity. Often vilified by the media, associated with extremist anti-communist activities, and accused of brainwashing tactics as well as tax evasion, Moon is viewed as a divinely inspired messiah by his followers.

The occult

Some new religious movements focus on the spirit world rather than the malfunctioning of human society. Through their presumed contacts with invisible realities, they feel they can bring healing for those who are suffering and insights for those who want to see beyond the material life. *Occult* means dealing with, or knowledgeable about, the supernatural – that which is beyond the experiences of the senses and is therefore mysterious to most people. Those who are interested in the occult seek to penetrate these mysteries. They do not necessarily intend to gain powers that can be used in "black magic" (destructive use of spiritual energies), but the word "occult" is often popularly associated with this negative connotation.

Magical Christianity

In the Caribbean and Latin America, many mixtures of African and Catholic traditions have evolved, with a prevailing interest in contacting and cooperating with spirits. *Santeria*, which literally means "worship of saints," blends some of the Yoruba gods of ex-Nigerian slaves with images of Catholic saints. *Voodoo* is the cult of various spirits to help regulate people's relationship with nature and with each other. Specialists in these traditions have techniques for "magical" intervention in people's lives to help solve problems that cannot be fixed by ordinary means. The santeros, for example, say they are able to clear away negative spiritual influences around people, help them get jobs, heal sickness, attract mates, block their enemies, and get ahead financially.

In occult understanding, what seems "evil" may be useful. Evil takes two forms, passive and active, each of which has negative and positive aspects. Even the word "negative," in this context, does not necessarily mean "bad." Passive evil in its negative aspect is the principle of inertia – that which offers resistance to movement. As Santeria scholar Migene Gonzalez-Wippler observes, we cannot walk on a slippery surface; we can only advance by pushing our feet against something resistant. In its positive aspect, passive evil is the principle of destruction. Like the Hindu goddess Kali, destruction is necessary to clear away that which has outlived its usefulness, allowing evolution to proceed.

As for active evil, its negative aspect is chaos, the state of imbalance from which all growth issues. If things always stay in secure balance, there is only stagnation; improvement is impossible. It is the positive aspect of active evil that is most feared: the demonic energies, which are thought to derive from hateful, vengeful, twisted human thoughts and which are attracted by fear itself.

The occult practitioner who fearlessly operates in invisible realms, shamanistically allowing himself or herself to be possessed by the spirits, can theoretically use all these energies to accomplish desired ends. But when these ends are harmful, as is sometimes the case, life can become difficult for those caught in the spiritual battles of black magicians. Some actually die from terror. The ultimate protection is not more black magic but rather "white magic." Invoking Jesus or Mary or another saint, or simply affirming the presence of goodness and light, is thought to be powerful counter-magic to protect oneself against terrorization by demonic entities.

Japanese sects

Many founders of these new religions are women with shamanistic gifts. Miki Nakayama, nineteenth-century founder of the *Tenrikyo* sect, was acting as a trance medium for the healing of her son when she was reportedly possessed by ten kami, including the chief God the Parent. They proclaimed through her, "Miki's mind and body will be accepted by us as a divine shrine, and we desire to save this three-thousand-world through this divine body."[10] It is said that she later spontaneously composed 1711 poems under divine inspiration, and that these became the sacred scriptures of a new religion. Tenrikyo has continued to be popular since her death, with Miki revered as the still-living representative of the divine will.

The *Mahikari* movement was founded in Japan in 1959 by Sukui Nushi Sama, who believes he is the successor to Buddha and Christ as God's representative on earth. The path he taught has become popular in the Caribbean. Although it does not claim to be a religion in itself, but rather to bring all religions together, it involves certain distinctive practices centering on spiritual "light." Mahikirians are taught to heal by radiating light out of their hands, to send light to disturbed ancestral spirits to help them find peace, and to spread the divine civilization through the world by transmitting light. Inverting the conventional opinion of such practices, Mahikirians are taught that the spiritual realm is the only reality; science and medicine are ignorant superstitions.

Great White Brotherhood groups

Certain Western occult traditions are said to link members with an invisible *Great White Brotherhood* ("white" refers to the light surrounding them, rather than their skin color). Elizabeth Claire Prophet, one of the "messengers" of these "Ascended Masters," explains that they include:

> *Gautama Buddha, Confucius, Moses, Mohammed, Jesus Christ, Saint Germain [a mysterious eighteenth-century European count believed to be the Master of the "Seventh Ray"], Mother Mary, to name but a few, who have mastered outer conditions and earned the right to ascend into the very Presence of God. . . . The Brotherhood is a spiritual fraternity of lightbearers. . . . They work hand in hand with their disciples in every nation, and of every race and religious persuasion. . . . As immortal, God-free beings living in the joy of the Eternal Now, they would lovingly, wisely, and safely guide you on the path to soul freedom.*[11]

Prophet's group, called the Summit University, owns a huge ranch next to Yellowstone National Park in Montana. People are invited to bring their recreational vehicles or tents for international conferences in which they work with practices such as visualization of the "violet flame" for healing and purification and "receive initiations from the Ascended Masters."[12] Yet the environmental impact of the camp and its alleged arsenal of weapons have invoked serious criticism. The *I AM* version of this tradition, founded in 1930 by Guy Ballard, envisions the United States as the potential spiritual salvation of the planet and teaches members to concentrate spiritual power into "decrees" to dissipate the power of "enemies of America."

Spiritualism

The tradition of communication with the spirits of the dead was revived in the United States in the nineteenth century as *Spiritualism* and is practiced through numerous Spiritualist churches today. The National Spiritualist Association of Churches defines Spiritualism as "The science, philosophy, and religion of continuous life." Its services resemble Christian worship services, with a sermon and the singing of devotional hymns, but without the focus on Jesus or sinfulness. They include periods of spiritual healing in which trained "healing vehicles" are believed to serve as channels for God's healing power by placing their hands on or near the head and shoulders of a seated person. Equally important are messages transmitted by a medium who speaks to members of the congregation on behalf of relatives "on the other side." Spiritualist medium Sandra Pfortmiller explains:

> *The gift and faculty of mediumship is to prove that life continues, that our loved ones are*

only a prayer away, that we do have help, guidance, communication and inspiration from another Plane of existence. It shows that we should not fear death but rather understand that the personality continues, always growing. [13]

Spiritualist doctrine includes a version of karma – "We affirm the moral responsibility of the individual, and that he makes his own happiness or unhappiness as he obeys or disobeys Nature's physical and spiritual laws" – with infinite possibility for positive change – "We affirm that the doorway to reformation is never closed against any human soul here or hereafter."[14]

Eckankar

A new Western offshoot from the Radhasoami tradition, *Eckankar*, centers on out-of-body "soul travel" as a way of exploring the supernatural planes of existence and unlocking their secrets. Its founder Paul Twitchell, an ex-devotee of the Sant Mat tradition, speaks of previous masters, including Kabir, Guru Nanak, Saint Paul, Christ, Zoroaster, and Buddha, as "explorers of the other worlds"[15] who "all teach that there is no means of spiritual liberation except through Soul Travel."[16] He explains the rationale for "leaving the physical body temporarily while Soul explores the worlds of this universe":

When we travel beyond the Soul plane, known as the fifth plane of God, into the higher realms of spirit, we will gain freedom, charity and wisdom. We can go anywhere we wish and do anything within the spiritual and material worlds that is within reason and authority of God. At least we are free of the lower world phenomenon. . . . [This] traveling leads to illumination, cosmic consciousness and eventually to becoming a co-worker with God. [17]

Twitchell claims that one can be taught by a living ECK Master to leave the body by use of the mind and the universal sound current (ECK); he says that this technique is an ancient science which preceded Sant Mat.

Mysticism

There is a fine line between mysticism and the occult, and the two are often confused. While occult practitioners try to study and manipulate the supernatural, mystics undertake spiritual disciplines in order to experience sacred union with the divine. Most of these meditation disciplines are quite ancient, developed by contemplatives within all the major religions. When Zen meditation or yoga or Christian contemplation are introduced into contemporary societies, they may seem "new," but they are not.

Subud

A truly new form of mysticism, *Subud*, was introduced in 1933 by an Indonesian named Muhammad Subuh. Some years earlier, he had been walking with friends at night when he had a spontaneous mystical experience. A globe of extremely bright light is said to have appeared over his head and then filled him with intense, vibrating energy.

He continued to feel it for years and was always in a state of ecstasy. Gradually, family, friends, and then people from throughout Indonesia heard of him by word of mouth and came for his guidance, calling him Bapak, meaning "Father." In 1957 he was invited to travel beyond his homeland to spread his gift farther. The way he taught has now been introduced in almost every country of the world.

The central Subud practice is *latihan*. Those who have prepared themselves for initiation into Subud are "opened" into spontaneous worship of God by a "helper" approved by Bapak. In a darkened room, they spend half an hour twice a week doing whatever comes, from shouting or jumping about to crying or singing wordless melodies. Subud helper June Saury-Cookson explains:

> The latihan cannot be taught or imitated, for it arises spontaneously from within after the contact with the Power of God has been received by transmission through a person in whom it is already established. . . . The latihan is true worship of God through our surrender to His will, and its action is one of purification and inward growth. [18]

Gurdjieff

Several mystics have introduced new dance forms as a means of communion with the Divine. One was Georges Ivanovitch *Gurdjieff*, a Russian who lived from 1872 to 1949. He traveled throughout central Asia and claimed to have been instructed by a Hidden Brotherhood of masters, probably Sufis. His writings are enigmatic, defying ordinary logic; realization of the divine was to be sought through his program of complicated dance and posture exercises, and the classical Sufi transmission of *baraka* (spiritual blessing) from teacher to student.

The Dances of Universal Peace are for sharing a sacred reality. Rahima Dziubany (left) led the dances at a British community of handicapped adults and said, "I met their hearts in the very first moment, and from that place we danced."

Dances of Universal Peace

Another to use dance as meditation and communion was Samuel Lewis (1896–1971), known to those who loved him as "Sufi Sam." Enthusiastic about all religions, he was recognized as a Zen master, a Hasidic rabbi, a master of Yoga, and a Christian teacher as well as a Sufi master. Murshid Sam was inspired not only to share traditional Sufi dervish dances, accompanied by chanting of the Names of God, but also to create the *Dances of Universal Peace* (often called "Sufi dancing"). These are simple circle dances to sacred phrases from all the world's religions; people interact in a way that can open their hearts to the divine in each other. He also taught Spiritual Walk: tapping into unknown reaches of the divine in oneself by walking in the attunement of various spiritual masters. The Dances and Walks have been taken around the world and are often used to bring groups into sacred harmony and celebration of unity. Because they offer a "safe" form of intimacy and are not confined to any one religion, they have been used in gatherings for peace studies, transpersonal counseling, and holistic health education, enrichment activities for psychiatric and mentally retarded clients, cross-cultural arts events, and interfaith conferences. The usual experience at the end is that people do not want to leave.

> *One of the reasons I am teaching this music and dancing is to increase Joy, . . . bliss in our own self. This is finding God within, through Experience. . . .*   Samuel L. Lewis[19]

Metaphysical study

In contrast to the experiential quality of mystical practices, another group of new religious movements focuses more on intellectual study. *Metaphysics* is a branch of philosophy: the systematic investigation of ultimate reality.

Theosophical Society

The major new school of metaphysics in the nineteenth and twentieth centuries is *Theosophy*, which means "divine wisdom." This is an ancient quest, given new form by Madame Blavatsky (1831–1891). Born into a noble Russian family, she was a holy terror with notable psychic powers. She claimed to have traveled around the globe studying with masters of esoteric schools and to have undergone initiations with Tibetan masters. In the United States, she founded the Theosophical Society with the motto, "There is no religion higher than truth." It was an attempt, she said, "to reconcile all religions, sects and nations under a common system of ethics, based on eternal verities."[20]

In its search for truth, the Theosophical Society studies religions of all times and places. It introduced ancient Eastern ideas to Western seekers, especially Hindu beliefs such as karma, reincarnation, and subtle energy bodies. Madame Blavatsky was particularly interested in the secret esoteric teachings of each religion, which collectively she called the "Wisdom Religion" or the "secret doctrine." Blavatsky's book *The Secret Doctrine* describes an elaborate cosmology of levels or "rays" through which humans can rise by consciousness-expanding initiation from invisible Masters.

An early meeting of The Theosophical Society in Madras, 1884. Fourth from the left in the back is its founder, Madame H. P. Blavatsky, who wrote of the boundless eternal Principle, innumerable universes, and the identity of souls with the Universal Oversoul.

Anthroposophical Society

Theosophical concepts influenced many later movements, including Rudolf Steiner's *Anthroposophical Society.* Steiner, an Austrian, headed the German branch of the Theosophical Society early in the twentieth century. His views of the cosmos are similar to those of Theosophy, and therefore, of Hinduism. But Steiner developed his own blend of science and spirituality and sought to initiate people to higher levels of spiritual understanding and achievement by the use of music, art, and imagination as well as study. His Waldorf Schools offer a highly creative, artistic environment for children, with attention to such details as the colors surrounding them. Unlike Theosophy, the Anthroposophical Society offers worship services, based on a Christian model. The priests administer a communion ceremony designed to help people become like Christ, whom they see as a fully developed human.

Nature spirituality

If religion is defined in the broadest sense as that which ties us back to the sacred, one of the strongest trends in our time is that of the religion of nature. Many who are experiencing a reconnection with the natural world do not think of this path as a religion, for it has no clear structure. It is growing spontaneously, from within.

Revival of old models

Some who seek to practice a nature-oriented spirituality look to the past for models. This trend is sometimes called *Neo-Paganism*, although many who practice these ways would not think of applying this label (with its old pejorative connotations) to what they are doing. It is an attempt to return to the spiritual ways of ancient peoples who were suppressed by more powerful organized religions. Some, particularly women, believe that the divine was once worshipped as a female power. They feel that by worshipping the Goddess they are reviving an ancient tradition, rejecting what they see as the negative aspects of patriarchal religions. They may call their way *Witchcraft*. As Starhawk, minister of the Covenant of the Goddess, explains:

> *Modern Witches are thought to be members of a kooky cult, ... lacking the depth, the dignity and seriousness of purpose of a true religion. But Witchcraft is a religion, perhaps the oldest religion extant in the West ... and it is very different from all the so-called great religions. The Old Religion, as we call it, is closer in spirit to Native American traditions or to the shamanism of the Arctic. It is not based on dogma or a set of beliefs, nor on scriptures or a sacred book revealed by a great man. Witchcraft takes its teachings from nature, and reads inspiration in the movements of the sun, moon, and stars, the flight of birds, the slow growth of trees, and the cycles of the seasons.*[21]

Some Neo-Pagans honor pantheons such as the Egyptian gods and goddesses, balancing "masculine" and "feminine" qualities. Some try to reproduce some of the sacred ways of earlier European peoples, such as the Celts of the British Isles or the ancient Scandinavians. Reconstructing these ways is difficult, for they were largely oral rather than written traditions. After religions such as Christianity were installed, the remaining practitioners of the old ways were often tortured and killed as witches, blamed for social ills such as the plague. They were said to be in league with the devil against God, but the pagan pantheons had no devil; he was introduced by the Judeo-Christian-Muslim traditions.

Teachers from life-affirming religions that were never totally destroyed, such as certain Native American sacred ways, are highly valued as guides to worship for the natural world. From them, contemporary seekers have learned to use traditions such as vision quests, sweat lodges, and medicine wheels. But the traditions are complex, requiring life-long training and interwoven with ways of life that have passed; Neo-Pagans from non-native backgrounds usually cannot experience them in their original fullness. What remains is the intent: to honor and cooperate with the natural forces, to celebrate the circle of life rather than destroy it, as "civilization" has done.

In the absence of sure knowledge of ancient ways of honoring Spirit, Neo-Pagans often make up their own forms of group ritual, attempting to draw on divine inspiration for these new ceremonies. Usually they are held outside, with the trees and rocks and waters, the sun, moon, and stars as the altars of the sacred. Speakers may invoke the pantheistic Spirit within all life or the invisible spirits of the place. At ceremonies dedicated to a phase of the moon or the change of the seasons, worshippers may be reminded of how their lives are interwoven with and affected by the natural rhythms. Prayers and ritual may be offered for the healing of the earth, the creatures, or the people.

Certain spots have traditionally been known as places of high energy, as indicated in

Chapter 2, and these are often used for ceremonies and less structured sacred experiences. Ancient ceremonial sites in the British Isles, such as Stonehenge and Glastonbury Tor, draw a new breed of tour groups wanting to experience the atmosphere of the places. In New Zealand, the traditional Maori people know of the revivifying power of running water, such as waterfalls (now understood by scientists as places of negative ionization, which do indeed have an energizing effect). The Maori elders have told the public of the healing power of a certain waterfall on the North Island; the area is dedicated to anyone who needs healing. The government has built a special parking area and walkway for access to the falls, explicitly for spiritual healing purposes.

Deep ecology

In addition to groups that are looking to replicate or re-invent past ways of earth-centered worship, many people in non-traditional societies are now feeling their way toward new ways of connecting themselves with the cosmos. This rapidly-developing global phenomenon has been labeled *deep ecology*. If ecology is the science of the interconnectedness of all living things, deep ecology is the *experience* of oneness with the natural world. By contrast, most Western religions have cast humans as controllers of the natural world, of a different order of being than bears and flowers, mountains and rivers. Australian deep ecologist John Seed calls this attitude *anthropocentrism* – "human chauvinism, the idea that humans are the crown of creation, the source of all value, the measure of all things."[22]

> *What is man without the beasts? If all the beasts were gone, men would die from a great loneliness of spirit. For whatever happens to the beasts soon happens to the man . . . The earth does not belong to man; man belongs to the earth. This we know. All things are connected like the blood which unites one family.*
>
> Chief Seattle[23]

Many of us came to a new awareness of our planetary home when we first saw it photographed from space. Rather than a globe divided by national political boundaries, it appeared as a beautiful being, its surface mostly covered by oceans, wreathed in clouds, floating in the darkness of space. Some scientists have taken up this metaphor of the earth as a being and are finding evidence of its scientific plausibility. Biogeochemist James Lovelock proposed in 1969 that the *biosphere* ("the entire range of living matter on Earth, from whales to viruses, and from oaks to algae") plus the earth's atmosphere, oceans, and soil can be viewed as "a single living entity, capable of manipulating the Earth's atmosphere to suit its overall needs and endowed with faculties and powers far beyond those of its constituent parts."[24] Lovelock named this complex, self-adjusting entity *Gaia*, after the Greek name for the Earth Goddess. His *Gaia hypothesis* was initially scorned by scientists but is now receiving some consideration as a useful model.

"New Age" planetary consciousness

A corollary to the Gaia hypothesis is the concept that humans are becoming the global brain of the planet, its mode of conscious evolution. In the "body" of Gaia, the tropical rainforests function as the liver and/or lungs, the oceans as the circulatory system, and so on. As the evolving brain of the planet, we are becoming conscious of the dangers our activities pose to these other parts of "our body." Peter Russell, author of *The Global Brain*, warns that we have little time to become fully conscious of our potential destructiveness, our connectedness to everything else, and to take appropriate action to forestall environmental disaster:

> As a species we are facing our final examination; . . . it is in fact an intelligence test – a test of our true intelligence as a species. In essence we are being asked to let go of our self-centred thinking and egocentric behaviour. We are being asked to become psychologically mature, to free ourselves from the clutches of this limited identity, and express our creativity in ways which benefit us all. [25]

Russell acknowledges that "the wisdom of the human psyche" is already embodied in many of our religions, philosophies, and psychologies. But he feels that this understanding of our sacred oneness must be re-interpreted in contemporary language and scientific terms if it is to be grasped by enough people to make a difference.

How many people does it take to shift the consciousness of the earth? Many believers in planetary consciousness now think in terms of the *Hundredth Monkey Effect*. That is, they believe that there is some mechanism by which the consciousnesses of all members of our species are interlinked, and if enough of us change our way of thinking, the rest of us will spontaneously change as well. The "Harmonic Convergence", August 16 and 17, 1987, seemingly predicted by the Mayan calendars as a time of major transition in the consciousness of humanity toward less anthropocentric thinking, drew hundreds of thousands of people to gatherings and sacred power spots around the earth. They were attempting to raise their own awareness above self-centeredness to planetary and even cosmic consciousness, in the hope that this mental/spiritual energy would have an impact on the whole globe. Each December 31 since then, there has been another such global attempt at simultaneous meditation for the peaceful transformation of the world. Other groups join each month on the full moon for simultaneous meditation around the planet. One of these links people in the United States and the Soviet Union.

In addition to group meditations, what has been called the "New Age" spirituality often blossoms in individual mystical experiences of union with the cosmos. Some people find that if they commune non-verbally in a friendly spirit of oneness, they transcend the cultural boundaries between humanity and the rest of nature. It seems that those who have such experiences have often prepared themselves by spiritual disciplines, such as meditation practices, but the mystical experience itself comes spontaneously. Dorothy Maclean studied with Sufi masters, learning how to receive "inner guidance," before joining with Eileen and Peter Caddy in developing *Findhorn* – a transformation of desolate dunes on the coast of Scotland into an extraordinarily lush farming community. Dorothy's role was to receive communications from the energies that she called the plant "devas," after the Hindu term for the invisible "shining ones." Dorothy developed a cooperative relationship with the devas, asking for their "advice" on matters such as what nutrients the plants needed.

Those who have opened to the oneness of all life are often inspired to take political action to protect other members of the earth's body. Many support "Green" political agendas on behalf of the environment. In Oregon, people have chained themselves to giant trees to try to keep loggers from cutting them down. In 1974, the women and

The Findhorn Community in Scotland draws people from all around the world to share in its spiritual ways of listening to and cooperating with nature.

children of Reni, a Himalayan village, wrapped themselves around trees to protect them from woodcutters seeking wood for the cities. They knew that the trees' roots were like hands that kept the hillside from washing away, that they provided shade for the plants they used for medicine and homes for the animals and birds. They said, "The trees are our brothers and sisters."[26] Although some view such actions as romantically naive and hopeless, the "Tree Hugging" movement grew to such proportions in northern India that the government stopped commercial wood-cutting in Uttar Pradesh, a heavily populated state.

Universalist religions

At the same time that an amorphous new religious movement toward "Green" spirituality is bringing humans into connection with all beings, there are efforts being made to harmonize the world's religions. To cite some examples, the Theosophical Society encourages study of all religions and maintains a large interfaith library in Illinois. Its holdings are made available to all who are interested in world religions, not just to Theosophists. Many Protestant ministers are trained at interfaith theological seminars. A number of temples are being built to honor all religions, such as the Light of Truth Universal Shrine at the Satchidananda Ashram in Virginia. In addition, several groups have religious unity as their major focus.

Universal Worship

The Sufi Order of the West trains ministers who offer Universal Worship services, at which the scriptures of all the major religions (including indigenous ways and worship of the "Divine Feminine Principle") are placed side-by-side on an altar. Candles are lit for each tradition from one light, representing what is believed to be the common source of all religions, all life. Participants share scriptural readings, songs, stories, and meditations from all the religions on a particular theme, such as the idea of spiritual sacrifice. Murshid Hazrat Inayat Khan, who initiated the Universal Worship early in the twentieth century, explained:

> *Instead of giving a new form of worship, it collects all forms in one, so that no one may say, "My form of worship is left out." It gives examples so that the followers of all religions may worship at the same time. It also brings all teachers known and unknown to the world as different beads in the same rosary. Imagine this idea spreading and penetrating through those separated because of differences of faith! . . . This is the fulfillment of the prayer of Moses, the aspiration of Jesus Christ, the desire of Muhammad, the dream of Abraham. They all desired that one day there would come a time when humanity would no longer be divided into different sections.* [27]

Baha'i

One new religion has been developed that attempts to unite all of humanity in the belief that there is only one God, the foundation of all religions. This is *Baha'i*. It was foreshadowed in Persia in 1844 when a young man named the Bab announced that a new messenger of God to all the peoples of the world would soon appear. Because he proclaimed this message in a Muslim state, where Muhammad was considered the Seal of the Prophets, he was arrested and executed. Some twenty-two thousand of his followers were reportedly massacred as well. One of his imprisoned followers was Baha'u'llah, a member of an aristocratic Persian family. He was stripped of his worldly goods, tortured, and banished to Baghdad. From prison, he revealed himself as the messenger proclaimed by the Bab. He wrote letters to the rulers of all nations, asserting that humanity was becoming unified and that a single global civilization was emerging.

This message gradually spread, until today it has four million followers in most of the world's races, cultures, and geographic regions. They were formerly members of all the different religions, or none at all. They have no priesthood but they do have their own sacred scriptures, revealed to Baha'u'llah. He did not declare himself to be the ultimate messenger. Rather, he prophesied that another would follow in a thousand years. Baha'u'llah taught that all religions are culturally shaped and therefore relative to the times and societies in which they develop. They are one in essence: universal love.

Baha'i Houses of Worship are open to all, with nine doors and a central dome symbolizing the simultaneous diversity and oneness of humanity. Devotional services include readings from the scriptures of all religions, meditations, unaccompanied singing, and prayers by the Bab, Baha'u'llah, and his successor 'Abdu'l-Baha, his oldest son. A prayer of 'Abdu'l-Baha ends with this plea: "O Thou kind Lord! unite all, let the religions agree, make the nations one so that they may be as one kind and as children of the same fatherland." [28]

The World Center of Baha'i is in Israel. This fact does not endear Baha'is to Arabs. Baha'is in Iran have been subjected to persecution since the 1979 Revolution, and 170 were reportedly killed in the first five years after the revolution. Baha'is' attempts to unite the earth in faith do extend into the political sphere, where they actively support the United Nations' efforts to unify the planet. Their goal is the building of a unified, peaceful global society. To this end, they work for these principles:

1 The end of prejudice in all forms.
2 Equality for women.
3 Acceptance of the relativity and unity of spiritual truth.
4 Just distribution of wealth.
5 Universal education.
6 The individual responsibility to seek truth.
7 Development of a world federation.
8 Harmony of science and true religion.[29]

Baha'is' efforts are partly devotional and partly worldly, such as the sponsorship of a radio station in Ecuador. Its programs range from information about vaccination of livestock to revitalization of traditional Quechua music.

> *If the religions are true it is because each time it is God who has spoken, and if they are different it is because God has spoken in different ''languages'' in conformity with the diversity of the receptacles. Finally, if they are absolute and exclusive, it is because in each of them God has said ''I.''*
>
> *Frithjof Schuon*[30]

Interfaith dialogue

The most exciting trend today for a student of all religions is the rapid acceleration of *interfaith dialogue* – the willingness of people of all religions to meet, explore their differences, and appreciate and find enrichment in each other's ways to the divine. This approach has been historically difficult, for many religions have made exclusive claims to being the best or only way, out of zealous belief and in order to gain a following. However, many people of broad vision have noted that many of the same principles reappear in all traditions. Every religion teaches the importance of setting one's own selfish interests aside, loving others, and harkening to the divine.

Diana Eck, Professor of Comparative Religion and Indian Studies of Harvard Divinity School and Chair of the World Council of Churches committee on interfaith dialogue, observed at a 1988 interfaith conference in Wichita, Kansas, that there are three responses to contact between religions. One is *exclusivism*: "Ours is the only true way." In Christianity, for instance, a few lines in the New Testament have been interpreted thus. There are passages such as John 14:6: "I am the way, the truth, and the life; no one comes to the Father but by me." But some Christian scholars now feel that it is inappropriate to take this line out of its context (in which Jesus's disciples were asking how to find their way to him after they died) and to interpret it to mean that the ways of Hindus, Buddhists, and Subuds are invalid. Relationships with other faiths was not the question being answered. Nevertheless, Eck feels that the first essential step in interfaith dialogue is faith, deep personal commitment to one's own faith.

Eck sees the second response to interfaith contact as *inclusivism*. This may take the form of trying to create a single world religion, such as Baha'i. Or it may appear as the belief that our religion is spacious enough to encompass all the others, that it supersedes all previous religions, as Islam said it was the culmination of all monotheistic traditions. In this approach, the inclusivists do not see other ways as a threat. They feel that all diversity is included in a single world view – their own. All other religions are interpreted in their terms; they do not really listen to them.

The third way Eck discerns is *pluralism* – to hold one's own faith and at the same time ask people of other faiths about their path, about how they want to be understood. As Eck sees it, this is the only point from which true dialogue can take place. And it is a place from which true cooperation, true relationship can happen. Uniformity and agreement are not the goals – the goal is to collaborate, to combine our differing strengths for the common good. For effective pluralistic dialogue, people must have an openness to the possibility of discovering sacred truth in other religions. This is the premise on which this book has been written.

Raimundo Panikkar, a Catholic/Hindu/Buddhist doctor of science, philosophy, and theology, has written extensively on this subject. He concludes:

> We realize that, by my pushing in one direction and your pushing in the opposite, world order is maintained and given the impulse of its proper dynamism . . . One animus *does not mean one single theory, one single opinion, but one aspiration (in the literal sense of one breath) and one inspiration (as one spirit). Consensus ultimately means to walk in the same direction, not to have just one rational view . . . To reach agreement suggests to be agreeable, to be pleasant, to find pleasure in being together. Concord is to put our hearts together.* [31]

People of all faiths have begun to put their hearts together. Initially, ecumenical conferences involved pairs of related religions who were trying to agree to disagree, such as Judaism and Christianity. Now interfaith meetings draw people from all religions in a spirit of mutual appreciation. Some are intimate gatherings, such as the yearly get-togethers of the *Snowmass Group* – a standing group of twelve men and women whose lives are deeply imbued with their own traditions: Episcopalian, Quaker, Roman Catholic, Dutch Reformed Calvinist, Orthodox Christian, Native American, Tibetan Buddhist, Zen Buddhist, Vedanta, Hasidic Jewish, Islamic Sufi, and non-aligned spirituality. They live together for a week, meeting twice a day for an hour of silent meditation and, if they wish, participating in the liturgy of the spiritual community where they are staying. Their conversations are never taped, at the request of Grandfather Red Elk; they are "like a birdsong in the heart."[32] Once or twice during the week they open their dialogue to the public.

Some interfaith dialogues are open only to those at the highest levels. In 1986 Pope John Paul II invited 160 representatives of all religions to Assisi in honor of the humble St. Francis, to pray together for world peace. "If the world is going to continue, and men and women are to survive in it, it cannot do without prayer. This is the permanent lesson of Assisi," declared the pope.[33]

Two years later, the Assisi idea was extended to include governmental leaders, scientists, artists, business leaders, and media specialists as well as spiritual leaders. Some two hundred of them from around the globe met in Oxford, England, in 1988 at the Global Forum of Spiritual and Parliamentary Leaders on Human Survival. They held their plenary sessions beneath an enormous banner with the image of the earth as seen from space. Statements of concern for the environment brought participants to the conclusion that the ecological dangers now threatening the entire human race may be the key that draws us together. But it was spiritual camaraderie rather than shared fear

Scientist Carl Sagan announces a new pact of cooperation between scientists and spiritual leaders at the Global Forum of Spiritual and Parliamentary Leaders on Human Survival, held in Moscow, January 1990.

that brought the participants together. Dr. Wangari Maathai, leader of the Green Belt movement in Kenya, observed:

> *All religions meditate on the Source. And yet, strangely, religion is one of our greatest divides. If the Source be the same, as indeed it must be, all of us and all religions meditate on the same Source.* [34]

Yearly International Human Unity conferences have been convened for the general public by various spiritual groups. The first was held in India in 1974, sponsored by Sant Kirpal Singh. Over one hundred thousand people gathered to explore and honor spiritual ways to peace, unity, and service. Since then, similar conferences have been held in Brazil, Mexico, Canada, Great Britain, and the United States.

In January, 1990, an astonishing assembly of spiritual leaders of all faiths with scientists and parliamentarians took place in what, until a few years before, would have been the most unlikely place in the world for such a gathering – Moscow, capital of the previously officially atheistic Soviet Union. The final speaker was Mikhail Gorbachev, who called for a merging of scientific and spiritual values in the effort to save the planet.

As the Dalai Lama stated in Costa Rica in 1989 at an international interfaith gathering entitled "Seeking the True Meaning of Peace,"

> *How can we eliminate religious prejudice when each religion wants to dominate? We need to see others as people like ourselves – not as opponents or aliens. We need constant communication, meeting, dialogue for deeper understanding of each other's religion. Then you can develop genuine respect, genuine harmony. And from that, genuine brotherhood will develop.* [35]

Gordon Kaufman, Harvard professor and Mennonite Christian minister, sees interfaith dialogue as crucial in solving the problems of the planet:

> *The problems with which modernity confronts us – extending even to the possibility that we may obliterate mankind completely in a nuclear holocaust – demand that we bring together all the wisdom, devotion, and insight that humanity has accumulated in its long history ... We simply cannot afford not to enter into conversation with representatives of other traditions, making available to each other whatever resources each of our traditions has to offer, and learning from each other whatever we can.* [36]

To make a difference in the world, interfaith dialogue must not be just armchair scholarship. In some places, it is being applied directly to difficult real-life situations, such as the fighting between Protestants and Catholics in Northern Ireland and between Muslims and Christians in parts of Africa. In Mayfair, a neighborhood of Washington, D.C., people lived in fear of drug dealers armed with semi-automatic weapons. A group of African American Muslims went into the area and chased out the drug dealers, making Mayfair a safe place to live. Then, rather than consolidating their own power, they invited African American Baptist ministers to come in and help teach the people of Mayfair about the spiritual life.

True interfaith dialogue is a grassroots phenomenon. It is most immediately fruitful when it takes place between individuals rather than between representatives of large official groups. Religions have institutionalized their differences, but people of different faiths can meet face-to-face and recognize their common humanity, and together celebrate, honor, and serve their common source.

Suggested reading

Beckford, James A., ed, *New Religious Movements and Rapid Social Change,* Paris; UNESCO and London: Sage Publications, 1986. Descriptions and sociological analyses of many new religious movements, from the Unification Church to sects in Nigeria, the Caribbean, and Sri Lanka.

Blavatsky, H.P., *The Key to Theosophy*, Los Angeles: The United Lodge of Theosophists, 1920. A wide-ranging survey of esoterica from many of the world's religions.

Eddy, Mary Baker, *Science and Health with Key to the Scriptures*, Boston: Trustees under the Will of Mary Baker G. Eddy, 1875. A prime example of New Thought beliefs in the spiritual power of the mind.

Ellwood, Robert S., Jnr., *Religious and Spiritual Groups in Modern America*, Englewood Cliffs, New Jersey: Prentice-Hall, 1973. Somewhat dated but still useful source of information and appreciation of new religions that have flourished in the United States.

Gaver, Jessyca Russell, *The Baha'i Faith: Dawn of a New Day*, New York: Hawthorn Books, Inc., 1967. The history and beliefs of Baha'is, in appreciative detail.

Ikeda, Daisaku, *A Lasting Peace*, vol. 2, New York and Tokyo: John Weatherhill, 1987. Addresses by the head of Soka Gakkai on the major issues of our times, including the nuclear threat, environmental destruction, and east-west north-south polarization, in the context of the solutions that could arise through universal spiritual renewal.

Khan, Hazrat Inayat, *The Unity of Religious Ideals*, New Lebanon, New York: Sufi Order Publications, 1927, 1979. A master of Sufi mysticism explores the underlying themes in the religious quest which are common to all religions.

Seed, John, Macy, Joanna, Fleming, Pat, Naess, Arne, *Thinking Like a Mountain: Towards a Council of All Beings*, Philadelphia: New Society Publishers, 1988. Some of the leaders of the deep ecology movement offer a collection of thoughts and exercises leading one into the experience of kinship with all life.

Starhawk, *The Spiral Dance: A Rebirth of the Ancient Religion of the Great Goddess,* San Francisco and London: Harper and Row, 1979. A lyrical, experimental introduction to the interweaving of the God and Goddess principles.

Swidler, Leonard, ed., *Toward a Universal Theology of Religion* Maryknoll, New York: Orbis Books, 1988. Leaders in the evolving interfaith dialogue grapple with the issues of transcending differences.

NOTES

CHAPTER 1: THE RELIGIOUS RESPONSE

1 Karl Marx, from "Contribution to the Critique of Hegel's Philosophy of Right," 1884, *Karl Marx, Early Writings*, translated and edited by T. B. Bottomore, London: C. A. Watts and Co., 1963, pp. 43–44; *Capital*, vol. 1, 1867, translated by Samuel Moore and Edward Aveling, ed. F. Engels, London: Lawrence and Wishart, 1961, p. 79; "The Communism of the Paper 'Rheinischer Beobachter'," *On Religion*, London: Lawrence and Wishart, undated, pp. 83–84.
2 Jiddu Krishnamurti, *The Awakening of Intelligence*, New York: Harper and Row, 1973, p. 90.
3 Buddha, *The Dhammapada*, translated by P. Lal, 162/92 Lake Gardens, Calcutta, 700045 India. (Originally published by Farrar, Straus and Giroux, 1967, p. 97). Reprinted by permission of P. Lal.
4 Mahatma Gandhi, quoted in Eknath Easwaran, *Gandhi the Man*, Petaluma, California: Nilgiri Press, 1978, p. 121.
5 *The Bhagavad Gita*, portions of Chapter 2, translated by Eknath Easwaran, quoted in Easwaran, *ibid.*, p. 121–122.
6 "Tilang Nam Dev Jee," AK 126, SGGS 727.
7 William James, *The Varieties of Religious Experience*, New York: New American Library, 1958, p. 49.
8 Philippians 4: 7, *The Holy Bible*, King James Version.
9 From *The Kabir Book* by Robert Bly, copyright 1971, 1977 by Robert Bly, copyright 1977 by Seventies Press. Reprinted by permission of Beacon Press.
10 William Wordsworth, "Ode on Intimations of Immortality".
11 St. Francis of Assisi, "Canticle to all Creation," quoted in Rosemary Ruether, *Women-Church: Theology and Practice of Feminist Liturgical Communities*, San Francisco: Harper and Row, 1985, p. 271.
12 Pierre Teilhard de Chardin, *The Heart of Matter*, translated by Rene Hague, New York and London: Harcourt Brace Jovanovich, 1978, pp. 66–67.
13 AE (George William Russell), *The Candle of Vision*, Wheaton, Illinois: The Theosophical Publishing House, 1974, pp. 8–9.
14 William James, op. cit., p. 298.
15 Rudolf Otto, *The Idea of the Holy*, second edition, translated by John W. Harvey, London: Oxford University Press, 1950, pp. 12–13.
16 John White, "An Interview with Nona Coxhead: The Science of Mysticism — Transcendental Bliss in Everyday Life," *Science of Mind*, September 1986, pp. 14, 70.
17 Lucien Cuenot, *Invention et finalite en biologie*, Translated by Robert Augros and George Stanciu, Paris: Flammarion, 1941, pp. 240–241.
18 Robert Augros and George Stanciu, *The New Biology*, Boston: Shambhala, New Science Library, 1987,

pp. 209, 213.
19 Quoted in John Gliedman, "Mind and Matter," *Science Digest*, March 1983, p. 72.
20 Albert Einstein, *The World as I See It*, New York: Wisdom Library, 1979; *Ideas and Opinions*, translated by Sonja Bargmann, New York: Crown Publishers, 1954.
21 Bede Griffiths, *Return to the Center*, Springfield, Illinois: Templegate, 1977, p. 71.
22 Pir Vilayat Inayat Khan, "The Significance of Religion to Human Issues in the Light of the Universal Norms of Mystical Experience." *The World Religions Speak on the Relevance of Religion in the Modern World*, ed. Finley P. Ounne, Jr., The Hague: Junk, 1970, p. 145.
23 Joseph Campbell, *The Hero with a Thousand Faces*, second edition, Princeton, New Jersey: Princeton University Press, 1972, p. 29.
24 Quoted in Merlin Stone, *When God was a Woman*, San Diego, California: Harcourt Brace Jovanovich, 1976, p. x.
25 Rosemary Radford Ruether, *Women-Church: Theology and Practice of Feminist Liturgical Communities*, San Francisco: Harper and Row, 1985, p. 3.
26 Jonathan Edwards, sermon in Enfield, Connecticut, July 8, 1741. Reproduced in Charles Hurd, *A Treasury of Great American Speeches*, New York: Hawthorn Books, 1959, pp. 19–20.
27 John Welwood, "Principles of Inner Work: Psychological and Spiritual," *The Journal of Transpersonal Psychology*, 1984, vol. 16, no. 1, pp. 64–65.

CHAPTER 2: INDIGENOUS SACRED WAYS

1 Vine Deloria, Jr., *God is Red*, New York: Grosset and Dunlap, 1973, p. 267.
2 Lorraine Mafi Williams, personal communication, September 16, 1988.
3 Quoted by Bob Masla, "The Healing Art of the Huichol Indians," *Many Hands: Resources for Personal and Social Transformation*, Fall 1988, p. 30.
4 Dhyani Ywahoo, personal communication, May 31, 1988.
5 Ibid.
6 Williams, op. cit.
7 John (Fire) Lame Deer and Richard Erdoes, *Lame Deer — Seeker of Visions*, New York: Pocket Books, 1972, p. 100.
8 Black Elk, recorded by Joseph Epes Brown, *The Sacred Pipe*, Harmondsworth, England: Penguin Books, 1971. p. xx.
9 Knud Rasmussen, *Across Arctic America*, New York: G. P. Putnam and Sons, 1927, p. 386.
10 John Redtail Freesoul, *Breath of the Invisible: The Way of the Pipe*, Wheaton, Illinois: Theosophical Publishing House, 1986, p. 50.
11 Jo Agguisho/Oren R. Lyons, spokesman for the

Traditional Elders Circle, Wolf Clan, Onondaga Nation, Haudenosaunee, Six Nations Iroquois Confederacy, from the speech to the Fourth World Wilderness Conference, September 11, 1987, p. 2.

12 Quoted by Oren Lyons, ibid., p. 9.

13 Jaime de Angulo, "Indians in Overalls," *Hudson Review*, II, 1950, p. 372.

14 Kahu Kawai, interviewed by Mark Bochrach in *The Source*, as quoted in *Hinduism Today*, Dec. 1988, p. 18.

15 Quoted in Matthew Fox, "Native teachings: Spirituality with power," *Creation*, January/February 1987 vol. 2, no. 6.

16 *Macrofax* March/April 1989, as quoted in *Hinduism Today*, May 1989, p. 20.

17 Lame Deer with Richard Erdoes, op. cit., p. 116.

18 Tlakaelel, talk at Interface, Watertown, Massachusetts, April 15, 1988.

19 Ibid.

20 Leonard Crow Dog and Richard Erdoes, *The Eye of the Heart*, unpublished manuscript, quoted by Joan Halifax, *Shamanic Voices: A Survey of Visionary Narratives*, New York: E. P. Dutton, 1979, p. 77.

21 Quoted in John Neihardt, *Black Elk Speaks*, op. cit., pp. 208–209.

22 Mado (Patrice) Somé, interviewed Sept. 14, 1989.

23 Lame Deer with Richard Erdoes, op. cit., pp. 145–46.

24 Uvavnuk, in Knud Rasmussen, *Across Arctic America*, report of the Fifth Thule Expedition 1921–1924, trans. W. E. Calvert, ed. from *Fra Groland till Stillehavet*, Copenhagen, 1925, reprint New York: Greenwood Press, 1969, p. 34.

25 Igjugarjuk, in Knud Rasmussen, *Intellectual Culture of the Hudson Bay Eskimos*, report of the Fifth Thule Expedition, 1921–1924, trans. W. E. Calvert, vol. 7, Copenhagen: Gylendal, 1930, p. 52.

26 Ruth M. Underhill, *Papago Woman*, New York: Holt, Rinehart and Winston, 1979, p. 9.

27 Dhyani Ywahoo, personal communication May 31, 1988.

28 Dhyani Ywahoo, *Voices of Our Ancestors*, Boston: Shambhala Publications, 1987, p. 89.

29 Leonard Crow Dog and Richard Erdoes, in Joan Halifax, *Shamanic Voices*, op. cit., p. 77.

30 Quoted by Black Elk in Joseph Epes Brown, *The Sacred Pipe*, op. cit., p. 71.

31 Tlakaelel, op. cit.

32 Brooke Medicine Eagle, quoted in Joan Halifax, *Shamanic Voices*, op. cit., p. 89.

33 Excerpted from Traditional Circle of Indian Elders and Youth, *Communique No. 12*, Haida Gwaii, Queen Charlotte Islands, June 14, 1989, pp. 5–6.

CHAPTER 3: HINDUISM

1 English transliteration of the Sanskrit ṣ as "s" or "sh" varies widely and is by no means consistent. In accordance with the inconsistencies long found, this chapter follows existing usage and does not try to standardize it, to conform with popular though inconsistent English usage.

2 Sukta-yajur-veda XXVI, 3, as explained by Sai Baba in *Vision of the Divine* by Eruch B. Fanibunda, Bombay: E. B. Fanibunda, 1976.

3 Sukta III (LXIV), Anuvaka VI, Mandala VI, First Adhyaya, Fifth Ashtaka. *Rig-Veda Sanhita*, translated by H. H. Wilson, London: N. Trubner and Company, 1866. vol. 4, pp. 6–7.

4 Excerpted from Sri Aurobindo, *The Immortal Fire*, Auroville, India: Auropublications, 1974, pp. 3–4.

5 Rig Veda, 10.90.

6 *The Upanishads*, translated by Swami Prabhavananda and Frederick Manchester, The Vedanta Society of Southern California, New York: Mentor Books, 1957.

7 Ibid., p. 46.

8 Mundaka Upanishad, ibid., p.51.

9 Ibid., p. 59.

10 Taittiriya Upanishad, ibid., p. 68.

11 Brihadaranyaka Upanishad, ibid., p. 109.

12 Brihadaranyaka Upanishad, ibid., p. 109.

13 T. M. P. Mahadevan, *Outlines of Hinduism*, second edition, Bombay: Chetana Ltd., 1960, p. 24.

14 A condensation by Heinrich Zimmer of the Vishnu Purana, Book IV, Chapter 24, translated by H. H. Wilson, London, 1840, in Zimmer's *Myths and Symbols in Indian Art and Civilization*, New York: Pantheon Books, 1946, p. 15.

15 From the Ramayana, as quoted in P. Thomas, *Epics, Myths and Legends of India*, Bombay: D. B. Taraporevala Sons and Co., 1961, p. 30.

16 Uttara Kandam, *Ramayana*, third edition, as told by Swami Chidbhavananda, Tiriuuparaitturai, India: Tapovanam Printing School, 1978, pp. 198–199.

17 Chapter III:30, p. 57. All quotes from the *Bhagavad-Gita* are from *Bhagavad-Gita as It Is*, translated by A. C. Bhaktivedanta Swami Prabhupada, New York: Copyright 1972, The Bhaktivedanta Book Trust. Reproduced with permission of The Bhaktivedanta Book Trust International.

18 Ibid III:30, p. 57.

19 Ibid., IV: 3, p. 64.

20 Ibid., IV: 7–8, pp. 68–69.

21 Ibid., VII: 7–8, 12, pp. 126, 128.

22 Ibid., IX: 26, p. 157.

23 Ibid., X:10, p. 167.

24 *Srimad-Bhagavatam*, second canto, "The Cosmic Manifestation," part one, chapter 6:3 and 1:39, translated by A. C. Bhaktivedanta Swami Prabhupada, New York: Bhaktivedanta Book Trust, 1972, pp. 275–276 and 59.

25 Commentary by Swami Prabhupada, ibid., p. 79.

26 *Thus Spake Sri Ramakrishna*, fifth edition, Madras: Sri Ramakrishna Math, 1980, p. 54.

27 Swami Prajnananda, introduction to *Light on the Path*, Swami Muktananda, South Fallsburg, New York: SYDA Foundation, 1981, p. x.

28 Swami Satchidananda, ed. Philip Mandelkorn, *To Know Your Self*, Garden City, New York: Anchor Press/Doubleday, 1978, p. 42.

29 Swami Sivananda, *Dhyana Yoga*, fourth edition, Shivanandanagar, India: The Divine Life Society, 1981, p. 67.

30 Ramana Maharshi, *The Spiritual Teaching of Ramana Maharshi*, Boston: Shambhala, 1972, pp. 4, 6.

31 Swami Vivekananda, *Karma-Yoga and Bhakti-Yoga*, New York: Ramakrishna-Vivekananda Center, 1982, p. 32.

32 *Bhagavad-Gita as It Is*, op. cit., Chapter 2:49 (p. 36), Chapter 5:8, 12.

33 Ramakrishna, quoted in Carl Jung's introduction to *The Spiritual Teaching of Ramana Maharshi*, op. cit., p. viii.

34 Swami Sivasiva Palani, personal communication,

Oct. 26, 1989.

35 Gerard Blitz, April 2, 1988, talk at Satchidananda Ashram, Yogaville, Virginia.

36 Swami Palani, op. cit.

37 Robert N. Minor, "Sarvepalli Radhakrishnan and 'Hinduism': Defined and Defended," in Robert D. Baird, ed., *Religion in Modern India*, New Delhi: Manohar Publications, 1981, p. 306.

38 *Condensed Gospel of Sri Ramkrishna*, Mylapore, Madras: Sri Ramkrishna Math, 1911, p. 252.

39 Ramakrishna, as quoted in Swami Vivekananda, *Ramakrishna and His Message*, Howra, India: Swami Abhayananda, Sri Ramakrishna Math, 1971, p. 25.

40 Paraphrased from brochure from Vedanta Centre, Ananda Ashram, Cohasset, Massachusetts.

CHAPTER 4: JAINISM

1 Acaranga Sutra, tranlated by Padmanabh S. Jaini in *The Jaina Path of Purification*, Berkeley: University of California Press, 1979, p. 26.

2 Akaranga Sutra, Fourth Lecture, First Lesson, in *Sacred Books of the East*, ed. F. Max Muller, vol. XXII, Gaina Sutras part 1, Oxford: Clarendon Press, 1884, p. 36.

3 Address to the North American Assissi Interfaith Meeting in Wichita, Kansas, October 31, 1988.

4 Gurudev Shree Chitrabhanu, *Twelve Facets of Reality: The Jain Path to Freedom*, New York: Dodd Mead and Company, 1980, p. 93.

5 Padma Agrawal, "Jainism: Mahavira as Man-God," *Dialogue and Alliance*, p. 13.

6 Ibid., p. 11.

7 Acharya Shri Sushil Kumar, personal communication, October 30, 1989.

CHAPTER 5: BUDDHISM

1 Muhaparinibbana Sutta, Digha Nikaya, 2.99f, 155–56, quoted in *Sources of Indian Tradition*, ed. William Theodore de Bary, New York: Columbia University Press, 1958, pp. 110–11.

2 Ibid.

3 Majjhima-Nikaya, "The Lesser Matunkyaputta Sermon," Sutta 63, translated by P. Lal in the introduction to *The Dhammapada*, op. cit., p. 19.

4 Ven. Ajahn Sumedho, "Now is the Knowing," undated booklet, pp. 21–22.

5 Sigalovada Sutta, Dighanikaya III, pp. 180–193, quoted in H. Saddhatissa, *The Buddha's Way*, New York: George Braziller, 1971, p. 101.

6 *The Dhammapada*, translated by P. Lal, op. cit., p. 152.

7 Ibid., p. 49.

8 Achaan Chah, *A Still Forest Pool*, eds. Jack Kornfield and Paul Breiter, Wheaton, Illinois: Theosophical Publishing House, 1985.

9 *The Dhammapada*, translated by P. Lal, op. cit., pp. 71–72.

10 Samyutta Nikaya, quoted in the introduction to *The Dhammapada*, translated by P. Lal, op. cit., p. 17.

11 Vinaya-pitaka I., 20–21, quoted in *Buddhist Texts Through the Ages*, ed. Edward Conze, New York: Philosophical Library,

1954, p. 33.

12 "Khandhaparitta, The Group Protection," from *Pali Chanting with Translations*, Bangkok, Thailand: Mahamakut Rajavidyalaya Press, pp. 18–19.

13 Sikshasamuccaya, 280–81 (Vajradhvaja Sutra), in Edward Conze, ed., *Buddhist Texts*, op. cit., pp. 131–32.

14 Pancavimsatisahasrika, 263–64, ibid., p.137.

15 *Lalitavistara*, 13: 175. Quoted in ed. Wm. Theodore de Bary, *Sources of Indian Tradition*, vol 1, New York: Columbia University Press, 1958, p. 173.

16 *Dharmasangiti Sutra, Siksamuccaya*, p. 264. Quoted in de Bary, op. cit., p. 175.

17 Zen Master Seung Sahn, remarks in Moscow, USSR, The Global Forum of Spiritual and Parliamentary Leaders, Jan. 18, 1990.

18 *Stories and Songs from the Oral Tradition of Jetsun Milarepa*, translated by Lama Kunga Rimpoche and Brian Cutillo in *Drinking the Mountain Stream*, New York: Lotsawa, 1978, pp. 56–57.

19 Platform Scripture of the Sixth Patriarch, Hui-neng, quoted in *World of the Buddha*, ed. Lucien Stryk, New York: Doubleday Anchor Books, 1969, p. 340.

20 From "Hsin hsin ming" by Sengtsan, third Zen patriarch, translated by Richard B. Clarke.

21 Roshi Philip Kapleau, *The Three Pillars of Zen*, New York: Anchor Books, 1980, p. 70.

22 Bunan, quoted in *World of the Buddha*, Stryk, op. cit., p. 343.

23 Zen Master Seung Sahn, personal communication, Jan. 18, 1990.

24 Genshin, *The Essentials of Salvation*, quoted in ed. William de Bary, *The Buddhist Tradition in India, China, and Japan*, New York: Modern Library, 1969, p. 326.

25 Taitetsu Unno, personal communication, March 28, 1988.

26 The Most Venerable Nichidatsu Fujii, quoted in a booklet commemorating the dedication for the Peace Pagoda in Leverett, Massachusetts, October 5, 1985.

27 Richard B. Clarke, personal communication, Oct. 2, 1981.

CHAPTER 6: TAOISM AND CONFUCIANISM

1 *The I Ching*, translated by Richard Wilhelm (German)/ Cary F. Baynes (English), Princeton, New Jersey: Princeton University Press, 1967, pp. 620–621.

2 Excerpt from verse 1 in *Tao Te Ching*, translated by Stephen Mitchell. Translation copyright 1988 by Stephen Mitchell. Reprinted by permission of Harper and Row, Publishers, Inc.

3 *Tao-te Ching*, translated by Lin Yutang, New York: Modern Library, 1948, verse 1, p. 41.

4 Ibid., Chapter 25, p. 145.

5 *Tao-te Ching*, translated by Stephen Mitchell, op. cit., verse 14.

6 Chang Chung-yuan, *Creativity and Taoism*, New York: Harper Colophon, 1963, p. 5.

7 *Chuang-tzu, Inner Chapters*, translated by Gia-fu Feng and Jane English, New York: Vintage Books, 1974, p. 29.

8 Ibid., p. 40.

9 *The Way to Life: At the Heart of the Tao-te Ching*, non-literal translation by Benjamin Hoff, New York/Tokyo: Weatherhill,

1981, p. 52, chapter 78.
10 *Tao-te Ching*, translated by Stephen Mitchell, op. cit., chapter 15.
11 Chuang-tzu, op. cit., p. 150.
12 *Tao-te Ching*, chapters 19 and 20, as translated by Chang Chung-yuan, *Creativity and Taoism*, op. cit., pp. 39–40.
13 *The Way of Life*, translated by Benjamin Hoff, op. cit., p. 33, chapter 35.
14 *Tao-te Ching*, translated by Stephen Mitchell, op. cit., Chapter 15.
15 *The Secret of the Golden Flower*, translated by Richard Wilhelm/Cary Baynes, New York: Harcourt Brace Jovanovich, 1962, p. 21.
16 Chuang-tzu, op. cit., p. 59.
17 Excerpted from Huai-Chin Nan, translated by Wen Kuan Chu, *Tao and Longevity: Mind-Body Transformation*, York Beach, Maine: Samuel Weiser, 1984, pp. 4–5.
18 Quoted in *T'ai-chi*, Cheng Man-ch'ing and Robert W. Smith, Rutland, Vermont: Charles E. Tuttle, 1967, p. 106.
19 Ibid., p. 109.
20 Excerpted from Al Chung-liang Huang, *Embrace Tiger, Return to Mountain*, Moab, Utah: Real People Press, 1973, pp. 12, 185.
21 Quoted by Da Liu, *The Tao and Chinese Culture*, London: Routledge and Kegan Paul, 1981, p. 161.
22 *The Analects*, VII: 1, in *Sources of Chinese Tradition*, vol. 1, eds. William Theodore de Bary, Wing-tsit Chan, Burton Watson, p. 23.
23 Ibid. XV: 23, p. 25.
24 Ibid. XIII: 6, p. 32, and Analects II: 1, as translated by Ch'u Chai and Winberg Chai in *Confucianism*, Woodbury, New York: Barron's Educational Series, 1973, p. 52.
25 Analects I: 6, translated by Chai and Chai, op. cit., p. 35.
26 The Analects XII: 11, in De Bary et al., op. cit., p. 33.
27 *Chung Yung* (The Doctrine of the Mean), translated by Ch'u Chai and Winberg Chai, *The Sacred Books of Confucius and Other Confucian Classics*, New Hyde Park, New York: University Books, 1965, pp. 11–12.
28 The Analects, XI–11, in Chai and Chai, ibid., p. 46.
29 The Mencius, in De Bary, op. cit., p. 91.
30 Ibid., p. 89.
31 From the Hsun Tzu, Chapter 17, in De Bary, op. cit., p. 101.
32 A prayer offered by the Ming dynasty emperor in 1538, in James Legge, *The Religions of China*, London, 1880, pp. 43–44.
33 *Quotations from Chairman Mao tse-Tung*, second edition, Peking: Foreign Languages Press, 1967, pp. 172–173.
34 *China Daily*, January 30, 1989, p. 1.
35 "Surgeon with pure heart," *China Daily*, January 19, 1989, p. 6.
36 Peimin Ni, personal communication, January 27, 1988.
37 Uno Sosuke, quoted in *Asiaweek*, June 16, 1989, p. 52.

CHAPTER 7: SHINTO

1 Yukitaka Yamamoto, *Way of the Kami*, Stockton, California: Tsubaki America Publications, 1987, p. 75.
2 Adapted from the *Nihon Shoki* (Chronicles of Japan), I: 3, in Stuart D. B. Picken, *Shinto: Japan's Spiritual Roots*, Tokyo: Kodansha International, 1980, p.10.
3 Ise-Teijo, *Gunshin-Mondo, Onchisosho* vol. x, quoted in Genchi Kato, p. 185.
4 Yamamoto, op. cit., pp. 73–75.
5 Unidentified quotation, Stuart D. B. Picken, ed., *A Handbook of Shinto*, Stockton, California: The Tsubaki Grand Shrine of America, 1987, p. 14.
6 Ibid.
7 Hitoshi Iwasaki, "Wisdom from the night sky," Tsubaki Newsletter, June 1, 1988, p. 2.
8 Yamamoto, op. cit., p. 97.
9 Motoori Norinaga (1730–1801), *Naobi no Mitama*, quoted in Tsubaki Newsletter, November 1, 1988, p. 3.
10 Yamamoto, op. cit., p.65.

CHAPTER 8: ZOROASTRIANISM

1 Framroz Rustomjee, *The Life of Holy Zarathushtra*, third edition, Bombay: Nirnaya Sagar Press, 1961, p. 26.
2 *The Hymns of Zarathushtra*, translated by Jacques Duchesne-Guillemin/Mrs. M. Henning, London: John Murray Publishers, 1952, p. 7.
3. Yasna 46: 1–2, *Songs of Zarathushtra*, The Gathas translated by Dastur Framroze Ardeshir Bode and Piloo Nanavutty, London: George Allen and Unwin, 1952, p. 83.
4 Yasna 31: 8, 45: 6, 46: 9, translated by Bode and Nanavutty, ibid., p. 33.
5 Yasna 33: 14, ibid., p. 66.
6 Yasna 34: 5, 4, p. 67.
7. Yasna 31: 18, translated by Bode and Nanavutty, op. cit., p. 55.
8 T. R. Sethna, *Book of Instructions on Zoroastrian Religion*, Karachi: Informal Religious Meetings Trust Fund, 1980, p. 87.
9 Zamyad Yasht, quoted in Rustom Masani, *Zoroastrianism: The Religion of the Good Life*, New York: Macmillan, 1968, pp. 75–76.
10 I. J. S. Taraporewala, *The Religion of Zarathushtra*, Madras, India: Theosophical Publishing House, 1926, p. 70.
11 Dr. Framroze A. Bode, "Mazdayasna Today," Eugene, Oregon: Mazdayasnan Anjoman Press, p. 5.

CHAPTER 9: JUDAISM

1 Genesis 1: 1. *Tanakh — The Holy Scriptures*: The New JPS Translation According to the Traditional Hebrew Text, Philadelphia: The Jewish Publication Society, 1985. This translation is used throughout this chapter.
2 Genesis 1: 28.
3 Genesis 3:22.
4 Genesis 6: 17.
5 Genesis 9: 17.
6 Genesis 22: 12.
7 Personal communication, March 24, 1989.
8 Genesis 1: 26.
9 Deuteronomy 7: 7.
10 Exodus 3: 5.
11 Exodus 3: 10.
12 Exodus 3: 12.
13 Exodus 3: 14–15.
14 Exodus 34: 13.

15 Adapted from Leo Trepp, *A History of the Jewish Experience: Eternal Faith, Eternal People*, New York, N. Y.: Behrman House Inc., 1962 and 1973, pp. 133–135.

16 Martin Buber, "Jews and Christians," in *The Way of Response: Martin Buber*, selections from his writings ed. N. N. Glatzer, New York: Schocken Books, 1966, p. 149.

17 Joshua Loth Liebman, quoted in adapted form in *Likrat Shabbat*, compiled and translated by Rabbi Sidney Greenberg, Bridgeport, Connecticut: Media Judaica/Prayer Book Press, 1981, p. 65.

18 From the Talmud and Midrash, quoted in *The Judaic Tradition*, ed. Nahum N. Glatzer, Boston: Beacon Press, 1969, p. 197.

19 Edict of Theodosius II, quoted in Jacob R. Marcus, ed., *The Jew in the Medieval World*, New York: Harper and Row, 1965, p. 5.

20 Maimonides, Introduction to the Mishnah, Chapter VIII, quoted in *Maimonides: His Wisdom for Our Time*, Gilbert S. Rosenthal, ed., New York: Funk and Wagnalls, 1969, pp. 20–21.

21 Quoted in S. A. Horodezky, *Leaders of Hasidism*, London: Ha-Sefer Agency for Literature, 1928, p. 11.

22 Verax, "The Jews and Bolshevism," *The Times*, London, November 27, 1919.

23 Reeve Robert Brenner, *The Faith and Doubt of Holocaust Survivors*, New York and London: Free Press/Macmillan, 1980, p. 76.

24 Elie Wiesel, speech for the UConn Convocation, September 7, 1988, University of Connecticut, Storrs, Connecticut.

25 Ibn Gabirol, *Keter Malkhut*, quoted in Abraham J. Heschel, "One God," in *Between God and Man: An Interpretation of Judaism, from the Writings of Abraham J. Heschel*, ed. Fritz A. Rothschild, New York: Free Press, 1959, p. 106.

26 Heschel, ibid., p. 37.

27 Ibid., p. 105.

28 Ibid., p. 104.

29 Martin Buber, in *The Way of Response: Martin Buber – Selections from His Writings*, ed. Nahum N. Glatzer, New York: Schocken Books, 1968, p. 53.

30 Translated from the Hebrew by Rabbi Sidney Greenberg, *Likrat Shabbat*, Bridgeport, Connecticut: Media Judaica/The Prayer Book Press, 1981, p. 61.

31 Job 1: 20–21.

32 Harold S. Kushner, *When Bad Things Happen to Good People*, New York: Schocken Books, 1981, pp. 2–3.

33 Perle Epstein, *Kabbalah: The Way of the Jewish Mystic*, Boston and London: Shambhala, 1988, p, xvi.

34 Talmud Berakhoth 11a, in *Ha-Suddur Ha-Shalem*, translated by Philip Birnbaum, New York: Hebrew Publishing Company, 1977, p. 14.

35 Sanhedrin 22a, quoted in *The Second Jewish Catalog*, eds. Sharon Strassfeld and Michael Strassfeld, Philadelphia: The Jewish Publication Society, 1976.

36 Rabbi Yochanan ben Nuri, Rosh Hashanah prayer quoted by Arthur Waskow, *Seasons of Our Joy*, New York: Bantam Books, 1982, p. 11.

37 Ibid., p. 175.

38 Marc Chagall, 1962 speech, quoted in Glatzer, *The Judaic Tradition*, op. cit., p. 798.

39 Mordecai M. Kaplan, "The Way I Have Come," in *Mordecai M. Kaplan: An Evaluation*, eds. I. Eisenstein and E. Kohn, New York, 1952, p. 293.

40 Gersom Scholem, "Judaism," *Contemporary Jewish Religious Thought*, op. cit., p. 507.

41 Arthur Waskow, "A Seder for Peace in the Mideast," *The Nation*, April 24, 1989, p. 559.

CHAPTER 10: CHRISTIANITY

1 *The Gospel According to Thomas*, Coptic text established and translated by Guilloaumont et al., Leiden: E. J. Brill; New York: Harper and Row, 1959, verse 77.

2 Luke 2: 47, 49. Biblical scripture quotations in this chapter are from the Revised Standard version of the Bible, copyright 1946, 1952, 1971 by The Division of Christian Education of the National Council of the Churches of Christ in the USA. Used by permission.

3 Mark 1: 10–11.

4 Luke 9: 17.

5 John 6: 48.

6 William, quoted in *The Gospel in Art by the Peasants of Solentiname*, eds. Philip and Sally Scharper, Maryknoll, New York: Orbis Books, 1984, p. 42.

7 Mark 1: 15.

8 Luke 4: 43.

9 Matthew 6: 10.

10 Matthew 24: 29–31.

11 Mark 8: 29–30.

12 Matthew 17: 2–5.

13 Mark 2: 27–28.

14 John 2: 14–16.

15 John 7: 16, 8: 12, 8: 23, 8: 58.

16 Mark 11: 10.

17 Mark 14: 36.

18 Matthew 26: 64.

19 Matthew 27: 11.

20 Matthew 27: 46.

21 Matthew 28: 18–20.

22 Luke 17: 20–21.

23 Matthew 13: 40–43.

24 Matthew 6: 25–27.

25 Matthew 7: 7.

26 Matthew 11: 29–30.

27 Matthew 5: 21–22.

28 Matthew 5: 44–45.

29 Matthew 22: 39.

30 Matthew 25: 37–40.

31 Quotations of Mother Teresa in this box are taken from the film *Mother Teresa*, Petrie Productions, 1986.

32 Matthew 26: 28.

33 John 14: 1–6.

34 Matthew 5: 3.

35 Acts 2: 36.

36 Acts 26: 18.

37 Acts 17: 28.

38 *The Gospel According to Thomas*, op. cit., 82.

39 *Confessions of St. Augustine*, translated by Edward Bouverie Pusey, Chicago: Enclyclopedia Britannica, vol. 18 of Great Books of the Western World, 1952, p. 64.

40 Rowan Williams, *Resurrection*, New York: The Pilgrim Press, 1984, p. 46.

41 Archimandrite Chrysostomos, *The Ancient Fathers of the Desert*, Brookline, Massachusetts: Hellenic College Press, 1980, p. 78.
42 Ibid., p. 80.
43 Mikhail S. Gorbachev, quoted in Michael Dobbs, "Soviets, Vatican to Establish Ties," *The Hartford Courant*, Dec. 2, 1989, p. 1.
44 St. Gregory Palamas, "Homily on the Presentation of the Holy Virgin in the Temple," ed. Sophocles, *22 Homilies of St. Gr. Palamas*, Athens, 1861, pp. 175–7, quoted in Vladimir Lossky, *The Mystical Theology of the Eastern Church*, New York: St. Vladimir's Seminary Press, 1976, p. 224.
45 Jim Forest, *Pilgrim to the Russian Church*, New York: Crossroad Publishing Company, 1988, p. 50.
46 From *A Hopkins Reader*, ed. John Pick, New York: Oxford University Press, 1953, quoted in D. M. Dooling, ed., *A Way of Working*, New York: Anchor Press/Doubleday, 1979, p. 6.
47 St. Francis, *Testament*, April 1226, p. 3, quoted in eds. Jean Leclerc, Francois Vandenbroucke, and Louis Bouyer, *The Spirituality of the Middle Ages*, vol. 2 of *A History of Christian Spirituality*, New York: Seabury Press, 1982, p. 289.
48 *The Cloud of Unknowing and The Book of Privy Counseling*, Garden City, New York: Image Books, 1973 edition, p. 56.
49 Martin Luther, *A Treatise on Christian Liberty*, quoted in John Oillenberger and Claude Welch, *Protestant Christianity*, New York: Charles Scribner's Sons, 1954, p. 36.
50 Huldreich Zwingli "On True and False Religion," quoted in ed. Harry Emerson Fosdick, *Great Voices of the Reformation* New York. Random House, 1952, p. 169.
51 John Calvin, "Instruction in Faith," quoted in Fosdick, op. cit., p. 216.
52 St. Teresa of Avila, *Interior Castle*, translated by E. Allison Peers from the critical edition of P. Silverior de Santa Teresa, Garden City, New York: Image Books, 1961, p. 214.
53 John Wesley, as quoted in John Dillenberger and Claude Welch, *Protestant Christianity*, New York: Charles Scribner's Sons, 1954, p. 134.
54 Sarah Grimke, "Letters on the Equality of the Sexes and the Condition of Women" (1836–37), in *Feminism: The Essential Historical Writings*, ed., M. Schneir, New York: Vintage, 1972, p. 38.
55 The Documents of Vatican II, ed. Walter M. Abbott, New York: Guild Press, 1966, p. 665.
56 Ibid., pp. 661–662.
57 Thomas Keating, *The Mystery of Christ: The Liturgy as Spiritual Experience*, Amity, New York: Amity House, 1987, p. 5.
58 Luke 1: 38.
59 Quoted in Jim Forest, *Pilgrim to the Russian Church*, New York: Crossroad Publishing Company, 1988, p. 63.
60 Thomas Merton, *Contemplative Prayer*, Garden City, New York: Image Books, 1969, p. 67.
61 World Council of Churches, *Baptism, Eucharist and Ministry*, Faith and Order Paper No. 111, Geneva, 1982, p. 2.
62 Julia Gatta, personal communication, July 22, 1987.
63 "Brief Order for Confession and Forgiveness," *Lutheran Book of Worship*, Prepared by the churches participating in the Inter-Lutheran Commission on Worship, Minneapolis, Minnesota: Augsburg Publishing House, 1978, p. 56.
64 John 1: 9.
65 Jim Forest, *Pilgrim to the Russian Church*, op. cit., p. 72.
66 Quoted in Don A. Schanche and Russell Chandler, Los Angeles Times, "Tensions confront pope in U.S.," *The Hartford Courant*, September 11, 1987, p. 1.
67 Roland Q. Leavell, *Winning Others to Christ*, Nashville, Tennessee: The Sunday School Board of the Southern Baptist Convention, 1936, p. 5.
68 Excerpted from George Marsden, *Evangelism and Modern America*, Grand Rapids, Michigan: William B. Eerdmans Publishing Company, 1984, pp. ix–x.
69 Quoted by Geraldine Baum, "Fallen fundamentalists: solving the puzzle," *The Hartford Courant*, March 8, 1988, p. C1.
70 Members of African Independent Churches Report on their Pilot Study of the History and Theology of their Churches, "Speaking for Ourselves," Braamfontein, South Africa: Institute for Contextural Theology, 1985, pp. 23–24.
71 Martin Luther King, Jr., "An Experiment in Love," in *A Testament of Hope: The Essential Writings of Martin Luther King, Jr.*, ed. James Melvin Washington, San Francisco: Harper and Row, 1986, p. 16.
72 Gustavo Gutierrez, quoted in Phillip Berryman, *Liberation Theology*, New York: Pantheon Books, 1987, p. 33.
73 Bakole Wa Ilunga, *Paths of Liberation: A Third World Spirituality*, Maryknoll, New York: Orbis Books, 1984, p. 92.
74 Thomas Berry, remarks at "Seeking the True Meaning of Peace" conference in San Jose, Costa Rica, June 27, 1989.
75 The Lambeth Conference 1988, *The Truth Shall Make You Free*, published for the Anglican Consultative Council, London, 1988, p. 131.

CHAPTER 11: ISLAM

1 *The Holy Qur'an*, XCVI: 1–5, English translation by Abdullah Yusuf Ali, Durban, R.S.A.: Islamic Propagation Centre International, 1946. This translation is used throughout this chapter, by permission.
2 Abu Abdallah Muhammad Bukhari, *Kitab jami'as-sahih*, translated by M. M. Khan as *Sahih al-Bukhari*, Lahore: Ashraf, 1978–80, quoted in Annemarie Schimmel, *And Muhammad is His Messenger*, Chapel Hill, North Carolina: University of North Carolina Press, 1985, p. 11.
3 Maulana M. Ubaidul Akbar, *The Orations of Muhammad*, Lahore: M. Ashraf, 1954, p. 78.
4 Quoted by Mahmoud Ayoub, *The Qur'an and Its Interpreters*, Albany: State University of New York Press, 1984, vol. 1, p. 14.
5 Sura 1, *The Holy Qur'an*.
6 Footnote 5778, Sura 74: 1, p. 1640.
7 Sura 19: 30–31.
8 Footnote 390, Sura 3: 48, p. 135.
9 Islamic Society of North America, "Islam at a Glance," Plainfield, Indiana: Islamic Teaching Center.
10 Abu Hashim Madani, quoted in Samuel L. Lewis, *In the Garden*, New York: Harmony Books/Lama Foundation, 1975, p. 136.
11 Frithjof Schuon, *Understanding Islam*, translated by D. M. Matheson, London: George Allen and Unwin, 1963, p. 59.
12 Sura 2: 136.
13 Seyyed Hossein Nasr, *Ideals and Realities of Islam*, second edition, London: Unwin Hyman Limited, 1985, p. 23.
14 Quoted by Abdur-Rahman Ibrahim Doi, "Sunnism," *Islamic Spirituality: Foundations*, ed. Seyyed Hossein Nasr,

New York: Crossroad, 1987, p. 158.
15 Sura 75: 3–4.
16 Sura 41: 30–32.
17 Sura 24: 24.
18 Quoted by Muhammad Rida al-Muzaffar, *The Faith of Shi'a Islam*, London: The Muhammadi Trust, 1982, p. 35.
19 al-Muzaffar, ibid., p. 42.
20 Hadith #535 cited in Badi'uz-Zaman Furuzanfar, *Ahadith-i Mathnawi*, Tehran, 1334 sh./1955, in Persian, quoted in Annemarie Schimmel, *Mystical Dimensions of Islam*, Chapel Hill: University of North Carolina Press, 1975, p. 118.
21 Rabi'a al-'Adawiyya al-Qaysiyya, quoted in Abu Talib, *Qut al-Qulub*, II, Cairo, A. H. 1310, p. 57, as quoted in Margaret Smith, *Rabi'a the Mystic and her Fellow-Saints in Islam*, Cambridge: Cambridge University Press, 1928, 1984, p. 102.
22 Mevlana Jelaluddin Rumi, opening lines of the *Mathnawi*, as translated by Edmund Helminski, *The Ruins of the Heart: Selected Lyric Poetry of Jelaluddin Rumi*, Putney, Vermont: Threshold Books, 1981, p. 20.
23 Jalaluddin Rumi, *Mathnawi-i ma'nawi*, ed. and translated by Reynold A. Nicholson, London, 1925–40, vol. 4, line 2102.
24 Hadith of the Prophet, #352 in Zam Furuzanfar, *Ahadith-i Mathnawi*, op. cit.
25 Abu Sa'id Abel-Khayr, as quoted in Javad Nurbakhsh, *Sufism: Meaning, Knowledge, and Unity*, New York: Khaniqahi-Nimatullahi Publications, 1981, pp. 19, 21.
26 Idries Shah, *The Sufis*, London: Jonathan Cape, 1964, p. 76.
27 Rumi, Mathnawi, VI, 3220–3246, as translated by Coleman Barks in *Rumi: We are Three*, Athens, Georgia: Maypop Books, 1987, pp. 54–55.
28 Sura 2: 256.
29 Hadith quoted by Syed Ali Ashraf, "The Inner Meaning of the Islamic Rites: Prayer, Pilgrimage, Fasting, Jihad," in *Islamic Spirituality: Foundations*, op, cit., p. 114.
30 Hammudah Abdalati, *Islam in Focus*, Indianapolis, Indiana: American Trust Publications, 1975, p. 88.
31 Seyyed Hossein Nasr, *Traditional Islam in the Modern World*, London: KPI Ltd., 1987, p. 33.
32 Sura 22: 39–40.
33 M. R. Bawa Muhaiyaddeen, "Islam's Hidden Beauty: The Sufi Teachings of M. R. Bawa Muhaiyaddeen," tape from New Dimensions Foundation, San Francisco, 1989, side 1.
34 Treaty cited in Philip K. Hitti, *Islam and the West*, Princeton, New Jersey: D. Van Nostrand, 1962, p. 112.
35 Indonesian President Suharto, quoted in *Hinduism Today*, July 1989, p. 20.
36 Annemarie Schimmel, speaking in "Islam's Hidden Beauty," tape from New Dimensions Foundation, San Francisco, 1989, side 1.
37 Jelaluddin Rumi, *Mathnawi*, IV, in *Rumi: We are Three*: op. cit., Barks, p. 52.
38 Ahmed Abdulla, *The Heights: Glory of Muslim World*, Karachi, Pakistan: Tanzeem Publishers, 1984, pp. 258–259.
39 Seyyed Hossein Nasr, "The Pertinence of Islam to the Modern World," *The World Religions Speak on the Relevance of Religion in the Modern World*, ed. Finley P. Dunne, Jr., The Hague: Junk, 1970, p. 133.
40 The First World Conference on Muslim Education,
quoted in Syed Ali Ashraf, *New Horizons in Muslim Education*, Cambridge, England: Hodder and Stoughton/The Islamic Academy, 1985, p. 4.
41 From a speech by Ayatollah Khomeini, Foreign Broadcast Information Service, *Daily Report*, South Asia, August 17, 1983.
42 Ibid., June 20, 1983.
43 Dr. A. K. Aboulmagd, quoted in the video "Islam," Smithsonian World series, Smithsonian Institution and WETA, Washington, D.C., originally broadcast July 22, 1987, transcript pp. 6, 17.

CHAPTER 12: SIKHISM

1 Kabir, in modern translation by Robert Bly, *The Kabir Book: Forty-four of the Ecstatic Poems of Kabir*, Copyright 1971, 1977 by Robert Bly, copyright 1977 by Seventies Press. Reprinted by permission of Beacon Press, p. 33.
2 Puratan, quoted in Khushwant Singh, *Hymns of Guru Nanak*, New Delhi: Orient Longmans Ltd., 1969, p. 10.
3 Guru Nanak, as quoted in W. Owen Cole and Piara Singh Sambhi, *The Sikhs: Their Religious Beliefs and Practices*, London: Routledge and Kegan Paul, 1978, p. 39.
4 As quoted by V. K. R. V. Rao, Foreword to *Hymns of Guru Nanak*, ibid., p. vi.
5 Var Maji 7: 1, *Adi Granth*, quoted in *Textual Sources for the Study of Sikhism*, translated and edited by W. H. McLeod, Totowa, New Jersey: Barnes and Noble, 1984, p. 43.
6 Sri Rag, p. 59, quoted in Trilochan Singh, Jodh Singh, Kapur Singh, Bawa Harkishen Singh, and Kushwant Singh, trans., *The Sacred Writings of the Sikhs*, reproduced by kind permission of Unwin Hyman Ltd., 1973, p. 72.
7 Mool mantra, quoted in *Hymns of Guru Nanak*, op. cit., p. 25.
8 Adi Granth 684, quoted in Cole and Sambhi, op. cit., p.74.
9 Ralph Singh, interview October 30, 1988.
10 Guru Arjan, Rag Majh, p. 102, quoted in Singh et al, *Sacred Writings of the Sikhs*, op. cit., p. 180.
11 Kiran Gill, April 14, 1985 interview quoted in Harold Coward, *Sacred Word and Sacred Text: Scripture in World Religions*, Maryknoll, New York: Orbis Books, 1988, p. 134.
12 Japji 9, 10, quoted in Singh et. al., op. cit., pp. 33–34.
13 Shri Surendra Nath, *Gobind Sadan: The Abode of Love, Peace and Miracles*, New Delhi: Gobind Sadan Publications, p. 16.

CHAPTER 13: NEW RELIGIOUS MOVEMENTS

1 Friday M. Mbon, "The Social Impact of Nigeria's New Religious Movements," in ed. James A. Beckford, *New Religious Movements and Rapid Social Change*, Paris and London: Unesco/Sage Publications, 1986, p. 177.
2 Antonio Maciel ("Conselheiro"), as quoted in Roger Bastide, *The African Religions of Brazil*, translated by Helen Sebba, Baltimore and London: The John Hopkins University Press, 1978, p. 359.
3 Quoted in Ernest Cashmore, *Rastaman*, London: Unwin Paperbacks, 1983, p. 22.
4 "Introduction to NSA" (Nichiren Shoshu Soka Gakkai of America).

5 Ibid.

6 Ernest Holmes, excerpt from "I am Vitalized by the Strength of God," reprinted in *Science of Mind*, October 1981, p. 59.

7 Tom Johnson, personal communication, February 19, 1990.

8 Paramhansa Yogananda, *Sayings of Paramhansa Yogananda*, fourth edition, Los Angeles: Self-Realization Fellowship, 1980, p. 9.

9 Reverend Sun Myung Moon, *Divine Principle*, New York: Holy Spirit Association for the Unification of World Christianity, 1973, p. 530.

10 *Tenri kyoso den* ("Life of the Founder of the Tenri-kyo Sect"), compiled by the Tenri-kyo doshi-kai, Tenri, 1913, quoted in Ichiro Hori, *Folk Religion in Japan*, Chicago: University of Chicago Press, 1968, p. 237.

11 Elizabeth Claire Prophet, brochure from The Summit Lighthouse, Livingston, Montana.

12 "The Chart of Your Divine Self," Summit University, Livingston, Montana.

13 Sandra Pfortmiller, "Messages," *The National Spiritualist Summit*, January 1989, p. 31.

14 Principles 7 and 8 of the Declaration of Principles, National Spiritualist Association of Churches.

15 Paul Twitchell, *Eckankar: Compiled Writings*, vol. 1, San Diego, California: Illuminated Way Press, 1975, p. 26.

16 Ibid., p. 135

17 Ibid., pp. 34–35.

18 June Saury-Cookson, "A First Introduction to Subud," p. 2.

19 Samuel L. Lewis, *In the Garden*, New York: Harmony Books/Lama Foundation, 1975, p. 122.

20 H. P. Blavatsky, *The Key to Theosophy*, Los Angeles: The United Lodge of Theosophists, 1920, p. 3.

21 Starhawk, *The Spiral Dance: A Rebirth of the Ancient Religion of the Great Goddess*, San Francisco: Harper and Row, 1979, p. 2–3.

22 John Seed, "Anthropocentrism," *Awakening in the Nuclear Age*, Issue #14 (Summer/Fall 1986), p. 11.

23 Chief Seattle, "Chief Seattle's Message," quoted in eds. John Seed, Joanna Macy, Pat Fleming, Arne Naess, *Thinking Like a Mountain: Toward a Council of All Beings*, Santa Cruz, California: New Society Publishers, 1988, p. 71.

24 J. E. Lovelock, *Gaia: A new look at life on Earth*, Oxford: Oxford University Press, pp. 9, 11.

25 Peter Russell, "Endangered Earth: Psychological roots of the environmental crisis," Link Up, Issue #38 (Spring 1989), pp. 7–8.

26 David Albert, "A Children's Story: Gaura Devi Saves the Trees," *Awakening in the Nuclear Age*, op. cit., p. 15.

27 Hazrat Inayat Khan, "A New Form," *Addresses to Cherags*, Lebanon Springs, New York: Sufi Order, p. 75.

28 'Abdu'l-Baha, prayer in *Baha'i Prayers*, Wilmette, Illinois: Baha'i Publishing Trust, 1979, p. 45.

29 Adapted from "The Baha'i Faith," New York: Baha'i International Community (unpaginated).

30 Frithjof Schuon, *Understanding Islam*, London: George Allen and Unwin Ltd., translated from French, 1963, p. 41.

31 Raimundo Panikkar, "The Invisible Harmony: A Universal Theory of Religion or a Cosmic Confidence in Reality?", *Toward a Universal Theology of Religion*, ed. Leonard Swidler, Maryknoll, New York: Orbis Books, 1987, p. 147.

32 Sister Sudha, Vedanta Center, interview June 16, 1988.

33 Pope John Paul II, quoted in Richard N. Ostling, "A Summit for Peace in Assisi," *Time*, November 10, 1986, p. 78.

34 Wangari Maathai, speaking at the Oxford Global Survival Conference, quoted in The Temple of Understanding Newsletter, Fall 1988, p. 2.

35 His Holiness Tenzin Gyatso, the Dalai Lama, remarks in San Jose, Costa Rica, June 26, 1989, Seeking the True Meaning of Peace Conference.

36 Gordon Kaufman, The Myth of Christian Uniqueness Maryknoll, New York: Orbis Books, 1987.

GLOSSARY

AGNI The god of fire in Hinduism.

AGNOSTICISM The belief that if there is anything beyond this life, it is impossible for humans to know it.

AHIMSA Non-violence, a central Jain principle.

AMIDA (Sanskrit: Amitabha) The Buddha of infinite light, the personification of compassion whom the Pure Land Buddhists revere as the intermediary between humanity and Supreme Reality; esoterically, the Higher Self.

ANATTA In Buddhism, the doctrine that nothing in this transient existence has a permanent self.

ANEKANTWAD The Jain principle of relativity or open-mindedness.

ANICCA In Buddhism, the impermanence of all existence.

ANIMISM The belief in usually invisible spirits present within things and people.

APARIGRAHA The Jain principle of non-acquisitiveness.

APOCALYPSE In Judaism and Christianity, the dramatic end of the present age.

ARHANT (Sanskrit; Pali: arhat or arahat) A "Worthy One" who has followed the Buddha's Eightfold Path to liberation, broken the fetters that bind us to the suffering of the Wheel of Birth and Death, and arrived at Nirvana; the Theravadan ideal.

ARYANS The Indo-European pastoral invaders of many European and Middle Eastern agricultural cultures during the second millenium B.C.E.

ATHEISM Non-belief in any deity.

ATMAN In Hinduism, the soul.

BAPTISM A Christian sacrament by which God cleanses all sin and makes one a sharer in the divine life, and a member of Christ's body, the Church.

BARAKA In Islamic mysticism, the spiritual wisdom and blessing transmitted from master to pupil.

BHAGAVAD-GITA A portion of the Hindu epic Mahabarata in which Lord Krishna specifies ways of spiritual progress.

BHAKTI In Hinduism, intense devotion to a personal aspect of Deity.

BHIKKHU (Sanskrit: bhikshu; feminine; bhikkhuni or bhikshuni). A Buddhist monk or nun who renounces worldliness for the sake of following the path of liberation and whose simple physical needs are met by lay supporters.

BODHISATTVA In Mahayana Buddhism, one who has attained enlightenment but renounces Nirvana for the sake of helping all sentient beings in their journey to liberation from suffering.

BRAHMAN The impersonal Ultimate Principle in Hinduism.

BRAHAMANAS The portion of the Hindu Vedas concerning rituals.

BRAHMIN (brahman) A priest or member of the priestly caste in Hinduism.

BUDDHA-NATURE A fully awakened consciousness.

CALIPH In Sunni Islam, the successor to the Prophet.

CATHOLIC Universal, all-inclusive. Christian churches referring to themselves as Catholic claim to be the representatives of the ancient undivided Christian church.

CHAKRA An energy center in the subtle body, recognized in kundalini yoga.

CH'I (ki) The vital energy in the universe and in our bodies, according to Far Eastern esoteric traditions.

COMMUNION See "Eucharist."

CREED A formal statement of the beliefs of a particular religion.

DARSAN Visual contact with the divine through encounters with Hindu images or gurus.

DAVENING In Hasidic Judaism, prayer.

DENOMINATION One of the Protestant branches of Christianity.

DERVISH A Sufi ascetic, in the Muslim tradition.

DEVA Vedic term for god or goddess in Hinduism.

DHIMMI A person of a non-Muslim religion whose right to practice that religion is protected within an Islamic society.

DHARMA (Pali: Dhamma) The doctrine or law, as revealed by the Buddha; also the correct conduct for each person according to his or her level of awareness.

DHYANA YOGA The path of meditation, in Hinduism.

DOGMA A system of beliefs declared to be true by a religion.

DUALISM The separation of reality into two categories, particularly the concept that spirit and matter are separate realms.

DUKKHA According to the Buddha, a central fact of human life, variously translated as discomfort, suffering, frustration, or lack of harmony with the environment.

DURGA The Great Goddess as destroyer of evil, and sometimes as sakti of Siva.

EUCHARIST The Christian sacrament by which believers are renewed in the mystical body of Christ by partaking of bread and wine, understood as his body and blood.

FUNDAMENTALISM A literal interpretation of scriptures.

GAYATRIMANTRA The daily Vedic prayer of upper-caste Hindus.

GOSPEL In Christianity, the "good news" that God has raised Jesus from the dead and in so doing has begun the transformation of the world.

GUNAS In Yoga, the three states of the Cosmic Substance: sattva, rajas, tamas.

GURU In Hinduism, an enlightened spiritual teacher.

HADITH In Islam, a tradition report about a reputed saying or action of the Prophet Muhammad.

HAGGADAH The non-legal part of the Talmud and midrash.

HAJJ The holy pilgrimage to Mecca, for Muslims.

HALAKHA Jewish legal decision and the parts of the Talmud dealing with laws.

HATHA YOGA Body postures, diet, and breathing exercises to help build a suitable physical vehicle for spiritual development.

HERETIC A member of an established religion whose views are unacceptable to the orthodoxy.

HEYOKA "Contrary" wisdom or a person who embodies it, in some Native American spiritual traditions.

HINAYANA In Mahayana Buddhist terminology, the label "lesser vehicle," given to the orthodox Southern tradition now represented by Theravada; in Tibetan terminology, one of the three vehicles for salvation taught by the Buddha.

HOLOCAUST The genocidal killing of six million Jews by the Nazis during World War II.

ICON A sacred image, a term used especially for the paintings of Jesus, Mary, and the saints of the Eastern Orthodox Christian Church.

IMAM A leader of Muslim prayer; in Shi'ism, the title for the person carrying the initiatic tradition of the Prophetic Light.

IMMANENT Present in Creation.

INDIGENOUS Native to an area.

INDRA The old Vedic thunder god in the Hindu tradition.

INFIDEL The Muslim and Christian term for "non-believer," which each of these traditions often applied to the other.

JEN Humanity, benevolence — the central Confucian virtue.

JIHAD The Muslim's battle against the inner forces that prevent God-realization and the outer barriers to establishment of the divine order.

JINA In Jainism, one who has realized the highest, omniscient aspect of his or her being and is therefore perfect.

JIVA The soul in Jainism.

JNANA YOGA The use of intellectual effort as a yogic technique.

KABBALAH The Jewish mystical tradition.

KALI Destroying and transforming Mother of the World, in Hinduism.

KALI YUGA In Hindu world cycles, an age of chaos and selfishness, including the one in which we are now living.

KAMI The Shinto word for that invisible sacred quality which evokes wonder and awe in us, and also for the invisible spirits throughout nature that are born of this essence.

KANNAGARA Harmony with the way of the kami in Shinto.

KARMA In Hinduism and Buddhism, our actions and their effects on this life and lives to come.

KARMA YOGA The path of unselfish service in Hinduism.

KEVALA The supremely perfected state in Jainism.

KOSHER Ritually acceptable, applied to foods in Jewish Orthodoxy.

KSHATRIYA A member of the warrior or ruling caste in traditional Hinduism.

KUNDALINI In Hindu yogic thought, the life force that can be awakened from the base of the spine and raised to illuminate the spiritual center at the top of the head.

LAMA A Tibetan Buddhist monk, particularly one of the highest in the hierarchy.

LI Ceremonies, rituals, and rules of proper conduct, in the Confucian tradition.

LINGAM A cylindrical stone or other similarly shaped natural or sculpted form, representing for Saivite Hindus the unmanifest aspect of Siva.

MAHABARATA A long Hindu epic which includes the *Bhagavad-Gita*.

MAHAYANA The "greater vehicle" in Buddhism, the more liberal and mystical Northern School which stressed the virtue of altruistic compassion rather than intellectual efforts at individual salvation.

MANTRA(M) A sound or phrase chanted to evoke the sound vibration of one aspect of creation or to praise a deity.

MASS The Roman Catholic term for the Christian Eucharist.

MEDICINE Spiritual power, in some indigenous traditions.

MESSIAH The "anointed," the expected king and deliverer of the Jews, a term later applied by Christians to Jesus.

METAPHYSICS A branch of philosophy that deals with the systematic investigation of ultimate reality.

METTA In Buddhist terminology, loving-kindness.

MIDRASH The literature of delving into the Jewish Torah.

MILLENIUM One thousand years, a term used in Christianity and certain newer religions for a hoped-for period of a thousand years of holiness and happiness, with Christ ruling the earth, as prophesied in the book of Revelation.

MISOGI The Shinto waterfall purification ritual.

MITZVA (plural: *mitzvot*) In Judaism, a divine commandment or sacred deed in fulfillment of a commandment.

MOKSHA Liberation of the soul from illusion and suffering, in Hinduism.

MONISM The concept of life as a unified whole, without a separate "spiritual" realm.

MONOTHEISM The concept that there is one God.

MURSHID A spiritual teacher, in esoteric Islam.

MYSTIC One who values inner spiritual experience in preference to external authorities and scriptures.

NAGA A snake, worshipped in Hinduism.

OCCULT Involving the mysterious, unseen, supernatural.

OM In Hinduism, the primordial sound.

ORIGINAL SIN The Christian belief that all human beings are bound together in prideful egocentricity. In the Bible, this is described mythically as an act of disobedience on the part of Adam and Eve.

ORTHODOX Adhering to the established tradition of a religion.

PALI The Indian dialect first used for writing down the teachings of the Buddha, which were initially held in memory, and still used today in the Pali Canon of scriptures recognized by the Theravadins.

PANTHEISM The concept that One Absolute Reality is everywhere.

PARVATI Siva's spouse, sweet daughter of the Himalayas.

PENTATEUCH The five books of Moses at the beginning of the Hebrew Bible.

POLYTHEISM Belief in many deities.

POPE The Bishop of Rome and head of the Roman Catholic Church.

PRAKRITI In Samkhya Hindu philosophy, the cosmic substance.

PRANA In yogic thought, the invisible life force.

PRANAYAMA Yogic breathing exercises.

PUJA Hindu ritual worship.

PURANAS Hindu scriptures written to popularize the abstract truths of the Vedas through stories about historical and legendary figures.

PURE LAND A Buddhist sect in China and Japan that centers on faith in Amida Buddha, who promised to welcome believers to the paradise of the Pure Land, a metaphor for enlightenment.

PURGATORY In some branches of Christianity, an intermediate after-death state in which souls are purified from sin.

PURUSHA The Cosmic Spirit, soul of the universe in Hinduism.

RABBI Historically, a Jewish teacher; at present, the ordained spiritual leader of a Jewish congregation.

RAJAS The active state, one of the three gunas in Hinduism.

RAMAYANA The Hindu epic about Prince Rama, defender of good.

REINCARNATION The transmigration of the soul into a new body after death of the old body.

RIG VEDA Possibly the world's oldest scripture, the foundation of Hinduism.

RISHI A Hindu sage.

SACRAMENT Outward and visible signs of inward and spiritual grace in Christianity. Almost all churches recognize baptism and the Eucharist as sacraments; some churches recognize five others as well.

SACRED THREAD In Hinduism, a cord worn over one shoulder by men who have been initiated into adult upper-caste society.

SADHU An ascetic holy man, in Hinduism.

SAIVITE A Hindu worshipper of the Divine as Siva.

SAKTA A Hindu worshipper of the female aspect of Deity.

SAKTI The creative, active female aspect of Deity in Hinduism.

SAMADHI In yogic practice, the blissful state of superconscious union with the Absolute.

SAMKHYA One of the major Hindu philosophical systems, in which human suffering is characterized as stemming from the confusion of Prakriti with Purusha.

SAMSARA The continual round of birth-and-death existence, in Hinduism, Jainism, and Buddhism.

SANATANA DHARMA The "eternal religion" of Hinduism.

SANGHA In Theravada Buddhism, the monastic community; in Mahayana, the spiritual community of followers of the Dharma.

SANNYASIN In Hinduism, a renunciate spiritual seeker.

SANSKRIT The literary language of classic Hindu scriptures.

SATI The Hindu tradition of live cremation of a widow with her dead husband.

SATTVA The state of purity and illumination, one of the three gunas in Hinduism.

SEMITIC Referring to Jews, Arabs, and others of eastern Mediterranean origin.

SHAYK A spiritual master, in the esoteric Muslim tradition.

SHAKTIPAT In the Siddha Yoga tradition of Hinduism, the powerful, elevating glance or touch of the guru.

SHAMAN A "medicine person," a man or woman who has undergone spiritual ordeals and can communicate with the spirit world to help the people in indigenous traditions.

SHARI'AH The divine law, in Islam.

SHEKKHINAH God's presence in the world, in Judaism.

SHUDRA A member of the manual laborer caste in traditional Hinduism.

SIVA In Hinduism, the Supreme as lord of yogis, absolute consciousness, creator, preserver, and destroyer of the world; or the destroying aspect of the Supreme.

SOMA An intoxicating drink used by early Hindu worshippers.

STUPA A rounded monument containing Buddhist relics or commemorative materials.

SUNNAH The behavior of the Prophet Muhammad, used as a model in Islamic law.

SUNYATA Voidness, the transcendental ultimate reality in Buddhism.

SURA A chapter of the Qur'an.

SUTRA Literally, a thread on which are strung jewels — the discourses of the Buddha.

SYNAGOGUE A meeting place for Jewish study and worship.

SYNCRETISM A form of religion in which otherwise differing traditions are blended, as, for instance, Sikhism is in some senses a syncretistic combination of Hinduism and Islam.

TAMAS The dull state, one of the three gunas in Hinduism.

TANAKH The Jewish scriptures.

TAO (Do) The way or path, in Far Eastern traditions. The

term is also used as a name for the Nameless.

TAO-CHIA The ancient philosophical Taoist tradition.

TAO-CHIAO The newer magically religious Taoist tradition.

THERAVADA The remaining orthodox school of Buddhism, which adheres closely to the earliest scriptures and emphasizes individual efforts to liberate the mind from suffering.

THIRD EYE The center of spiritual insight thought to reside between and slightly above the physical eyes.

TIRTHANKARAS The great enlightened teachers in Jainism, of whom Mahavira was the last in the present era.

TORAH The Pentateuch or the whole body of Jewish teachings and law.

TRANSCENDENT Existing outside the material universe.

TRANSPERSONAL Referring to an eternal, infinite reality, in contrast to the finite material world.

TRINITY The Christian doctrine that in the One God are three divine persons: the Father, the Son, and the Holy Spirit.

TRIPLE GEM The three jewels of Buddhism: Buddha, Dharma, Sangha.

TSUMI Impurity or misfortune, a quality that Shinto purification practices are designed to remove.

"TWICE-BORN" Upper-caste men who have been initiated into Aryan society in traditional Hinduism.

TZADDIK An enlightened Jewish mystic.

UMMAH The Muslim community.

UPANISHADS The philosophical part of the Vedas in Hinduism, intended only for serious seekers.

VAISHNAVITE (*Vaishnava*) A Hindu devotee of Vishnu, particularly in his incarnation as Krishna.

VAISHYA A member of the merchant and farmer caste in traditional Hinduism.

VAJRAYANA The ultimate vehicle used in Tibetan Buddhism, consisting of estoteric tantric practices and concentration on deities.

VARUNA The old thunder god of cosmic order in ancient Hinduism.

VEDANTA A Hindu philosophy based on the Upanishads.

VISHNU In Hinduism, the preserving aspect of the Supreme or the Supreme Itself, incarnating again and again to save the world.

VISION QUEST In indigenous traditions, a solitary ordeal undertaken to seek spiritual guidance about one's mission in life.

WEI WU WEI In Taoism, "not doing," in the sense of taking no action contrary to the natural flow.

YANG In Chinese philosophy, the bright, assertive, "male" energy in the universe.

YANTRA In Hinduism, a linear cosmic symbol used as an aid to spiritual concentration.

YI Righteous conduct (as opposed to conduct motivated by desire for personal profit), a Confucian virtue stressed by Mencius.

YIN In Chinese philosophy, the dark, receptive, "female" energy in the universe.

YOGA Ancient techniques for spiritual realization, found in several Eastern religions.

YOGA A systematic approach to spiritual realization, one of the major Hindu philosophical systems.

YONI Abstract Hindu representation of the female vulva, cosmic matrix of life.

YUGA One of four recurring world cycles in Hinduism.

ZAKAH Muslim almsgiving.

ZAZEN Zen Buddhist sitting meditation.

ZEN (Chinese: Ch'an) A Chinese and Japanese Buddhist school emphasizing that all things have Buddha-nature, which can only be grasped when one escapes from the intellectual mind.

ZENDO A Zen meditation hall.

CREDITS

The authors and publishers wish to acknowledge, with thanks, the following photographic sources.

INDEX